Action and Insight

Other Books by Paul L. Wachtel

Psychoanalysis and Behavior Therapy: Toward an Integration (1977)
Resistance: Psychodynamic and Behavioral Approaches (Editor; 1982)
*The Poverty of Affluence: A Psychological Portrait of
the American Way of Life* (1983)
Family Dynamics in Individual Psychotherapy: A Guide to Clinical Strategies
(with Ellen F. Wachtel; 1986)

ACTION AND INSIGHT

Paul L. Wachtel

THE GUILFORD PRESS
New York   London

© 1987 Paul L. Wachtel

Published by:
The Guilford Press
A Division of Guilford Publications, Inc.
200 Park Avenue South, New York, N.Y. 10003

Printed in the United States of America

Library of Congress Cataloging in Publication Data

Wachtel, Paul L., 1940–
    Action and insight.

    Bibliography: p.
    Includes index.
    1. Psychotherapy.   2. Insight in psychotherapy.
I. Title.
RC480.W26 1987   616.89′1   86-22828
ISBN 0-89862-685-4

PREFACE

As one of my children put it none too delicately recently, it has been a quarter of a century since I began my graduate studies in psychology at Yale. Over that period, my interests have ranged over a number of topics. The publication of this set of selected papers provides an opportunity to reflect on the compass of this work. It offers me, as well as the reader, the chance to reflect on the main themes and how they interact, and to consider the underlying assumptions that have energized and, inevitably, limited the work. It affords as well a chance to consider the important questions that remain unanswered and how they might be pursued.

For the convenience of the reader, the chapters have been organized according to five broad categories, but these should not be taken as representing completely separate areas of concern. In fact, the central themes that weave through the five sections bind them together in a variety of ways. My views on psychotherapy, for example, are obviously related to the particular perspective on psychodynamic theory that has guided my work as it has evolved over the years. So, too, has my understanding of social processes and the large social context been shaped by that theoretical perspective. Conversely, my view of psychodynamics—particularly my conviction that psychodynamic theories must take context into account more than has been typical—has itself been shaped by my concern about social issues and by experiences during the period of intense social activism of the 1960s; similarly, my views about needed revisions in psychodynamic thought have been significantly influenced by my experiences in practicing psychotherapy, even as that practice has itself been modified and guided by my evolving theoretical perspective. In this, perhaps, one sees an illustration of one of the overarching conceptions that has become increasingly compelling to me over the years—that causality in human behavior and experience must be understood as circular rather than linear, characterized by feedback loops and mutual influences rather than by the simple perpetuation of early experiences in later behavior. This conception of human affairs is evident in much of what follows.[1]

The title of this volume reflects another central assumption that runs as a thread throughout most of the chapters in one way or another. Specifically, in regard to the process of psychotherapy, this perspective stresses that actions and insights are mutually facilitative and that ways of approaching and understanding human phenomena that stress one to the relative exclusion of the other are not fully satisfactory. To put it differently, who we are cannot be separated from what we do; fundamental personality change requires fundamental change in how we handle the events of our daily lives. Change in overt behavior is not simply an epiphenomenal *reflection* of more basic "inner" change or the inevitable *result of* such change, but rather is part and parcel of the *process* of change. It is not a matter of one or the other, or of one first and then the other, but of both or neither.

The theoretical perspective reflected in this view of psychotherapeutic change is evident as well in the discussions of personality development and the nature of individual differences and consistencies. In development as in therapeutic change, internal organization and reorganization proceed apace with, and as complements to, actions in the world. As I hope to show, many of the formulations that have been dominant in the psychodynamic tradition have paid insufficient attention both to the role of context and to the way in which the developing child's early responses to the events of his life skew the responses of others, thereby altering both the world he encounters and the evolving self in fateful ways.[2] As one of the chapters puts it, there is no such thing as an "average expectable environment."

The role of the unique environment that comes to characterize the life of each of us is a pivotal concern of the explorations that follow. The position taken here is not, however, a simple "environ-

1. The therapeutic implications of a circular view of psychodynamics are also spelled out in considerable detail in a recent book written with my wife, Ellen F. Wachtel (E. F. Wachtel & Wachtel, 1986).

2. Wherever possible, I use in the introductory material the multiple form "he and she" to remind the reader of the ways in which our language biases us to slight half of the human race. In sentences such as the foregoing, however, which would become intolerably awkward that way, the more traditional phrasing is used. The chapters themselves are published in their original wording, which sometimes reflects the times in which they were written or the journals in which they appeared.

mentalist" position. Indeed, a central point of much of what follows
is that the environment is not simply an "external" influence or an
independent variable to which the individual reactively must conform. Rather, it is very largely in our understanding of how the
developing individual himself *shapes* his environment that our understanding of personality will be advanced.

The views developed in this book are the product of a multitude
of influences. From very early in my professional development, the
psychoanalytic tradition has been a lodestar in the confusing wilder-
ness of human behavior. Freud's observations and insights remain in
many ways the most basic source of my understanding of myself and
others. Over time, however, I experienced growing dissatisfaction
with a number of the particulars of Freudian theory and an increasing interest in the interpersonal tradition in psychoanalysis, as well
as in the related theories of Erik Erikson, who in important respects
provides a bridge between classical Freudian theory and the innovations of the interpersonalists. Erikson, Horney, and Sullivan—or at
least their ideas as filtered through my own theoretical lenses—
became central to my evolving point of view. Indeed, it is in important respects still quite accurate to describe my own position as that
of an interpersonal psychodynamic theorist.

Other influences have been important as well, however. From
early on, I have believed that the findings of controlled research
ought to have a bearing on how we think about clinical matters. This
was reflected initially in an interest in the psychoanalytically oriented empirical investigations in attention and cognitive style that
were going on at such places as the Menninger Foundation and the
Research Center for Mental Health at New York University. In-
trigued by the idea that what we attend to and *how* we attend to it
determines our conscious experience—to put it differently, that attention was the gateway to consciousness—I began to study attentional processes with the aim of understanding better the nature of
psychological defenses. The chapters in Part Four describe some of
this work.

Another fateful consequence of my conviction that our theoretical predilections must yield to the findings of empirical research was
my encounter with behavior therapy. Like many dynamically trained
clinicians, I had been brought up professionally to regard behavior
therapy as superficial and manipulative, and had given it little
thought until I began to read its literature in preparation for a
critique to be presented at an American Psychological Association
symposium. I was quite surprised to find that although some of the
behavioral literature fit my stereotyped image, much of it consisted
of very well-thought-out clinical innovations that seemed to hold

exciting promise. I was especially impressed with the efforts of behavior therapists to put their ideas to empirical test and with their initial demonstrations that their interventions did yield beneficial change. Faced with carefully gathered data, I felt a need to come to terms with this new approach.

For the next several years, I immersed myself in this literature and arranged to observe the work of the leading behavior therapists and to learn to use their methods myself. Concomitantly, I began efforts to articulate a dawning recognition of how some of the seeming incompatibilities between psychodynamic and behavioral points of view could be reconciled. The result was my first book, *Psychoanalysis and Behavior Therapy: Toward an Integration* (1977), and the beginnings of a journey along a path I had never thought I would tread.

A few of the papers presented here predate *Psychoanalysis and Behavior Therapy*, but most have appeared subsequent to the publication of that book, and the present volume can in some measure be viewed as a sequel. Many of the chapters amplify the conceptual approach introduced in the earlier book or explore further dimensions of the use of active methods in the context of a psychodynamically informed therapy.

Between the lines, and occasionally explicitly, the reader will find indications of an effort to extend the integrative framework to include perspectives other than the psychodynamic and behavioral. Although what I have learned from behavior therapy continues to nourish my work in important ways, I no longer think of what I am engaged in as specifically or exclusively an integration of psychodynamic and behavioral points of view. That project remains of importance to me, but is part of a larger effort to integrate active-intervention methods into a psychodynamically oriented therapy and to elaborate the theoretical implications of the various clinical and conceptual explorations in which I have been engaged. In a recent textbook, *Contemporary Psychotherapies: Models and Methods* (Lynn & Garske, 1985), my approach is described as "integrative psychodynamic therapy" and the theoretical position as that of "cyclical psychodynamics" (P. L. Wachtel, 1985).

When these various integrative efforts were first undertaken, I felt very much alone, if also supported by valued colleagues who were warmly respectful even when they did not share my views. Subsequently, I have been buoyed by learning of work along somewhat similar lines that has been going on throughout the United States and in various parts of the world. Moreover, in recent years the possibilities of integration have increasingly been capturing the imagination of large numbers of therapists, especially of younger people in the field. It is now possible to discern a worldwide movement toward integration in psychotherapy, embodied most recently in a new international organization, the Society for the Exploration of Psychotherapy Integration (SEPI).

The papers presented here are not placed in strictly chronological order even within sections, but rather according to a logic that should be evident from the introductions to each section. Different people contributed helpful assistance and suggestions to different chapters, and therefore the acknowledgments that appear can be found on the first page of the relevant chapters. Special thanks are due to my good friend Jim Blight for his participation and assistance at a stage when the preparation of this book was first being considered. Without his encouragement, the book might never have appeared.

Times change. For the new material in the book, my Compaq computer and WordPerfect word-processing program deserve the thanks that once went to secretaries. But some things fortunately remain the same. My family has as usual been a source of enormous support, pleasure, and encouragement.

Paul L. Wachtel

CONTENTS

PERSPECTIVES ON PSYCHODYNAMIC THEORY

Introduction to Part One

In the preface to this book, I state that the various parts of the book are interdependent, that ideas from each have influenced the others. This is true. But if I were to stretch to describe any of the sections as most basic, it would have to be this first one. The prism through which I view all of the other issues addressed in this book is most evident here.

Chapter 1 contains my first published foray into psychoanalytic theory, and perhaps for this reason it remains one of my favorites. It presages many of the themes that were to become central concerns in the ensuing years. The paper probably changed more from first draft to final publication than any other paper I have written, and the process of revising it constituted a valuable supplement to the education in psychoanalytic theory I had received at Yale. That education, reflecting the close ties between the Yale psychology and psychiatry departments and the Western New England Psychoanalytic Institute, had been strongly rooted in psychoanalytic ego psychology, and the work of David Rapaport had figured very prominently. (I recall borrowing from one of my professors a well-worn copy of *Organization and Pathology of Thought* in which Rapaport's dense concluding chapter, "Toward a Theory of Thinking," had been so thoroughly underlined that the very purpose of underlining—to highlight some *portion* of what was written—had been rendered useless.)

One of the great challenges for us as graduate students had been to master the murky concepts of "cathexis," "attention cathexis," and "countercathexis," and, if I recall honestly the original impetus for the paper that resulted in Chapter 1, it included in very large measure the wish to show off that I had indeed come to understand the energy concepts in psychoanalysis and was able to use them. The paper was initially written as a reply to a paper that had just appeared by Jane Loevinger, which was one of the early volleys in the assault on the metapsychological formulations that had dominated psychoanalytic theorizing not long before.

The early draft was very much a debater's brief that defended metapsychology to the hilt. I no longer have a copy of that draft, but, as I recall, given that it was defending a hopeless cause, it didn't do such a bad job. But it was much too rooted in the past—both my immediate past and the longer-term past of psychoanalysis—and it required extensive revision. I had long discussions about the paper with Jean Schimek, who at that time was the chief psychologist at Downstate Medical Center, where I was working when the paper was begun. These discussions served to loosen my ties to the conceptual allegiances of my graduate school days, and to point me toward a greater concern with the limitations of the metapsychological approach. By the time the paper was completed I was at the NYU Research Center for Mental Health, where close contact with George Klein, Bob Holt, and Merton Gill brought these issues very much to the forefront of my concerns.

In its final form, Chapter 1 embodies *both* a critique and a defense of metapsychology. It highlights ways in which metapsychological concepts have been misused to provide pseudoexplanations, but it also insists (as I would today) that in principle causal accounts are as appropriate and necessary as ones that stress the individual's purposes. Looking back at the paper from the present vantage point, it seems to me to stand up quite well. Upon rereading, the discussion of the difference between physicists' use of energy concepts employing an interval scale, and psychoanalysts' efforts using an ordinal scale (pp. 23-24), seems to me still to be one of the clearest statements of why energy concepts in psychoanalysis are of limited utility and of how they lend false prestige to rather simple and unremarkable formulations.

Unlike many of the other criticisms of metapsychology that were beginning to appear at about that time, this chapter does not take the view that a natural-science perspective in psychoanalytic discourse is simply a mistake; such a view, I believe, places enormous obstacles in the way of bringing about a *cumulative* development of psychoanalytic thought that could in any way be thought of as leading to progress. Neither does the chapter support the strategy of building psychoanalytic theory rather exclusively from the data of the psychoanalytic session, as so much of the literature critical of metapsychology seems to do. To be sure, the clinical data of the psychoanalytic hour provide a unique source of understanding of people's hidden aims and fantasies; however, their utility is diminished if we eschew other sources of data that can in fact help either to validate or to modify the formulations deriving from the analytic hour.

I was pleased as well to discover in this early work a criticism of the implicit assumption of "motivational omnipotence" that is prevalent in psychoanalytic discourse (p. 18). This is a matter that I have wanted to write about for some time, without recalling that at least in a cursory way I had already addressed it quite early. The alert reader will find significant connections between this aspect of Chapter 1 and the chapters in Part Four. As noted in Chapter 1, psychological functioning depends not only on the person's intentions, but on his capacity to carry out his intentions. The chapters in Part Four are very largely concerned with those capacities.

As the reader will see, some of the issues addressed in this chapter bear on the timeless knot of freedom and determinism in human behavior. The solution arrived at here—regarding neither as more "true" than the other, but rather seeing them as two complementary perspectives, two alternative ways of making sense of the body of observations available to us, not amenable to empirical disentanglement—may not be satisfactory to the philosopher. However, it seems to me a quite reasonable guiding assumption for the therapist, particularly because it is likely to prove relatively immune to patients' attempts either to wait passively for change to hit them like lightning or to blame themselves with a viciousness that is part and parcel of their problem.

All in all, in reviewing this early paper for the present volume, I was struck by the continuity of themes that became apparent. I chuckled a bit to find in the very first paragraph an emphasis on the importance of "integrative efforts" and the problems due to "the narrowed perspective and narrowed definition of problems that result from the limited sources of data upon which theories in psychology are generally built." Seeing such a focus in a paper begun in 1966, when I was just out of graduate school, helped demonstrate to me that there was indeed a coherence in the varied publications that have appeared since then. Similarly, I was struck by the case description (p. 21) that notes how the patient's "generally childlike manner called forth in her therapist some responses that were more appropriate to addressing a child." Both the reality basis on which transference reactions are based (cf. Gill, 1982; Hoffman, 1983) and the patient's role in bringing about that very behavior on the part of the therapist (and on the part of other significant people in the patient's life) are considerations that have been central to my evolving position over the years and are evident in considerable degree in the chapters that follow.

Indeed, these latter themes are the central ones in Chapter 2, which was written about 15 years later. The chapter recasts these questions in terms of the Piagetian notions of assimilation and accommodation. In this, it develops a theoretical strategy I first attempted in *Psychoanalysis and Behavior Therapy*, but it spells out the clinical and theoretical implications in considerably more detail. The chapter begins by examining how transference has traditionally been conceived by psychoanalysts, highlighting the usual emphasis on transferences as inappropriate to the situation and the problems with such formuations. It then goes on to show how the phenomena usually discussed in terms of transference can be understood in terms of Piaget's conception of schemas; transference reactions reflect schemas in which assimilation predominates over accommodation. This view, as the chapter develops, points the theorist or therapist to the necessity of seeing what role accommodation may play in the process as well, since from a Piagetian perspective pure assimilation without accommodation is an impossibility. Once the question is framed this way, considerably greater appreciation of the therapist's contribution to the patient's transference experience is afforded, as well as a more complex picture of just how the predominance of assimilation occurs and of how the therapist can play a more transformative role in the patient's life. This perspective also helps to illuminate ways in which the transference experience can be a disguised and highly symbolic representation of what is actually transpiring between patient and therapist without awareness.

Chapter 3 elaborates on some of these themes, but develops much more focally the circular nature of the processes that occur. This emphasis on circularity is, to be sure, a consistent thread through many of these papers, as it is in *Psychoanalysis and Behavior Therapy*.[1] Chapter 3, however, spells out more fully the implications of this pervasive circularity. The title originally given to the paper (it was changed by the journal editor) included the term "cyclical psychodynamics," and as far as I can recall this was in fact the first psychoanalytic publication in which I used that term to describe my theoretical point of view. Cyclical psychodynamics attempts to cast our understanding of the role of conflict, defense, and unconscious motives and thoughts in a way that also addresses what we have learned about the ways in which people's private reactions are responsive to the events of their lives and the ways in which their private reactions themselves *determine* in large part what those events will be.

1. See also Wachtel and Wachtel (1986), where its relation to the conceptions that have guided the work of family therapists is discussed in detail.

Central to the chapter is the spelling out of the implications of certain pervasive linguistic habits of psychoanalysts—in particular, the use of the terms "emerge" and "unfold" to describe what is revealed about the patient over the course of an analysis. Frequently those terms are used in ways that obscure the relation between what "unfolds" and the particular events in relation to which that unfolding occurs. Understanding the rhetorical use of these by now ritualistically pervasive terms enables us to see more clearly why Sullivan's conception of the therapist as a participant–observer raises serious doubts about the utility or validity of the notion of therapeutic neutrality.

Two other matters are highlighted in Chapter 3 as well. One is an effort to call attention to the major shift in the foundations of psychoanalysis that occurred when Freud recognized clearly the relation between anxiety and repression. As the chapter notes, Sullivan's and Horney's theories took as a starting point Freud's 1926 revisions of his anxiety theory, but in important respects they did not fully capitalize on the new insights that accrued to them from such a point of departure. Nonetheless, as the chapter also points out, both Sullivan and Horney were centrally concerned with issues that have only recently been focally addressed by the mainstream of psychoanalysis. Each of them, for example, developed a rather thorough-going psychology of the self decades before the term and the idea had become fashionable in psychoanalytic circles. Moreover, especially in the case of Horney, she did so in a way that did not pit a psychology of self and object relations against the prior psychoanalytic psychology of conflict and defense. Rather, she showed—as does the cyclical psychodynamic view spelled out in this book—how "the sense of self evolves gradually from experiences with other people, integrating a variety of experiences and reflecting as well the limitations set by anxiety and compulsive efforts to avoid it" (p. 53). As Chapter 3 shows, the conscious and unconscious experience of self can best be understood by understanding how it is guided and limited by the lines of conflict that characterize the evolving personality. At the same time, our understanding of conflict can itself be advanced by understanding how central is the shaping role of the dynamically evolving self.

Chapter 4 examines related questions from a different vantage point—in this case, that of the distinction between internal and external determinants of behavior and experience. One of the persisting sources of confusion in psychoanalytic thought has been the tendency to conceptualize an "internal world" that is in important respects unrelated to the ongoing events of the person's life. Much of what appears in this book can be seen as an effort to address the confusions that arise from such a conceptual strategy—an effort to preserve the *observations* that have made such a point of view compelling to many people, while at the same time to recast them in a way that is more logical and more inclusive of other observations that at first seem to point in a very different direction. The chapter is one of a series of papers (see also Chapters 17 and 18) written in the context of a great upsurge of interest by personality researchers in the 1970s in the development of an interactional approach to personality; it was an invited chapter for a volume called *Perspectives in Interactional Psychology*. As the conclusion of the chapter notes, however, it

> can be distinguished from much work that goes on under [the label of interactionism] by its reluctance to treat "person variables" and "situation variables" as thoroughly independent. In much personality research, the interactionism comes at the point of statistical analysis, when variables that are originally defined and conceptualized as very separate are combined additively and their statistical interaction viewed with interest. From the present perspective, however, it is hard to distinguish person variables and situation variables (or "internal" and "external" determinants). Aspects of the person and the situation he is in continuously interact. The appropriate mathematical representation for such interaction is not the statistical model of analysis of variance, but rather the model of the integral calculus. In most real-life situations, only for a diminishingly small instant is any person–effect manifested that is independent of the situation or does any situation unfold that is independent of the person who encounters (and changes) it. (p. 81)

Chapter 5 reflects the considerable influence of John Dollard and Neal Miller on my thinking. Both Dollard and Miller were at Yale when I was a graduate student, and Dollard was in fact one of my first therapy supervisors. Their contribution in providing a theoretical bridge between the concepts of psychoanalysis and those of the learning laboratory has continued to seem to me a major one, despite the recent tendency to downgrade it because it did not lead to much that was new in actual clinical practice. Such an evaluation underestimates the potential contribution of having a theoretical language in which to reorder observations, as well as the utility of re-examining false distinctions that can constrict future explorations. My own integrative efforts, which did yield a quite considerable change in the way I practiced, were greatly aided by Dollard and Miller's theoretical forays.

The analysis in Chapter 5 addresses a number of points of confusion in Dollard and Miller's model of conflict. Despite the many clarifying and heuristic features of their model, there were ambiguities that required elucidation, as well as a number of ideas whose consequences needed to be spelled out.

Dollard and Miller's conflict diagrams, for example, are of particular utility in clarifying the implications of both wanting and fearing the same object. They illuminate why conflicts of this sort are so difficult to resolve, as well as making much clearer how the therapeutic process facilitates such resolution and why in the middle of the process the patient can actually feel worse while progress is being made. But they do not make clear enough that there are in fact *two* kinds of avoidance, with differing implications—one that is simply one pole of the conflict and that is in dynamic tension with the tendency to approach; and one in which the person leaves the field of conflict altogether. Significantly, the latter kind of avoidance is not countered by an approach tendency and hence leads to more thorough avoidance. Their conflict diagrams, which depict avoidances of the first kind, can lead to an overestimation of patients' effective exposure to what is feared and hence to some puzzlement at the persistence of neurotic fears. As Chapter 5 points out, appreciation of this distinction has important implications for one's understanding of the therapist's role and raises questions about the efficiency of relying on free association as a primary therapeutic vehicle.

The analysis in this chapter also points out some ambiguities and potentially incorrect predictions in Dollard and Miller's model, which stem from their strong emphasis on an intrapsychic version of psychodynamic thought. It shows how consideration of interpersonal dynamics and circular feedback loops can enable Dollard and Miller's model to account for observations that would otherwise be problematic. Finally, the chapter is the only publication I know of that asks the rather odd question: Why don't patients sleep with their mothers after successful therapy?

1

Psychology, Metapsychology, and Psychoanalysis

Perhaps the most encouraging trend in psychoanalytic theory in the years since Freud's death has been the tendency to dismantle the iron curtain surrounding its brilliant insights, facilitating fruitful intercourse and integrative merger between the observations and viewpoints of psychoanalysts and those of academic psychologists. Such integrative efforts are essential to counter the narrowed perspective and narrowed definition of problems that result from the limited sources of data upon which theories in psychology are generally built. Thus, the structure of psychoanalytic theory, the nature of its assumptions and emphases, derives not only from the nature of Freud's personality and training (Amacher, 1965; Holt, 1965), but also from the fact that its primary data source is the free associations of neurotic patients. Other theories in psychology place similarly heavy emphasis on the bar pressing of rats, the problem solving of college students, etc., and such emphasis cannot help but constrict the range of questions asked and models proposed.

In the course of the development of psychoanalytic theory, it became the hope of Freud and his followers that psychoanalytic theory would become a general psychology, that it would account not only for neurotic phenomena but for all phenomena in the realm

Reprinted by permission from the *Journal of Abnormal Psychology*, 1969, 74(6), 651–660.

This chapter was written while I was a Fellow in the Program for Postdoctoral Study and Research in Psychology and on the staff of the Research Center for Mental Health at New York University. I wish to express my gratitude to George S. Klein, J. G. Schimek, Linda H. Schoeman, and Philip Bromberg for their valuable comments on earlier drafts of this chapter.

of psychological science. An almost inevitable result of such efforts will be a change in the structure of psychoanalytic theory. As the data base of the theory expands, as it attempts to encompass new observations—to include, for example, the data of laboratory experiments—the theoretical concepts that tie together the observations will require revision. This has been the case generally in the history of science, and even in the history of psychoanalytic theory itself. Thus, as psychoanalytic observation began to focus upon the mechanisms of defense, the topographic model of the conscious, preconscious, and unconscious systems (Freud, 1915/1959) had to be replaced by the structural model of ego, id, and superego; the former model was adequate to account for the early observations but could not survive new data. One can imagine that efforts to expand the explanatory realm of psychoanalytic theory may one day become so successful that the original theory will disappear of its own success. To the extent that the theory truly becomes a general psychology it will cease to be *psychoanalytic* theory, and will tend to be simply psychological theory. The total disappearance of separate theories in psychology and the emergence of a single psychological theory free of the parochial origins of its parts constitute, of course, an asymptote from which we are still quite distant, but it is important to keep the emerging goal in mind, for the goal determines what is the essential product of psychoanalytic research.

Freud was far less reverent toward his theoretical constructions than are many of his followers. He recognized (Freud, 1940/1949) quite clearly that it is the *facts* discovered by psychoanalytic work that will stand as his major achievement, rather than the theories. The latter were merely ingenious working principles to tie together the data that had emerged up until then and to point toward new observations. Freud's discoveries regarding unconscious motivation, the expressive meaning of dreams, and the organization of primitive thought will remain valuable long after the words "ego," "id," or "libido" have become obsolete. Concern with the distinction between psychoanalytic data and the theory used to account for it has led to increasing critical discussion of the basic theoretical assumptions of psychoanalytic theory in recent years. That aspect of the theory that Freud called his metapsychology has come under the most critical scrutiny. Some of this criticism has been helpful in clarifying assumptions and opening the way for theoretical formulation more suited to our present level of knowledge, but blanket dismissal of all metapsychological perspectives as "reductionistic" (Loevinger, 1966) may obscure some important issues. In particular, it will be suggested below that the energy constructs of Freudian metapsychology, while clearly in need of drastic revision and perhaps even amputation, have served to direct researchers to an important realm of questions. Without careful consideration of the role of energy constructs and other impersonal process descriptions in the theory, there is a danger that a poor formulation may be replaced not by a more adequate one, but by a reluctance to encompass the observations that led to the formulation in the first place.

MEANING AND METAPSYCHOLOGY

Psychoanalytic theory is characterized by two rather separate theoretical approaches. The clinical theory consists of "inferences of *directional* gradients in behavior, and of the *object-relations* involved in these directions" (Klein, 1966, p. 10); it represents a search for meaning and purpose in behavior. Psychoanalytic metapsychology, on the other hand, reflects Freud's view that purposive concepts are scientifically unacceptable. It is a mechanical quasi-thermodynamic model in the language of forces and energies. Klein (1966) has called it a theory to explain a theory, and has argued that, unlike the clinical propositions, metapsychological concepts are "impervious to the type of data obtainable from the psychoanalyst's hour" (p. 15).

Tension between a humanistic and a mechanistic view of man, between the sense that man is a choosing responsible moral agent and the idea that human actions are as impersonally determined as the motion of the planets, is woven tightly into the fabric of psychoanalysis. One could not expect such tension to be absent from any meaningful psychology, for the paradox of human choice has been a central problem in the study of man for many centuries. Klein (1966) has noted that the impersonal, metapsychological perspective on human behavior has been fallaciously put forth as more *basic* than the purposive explanations of the clinical theory. To understand a man's strivings and feelings, to know him from the inside, is somehow regarded as inferior to observing him as an object in the most literal sense.

Questions of freedom and determinism in psychoanalysis do not directly parallel the conflict between the clinical and metapsychological perspectives. Much of Freud's argument for a determinist position was in the service of building the *clinical* theory, of demonstrating that seemingly meaningless events such as dreams and slips of the tongue could be given meaning if the determining chain of associations were followed back to its source. Nonetheless, the role of metapsychological theorizing is related to the view of human behavior as ultimately determined by an impersonal "natural" process, even if "meanings" are a convenient description of the intervening events that occur. A brief examination of the psychoanalytic view of determinism and freedom is therefore in order.

FREEDOM AND DETERMINISM

Knight's (1946) discussion of the freedom–determinism issue is probably as close to a standard psychoanalytic position on this issue as one can find. Knight believed that determinism was an essential assumption for a scientific psychology. Yet like many other analysts and therapists (e.g., Mazer, 1960; Wheelis, 1956), Knight recognized that a deterministic viewpoint may be used by patients as resistance to effort at therapeutic change. Many patients claim that they simply cannot help what they are doing, that their behavior is determined and they have no choice or responsibility. Such an attitude may effectively inhibit necessary effort on the part of the patient and may function as a self-fulfilling prophecy that indeed results in the patient remaining the same.

In dealing with this dilemma, Knight emphasized the distinction between determinism as a construct and freedom as a subjective experience. For Knight, freedom is an experience of harmony between one's behavior and one's character, a sense that one is behaving in one's own best interests and is free from compulsion, anxiety, and irrational doubts;

> this kind of "freedom" is experienced only by emotionally mature, well-integrated persons, it is the goal sought for one's patients in psychotherapy; and this freedom has nothing whatever to do with free will as a principle governing human behavior, but is a subjective experience *which is itself determined.* (italics added; Knight, 1946, p. 372)

Knight claims that such freedom, while subjective, need not be spurious.

> The behavior of a well-integrated civilized person can be objectively assessed as "free." Observers see that such a person makes ego-syntonic choices, that his motives are "good," and that he is able to carry out what he wills to do. (p. 372)

Nonetheless, one is left with the impression from Knight's paper that man's every act and thought is *really* determined, and that freedom, however precious, is finally just an epiphenomenon.

Knight is certainly correct that the term "free will" confuses the issue. One can hardly use the term without calling up visions of medieval theological debate. But simply to define free will as a subjective experience, causally determined in the same way as the experience of pain upon being burned is determined, seems to be begging the question. Such an approach *assumes* determinism without ever questioning it, and deals with the perplexing issue of freedom by redefining it, and thereby essentially dismissing it.

Free will is a frustrating conception because no one is clear what is meant by "free." It is easy to topple the straw man who speaks of freedom as if it were caprice, of freely willed acts as those that are unrelated to a person's history, character, or environment. But the great hold that the concept of freedom has had on men does not stem from the belief that man's actions are random. It stems from the belief that men's choices are meaningful and that the agony of decision is not simply an interesting phenomenon, to be explained by causal laws external to it, but rather the central fact from which to launch an investigation of man.

In this light, it may be seen that the determinism subscribed to by Knight and other analysts and the freedom proclaimed, for example, by the existentialists are two different perspectives on the same set of observations. Both groups of theorists see men walk and talk and make love and war. In order to organize and make sense of these observations, the determinist views the men he observes as he views all other objects in the universe. They are to him (while he is wearing the cap of the determinist) ultimately understood as bits of moving matter whose motions are described in terms similar in principle (though far more complex and perhaps at a different "level") to those describing the motion of any other particles. From this perspective, free will is indeed simply a "subjective experience," to be explained causally like any other phenomenon.

But there is another perspective on human behavior, another way of organizing the data, which all (healthy?) determinists use in much of their personal lives, and which some psychologists (e.g., the phenomenologists) use in their professional lives as well. Starting not with what is similar between man and the rest of the universe, but rather with what seems unique to man, one may view men's actions as through their own eyes, one may attempt to construct their phenomenal world, to understand them as men who act and decide on the basis of what they see and feel. From this second perspective (one may call it a "common-sense" perspective, though modern psychoanalytic and phenomenological research have carried it far beyond common sense), determinism is neither right nor wrong—it is simply irrelevant, a different way of looking at things. The terms of discourse for such a perspective are feeling and decision rather than cause and effect.

Both perspectives on the facts of human behavior have their utility. As Klein (1966) seems to suggest in a different context, they are mutually incompatible ways of organizing and comprehending observations of human beings (including oneself). Perhaps (though it is doubtful) some day a synthesizing formulation will be created that resolves the contradiction and shows each perspective to be a special case of some general and consistent view. For the present, however, it seems necessary to recognize the need for both perspectives. No man can get along well with just one, and to reduce "psychological science" to those organizations of observations that employ the determinist perspective is simply to impoverish the realm of psychological inquiry. To completely exclude a determinist viewpoint is of course equally productive of sterility.

CAUSAL AND PURPOSIVE PERSPECTIVES

To the extent that metapsychology is, as Klein (1966) suggests, a theory to explain a theory, it reflects a nonrational, quasi-religious commitment to a determinist position. There is false hope (or fear) in the view that we have not *yet* explained all the nuances of human thought, feeling, and behavior in terms of energies and forces. I am in agreement with Klein that there are difficulties *in principle* with automatically "converting the terms of clinical observation to impersonal process terms." Neurophysiological or information-processing models, no less than energy models, represent only one perspective on human affairs, and have no greater claim to describing an *ultimate* truth than do descriptions of striving and meaning. Both perspectives, if used wisely, can provide useful insights.

Psychoanalytic observation is tuned in on a unique level of coherence (Klein, 1966). The structure of the analytic situation facilitates perception by the analyst of patterns of thought organization in the patient, and enables the analyst to notice characteristics of the patient's thinking and behavior that might otherwise go undetected. Certain seemingly unrelated ideas may be expressed in close contiguity with remarkable frequency. Or free association may lead to the expression of ideas and thoughts that are rarely directly expressed at all in any other context. Who would have expected, on the basis of other models of observation, that free-asssociating patients would so often express incestuous fantasies? On the other hand, psychoanalytic observations also highlights *gaps* in expression not generally as

visible elsewhere. The analyst may notice that every time his patient's thoughts seem to be leading toward criticism of an authority,
something happens to halt or deflect the progress of his associations.
Or he may notice that certain topics, or certain expected reactions,
simply never come up as the patient talks about himself and his life
day after day.

Such observations, and the generalizations derived from them,
are what give psychoanalytic thinking its special cast. Psychoanalysts
are trained to notice when a person says he is trying to do one thing
and consistently acts as if he were trying to do quite another (or
more frequently some odd combination of both). Greater knowledge
of the full range of human strivings and of the manifold fears and
compromises that bend, disguise, and complicate those strivings is
the special fruit of psychoanalytic research. For knowledge of mechanism, on the other hand, and for the building of models based on
physical and biological analogies, the data of psychoanalytic sessions
are largely irrelevant.

Klein (1966) is careful to point out that impersonal causal models of behavior are not without a place in psychology; they simply are
a poor strategy for dealing with the particular opportunities for
observation provided by the psychoanalytic session. Loevinger
(1966), however, seems to dismiss metapsychological perspectives
more categorically. She is concerned with finding a set of principles
that is distinctively psychoanalytic. But what does it mean for a
principle to be psychoanalytic? Does it mean that the data upon
which it is based came originally from psychoanalytic sessions? Are
other sources of data to be dismissed, with psychoanalytic principles
remaining "pure" but of little value for answering the more sophisticated questions called for by new observations? Or is a principle
psychoanalytic if it is in essence a theoretical statement formulated
by Freud or at least an elaboration of such? Then psychoanalytic
theory is destined to becoming an interesting historical curio, to be
respected for its eminence among early 20th-century efforts, but of
little interest to those concerned with understanding the latest observations of human behavior.

Psychoanalytic insights are far too important to be so embalmed
and preserved. The psychoanalytic tradition in psychological thought
has been one of the most vital and original. Perhaps the historical
accident of its isolation from the academic world and its development
into a "movement" contributed to that vitality. But there is now
danger that what was once a revolutionary way of thinking is becoming a conservative, consolidated "system," an outcome that is fostered by that same isolation. A psychoanalytic perspective, that is, a
view of human behavior based largely on psychoanalytic observa-

tions, and emphasizing the role of unconscious motivations, defenses, compromise formations, etc., is still vitally relevant to psychological inquiry. A separate psychoanalytic *theory*, however, at least to the extent that such a theory is not receptive to data from nonpsychoanalytic sources, seems increasingly a poor enterprise in which to invest effort. That some metapsychological propositions are "as congenial to many antianalytic psychologies as to psychoanalysis" (Loevinger, 1966, p. 433) is irrelevant. What matters is how congenial they are to the latest data.

Let us consider Loevinger's solution to "one of the most baffling theoretical problems of psychoanalysis" (p. 437), how an impulse contributes to its own control. She claims that notions such as bound cathexis and countercathexis add little to the explanation, and suggests instead that "one is controlled, simultaneously or in turn, by one's impulses and one's parents, and one therefore needs to control something in return, if not one's parents, then one's impulses" (Loevinger, 1966, p. 437). This may perhaps be an adequate account of why the developing personality *wants* to control the impulse, but it says nothing about why he *succeeds*. What is lacking in a psychology solely of meanings, as Loevinger calls for, is adequate consideration of *capacities*. As did early psychoanalytic writings, Loevinger's suggested system implies a kind of motivational omnipotence, whereby it is sufficient to explore the *motives* for behavior without considering the *ability* of the individual to efficiently order and execute all the wishes pressing for fulfillment at a given moment. As an example, if a person gets into an accident, it is certainly not always correct to say that he is expressing a wish to hurt himself. A self-destructive wish would no doubt lower the threshold for such events, but it is clear that such wishes are often kept from direct expression by a strong ego, and phenomena such as "distraction" may often play a more important role in accounting for accidents.

Phenomena such as distraction are at the heart of what is missing in Loevinger's scheme. Korchin (1964), for example, has summarized a great deal of evidence suggesting that anxiety may reduce the capacity to "do two things at once." The perceptual–cognitive effects he describes seem vitally relevant in understanding the kinds of behavior that psychoanalysts observe. Certainly, the exact form that behavior in an anxious state takes, as well as the origin of the anxiety itself, is largely a matter of meanings; but without consideration of the constriction of perspective and general narrowing of cognitive organization characteristic of the anxious individual, our understanding of his experience and behavior is incomplete. Similarly, the accounts of individual differences in the organization of attention attempted by Gardner, Klein, and their colleagues (e.g., Gardner,

Holzman, Klein, Linton, & Spence, 1959) represent a psychoanalytically oriented approach to character style complementary to and consistent with Freud's discussions of character in terms of libidinal organization. It is a strength rather than a weakness of such work that it is almost impossible to distinguish that part of the conceptual underpinning that comes from psychoanalytic theory and that which comes from other psychological approaches.

COGNITIVE STYLE AND MEANING

The need-in-perception studies were an effort to counter the overly impersonal view of perception prevalent at the time and to highlight the personal meaning of the stimulus for the perceiver. Many of these studies both explicitly and implicitly borrowed from psychoanalytic discoveries of the role of drive and wish in shaping perceptual and cognitive events. As Klein (1958) has pointed out, however, these corrective efforts themselves tended to be one-sided, erring in the direction of overemphasizing the role of drive and disregarding the structural constraints upon drive influence. More precisely, it was the recruiting or meaning-inducing activity of drives that was overemphasized, to the exclusion of the accommodative structures, for Klein's (1958) conception of drive is a unitary one, which emphasizes the coordination of intentions and the means of carrying them out.

One does not understand an individual very well if one knows only the wishes that dominate the recruitment aspects of his personality structure. One must also understand his modes of accommodation and the hierarchic ordering of his wishes and cognitions. Human perception is only sometimes distorted, but it is always selective, and such selection is always limited even if accurate. Regardless of what wishes are currently active, the field-independent individual (Witkin, Dyk, Faterson, Goodenough, & Karp, 1962) will perceive and experience a different world than the field-dependent, the world of the sharpener will differ from that of the leveler (Gardner *et al.*, 1959), etc. The origin of such differing modes of accommodation may well be largely a matter of the meaning to an individual of certain ways of experiencing the world.[1] Such characteristics of the individual's accommodative efforts, however, also enter into his encounters with the world as a kind of automatic filter that he can no longer readily change. Some aspects of personality often designated as styles may

1. Shapiro (1965), for example, has vividly illustrated the personal meaning of individual differences in cognitive style.

better be thought of as capacities than as stylistic preferences (Wachtel, 1968b).

The need for some impersonal process descriptions in personality theory (even for understanding the events of the psychoanalytic hour) is clearer, however, when one considers the somewhat automatic effects of such variables as anxiety upon cognitive functioning. To be sure, the effects of anxiety also are probably subject to individual differences related to the meaning of the anxiety-provoking stimulus. There are indications, for example, that anxiety due to a threat perceived as possible to avert seems to have different consequences than anxiety due to an inevitable harm (Wachtel, 1968a). Nonetheless, the breadth of the individual's cognitive and attentive field does seem to be usefully regarded as a dependent variable in a functional relationship between anxiety and attention (Easterbrook, 1959; Korchin, 1964; Wachtel, 1968a), and breadth of attention is important to consider in understanding phenomena of the therapy hour.

Consider the following clinical example: A female patient, in her early 20s, has a great stake in perceiving herself as a young child, though such an image is, of course, not experienced without considerable conflict. This image of herself helps to reassure her that she is not like her mother, whom she perceives as selfish, nasty, and controlling. She lives in a black and white world, where to be a child is to be innocent, pretty, and acceptable, and to be an adult is to be dirty, voracious, and despised.[2] Without full awareness, she often behaves in childish ways that call forth responses from others appropriate to dealing with someone much younger. Though she complains at times about such treatment, it seems to be quite comfortable for her. On several occasions, she has reported situations in which she was treated with greater respect than usual, and compliments, which she found gratifying, were combined with requests for her to assume responsibilities commensurate with her considerable talents. She found her distress on these occasions puzzling, and it was suggested to her that she would have preferred to receive a simple pat on the head that did not imply that she was an adult capable of making an adult's contribution. On each of these occasions, she became quite agitated and complained that her therapist was talking to her as if she were a child. Similar complaints were made at times about her husband, always at times when he asked her to behave like an adult, for example, by keeping track of her checkbook balance.

2. For purposes of exposition, the dynamics of the case must here be greatly simplified. There are, for example, many indications that her identification with her mother is also a cherished key to power, and further that her mother in many respects is also viewed as a kind of ideal.

Her response to her therapist, as to her husband, obviously had great personal meaning. Threatened with the exposure of and threat to her wish to be a child, she shifted her attention from the content of the therapist's comments to their tone; she further gratified her wish right in the hour by experiencing him as talking to her as if she were a child. But how did she manage to see her therapist in such a fashion? It is not sufficient merely to note that her perception was influenced by the pressure of strong wishes, for, as we noted earlier, there are considerable constraints upon the distorting effect of wishes. We must assume, I believe, that this patient focused upon some actual features of her therapist's behavior. No doubt her generally childlike manner called forth in her therapist some responses that were more appropriate to addressing a child. The rhythm, tone of voice, or style of phrasing must have provided the cues that led to her perception. That these aspects of the interaction, which meshed so well with her needs, should have become the focus of her attention is not surprising. What is worth noting, however, is the degree to which they remained unmodified by other aspects of the situation. Her field of attention was largely limited to these isolated cues. The larger context in which they occurred, including an explicit message directly opposite to her perceived meaning (i.e., you were being treated as an adult—people perceive you as an adult), was hardly noticed. In her state of arousal and anxiety, she experienced a narrower range of her therapist's behavior than she normally does, and this narrowing of her field of attention enabled her to focus exclusively on the infantalizing aspect of his remarks. Clearer understanding of the exact nature of the narrowing of attention occurring in anxious states (Wachtel, 1967) would clarify the structural limits within which her motivational and perceptual efforts were expressed, and would suggest what efforts would be needed to correct and amplify her perception of the interpersonal situation. Understanding of the "meaning" of infantilization to her would be necessary but not sufficient to guide the therapist's approach to such behavior.

ROLE OF ENERGY CONSTRUCTS

The aspect of psychoanalytic metapsychology that has come under the most intense and persistent criticism has been the economic viewpoint (Rapaport & Gill, 1959), or energy theory. Holt (1967) has pointed out that despite Freud's explicit commitment to physicalistic mechanistic explanation, his concept of psychic energy "is a vitalistic concept in the sense of being similar to and influenced by vital force, and being to a large extent functionally equivalent to it. They are at the least historically and methodologically homologous—buds from the same branch" (pp. 24–25). Holt has discussed in detail the limitations that are thereby inherent in the traditional psychoanalytic energy concept.

It should be noted, however, that the energy concepts of psychoanalysis have had several different functions in the theory. One main function of the energy concept was to deal with the mind–body problem. Freud referred to instincts as a borderland concept between mind and body; and as Holt (1967) points out, Freud often discussed libidinal energy as if it were not simply an abstract psychological concept but rather a form of physical–neural energy, transformed much as heat may be converted to kinetic energy. It is within this framework that loose metaphorical thinking and anthropomorphism have characterized discussion of psychic energy (libido seen as pushing, pressing for discharge, etc.).

There has been, however, another use of energy concepts by psychoanalytic thinkers that is less subject to the difficulties noted above. The concept of ego energies has been more consistently employed as an abstract nonexistential construct representing the capacity to do (psychological) work, and has thus played a role in theory construction somewhat more akin to the role of energy in physics. As we shall note, this use of an energy concept has its drawbacks too, but examination of the utility of the concept thus far and of the nature of its limitations can pave the way for a better replacement.

Consider the concept of attention cathexis, an aspect of ego energy emphasized by Rapaport (1967). It is based in a general way upon the obvious observation that at any given moment attention to certain aspects of the inner or outer world makes awareness of other aspects less likely. The energy construct is used to coordinate reciprocities among psychological phenomena, relating changes in different parts of the system to each other, much as physical energy is a hypothetical construct simplifying the coordination of reciprocities among physical phenomena. If we divest the concept of the controversial theories of the origins of such energies (cf. Hartmann, Kris, & Loewenstein, 1949; White, 1963), we seem to be left with a useful scheme for relating psychological phenomena, one that may lead to testable hypotheses.

For example, central to the psychoanalytic conception of defense and to the theory of neurosis is the idea that defenses use energy and require a constant effort to prevent the defended-against material from reaching awareness. Rapaport (1951) has described the psychoanalytic conception of consciousness as a matter of the distribution of attention cathexes, which are available only in a certain quantity. Evidence seems to suggest that these attention-cathexes are identical with those used in counter-cathecting and where excessive energies are required for the latter it limits those available for the former. (p. 699)

Gardner *et al.* (1959) have used this conception in accounting for the empirical relation between the cognitive style of leveling and repressive defenses, and many neurotic phenomena are also explained psychoanalytically by the impoverishment of the ego, which such diversion of energies implies (Fenichel, 1945). One might expect from this view that if an individual were defending against perceiving an aspect of the stimulus field, his responsiveness to the rest of the field would also be reduced, for part of his capacity to attend is engaged in preventing perception of the offending stimulus.[3]

Some authors, on the other hand (e.g., Kellner, Butters, & Wiener, 1964), have maintained that defenses do not involve a continuing struggle of the sort implied above, but rather are a matter merely of the individual's reinforcement history making some responses more likely and others less likely. If this is so, then defending would not consume any of the individual's capacity to attend, and no reduction in overall responsiveness to the field should be evident in those instances of conspicuous inattention to particular features from which defense is inferred. In fact, since some features are avoided, the rest of the field would have less competition for the individual's attention and should be *more* completely perceived. Defense studies that focus not on whether or not a particular brief stimulus is perceived, but rather on the individual's selective attention to a complex field through time, should be able to shed light on the merits of these two competing conceptions, and thereby on the important relation between defense on the one hand and character and neurosis on the other.

It is possible, then, to use energy concepts to guide empirical inquiry. A fair number of studies have originated at least in part from economic concepts (e.g., Lustman, 1957; Schimek & Wachtel, 1969; Schwartz & Schiller, 1970; Spence & Grief, 1968; Toman, 1954; Wachtel & Blatt, 1965). The utility of such concepts is considerably limited, however, by the difference in the kinds of quantitative statements made by physicists and psychologists. Energy in

---

3. The issue is of course far more complicated than can be described in this brief presentation. To maintain and reinforce the defense, for example, some *particular* aspect of the field might be *more* likely noticed when defending (e.g., loving implications when defending against hostility), but overall awareness of nuances in all aspects of the field might still be reduced.

physics is measured (indirectly, of course, as in psychology) on an interval scale. There is a precisely specifiable number of footpounds of potential energy embodied in an object suspended above the earth. If that body falls, its velocity upon hitting the ground can be exactly predicted by the formula $\frac{1}{2} mv^2$ (kinetic energy) $= ghM$ (potential energy). If these two numbers are not exactly equal, then one knows precisely what portion of the potential energy has been used in moving the resisting air particles, heating the falling object, etc. Since the same "quantity" is presumed to be involved in, for example, mechanical, electrical, and thermal phenomena, a powerful set of equations can be devised to precisely predict changes in seemingly diverse phenomenal realms. There are even "economic" consequences in the more common meaning of the term, for the electric company can bill people for a specific number of kilowatt hours of energy, regardless of whether they heated their house, lit their lamps, cooked a meal, ran electric trains, or brushed their teeth.

The case is quite different in psychology. Here energy is measured on an ordinal scale. One can say only that there is more or less energy used in a given process. To state, for example, the simple functional relationship that the more one exhibits signs of defending against forbidden wishes or ideas, the less one will be attentive to his (internal and external) environment, seems to be exactly equivalent to the proposition that defenses use attentional energy. The formulation in energic terms adds nothing. This is quite different from the situation in physics, where numerical specification of the quantity of energy involved leads to specific determination of other measures and to the possibility of checking whether all the energy in the system is accounted for. Physicists and engineers would not need an energy concept if the most that could be said was: The more water that falls on the generator, the more houses we can light. It is the possibility of measuring the energy on an interval scale that makes the postulation of such a quantity superior to simple functional description of the relationship between two observable variables. If one could actually quantify on an interval scale the amount of defensive activity, the amount of perceptual activity, the amount of organizing and structure formation, etc., and show their sum to be a constant, then psychological energy would be an invaluable construct. The day when such measurement is possible, however, seems at this point a matter for psychological science fiction.

At our present level of knowledge, the use of energy constructs may do more harm than good. That the term is used superfluously does not in itself seem a serious matter; it can still be consistently related to observations, and the imagery evoked by the particular metaphor may inspire original hypotheses in some investigators.

(Rapaport [1967], for example, created a complex set of hypotheses that might not have occurred without an energy notion.) It *is* a serious matter, however, if the illusion of an adequate explanation blinds investigators to the many unanswered questions that remain and delays seeking more precise descriptions of the state of affairs. It is not being unfaithful to an old friend to ask of a theoretical conception: What have you done for me lately? On the contrary, such irreverence is essential for scientific advance. Many concepts are perfectly adequate at an early stage of scientific investigation but may freeze progress if held on to too long. Energy statements have the ring of a finished system, and may perhaps best be held in abeyance until such a system is a more imminent possibility.

If the energy construct is discarded, however, it will be important to bear in mind the reasons for discarding it. In scientific endeavor it is often as important *why* a concept is abandoned as *whether* it is. The difficulties inherent in the use of an energy construct at this stage of theoretical development should not obscure the need for *some* kind of process description and causal analysis in psychological investigation.

The metaphor of a limited quantity of energy that may be deployed in various ways has its problems and limitations, but it does highlight some important issues that it is well to keep in mind. In particular, it is essential to explore the nature of the limits and consequences of human choices, to understand the price that one pays for committing oneself to a course of action, a style of life, or a mode of perception. The economic point of view emphasizes the limits or boundary conditions of human existence, and the importance of its message should not be dismissed because of the crudity of its formulation. Loevinger (1966) is correct that understanding the *meaning* of psychological events is an essential aspect of psychoanalytic research, perhaps the most important contribution that such research can make. But unless such understanding is integrated with a firm knowledge of the fabric of constraints within which meaning is given, the psychoanalytic endeavor is not likely to have much meaning at all.

2

Transference, Schema, and Assimilation: The Relevance of Piaget to the Psychoanalytic Theory of Transference

I

The Freudian concept of transference originated in observations of disturbed adults, obtained in the context of therapy, and was an attempt to account for certain distortions in their perception of reality. The Piagetian concept of schema derived from observations of healthy children, obtained in the context of research, and was an attempt to account for their increasingly accurate perception of reality. Two more disparate origins would be hard to find. Yet, I will argue, the Piagetian concept can provide a very useful and clarifying perspective on the phenomena to which Freud directed our attention.

Freud's first reports of transference phenomena were published in the *Studies on Hysteria* (Breuer & Freud, 1895/1955). There he referred to the patient establishing a *"false connection"* (p. 302) between the doctor and a figure from the past. Transference reactions were "a compulsion and an *illusion*, which melted away with the conclusion of the analysis" (p. 304; italics added).

In his discussion of the Dora case, Freud (1905/1953) elaborated somewhat on the concept and introduced an interesting complexity, related to the major theme of the present chapter. Though transferences were generally to be regarded as "facsimiles" which "replace some earlier person by the person of the physician," some were

Reprinted by permission from *The Annual of Psychoanalysis*, 1981, *8*, 59–76. Copyright © 1981 by International Universities Press.

found to be "more ingeniously constructed" and "may even become conscious, by cleverly taking advantage of some real peculiarity in the physician's person or circumstances and attaching themselves to that" (p. 116).

In "The Dynamics of Transference" (1912/1958) Freud states that "The peculiarities of the transference to the doctor, thanks to which it *exceeds, both in amount and nature, anything that could be justified on sensible or rational grounds* [italics added], are made intelligible if we bear in mind that this transference has precisely been set up not only by the *conscious* anticipatory ideas but also by those that have been held back or are unconscious" (p. 100).

Three years later, in further considering the idea that transference reactions should not be understood as real reactions to what is going on, Freud (1915/1958) discusses as an "argument against the genuineness of this love . . . the fact that it exhibits not a single new feature arising from the present situation, but is entirely composed of repetitions and copies of earlier reactions, including infantile ones. We undertake to prove this by a detailed analysis of the patient's behavior in love" (p. 167).

He then goes on to indicate, however, that in thus proceeding "we have told the patient the truth, but not the whole truth" (p. 168). The argument that transference love is not genuine because it is a repetition is weak, Freud says, because "this is the essential character of every state of being in love. There is no such state which does not reproduce infantile prototypes" (p. 168). Of particular relevance to the arguments to be advanced in the present discussion, Freud notes that the difference between transference love and what we call normal love is one of degree, and further adds, "it displays its dependence on the infantile pattern more clearly and is less adaptable and capable of modification; *but that is all and not what is essential*" (p. 168; italics added). Thus Freud indicates here that the processes responsible for the emotional and perceptual phenomena we label as transference are essentially the same as those in all relationships between two people, differing only in degree.

Yet only a year later, in his *Introductory Lectures*, Freud (1916/1963) repeats the kinds of statements which were the basis for the prevalent tendency (discussed below) to treat transference reactions as something quite distinct from "realistic" reactions to others. There, discussing transferences, Freud wrote that "we do not believe that the situation in the treatment could justify the development of such feelings. We suspect, on the contrary, that the whole readiness for these feelings is derived from elsewhere, that they were already prepared in the patient, and, upon the opportunity offered by the analytic treatment, are transferred on to the person of the doctor"

(p. 442). He goes on to say, discussing negative transferences, that there can be "no doubt that the hostile feelings towards the doctor deserve to be called a 'transference,' since the situation in the treatment quite clearly offers no adequate grounds for their origin" (p. 443). And in discussing how to deal with transferences in treatment, he says, "We overcome the transference by pointing out to the patient that his feelings do not arise from the present situation and do not apply to the person of the doctor, but that they are repeating something that has happened to him earlier" (pp. 443–444).

Increasingly, this latter emphasis became the standard and predominant psychoanalytic view. Transference reactions were regarded as inappropriate and unrealistic. They were not to be viewed as responses to the current reality of the analyst or the relationship he had established with the patient, but had to do with something in the patient's past which was being erroneously transferred to the present context. Despite developments in ego psychology, which have alerted us to the complex interaction between long-established psychic structures and current environmental input, contemporary formulations and definitions continue to treat transferences strictly as unfounded departures from reality. Greenson (1967), for example, states unequivocally that "transference reactions are always inappropriate" (p. 152). And Langs (1973a) says that "to identify a fantasy about, or reaction to, the therapist as primarily transference . . . we must be able to refute with certainty *any* appropriate level of truth to the patient's unconscious or conscious claim that she correctly perceives the therapist in the manner spelled out through her associations" (p. 415; italics added).

At the same time, however, it has been increasingly recognized that the actual behaviors and attributes of the analyst do play some role in evoking transference reactions. Informally, it is frequently pointed out that transference distortions often have a reality "hook" or "peg" on which they are hung; and, more formally, Langs (1973b) has referred to "reality precipitates" of patients' transference fantasies. Macalpine (1950) has pointed to the particular features of the psychoanalytic situation which foster and call forth regressive transference phenomena. Gill[1] has even suggested—correctly, I think—that unless the analyst acknowledges the role of his own behavior in evoking the patient's reaction, the patient's ability to accept and make use of the analyst's interpretation will be severely limited.

But the continuing emphasis on viewing transference as a distorted or inappropriate reaction, a displacement of something from

1. Gill makes this point in a monograph in preparation on the analysis of transference. See also Muslin and Gill (1978).

the past, has required the introduction of a number of other concepts to account for the patient's ability to react to the realities of the
treatment situation—to accept, for example, that the analyst's silence is a technical part of the procedure rather than a deprivation
aimed specifically at the patient and designed to hurt or punish him,
or to recognize after a while that the analyst does value him even if
he does not give overt reassurances.[2] Such concepts as the "therapeutic alliance," the "working alliance," and the "real relationship"
are designed to address these aspects of what occurs during the
course of an analysis (Greenson, 1965, 1971; Greenson & Wexler,
1969; Zetzel, 1956).

Since the same patient who is able to continue to cooperate in
the analysis because he recognizes the technical nature of the analyst's silence may also fantasize that the silence is really a sadistic act
or a retribution for sins, it is usually suggested that the transference
and the working alliance may exist, as it were, side by side, proceeding apace as two different features of the therapeutic process. Such a
way of conceptualizing does acknowledge the complexity of the
patient's manifold levels of reactivity to what is happening, but it
also creates serious dangers of reification, in which the transference,
the working alliance, and the real relationship are separate and
discrete "things."

Schafer (1977), from a slightly different perspective, has also
addressed the at once realistic and unrealistic aspects of the patient's
reactions to the analyst. He suggests that Freud had not quite reconciled two varying views of transference. "On the one hand, transference love is sheerly repetitive, merely a new edition of the old,
artificial and regressive . . . and to be dealt with chiefly by translating it back into its infantile terms. . . . On the other hand, transference is a piece of real life that is adapted to the analytic purpose, a
transitional state of a provisional character that is a means to a
rational end and as genuine as normal love" (p. 340). He notes that
integrating the two perspectives is an important theoretical problem,
and suggests that one major obstacle to such integration is the
tendency to draw too sharply such distinctions as "past and present,
old and new, genuine and artificial, repetition and creation, the
subjective world and the objective world" (p. 360), etc. As we shall
shortly see, applying the perspective of Piaget's theory to these

2. It is not simply a matter of having more "realistic" reactions. Also relevant is the
capacity to react—even if excessively—in coordination with the actual events of the
analysis. For example, patients are more likely to have memories and associations
regarding fears of abandonment stirred when the analyst's vacation is imminent than
at other times.

questions helps to transcend these dichotomies and to foster the integration of the different views of transference.

II

Piaget's concept of schemas, characterized by the two basic functions of assimilation and accommodation, seems particularly useful for understanding the diverse phenomena of transference and other more or less closely related relationship phenomena. Piaget's work in general highlights the active role of the developing individual in shaping and defining his experiential world. Neither as children nor as adults do we respond directly to stimuli per se. We are always *constructing* reality every bit as much as we are perceiving it. This emphasis on the importance of evolving structures which mediate the individual's experience and behavior is quite compatible with the psychoanalytic view. Both theories suggest that man is not stimulus-bound, that he does not just reflexly respond to external stimuli, but rather selectively organizes and makes sense of new input in terms of the experiences and structures which define who he is.

The concept of transference was an attempt to come to terms with an extreme version of this tendency to experience events in terms of structures and expectations based on earlier experiences. The observations which generated the concept seemed to suggest such an unusually strong role for internal mediating structures that the reality of who the analyst was or what he was doing was virtually ignored by the patient. The tendency to perceive the present in terms of the past became, in certain affectively laden areas of experience, so acute that it seemed to override all evidence of the analyst's actual neutral, investigative role.[3]

The difficulty with the concept of transference as it is usually formulated is that it is so *exclusively* focused on distortion, on the lack of perception of the real characteristics of the analyst. It is for this reason that the observation that the patient does also recognize the analyst as a real person in a professional helping relationship to him must be represented by a completely different concept than that of transference (e.g., therapeutic or working alliance, or real relationship). It is difficult, therefore, to know quite where or how to fit the observations that transference reactions do seem to have a "reality peg." The difficulty, discussed above, in integrating the varying

---

3. I shall later suggest that this neutrality has probably been exaggerated (see also Wachtel, 1977b).

perspectives on transference phenomena is a result of this dichotomous theorizing.

From a Piagetian perspective, one can readily see a continuity
between those phenomena usually described as "transference" and
those designated by terms such as "therapeutic alliance" or "real
relationship" (or indeed, more generally, between transference phenomena and the accurate gauging of other people's motives and
characteristics which facilitates effective adaptation). Transference
reactions, in Piaget's terms, may be seen simply as reflecting schemas which are characterized by a strong predominance of assimilation over accommodation. The experience with the analyst is assimilated to schemas shaped by earlier experiences, and there is very
little accommodation to the actualities of the present situation which
make it different from the former experience.

In part, of course, such a way of talking about transference
phenomena is simply a translation from one language system to
another. But it is a translation that has some important implications,
both in terms of pointing inquiry in somewhat different directions
and of facilitating the integration of varying views of the phenomena
of interest. Perhaps most importantly, once one views these phenomena in terms of schemas, one is confronted with the idea that
schemas can never be characterized *only* by assimilation. Assimilation
may at times predominate over accommodation, but there can be no
such thing as "pure" assimilation—or, for that matter, as "pure"
accommodation (Piaget, 1952, 1954).

> However necessary it may be to describe assimilation and
> accommodation separately and sequentially, they should be
> thought of as simultaneous and indissociable as they operate in
> living cognition. Adaptation is a unitary event, and assimilation
> and accommodation are merely abstractions from this unitary
> reality. As in the case of food ingestion, the cognitive incorpora-
> tion of reality always implies both an assimilation *to* structure and
> an accommodation *of* structure. To assimilate an event it is neces-
> sary at the same time to accommodate to it and vice versa. . . . [T]he
> balance between the two invariants can and does vary, both from
> stage to stage and within a given stage. Some cognitive acts show a
> relative preponderance of the assimilative component; others seem
> heavily weighted toward accommodation. However, "pure" assimi-
> lation and "pure" accommodation nowhere obtain in mental life.
> (Flavell, 1963, pp. 48–49)

Transference, seen in this light, can be understood as the result
of a state of affairs in which assimilation is strongly predominant,
but is nonetheless not inexorable. Some accommodation to the ac-

tual details of what is being experienced, and to how they differ from those of previous experiences assimilated to that schema, must also occur. Since assimilation is strongly predominant, it does not take a particularly close fit to activate the transference schema. So two very different analysts may, in separate analyses with the same patient, be subjectively experienced in very similar fashion by the patient. The schema is easy to activate, and it does not change very readily despite the lack of fit. But since "pure" assimilation cannot occur, it is not completely arbitrary. The range of activating events is wide but nonetheless does have some bounds. The occurrence of transference reactions can seem at times to be almost completely the playing out of an internal dynamic, so striking and deviant can it be from the reality of what is going on between patient and analyst; but it is never completely unrelated to what is transpiring. This is what Gill is calling our attention to in his emphasis on the importance of acknowledging the analyst's role in eliciting such reactions, and this is why a perceptive observer can often find a "reality peg" or "hook" in even the most extreme transference reaction.

This perspective also shows us why Gill's emphasis on the finding of a reality peg in no way undermines the important clinical core of the concept of transference; nor does it ignore Freud's insights about how the continuing effect of the patient's childhood way of experiencing reality is revealed in the transference. If anything, it provides a basis for making the traditional psychoanalytic formulation even more powerful by making it more precise: It points us to ask in all instances of transference precisely what aspect of the analytic situation or of the analyst's behavior or characteristics led to the occurrence of this particular transference reaction at this particular time. Since the predominance of assimilation is emphasized, no loss of the role of intrapsychic factors or the patient's unique individuality is entailed by this particular kind of effort to relate the patient's behavior to events currently going on about him. The schema notion implies responsiveness to environmental cues without positing stimulus-bound, slavish reactivity to environmental events. Thus, one can avoid the pitfall of the false and limiting dichotomy between understanding in terms of intrapsychic factors or "psychical reality" and understanding in terms of the "actual" situation, and appreciation of reality factors can enhance rather than compete with a psychodynamic perspective. An understanding of what particular features of the situation bring forth the transference reaction can in this way be seen as a legitimate part of what is pointed to by psychoanalytic understanding, rather than as the undermining or watering down of that understanding. A broader and firmer base is thus provided for the psychoanalytic view, which also gains increased power and utility.

Further clarity is also provided by this perspective regarding the question, both substantive and definitional, as to whether transference reactions are manifested only in the analytic situation or go on in the patient's daily life as well. From the present vantage point, one can readily see that *all* perceptions and behaviors are mediated by schemas which are the product of past experiences and which attempt to assimilate new input to them—as well as to accommodate to their novel features. Understanding just which aspects of the analytic situation make assimilation more likely or help to highlight the way in which it occurs in the patient's mental functioning (cf. Gill, 1954; Macalpine, 1950; Stone, 1961) has important clinical utility. Such understanding can also shed light on the question of how best to generalize from the data of the analytic session and integrate the formulations such data suggest with those deriving from other sources.

III

Much of the confusion which arises from the traditional way of talking about transference phenomena is a result of the cognitive and perceptual theory which underlay Freud's theorizing. As Schimek (1975) has recently clarified, Freud's view of cognition was at odds with the essential thrust of the rest of his theorizing, which was obviously strongly dynamic, motivational, and developmental in its emphasis. In contrast, his ideas about cognition, Schimek shows, were based on the simple associationism that one finds among many stimulus–response learning theorists who have been particularly opposed to psychoanalysis. This simple associational psychology has been sharply criticized by Piaget (1952), by critics of behavior therapy sympathetic to psychoanalysis (Breger & McGaugh, 1965), and recently even by a number of prominent behavior therapists who have seen the necessity of taking into account man's active role in defining what the effective stimulus is and how it will be experienced (Bandura, 1974; Mahoney, 1974). It would be unfortunate if psychoanalysis, to which such a view is really most alien, were to retain it.

Precisely because psychoanalysis is in its other aspects so strongly a dynamic, motivational psychology, this aspect of its conceptual underpinning went unnoticed for a long time. The stagnant, nonpersonalistic conception of perception and cognition was obscured because dynamic and personal factors were so strongly brought into the theory at the point *after* the percept or cognition was formed. As Schimek points out clearly, Freud assumed a simple, camera-like registration of reality and formation of memory traces which, again, stored "accurate" images of reality that were somewhere retained in their true and original form—but then he concentrated, in the more important and original aspects of his work, on how these images and representations were transformed or distorted under the pressure of drives and defenses. It was *here* that the dynamic features of the theory were evident. So powerful and original were Freud's ideas in this regard that it was little noticed that the perceptual building blocks for these dynamic processes were conceptualized by him in a far less dynamic fashion than they were by many academic psychologists in the developing area of cognitive psychology.

In conceptualizing transference phenomena, this camera-like view of perception and memory traces led to the formulation that a fully formed, pre-existing set of reactions is plucked from their original context and *displaced* from an early figure to the analyst. As Greenson (1967) puts it, "Transference is the experience of feelings, drives, attitudes, fantasies and defenses toward a person in the present which do not befit that person but are a repetition of reactions originating in regard to significant persons of early childhood, unconsciously displaced onto figures in the present" (p. 155).

Such a formulation leaves little room for any accommodation to the reality of the analyst and the interaction. Something static and pre-existing is simply "displaced," moved from one object to another. The postulation of a somewhat malleable and responsive structure, built up on the basis of prior experience, but shaped as well by new experiences that do not quite fit it, would permit a reconciliation and synthesis of observations of "distortion" in the transference, and observations of accurate perceptions and of realistic, cooperative engagement in the analytic process. But a "displacement" formulation, which implicitly requires a fully formed representation to be displaced, ends up leading to the proliferation of separate and discrete postulated quasi-entities—the transference, the therapeutic alliance, the real relationship, etc.

Rather than dichotomizing between perceptions that are accurate and those that are "distorted," the schema notion helps us to see that *all* perception is a selective construction, in some respects a creative act. It is not arbitrary, but it never lacks the personal element. Even the supposedly "objective" observations that underlie scientific theory building are richly suffused with the idiosyncratic and personal, as modern philosophers of science—Polanyi (e.g., 1958, 1966) in particular—have strongly emphasized. In the perception of other persons, and especially in the perception of their intentions and affective states and qualities, the variability from observer to observer is so great that it is extraordinary that a sharp distinction between "accurate" and "distorted" perceptions could have been retained for so long. To be sure, each patient's experience of the analyst is highly individual and shaped by personal needs and fantasies. But consider the enormous variation in perception of the analyst by those other than his patients—the differences in how he is experienced by his spouse, his children, his teachers, his students, his friends, his rivals. Which is the "undistorted" standard from which the transference distortion varies?

Discussing the phenomena traditionally designated as transference in terms of schemas, assimilation, and accommodation does not present us with such conundrums. It avoids the sharp dichotomizing implicit in most discussions of transference, yet retains the clinical core. To recognize a unity in the modes of apprehending reality that encompasses both the transference perceptions of the analysand and the observations of the physicist or chemist is not to ignore the differences between the two, or to blunt the problematic features of the former. Indeed, it enables us to incorporate the role of the analyst's real properties and behavior not as something which somehow limits, reduces, or "excuses" the patient's highly personal interpretation, but as a way of amplifying it and gaining a finer sense of its determinants.

IV

Ideally, one might expect to see a fairly even balance between assimilation and accommodation, with neither predominating to any great extent. In that case the individual would be able to be responsive to variations in environmental stimulation, while maintaining a certain consistency and managing to make sense out of new events on the basis of previous experience. The phenomena discussed in psychoanalytic writings under the rubric of transference suggest an imbalance in this ideal relationship, an excessive degree of assimilation that impedes efforts to adaptively gauge and deal with the events of the present. In attempting to account for how this imbalance comes about, two main lines of explanation seem to have developed.

The traditional psychoanalytic explanation stresses the role of repression and other defenses in creating a structural differentiation which, in effect, prevents accommodation. Accommodation per se is, of course, not referred to in most psychoanalytic accounts. Rather, what is stressed is that defenses relegate certain contents and processes to the id, preventing them from becoming part of the ego. Since it is the ego which is the part of the personality which is in touch with the perceptual world and which has well-developed properties of organization and coherence (Freud, 1923/1961), the result of repressing something is to prevent it from being modified by new perceptual input—i.e., to prevent accommodation. This is why the contents of the id are described as "timeless" and why, for change to occur, they must be integrated into the ego, where they are brought into contact with perceptual input and with the demands for logic and consistency. Freud's famous phrase "Where id was let ego be" reflects the view that only when id contents are integrated into the ego can they be modified to conform to current reality demands. If one employs (and extends) the conceptual scheme of Piaget in this context, it can be seen that one effect of defensive processes is to interfere with the accommodation of certain schemas to new input. When manifested as transference phenomena, these schemas are revealed in their original structure as they are applied inappropriately to stimulus objects which would be more appropriately assimilated by schemas which have undergone a developmental evolution.[4]

When viewed in the light of the Piagetian notions of schema, assimilation, and accommodation, some questions are raised about this traditional account of how transference reactions persist in unchanging form. Such an account seems to contradict Piaget's view that accommodation and assimilation must *both* be present. Now, of course, one need not postulate that transference schemas show *no* accommodation whatever. Even changes in the particular cues which serve to elicit the transference reaction reflect *some* degree of accommodation; and the postulation of at least a certain degree of evolution and change in transferential schemas (even apart from whatever change can be brought about by analysis) is not really inconsistent with the traditional psychoanalytic view. Moreover, transference schemas are ones in which affective and defensive processes—which Piaget did not address—are centrally implicated. It is certainly possible that in this realm Piaget's observations regarding the dual role of

---

4. It should be noted that although perception is clearly in the province of the ego in Freud's theorizing, id processes are not completely cut off from perceptual input. Were the separation total, there would be no way to account for the stimulation or stirring of repressed drives, even if such stirring occurred out of awareness. Moreover, the observations referred to earlier regarding the reality hooks or pegs for transference reactions would be difficult, if not impossible, to explain. Rather, what seems implied in the traditional psychoanalytic view is that current perceptual input may serve as a *trigger* for that which is repressed, releasing it to be played out in another repetition, but not serving to shape or modify it (see Wachtel, 1977b, pp. 42 ff.).

accommodation and assimilation might have to be modified. The question of precisely *how* defenses can impede accommodation would seem from this perspective a particularly important one.

A different way of accounting for the apparent lack of accommodation in transferential schemas relies less on structural differentiation and a conception of the id as a zone of nonaccommodation. Instead, one might assume that transference schemas, like any others, will show accommodation in response to clear, disconfirming feedback. In that case, a lack of change would imply that the actual feedback is either unclear or not really disconfirming. To understand how this might happen, it is useful to examine some contrasts between our interactions with the physical world and those with other persons.

The schemas which come to represent the physical world to the child, and which form the basis for much of our commerce with the world, do change a great deal as feedback requires accommodation of extant schemas. (At the same time, of course, this input is also assimilated to those evolving schemas.) Whether one is observing an infant learning to grasp an object, a child learning about conservation of various quantities, or an adult learning to drive or ski, one sees a process, varying in speed and efficiency, in which feedback shapes and changes the existing schema. Why then do the schemas associated with transference seem to change so little, despite their apparently poor match to the input with which they are coordinated?

One thing becomes clear if one pursues this line of thought: For the schemas that represent the physical world, disconfirmation is relatively clear and dramatic. The skier or driver who organizes input incorrectly falls or goes off the road; the infant fails to grasp the object he seeks; etc. In the realm of interpersonal and affective events, it is much harder to know one has been in error. Such events are highly ambiguous, and consensus is much harder to obtain. Almost everyone would agree when you have gone off the road. That is not the case as to whether you have incorrectly construed anger in another (or *failed* to construe anger). The ambiguity of affectively laden events and the consequent difficulty in determining when feedback requires accommodation make accommodation far less efficient in this realm and the persistence of old schemas in early form more likely.

It must further be noted that the nature of the affective and interpersonal stimuli which we encounter (and which we must assimilate and accommodate to) is substantially a function of our own actions. This is, of course, true to some extent in the physical realm as well. Driving presents us with different stimuli—and a different adaptive task—if we turn the wheel to the left or to the right. But with physical stimuli the process is not nearly as complex, and the potential input is more predictable and varies over a narrower range. Moreover, it is much easier to know when a change in input is due to our own actions and when it is an independent event—the difference, say, between the variation in direction of a hit tennis ball as a function of one's stroke or as a function of a sudden strong gust of wind.[5]

With affective and interpersonal events, however, the sorting-out process is particularly difficult. It is very easy to be convinced one has experienced what someone "is like" without realizing how much the experienced property (even if accurately gauged in this or other particulars) is a function of one's own actions when with him. Each of us tends to consistently elicit particular aspects of others' personalities, and must of necessity experience the sum of these elicitations as "the way people are." For relatively healthy personalities, the range of elicitations is fairly wide, and variable enough to be roughly representative and in agreement with the experience of others. But it is important to recognize that none of us really lives in an "average expectable environment." We all experience some particular idiosyncratic skewing of the possible kinds of encounters with others. And this skewing is not just accidental, but is a function of who we are. One of the ways in which consistency in personality is maintained is by the selective choice of situations and interactants and the elicitation of a particular side of those we do interact with. Given who we are, we select and create a particular kind of interpersonal world; and given that world, we experience the need to go on as we have—and thus elicit that same kind of personal world again.[6]

The persistence of transferential schemas, then, with little change over the years despite what one might expect to be consider-

---

5. The comparison between physical and interpersonal events is, to be sure, not a completely dichotomous one. In the former realm, too, difficulty in sorting out what is due to our own actions and what is fortuitous can be difficult (and indeed can make the difference between a good and a poor tennis player). In earlier times, a good deal of confusion existed as to what physical events were a result of our own actions. (What did I do to make the volcano erupt?) Complementarily, there are wide variations in how accurately people can gauge not only what someone is feeling but whether that feeling is primarily a reaction to one's own behavior.

6. In the academic psychology of personality, the question of consistency of personality across situations is currently a hotly debated topic, and the data of recent research have been construed by some as casting doubt on psychoanalytic assumptions. The conception of cyclically reconfirming events described here enables one to reconcile psychoanalytic conceptions with the findings of the academics, and points to areas in which their research strategy has been insufficient—though also to ways in which certain psychoanalytic assumptions may perhaps best be modified (cf. Endler & Magnusson, 1976; Magnusson & Endler, 1977; Mischel, 1968; Wachtel, 1973a, 1973b).

able pressure for accommodation, can be seen as due both to the ambiguity of interpersonal–affective feedback (making it easy not to notice that disconfirmation or lack of fit has occurred) and to the tendency for events to in fact confirm the seemingly inaccurate perception. If the world were, in effect, to "hold still" for the developing child rather than to change with his conceptions of it, *he* would change to accommodate to it. In learning about the physical world, this is in fact what happens, and it happens enough in the interpersonal world for most of us not to be grossly out of touch. But to a substantial degree, the world of affective and interpersonal events does not hold still. *It* accommodates to our initial conceptions and expectations (as they are translated into actions toward others) and short-circuits our accommodative activities in this realm. Our suspicions, and the actions they motivate, lead others to in fact be hostile; our expectations of seductive behavior lead to eroticized interactions with others; our submissive behavior, based on past experiences as well as defensive needs, induces others to expect more compliance from us than they do from others.

By the time the patient comes to see an analyst, he has probably had hundreds of such quasi-confirmatory experiences. I call them *quasi*-confirmatory because the patient's perceptions *are* in one sense anachronistic, even if they may turn out to be confirmed. For what happens is that the person encounters another who is initially quite ready to relate to him differently than the patient expects, but who over time responds to the patient's pattern of interaction with an all-too-familiar complementary pattern. What to the patient feels like an accurate *perception* may be inaccurate as that but fairly reliable as an implicit *prediction*: This is how the other will act toward him after some time in his interactive field (cf. Wachtel, 1977).[7]

V

The experience with the analyst is, one hopes, a major and dramatic disconfirmation that can permit accommodation to occur. The analyst facilitates accommodation in at least two ways. First, by interpreting unconscious fantasies (and by establishing the analytic situation, in which such fantasies are likely to become more intense and

---

7. Such patterns are, of course, not inexorable. The *other*, too, has an independent contribution and is not just putty in the hands of the patient's transferentially motivated actions. But, given the factor of ambiguity noted, it takes only a very rough approximation to confirmation to permit assimilation. Also, those people who have had the good fortune to have a sustained disconfirmatory experience with an important other are not likely to show up as analytic patients.

vivid), he helps the patient to be more aware of both the schemas that guide his transactions with others and the kinds of events that constitute confirmation or disconfirmation of his expectations. Thus he helps reduce the ambiguity which makes for easy assimilation and impedes accommodation. Second, he avoids falling into the complementary behavior pattern which the patient's style of relating has so frequently brought out in others. As I have described in more detail elsewhere (Wachtel, 1977b), every neurosis requires "accomplices" to maintain itself, and a good deal of the analyst's effectiveness may be seen as residing in his ability not to become one more accomplice. Both his neutral, analyzing stance and his skill in spotting and interpreting the patient's subtle and unconscious maneuvers enable him to accomplish this task.[8]

It is not necessary, however—nor do I think it is possible—for the analyst to *completely* avoid falling into complementary behavior patterns. Wolf (1966) has described particularly well how such unwitting participation in the neurotic pattern can occur. For therapeutic purposes, it is sufficient that (1) the analyst *for the most part* avoid becoming an accomplice to the neurotic process (in other words, that he do a better job at this than most of the people the patient encounters, even if he is not perfect); and (2) he be able to acknowledge when and how he has acted in a way consistent with the patient's transference expectations and to help the patient understand how such patterns come to be repetitive features of his life.[9] Thus, I would agree with Langs (1973a) that when the therapist's behavior "has been correctly and unconsciously perceived by the patient, his interventions will begin, as a rule, with an acknowledgment of the veracity of the perception and refer to the way it served as a stimulus for the patient's responsive fantasies and conflicts." I would further agree that "once the therapist has acknowledged his contribution to the situation . . . the patient's responsibility for his reactions must be recognized and subsequently analyzed" (p. 430). As a result of the considerations put forth in this paper, however, I would strongly disagree with Langs's contention that this is appropriate only when the therapist's or analyst's behavior has been "erroneous" or that all such occurrences are in fact errors in any useful sense of that term.

8. The advantages of "neutrality," however, may not outweigh the disadvantages (see Wachtel, 1977b).

9. I do not mean to imply here that this is all there is to the process of therapeutic change. Rather, the sufficiency I am referring to is with regard to the analyst's avoidance of the typical complementary pattern of behavior encountered by the patient. In *this* connection, the considerations described seem to me sufficient.

VI

Transferences can at times seem quite fantastic. All analysts have seen patients express feelings and ideas about them that seem grossly off the mark and appear to have much more to do with their experiences and fantasies with regard to other—usually earlier—figures. In order to understand this common sort of observation from the present point of view, several points must be considered. To begin with, one can recognize that transference reactions are indeed very often grossly inappropriate without drawing a theoretically problematic dichotomy between transferences and realistic perceptions. If one starts from the assumption that all perceptions and actions are mediated by schemas characterized by both assimilation and accommodation, then it would appear that we *label* as transference that portion of the continuum in which assimilation is predominant. Even in this range, however, assimilation is not inexorable, and a particular schema will be called into play only if there is something in the analytic situation that bears some resemblance to the stimuli which have nourished the schema in the past. Since, however, the dimension of similarity can be a highly personal one, there need not be much of an "objective" similarity. Hence the transference reaction may seem completely arbitrary and brought about by "internal" factors. Examination of what in the analytic interaction elicited it at this point, however, is likely to be richly rewarded, for it affords an understanding not only of the kinds of fantasies the patient is capable of, but also of the conditions for their arousal and the particular difficulties to which they may be related.

In considering just how unrealistic transferences really are, it is important to recognize that the transference reactions of most interest and concern to the analyst are those involving substantial anxiety and conflict. In such circumstances the patient is highly motivated not to see clearly what he is experiencing. Rather than communicating directly what his experience is with the analyst, he is likely to express it indirectly and symbolically. For defensive reasons, his statement about some aspect of his experience of the analyst may be so oblique it is unrecognizable. It simply sounds like an outlandish and incorrect perception that must really be about someone else. If the analyst is not prepared to translate the symbolism not only into childhood references but also into references to what is currently transpiring, he can easily be persuaded that the patient's reaction is simply a "displacement" from somewhere else and has little or nothing to do with actual occurrences in the analysis.

Thus, if the patient has the fantasy that the male analyst is a woman in disguise or has no penis, or that he is much older than he really is, or is a notorious and immoral seducer, the analyst, feeling secure that the fantasy as stated is not true, may not recognize how it symbolically reflects the patient's reaction *to some particular action or pattern of actions by the analyst*.[10] Depending on the specific meaning of "woman" to the patient in that context, for example, his fantasy that the analyst is a woman might mean he viewed something about the analyst as weak, or soft, or emotional, or nurturing, or smart or whatever.

It is, of course, important for the analyst to determine the *meaning* of "woman" to the patient in order to understand fully the transference reaction. But, having done so, it is also important to know *just what he did* that seemed weak, nurturing, or whatever to the patient; and this not primarily for the purpose of discovering his "error" and attempting to weed it out in the future by more self-analysis (though either of these aims is certainly at times appropriate), but rather for the purpose of understanding just what kind of input the patient's schemas assimilate in just what way (for not just *any* behavior on the analyst's part would get registered as "weak" or as "woman"). Such understanding enables the analyst to apprehend much more precisely how and when the patient's psychic processes create problems for him, and importantly, the range of situations in which problems and misperceptions are *not* likely to occur. All too often, lack of specificity and failure to understand intrapsychic organizing processes in their situational context interfere with an appreciation of the patient's *strengths*, of where and how intact functioning is manifested (see Wachtel, 1973b, 1980).

In addition, understanding what behavior of the analyst elicited the patient's transference reaction can enable analyst and patient to explore whether other people in the patient's life have tended to behave as the analyst did, and what meaning the patient has given to their behavior. The analytic work can then examine both the kinds of behavior the patient elicits from others and the impact of such behavior as filtered by the patient's complexly motivated perceptual

---

10. It is worth noting, regarding fantasies of this sort and even many others that are less extreme, that frequently the patient, too, recognizes that his thought or feeling is not "realistic." Not all transference reactions imply a loss of distance. Many are *experienced* by the patient as fantasies rather than perceptions (i.e., they are categorized by him as products of his imagination). The distinction between transference perceptions which are registered by the patient as "real" and those registered as "fantasy" (and the range of phenomenological experiences in between) is itself a topic worthy of a whole paper. It is related to the common distinction between transference and the therapeutic alliance but not reducible to it.

processes, as well as the way in which this in turn leads to behavior on the patient's part which is likely to again elicit similar behavior from others—thus starting the cycle all over again. One then gets a picture of transference reactions as not just the residue of some early experience which is being displaced or replayed, but as part of a *continuous* process that has characterized the patient's life for years yet has only become fully explicated in the experience with the analyst. Such a perspective, I would contend, provides both a more complete understanding of transference reactions and improved possibilities for facilitating therapeutic change (see Wachtel, 1977b).

VII

The considerations presented here do not pose a challenge to the basic observations of psychoanalysis regarding transference phenomena. I regard as soundly based on clinical observation such central psychoanalytic tenets as that patients regularly show rather substantial distortions in their perceptions of the analyst; that such distortions are personally meaningful and related to the person's history; and that they are in important ways the product of unconscious conflicts and fantasies.

The present perspective does suggest, however, certain modifications in how we *think about* our observations, and points toward the inclusion of a *wider range* of observations than has been typical in psychoanalytic practice. It also suggests that the path between early experiences and later transference reactions may be more *continuous* than has been typically portrayed; that interactions with many figures throughout the person's life tend to occur in such a way as to confirm and perpetuate the modes of perception and reaction that eventually appear as transferences in the patient's analysis; that transference reactions, even when seemingly unrelated to the reality of the analyst or the analysis, are often symbolic expressions of conflicted perceptions of what has actually transpired, or at least of the personal meanings which actual events and characteristics have had for the patient; that accommodation occurs to such a slight degree in some interpersonal and affective schemas both because of the ambiguity in this realm, which makes it harder to know when disconfirmations have occurred, and because of the reactivity of events in this realm to our own actions: What we expect to occur is likely to happen even if it would not have been likely to occur if it were *not* expected (and if we did not act accordingly).

The potential value of conceptualizing transference phenomena as reflecting schemas in which assimilation predominates over accommodation has not been exhausted by the considerations put forth here. It is to be hoped that future efforts will carry this work forward.

SUMMARY

Transference phenomena have traditionally been viewed as reactions which are inappropriate and based on the distorting effect of the patient's past. At the same time, they convey an important reality about the patient's life (or at least his subjective life) and—it has been increasingly recognized—an important reality about the therapeutic interaction as well. Integrating these varying perspectives on transference has created some (not always clearly understood) theoretical difficulties. The present discussion has suggested that Piaget's notion of schema, with its stress on the simultaneous processes of assimilation and accommodation, can help to clarify these theoretical issues. By regarding transferences as schemas in which assimilation predominates over accommodation to an inordinate degree, one can incorporate both the traditional clinical knowledge about the distorting effects of transference and an emerging recognition of the importance of what actually transpires between patient and analyst. Such a way of looking at transference both points to and is aided by an understanding of the differences between the ways in which we learn about the physical world and the world of people and emotions. It also leads to a number of other important new questions for psychoanalytic inquiry and new perspectives on psychoanalytic practice.

3

Vicious Circles:
The Self and the Rhetoric
of Emerging and Unfolding

I wish to discuss certain implications of a point of view I have come to call "cyclical psychodynamics" because it locates the heart of the psychodynamic process not in the patient's preserved past but in the vicious cycles which past events set in motion. This approach is rooted in the theoretical contributions of writers such as Horney (1939), Sullivan (1953), and Erikson (1950), but departs from their views at significant junctures and reworks them in ways they themselves might find uncongenial. The result has a great debt to each but makes no claim to being true to any.

Central to this point of view is the notion that the seemingly infantile wishes and ideas that are revealed in psychoanalytic work persist not in spite of the person's present reality but precisely because of it. When one looks closely enough at the person's daily interactions, one finds that each person skews his experiences in distinctive fashion, selecting with whom to interact and evoking particular sides of those he does encounter so as to make his environment as unique and pathognomonic as a fingerprint. When one looks carefully at the fine details of the patient's daily interactions, there turns out to be no "average expectable environment."

Reprinted by permission from *Contemporary Psychoanalysis*, 1982, 18(2), 259–273. Copyright © 1982 by The William Alanson White Institute.

An earlier version of this chapter was given as part of a scientific lecture series at the Postgraduate Center for Mental Health, on April 22, 1981.

Hartmann's (1939) introduction of that term was, to be sure, part of an effort to bring reality back into psychoanalytic theory, to amplify the perspective—never fully absent from psychoanalysis but kept well in the background until the 1920s—that looked for the roots of our actions not just in drives welling up from within, but in the adaptive tasks, and even opportunities, presented by the world in which we live.[1] But in the very notion of an average expectable environment lies the basis for canceling out the role of the environment even as it is being brought in.

Hartmann's conceptualizations have significant structural parallels with the Freudian strategy for understanding transference: The patient's reactions to the therapist are not primarily understood in terms of the idiosyncratic features of the particular analyst or the particular relationship which has developed between analyst and patient; rather, what is assumed is, in effect, an "average expectable analyst," and the specific, particular way that any given patient reacts is understood primarily in terms of the intrapsychic constellation that the patient brings. The actual characteristics of the analyst, like the environment in Hartmann's broader account, are necessary as the setting within which the patient's reactions can occur. If they are too deviant from what is "expectable," the predicted psychological processes or events will not be manifested. But in most instances, where the environment—or the analyst—is conceived of as average and expectable, the idiosyncratic specifics are attributed to intrapsychic rather than environmental particularities.

When, however, the very notion of an average or expectable environment is challenged, when the particular subtle variations in the responses we elicit from others become our focus, then the entire picture of how personality is formed and maintained looks very different. The behavior of other people is the most critically important feature of the environment in understanding most of the phenomena which are of particular interest to psychotherapists. Where what is emphasized is whether it falls within an average range of expectations, variations in individual behavior will be attributed largely to intrapsychic factors. Where what is emphasized is the variation from person to person in what is encountered—a variation that is in effect canceled out by the question of whether it is a variation that falls within the "expectable" range—then particularities in individual personalities are seen instead as residing largely in the interactions in which the person finds himself enmeshed, rather than primarily in properties describable solely as "his."

1. Certainly Erikson had much more to say on this score than Hartmann, but it was not absent from Hartmann's perspective either.

ANXIETY IN NEO-FREUDIAN AND CYCLICAL
PSYCHODYNAMIC THEORIES

It is important to note that the theories of Horney and of Sullivan were primarily formulated after Freud wrote *Inhibitions, Symptoms and Anxiety*. Freud himself was 70 when that work appeared, and it was too late for him to engage in the substantial overhaul of his theory which his latent conceptual clarification pointed toward. His followers in what was to be regarded as the orthodox or classical line did not undertake such a revision either. Sullivan and Horney, unencumbered by constraining theoretical commitments, did, in important ways, take as their starting point the revised theory of anxiety of the 1920s.

In clarifying that anxiety leads to repression rather than the other way round, Freud implicitly set the stage for a change in what would be the "cornerstone" of psychoanalysis (Freud, 1914/1958). For the theories of Horney and of Sullivan *anxiety*, rather than repression, seemed to be the cornerstone. This is not to say that repression—or in Sullivan's case, equivalent concepts with different names—did not play a major role in these theories. They were no more slighted in neo-Freudian theory than was anxiety in Freud's. But the emphasis, the basic structure on which the theory is cast, did differ. For both Sullivan and Horney, the experience of anxiety, and the actions undertaken to quell it, were the central shaping forces of personality. Horney in particular stressed that the very wishes and strivings defended against—and whose arousal later stirred such anxiety in their own right—were originally the product of efforts to quell anxiety rather than unmodified upwellings of raw human nature.

While shifting the cornerstone, though, these theories had a firm foundation in the psychoanalytic tradition. Sullivan is less explicit than Horney in acknowledging his debt to Freud, but both theorists, in their own languages, were very centrally concerned with unconscious motivation and fantasy, with psychological conflict, and with the non-normative wishes and ideas that more rationalistic theories excluded. Put differently, they concerned themselves with transference and resistance, the defining properties of psychoanalysis according to Freud. "Any line of investigation," Freud said, "no matter what its direction, which recognizes these two facts and takes them as the starting point of its work may call itself psycho-analysis, though it arrives at results other than my own" (Freud, 1914/1958, p. 298).

It would be closer to the truth, I believe, to say that the problem with Horney's and Sullivan's approach—and the approaches of those who followed—was not that they deviated too far from the central roots of psychoanalysis, but that they stayed too close. Their reformulations could—and should—have led to greater technical innovation than they did. Several features of the neo-Freudian conceptualizations point to a considerably more active role for the therapist not only than in Freudian analysis but than in the practice of most contemporary neo-Freudians.

Firstly, in their emphasis on anxiety as at least a dual cornerstone of clinical theory along with repression, there is implicit a concomitant shift in therapeutic strategy. The emphasis in psychoanalysis on insight, on self-knowledge, is a corollary of the emphasis on repression, that is, on not-knowing; the cure for not-knowing is to know. In contrast, when one takes anxiety as one's starting point, then one sees—or should see—the essence of therapeutic change in becoming less afraid. The two are certainly correlated, but they are not identical. To facilitate the search for self-understanding, for example, analysts tend to refrain from reassuring the patient, adopting instead a stance of neutrality. Here again, the two perspectives are not simply at odds. It can be argued that refraining from reassuring permits fuller exploration that ultimately results in the patient's feeling more profoundly reassured. But a perspective that places anxiety more centrally would nonetheless point to a greater concern with assuring that the patient does not just confront what has been repressed but has experienced the conditions that will enable him to be less afraid of it. Elsewhere (Wachtel, 1980) I have shown how the way in which interpretations are worded can contribute to this goal in a way quite separate from the content or accuracy of the interpretation.

THE LANGUAGE OF "EMERGING" AND "UNFOLDING"

Concern with more explicit reassurances, and with a further wide range of anxiety-reducing procedures, is discouraged by the conceptual framework of the classical psychoanalytic tradition. Psychoanalytic writings are replete with references to the transference, or to other aspects of the patient's psychological life, as "emerging" or "unfolding." The analyst is directed to assume a nonintrusive, neutral stance in large measure to avoid interfering with this unfolding, and to assure that "changing manifestations in the transference cannot be attributed to an external situation, to some changed factor in the interpersonal relationship, but the analysand must accept responsibility himself" (Gill, 1954, p. 781).

From the perspective offered by Sullivan, however, the language of "unfolding" and "emerging" is revealed as a bit of verbal sleight of hand. Psychological events are never just a function of inner forces and structures; they always occur in relation to other people. In highlighting the inevitability of the therapist's being a participant–observer, Sullivan sets the stage for a psychodynamic rationale for a much more active therapy. So-called "neutrality" is but one more way of participating in the events of the therapeutic process, and is no less likely to influence ensuing events than any other way of participating. Indeed, to call "neutral" someone who offers himself as a source of help to distressed souls, who frequently as well requests a substantial portion of the person's income, and who then avoids giving a direct answer to questions, refuses to give any sort of advice or reveal anything of his own life or his own opinions, and otherwise vetoes the everyday rules of social exchange is to stretch the word "neutral" beyond recognition.

Appreciation of the patient's tendency to distort or to interpret what is transpiring in a personal and idiosyncratic fashion does not require an effort to cancel out—or to pretend to cancel out—the therapist's impact. As I have discussed elsewhere (Wachtel, 1981), Piaget's concept of schema can help us understand the phenomena of transference in ways that acknowledge both the personal equation and the situational context. Piaget notes that all schemas all patterns of action and/or ways of apprehending the world—entail both assimilation and accommodation. We make sense of the world by *assimilating* new input to the schemas already available, by translating it into our own terms or finding in it possibilities consistent with what we can understand and what we can do. At the same time, we continuously *accommodate* to the ways in which the concrete details of the world we encounter vary in slight or not so slight ways from our expectations and previous experiences; we never have it all totally figured out and are in trouble if we think we do. Our survival depends on the balance of these two basic functions. They cannot occur in isolation. As the Piaget scholar John Flavell has pointed out, "'pure' assimilation and 'pure' accommodation nowhere obtain in mental life" (Flavell, 1963, pp. 48–49).

But psychoanalytic accounts of transference frequently read as if transferential structures were purely assimilative. The rhetoric of unfolding and emerging implicitly denies accommodation: The patient's reactions do not develop in the context of what is actually transpiring between the two people (or in the broader context of the general circumstances of the person's life); they "emerge" or "unfold" from within—or at least they do if only the analyst will get out of the way and let it happen.

Now it is true that accommodation is much harder to achieve in the realm of interpersonal and affective events than in coming to terms with the physical world, where Piaget concentrated most of his efforts. I have elsewhere discussed in detail why this is so (Wachtel, 1981). But understanding the difference between the feedback processes in these two realms—a difference that is one of degree, not kind—actually highlights the therapist's role as an inevitable participant as well as observer. It is the fact that the physical world is mostly nonreactive to our expectations about it, whereas other people are quite reactive to those expectations—or to the actions and signs inevitably associated with them—that accounts for the difficulty in accommodation; even if we are "wrong," the cumulative effect of our acting over and over in a trusting, or a suspicious, or a sexy, or whatever kind of way tends eventually to lead other people to act in ways that prove we were "right." And analysts, being people, are not immune to this. The best they can do is to try to comment on the wave that carries them. That is participant–observation. "Neutrality" is walking on water; and it's been almost 2000 years since that feat was last claimed.

If one abandons the quixotic quest for neutrality, and the corollary rhetoric of unfolding or emerging, one then can try to help in a far broader range of ways. Behavioral methods are but one kind of way to expand the therapist's helping role. Simple advice; directing the patient's thoughts and imagery; providing the patient with support and comfort; seeing other family members—these and a host of other ways of interacting with the patient all can be used synergistically with the more traditional psychoanalytic stance within the framework of cyclical psychodynamics. Such things do go on in analytically oriented therapies even now, but they are usually viewed as compromises which for various reasons are essential but which set limits to the degree of "structural change" which can be achieved. In contrast, I regard them as adding to, rather than subtracting from, the depth and range of the therapeutic process. Even for those patients who do not "require" them, who are capable of withstanding the privations of more classical methods, active interventions are valuable additions to the process of change.

Precisely when to use them cannot, of course, be given in a formula. I have spelled out some of the considerations elsewhere (Wachtel, 1979a), but much work remains to be done. I do not regard these various methods as "parameters," essentially to be undone as quickly as possible. Rather, they are an intrinsic part of the process, no harder or easier to analyze than is silently listening and interpreting. To "analyze" in this framework is not to persuade the patient that what has unfolded or emerged has little to do with the present reality; it is to help him examine the schemas by which he apprehends the events and figures he encounters, to see just how he assimilates what input to what set of rules and expectations. For this purpose, varied input in the sessions—opportunities for both parties to observe what the patient makes of advice as well as silence, for example, or of approval as well as interpretation—is actually useful. I am not advocating going out of one's way to alter one's stance as a means of probing the relation between schemas and interpersonal input; that would lead to a very inauthentic interaction and is, in addition, unnecessary. Simply being ready to help in a wider variety of ways will suffice for that purpose. I hope it is also unnecessary to say that I do not advocate speaking to patients in the highly intellectual language of schemas, assimilation, and accommodation. That is a language for talking *about* therapy, not for talking *in* therapy, where the language of emotion and experience is foremost.

PSYCHOLOGIES OF THE SELF

Psychoanalysis was Freud's research tool as well as his therapeutic method. An analysis was undertaken as an investigation, and the assumption has always been that this investigation is also therapeutic. To some degree, of course, this is the case. But it is also an assumption that is far too convenient to be trusted. There is more to the process of change even in a classical analysis than just the gaining of understanding (even "emotional" understanding), and the degree of change that is achievable could be increased further by more explicit efforts to mobilize these other therapeutic forces. Franz Alexander was one of the first in the analytic community to begin to make these matters explicit; in more recent years, a second wave of innovation has reached us from Chicago, again (in a somewhat different way) suggesting the importance of corrective emotional experiences.

There is much that is important and useful in the "psychology of the self" that has attracted so much attention recently. Both in its attention to the experience of self and in its concern with the actual facilitative behavior of the analyst, this approach raises matters which deservingly ring a responsive chord in many analysts (though I think it is the case that these matters are more absent in today's guardians of orthodoxy than they were in Freud's own work). Like the interest that has recently been generated by the writings of the British object-relations school, the interest in Kohut's work stems from his having addressed phenomena which many analysts felt were insufficiently attended to in what had been the mainstream of American psychoanalytic thought. But useful as these developments are in pointing the analyst to significant and somewhat overlooked clinical phenomena, I believe that they are flawed as theory. Further,

I believe that the earlier writings of Horney and of Sullivan covered much the same ground and did so more clearly and, potentially, in a way therapeutically more useful.[2]

One of Sullivan's central ideas, for example, was that the difficulties people got into stemmed from efforts to protect a particular sense of self, a sense that made interpersonal relations feel manageable and relatively free from anxiety. It was not disruptive biological impulses that posed the greatest threat in Sullivan's view, but the emergence of experiences inconsistent with the sense of self. Thus even "positive" experiences and attributes could be threatening and warded off if they presented a challenge to the person's stable experience of self. (Sullivan's view in this regard is similar to Carl Rogers's. As Arkin [1981] has recently noted, there are unacknowledged similarities between Kohut's and Rogers's view as well.)

The centrality of the sense of self in Sullivan's theorizing has at times been obscured by Sullivan's own rhetoric and the way in which it has been read by subsequent clinicians concerned with the self. "The unique individuality of the other fellow," Sullivan said, "need never concern us as scientists." Viewing these and similar statements, Friedland (1978) states, "the self in intra-psychic life was lost." Others (e.g., Klenbort, 1978; Wolstein, 1971) have voiced similar concerns.

In fact, I would argue, despite these rhetorical excesses Sullivan's shortcomings—and particularly those of his followers—were primarily in the opposite direction: failure to really carry through on the implications of an interpersonal perspective, retreating to a largely intrapsychic approach instead of building a truly interpersonal psychotherapy. As Sullivan noted, a genuinely interpersonal approach is essentially a field-theoretical approach. Such an approach would look at how past experiences have been carried forth into the present and would treat all the relevant forces as contemporaneous. Sullivan, however, largely adopted a traditional stance toward exploring the patient's past, and, from my experience, present-day therapists who describe themselves as interpersonal or Sullivanian in orientation exhibit a concern with reconstructing the patient's history (albeit *sans* libido theory) that would fit well on the staunchest Freudian, as they also indulge quite comfortably in the language of "exploring the patient's inner world."

Horney, in many respects, is actually more aptly viewed as a field theorist, though in other ways she was less thoroughly inter-

2. Mitchell (1979), in an interesting analysis of Kohut's and Kernberg's theories, has also called attention to the way in which these theorists have in large measure dealt with matters earlier addressed by the interpersonalists.

personal than Sullivan. Horney consistently argued that the patterns that constitute the neurosis, and that need to be understood for therapeutic change to occur, are fully present in the patient's current life. Events in the past set present patterns into motion, but their effect is indirect—not through a persistence of something belonging to the past but through a cumulative skewing of the person's character, yielding a concatenation of choices that keep the patient unable to see new options and that, due to present dynamics and forces, keep the neurosis going.

Horney was one of the earliest psychoanalytic theorists to concentrate focally on the experience of self, and that focus gained in importance in her writings through the years. Moreover, in her brief chapter on narcissistic phenomena in *New Ways in Psychoanalysis* (1939), she concisely conveys, without relying on libido theory, a sense of the experience of the narcissistic individual and of the causes and consequences of the narcissistic solution to neurotic tensions. Horney's (1939) discussion of self-inflation and its relation to feelings of worthlessness seems even more relevant today than when it was written.

There are several reasons why the ways of addressing the self and narcissistic phenomena suggested in Horney's and Sullivan's writings are potentially more useful than those of Kohut (1971, 1977) and of the object-relations theorists. For one thing, there is far less reification in the former than in the latter. The language, especially in Horney's case, is closer to plain English, and it is thus considerably easier to evaluate the various formulations. Kohut's theorizing, on the other hand, like that of the object-relations theorists, is heavily weighted with jargon and far more difficult to pin down.

Horney's approach also seems to me in some ways to be more comprehensive and integrative. Kohut, for example, treats the evolution of the self and the evolution of conflict as rather independent processes. Two different psychologies, in essence, are needed to account for them. In Horney's theory, as in the cyclical psychodynamic view deriving from it, conflict and self are actually not separated. From the point of view of cyclical psychodynamics, the sense of self evolves gradually from experiences with other people, integrating a variety of experiences and reflecting as well the limitations set by anxiety and compulsive efforts to avoid it. These latter influences make certain organizations of experience more possible than others, and the organizations they permit are not always those most consonant with the data of lived experience. The sense of self is built upon reflected appraisals by others as well as the person's own apperceptions of his characteristics, his desires and aspirations, and his possibilities. When this evolving center of the organization of experience is coherent and relatively free from anxiety-generated restrictions, the person's sense of self can accommodate to and incorporate both the demands and directives from the environment and the person's own varying desires. However much he may vary from context to context—and the healthy person in fact varies far more than the person suffering from serious psychopathology—he feels generally coherent and whole, self-consistent despite the variation.

When, however, the reflected appraisals he experiences conflict significantly with his own evolving apperceptions of himself and the events of his life, it becomes difficult to achieve a coherent sense of self. When such "failures of empathy" occur, the child feels neither understood nor accepted. Whether the parent sees him as "better" or "worse" than he really is, the result is roughly the same. If the parent sees him as worse, he will feel that his positive feelings cannot be trusted, that he is somehow "bad" and cannot really do anything about it (since the communicated sense of badness is not in response to his real characteristics and so not in his control).

But things are not much better if the parent sees the child as "better"—e.g., as smarter, stronger, more kindly, more capable. It is one thing for the parent to give a positive *interpretation* to the child's characteristics if they are more or less accurately perceived and reflected. Then the child learns to regard himself in a positive and optimistic fashion, and the foundation for feelings of well-being is laid. But when the parents' perceptions are actually disjunctive with the child's evolving sense of his own reality, then what he experiences is that who he thought he was is simply not good enough. He senses in some dim way that the parents need him to be someone he is not, and whatever real attributes he has will be experienced as insufficient and unimportant. Rather than building on the solid core of his actual experiences and attributes, he begins to chase a will-of-the-wisp and to experience self-alienation and a sense of falseness or hollowness.

But the difficulty in achieving a coherent sense of self, capable of reflecting and integrating the full range of one's attributes and aspirations, does not arise only from the disjunction between the appraisals of others and one's own beginning self-conceptions. It stems as well from conflicting self-generated imperatives as to how one must be. The lines of conflict traced by Horney are not between pre-existing impulses and defenses against them, but between different peremptory strategies for warding off the sense of helplessness and isolation that is inevitable to at least some degree in the years of childhood dependency (as it is in the face of the existential threats of later life as well). These strategies or trends, driven by anxiety as they are, do not have the flexibility to work smoothly or adaptively and tend to conflict with each other in serious ways. As an important key to how we reassure ourselves that we are acceptable or strong or invulnerable enough to feel safe, these trends are centrally implicated in our sense of who we are. When the conflict is very intense, we feel torn apart, fragmented, lacking solidity in the very ground of our being. When these driven, unbending tendencies occupy too much of our time and effort, preventing us from establishing a more genuine and reliable basis for security, we feel vulnerable, and our self-esteem is shaky. At times it is bolstered by a defensive self-inflation, a "narcissism" if you will, but one whose meaning has little to do with self-love.

When these neurotic trends are too dominant, they also compel us to act in stereotyped ways that have little to do with our deeper or more genuine inclinations, and we feel alienated from ourselves, hollow and unreal. In all these instances the experience of self and the vicissitudes of conflict are inextricably related. There is no need to formulate a self psychology separate from the psychology of conflict. That is an artifact of conceiving of drives that have little to do with self.

THE DECLINING INFLUENCE OF NEO-FREUDIANISM

It is easy to see why interpersonally oriented therapists should be drawn to such writers as Kohut or the object-relations theorists. They do seem in some ways to be concerned with matters that have been at the heart of the interpersonal approach from its inception—the sense of self and the shaping of that sense, and of personality generally, by the quality of our interactions with key others. But a close inspection of those theoretical perspectives suggests that the compatibility with the interpersonal approach is more apparent than real. They are, to some degree, interpersonal in their approach to the earliest years of life. But they are to a preponderant degree intrapsychic theories with regard to the rest of our three score and ten. Apart from the special circumstances thought to obtain when a therapeutic regression occurs, these theories treat most of our significant interactions not in terms of a transaction between two (or more) individuals who jointly determine what ensues and what is experienced via schemas, but also a present reality and a present relation to perceptual input; rather, they emphasize the playing out of a destiny sealed by the time the few years at all viewed interpersonally have drawn to a close. In the language used earlier, they are theories whose rhetoric is that of unfolding and emerging.

The eagerness of interpersonally oriented therapists to embrace such approaches suggests to me that the interpersonal movement has (unnecessarily) been brought to a cul-de-sac which leads back out to the intrapsychically dominated theorizing it was designed to transcend. The ferment that neo-Freudianism generated in the 1930s and 1940s, both among clinicians and in the general intellectual community, is hardly evident today. Though it has certainly yielded some substantial contributions, there is no canon of neo-Freudian works in the three decades since the deaths of Horney and Sullivan at all comparable to contributions over the same period of such writers as Hartmann, Waelder, Kris, Anna Freud, Spitz, Jacobson, Mahler, Kernberg, Kohut, Loewald, Schafer, Gill, and numerous other distinguished Freudians. I say this not to endorse this body of work—much of which I disagree with rather fundamentally—but simply to acknowledge its seriousness and substance. Freudianism has remained an intellectual force to be reckoned with in a way that neo-Freudianism really has not.

The reasons for this are complex and manifold and cannot be detailed here. But one which is particularly relevant to the present discussion is the tendency of followers of Horney and of Sullivan to define themselves largely in terms of their departure from the Freudian instinct theory. From that perspective the work of the British object-relations theorists and, to a somewhat lesser extent, of Kohut does seem relevant.

But more significant, I suggest, was the contextual element in both Horney's and Sullivan's writings, the insistence on seeing people in their interpersonal and cultural context. They both showed us how to explore the full richness of subjective experience and of the unconscious processes which lie behind it without assuming that these events simply "unfold." Potentially at least, they provided a means of integrating the intrapsychic perspective of Freud with an appreciation of our attunement to social and cultural events and to the subtle cues and exchanges between people. They provided—again at least potentially—a way of reconciling the discoveries of depth psychology regarding our ties to the past with the discoveries of other students of human behavior regarding our complex adaptation to the present.

Implicit in the best of Horney's and Sullivan's theorizing was a critique of the narrow individualism that characterized Freudian thought. As I have discussed elsewhere (Wachtel, 1983), there are fascinating parallels between aspects of Freudian thought and the individualistic conceptions that governed 19th-century economics. It was, as it were, a depth psychology for *laissez-faire* capitalism. Despite the recent upsurge of this anachronistic economic conception in our present political life, the long-run trend is that we are increasingly being forced to recognize the facts of our interdependency. We are in an era in which ecological modes of thought rather than models stressing autonomy are called for. Neo-Freudianism could have provided us with a basis for such a psychology. But it has largely retreated to the individualism which still dominates our society, and in so doing it has tended to yield little more than watered-down Freudianism, a soup of sentimentality and humanistic posturing in which its keenest insights have been dissolved (cf., Wachtel, 1979b).

Freudianism has shown greater intellectual vitality in the past few decades largely because it has remained true to its own paradigm. The interpersonal paradigm—which is quintessentially a contextual paradigm—still seems to me to hold great promise of incorporating what was valuable in the older, intrapsychic approach while opening new vistas both for therapeutic intervention and for the psychoanalytic examination of broader social issues (e.g., Wachtel, 1983). The cyclical psychodynamic approach is an effort to return to the contextual core of neo-Freudian theory from which so many putatively interpersonally oriented therapists have strayed. Some applications of this approach may be particularly controversial in present-day psychoanalytic circles—for example, the development of a rationale for utilizing behavioral interventions in a psychodynamically oriented therapy (Wachtel, 1977b). But the broader theme of active intervention in the context of psychoanalytic exploration, and the synergistic therapy this suggests—along with the theoretical reexamination of the roots of psychoanalysis and of interpersonal variants of it—offers, I believe, important possibilities for revitalizing interpersonal theory and psychoanalysis more generally.

4

Internal and External Determinants of Behavior in Psychodynamic Theories

INTRODUCTION

The distinction between inner and outer determinants of behavior, or some variant of that distinction, has been common in discourses on human behavior from the time of the Greek philosophers to the most recent American Psychological Association journal. Although not identical to the inner–outer question, questions of freedom versus determinism, of responsibility and punishment versus rehabilitation, of environmentalism versus instinctualism or environmentalism versus mentalism, of organismic versus conditioning models, and many other recurrent themes and debates are clearly recognizable as, so to speak, loading on the same factor.

The inner–outer distinction is common because it is in many respects a useful one; and whether due to a Kantian imperative or a widespread habit, it seems to present itself almost as a kind of perceptual given. Yet, it is also a very tricky distinction. The terms "inner" and "outer" may have very different meanings for different theorists or in different contexts.

It is easy enough to make a distinction between events "inside the skin" and all others. Often, more "hard-headed" or operationalist writers do just that, and it suits their purposes fairly well, largely because one of their purposes is to minimize the role of "inner"

Reprinted by permission from L. A. Pervin & M. Lewis (Eds.), *Perspectives in Interactional Psychology*. New York: Plenum Press, 1978.

Part of the form and focus of the present chapter was a function of the originally proposed title of the volume in which it first appeared: *Internal and External Determinants of Behavior*.

factors, in the pursuit of a psychology predominantly concerned with the impact of environmental events. To a growing number of psychologists, however, the distinction between internal and external determinants is not a prelude to the separation of the internal chaff from the external wheat, but a serious effort to include in their theorizing all of the events and processes that are important in determining who we are and what we do. Once such a course is undertaken, deciding what is meant by "inner" and "outer" becomes much more difficult. For a concern with what is inner that is not a dismissive concern introduces the investigator to a host of complexities.

Consider a stomach pain, for example. In one sense, this seems to be an event "inside the skin." Yet, in seeking to determine why a person left the room at a particular point in the conversation, the occurrence of the pain seems an explanation more extrinsic[1] to his personality than would be an explanation stressing his discomfort about the topic being discussed. If he "really" left because his stomach hurt rather than because the topic made him uncomfortable, this seems to tell us less about "him."

Were we to be told, however, that his stomach pain should be understood not as a purely physical complaint but rather as something "psychosomatic" or (even more so) as something "hysterical," then the locus of our understanding seems to shift, especially if we learn that he tends to get such pains (and "therefore" to have to leave) primarily when certain topics come up in conversation. The pain occurs in the same "place" in either event (or perhaps—we don't really know how to talk about such matters—in the stomach in one case and "in the head" in the other, but clearly "within the skin" as that term is used in its simplest version). Yet, the locus of our explanation and our understanding has shifted considerably.

The concepts of internal and external determinants of behavior, therefore, do not, in much of the psychological literature, refer necessarily to inside and outside of the body. What, then, do they refer to? Inside and outside of what? Schafer (1972), in examining the use of such concepts in psychoanalytic theorizing, asks a similar question. He concludes that there is no really satisfactory answer. To locate the events inside or outside of the body, or organism, or even brain, will miss the point of the distinction the theorist is concerned with (cf. the above example of the stomach pain). "Mind" or "ego"

---

1. The distinction between *intrinsic* and *extrinsic* factors may be a more useful one than that between *internal* and *external* factors, especially in light of the important role that the person himself plays in bringing about what can seem to be an "external" event (see below and Wachtel, 1973b, 1977a).

are somewhat closer, but to place events "within" them is to treat them as places or things, whereas they are more appropriately viewed as concepts designating "classes of events" (p. 411). Schafer argues that terms such as "inner" and "outer" in psychoanalytic theorizing are not merely harmless metaphors but rather habits of thought with rather serious consequences: They are confusing, unnecessary, and lead to concreteness of thinking and reification of abstract concepts; they introduce extra assumptions that complicate theorizing and require the elaborate pursuit of irrelevant questions; they confuse theory and observation, and lead to theorizing that has the primitive, primary-process qualities of the archaic fantasies that are being theorized about, and thus they represent "more a repetition or continuation of the problem than a clarification or explanation of it" (p. 423).

Schafer in no way minimizes the distinctions and experiences that the concepts of inner and outer are designed to approach. Rather, he contends that this particular way of talking about the issue is inelegant and mischievous. Schafer, the author of an entire book on "internalization" (1968), is very much concerned with notions of "inner" and "outer" as categories of human thought, and in his view it makes an enormous difference for how people act and feel whether they experience something as "within" them or not. But he views much of this kind of thinking by all of us as a residue of early, primitive forms of mental activity, and hence hardly a basis for mature theorizing. Thus, for Schafer, it is important that theories take into account that people will think of things as inside or outside, as taken in, swallowed up, spit out, etc. But in theorizing about such primary-process events, one must use the secondary-process modes of thought that are essential to rational understanding (even of the irrational).

The linguistic reforms in psychoanalytic theorizing that Schafer advocates seem potentially of considerable value, and may well help to clarify the empirical referents of psychoanalytic propositions and thereby to aid in the evaluation of which propositions are of lasting value and which should be relinquished as false leads or hunches. This would be a valuable outcome not just for psychoanalytic theory but for psychology as a whole. For the serious flaws in psychoanalytic theory making, and the tendency of many analysts to persist in advocating improbable propositions with little reliable empirical support, have led many academic psychologists to overreact, rejecting all concepts of unconscious motivation, motivational conflict, or (in some cases) even conceptions such as fantasy, expectancy, etc. This has led to an impoverishment of psychological theorizing and to an academic psychology that is precise about trivial matters but that, when it turns to such realms as psychotherapy, must smuggle in contraband clinical concepts in the dark of night (not a condition that leads to close or effective scrutiny; see Wachtel, 1977b, especially Chapters 6 and 7).

But a close re-examination of psychoanalytic theory will, I think, suggest that the prevalence of theorizing in terms of inner and outer worlds is due not only to the unfortunate influence of Freud's "metapsychology" (that aspect of Freud's theorizing that writers such as Schafer and Klein [e.g., Klein, 1976] view as an effort to put a natural-science cloak over a discipline more akin to the humanities, an effort strongly criticized by Schafer and by Klein). It is due, as well, to a substantive feature of Freudian theorizing that minimizes the role of things presently happening in the person's life as determinants of the psychological processes that are the central concern of psychoanalytic theory.

A HISTORICAL GLIMPSE AT PSYCHOANALYTIC THOUGHT

Closer examination of the role of concepts of inner and outer in psychoanalysis requires a brief historical look at the evolution of psychoanalytic ideas.

Freud's initial psychological theorizing was organized around the conception that "hysterics suffer from reminiscences" (Breuer & Freud, 1895/1955). This was a conception that derived rather directly from empirical observations, and made a great deal of sense in terms of what Freud observed. His patients came to him with a variety of distressing symptoms, which disappeared only when, after much effort, they came to remember certain important childhood events that they were at first unable to recall.

As is well known, the hypothesis that behind the patient's symptoms lay inaccessible memories of real events did not stand up to further scrutiny, and was shortly revised by Freud. Before it was, however, a distinct cast was given to psychoanalytic thought, a mode of thinking still persistent in much psychoanalytic writing and in large measure responsible for the gulf between psychoanalytic thought about personality change and other points of view on these matters dominant in academic circles. The specific aspect of psychoanalytic thought to which I am referring is its emphasis on the continuing effect of the past upon the present (and the implicit, if not absolutely logically necessary, corollary, of a relative lack of importance attributed to current events in the patient's life).

Freud's initial observations led him to seek historically earlier for the real explanation of the patient's problems and for their cure. When he reconceptualized his patients' reports as fantasies derived from childhood wishes, Freud retained his conceptual and methodological strategy of seeking for understanding in the patient's history rather than in current factors. In some ways this had highly salutary consequences. For one, it shed a good deal of light on childhood, pointing us to notice things that had been overlooked theretofore (and even providing some interesting perspectives on why such dramatic and obvious things should have been so largely overlooked for so long). I for one believe that Freud's insights, especially as modified and elaborated by Erikson (e.g., 1963), and as developed by child-observation work, provide a crucial foundation for any understanding of childhood; my conviction on this score has increased greatly since becoming a father of two small children.

But if Freud's emphasis on his adult patients' pasts had some very positive consequences, his particular way of conceptualizing how the past was influential was more questionable. It was, I believe, one of the important, and poorly understood, factors responsible for the unnecessary and counterproductive hostility of many academic psychologists to the idea of unconscious motivation. For Freud in many important respects retained the model of the traumatic memories period almost unchanged into the theory of conflict over infantile wishes, and even into the ego psychology that emerged in 1923 and has been increasingly dominant in psychoanalytic thought over the past half century.

In the hysteria period, Freud postulated that certain memories that were unacceptable to the patient's conscious sense of himself were intentionally repressed. Importantly, this did not just make them unconscious. It also somehow separated the psychological processes associated with such memories from the rest of everyday psychological functioning, so that they were not subject to the constraining and modifying effects of the organized nature of psychological processes. Whereas ordinary memories are subject to modification and reduction in intensity in a variety of ways (e.g., by comparison with other memories and/or with new perceptual input, by the application of logic, by the placing of things into perspective, by the reduction in importance of something once action is taken or it is "cried out," or by whatever is involved in simply "forgetting"), these memories did not seem to be. Their hypothesized effects (i.e., the symptoms that observation and theory suggested were linked to them) persisted powerfully so long as they remained in this split-off state, and when the memories were finally recovered, they appeared with an intensity and clarity quite different from what one might expect from everyday remembering. Elsewhere (Wachtel, 1977b), in a more extended discussion of the implications of the history of psychoanalytic thought, I have likened this picture of the preservation of memories in their original form (keeping them fresh and like new) to the discovery by Arctic explorers of woolly mammoths frozen in the ice, whose meat was almost as fresh and edible as the day millennia before when they were frozen; I have therefore referred to this early model of preservation of memories in their original form as the "woolly mammoth" model.

Now, it is important to recognize that when Freud revised his view of what it was that was repressed, he did more than just salvage his theory. He also expanded its range so that for the first time it had the possibility of being a general psychology. The traumatic-memories theory has a necessarily limited application. It was relevant only to those unfortunates who happened to have particular unusual things happen to them in childhood, and it was of necessity a theory of neurosis only, not a general theory of personality. The new theory, in contrast, dealt with the child's way of dealing with aspects of his own development. The wishes and fantasies Freud felt he detected in the histories and in the dreams of his neurotic patients, he found evident as well in the behavior and the creative products of mankind in general. Had Freud's first theory been correct, had neurotic symptoms in fact been due to the repression of real childhood traumas, Freud would have been a great name in the history of medicine, but would have had little impact upon our conception of human nature, our views of human development, or our social mores and child-rearing practices (other than to make us more careful in hiring governesses or nursery school teachers). The untenability of his initial theory led him to develop a conceptual framework whose legitimate scope was the entire range of cultural and psychological phenomena.

In one crucial way, however, Freud's theorizing did not change after the rejection of the traumatic-memories theory: He retained the essential features of the "woolly mammoth" model; only now, *impulses* were seen as preserved in their original state instead of veridical memories. Childhood wishes, which under ideal circumstances would evolve, change with new experiences, be integrated into, modified by, and coordinated with the evolving structure of aims and adaptive efforts, were, if repressed, preserved in their original form, to exert a continuing and unmodified influence and demand upon psychological functioning.

As in the earlier model, it was not just their unconsciousness that was viewed as important. Perhaps even more important was their unmodifiability, their persistence in primitive form and lack of accommodation to everything else that the person felt, wanted, and believed. Freud saw his patients as showing signs of continuing to strive for and long for things that were quite incompatible not only with their moral codes but with their realistic picture of what is possible or even desirable (e.g., what they had observed since the age of 4 might lead them to be much more interested in other women than in their mothers, but in an isolated, unacknowledged, yet crucially important way they continued to exhibit the old yearnings). Such considerations led Freud to refer to unconscious processes, in perhaps too colorful or potentially reifiable language, as "timeless," allowing of contradictory impulses side by side, etc.

The final, and most sophisticated, development of the "woolly mammoth" model, and its logical outcome, appeared when Freud recast his theory in 1923 in terms of the ego, id, and superego. Now it was made explicit that adaptation to reality was accomplished by a coordinated, organized system of psychological processes (the ego), grounded in perception, including, but not limited to, the experience of self-feeling, and from which certain psychological processes (e.g., repressed wishes) were excluded. Being excluded, they did not (like those wishes that were part of the organized ego system) get modified and coordinated with the rest of what we saw, felt, and wanted, but persisted instead as (to use an earlier metaphor of Freud's) a foreign body. To make very clear that it was this cut-off, uncoordinated aspect of repressed wishes that was most crucial, Freud revised his slogan for the goal of the psychoanalytic process from that of "making the unconscious conscious" to "where id was, let ego be." Thus, while consciousness was still important in the theory, what was more important than consciousness per se was the reintegration of psychological functioning, the resolution of the split in our functioning that enabled certain of our activities to go on in opposition to, rather than in coordination with, other of our activities. (I have discussed these issues, and their clinical implications, at greater length elsewhere [Wachtel, 1977b].)

This reconceptualization called the attention of analysts to the ego, that is, to coordinated adaptational efforts and to their link to (in fact their organization around) perception of environmental (as well as organismic) events. And analysts have indeed since then studied adaptation and perception in meaningful ways. But these have to a large degree been studied as aspects that modify the great core issues posed by repression, intrapsychic conflict, and the demands of the id. Psychoanalytic technique still aims to foster a regressive transference neurosis, in which the original childhood longings and fantasies can emerge and be reintegrated with the rest of the personality. Despite some recognition by modern analysts that transference manifestations usually are linked to some actual characteristic or action of the analyst, transferences are still seen as essentially occurring despite the current reality rather than because of it. This feature of the psychoanalytic view, and its link to the early "woolly mammoth" model, is particularly clear in the following quotation from Stone (1961), which is especially noteworthy since his monograph was a particularly well-regarded effort to modernize the psychoanalytic relationship and bring it closer to what would be implied by modern ego psychology. Stone writes that

> true transference . . . retains unmistakably its infantile character. However much the given early relationship may have contributed to the genuinely adult pattern of relationships (via identification, limitation, acceptance of teaching; for example), its transference derivative differs from the latter, *approximately in the sense which Breuer and Freud (1895) assigned to the sequelae of the pathogenic traumatic experience, which was neither abreacted as such, nor associatively absorbed in the personality.* (p. 67, italics added)

This stress on the locked-in, persistent, and unchanging remnant of the past is, I believe, the major and perhaps only substantive obstacle to the integration of the psychoanalytic approach with the approaches to psychological phenomena dominant in the academic world. Not only does the "woolly mammoth" model de-emphasize environmental control, and hence clash with the observations that have most influenced academic psychologists; it also influences what analysts observe and look for, and thus perpetuates itself. Classical analysts, guided by this model, emphasize free association and attempts to discern the inner dynamics of the patient. The patient's behavior is of interest primarily as a reflection of what is going on within him. With such a method and focus, it is difficult to discern the subtle influence of interpersonal cues, not only upon the patient's actions, but upon his motives and fantasies as well. The analyst's theory sets him to look predominantly for sequences from inside out, so to speak, and his method and viewpoint lead him to see just that (just as most experimentally grounded conceptions lead one to see primarily the outside-in-sequences—see Wachtel, 1973a, b, 1977a).

Moreover, this kind of theorizing unnecessarily sharpens the distinction between "inner" and "outer" and seems to imply that these are two entirely separate realms. The radical linguistic surgery that Schafer proposes would perhaps not seem so essential were this not the case. Although metaphors can, as Schafer indicates, be a source of considerable confusion and mischief, they can also spur creative thought; indeed, we can hardly do without them. Notions of internal and external have reached such a problematic state in psychoanalysis at least in part because of the considerations just discussed. I will try to indicate below some of the ways in which psychodynamic concepts may be employed in a somewhat different theoretical context, in which some of these difficulties may be less prevalent.

WISHES AS CAUSE AND EFFECT

Traditionally, psychoanalysts have sought to understand unconscious fantasies or wishes essentially as independent variables. They have been concerned with the effects produced by such phenomena far more than with understanding what leads to their occurrence, at least when trying to understand phenomena of adult behavior and personality. Although there has been a good deal of interest in what causes such wishes and fantasies to develop in childhood, and in what conditions at that time make them likely to remain of persisting importance, there has been little effort to account for the adult's unconscious fantasies and wishes as a function of the way the person is currently living his life. These wishes and fantasies are treated essentially as a given, something within the person that accounts for the behavior he manifests.

In modern psychoanalytic theorizing, the internal givens are not just wishes and fantasies, but a variety of ego processes, of both a defensive and adaptive nature. It is recognized far more explicitly that perception of environmental events will play a role in how the individual behaves and feels. But the emphasis is largely on these events as triggers for releasing or evoking particular impulses or conflicts that are structural features of the personality. There is little consideration of how these structures may themselves be a function of the manifest events of the patient's life at present (see Wachtel, 1977b).

It has been my experience, however, that closer scrutiny of the conditions under which a particularly troublesome impulse tends to be triggered suggests that the situation that evokes the impulse can be understood as a self-created situation. The relations among the person's manifest behavior, the situations it leads to, the desires that are aroused, and the fantasies that guide and interpret experience are interlocking ones in which no aspect is more basic or causal than any other. A cycle of events can usually be discerned as a common pattern in the person's life such that the situation that tends to evoke an impulse tends to be the situation that the arousal of that impulse tends to lead to (see Wachtel, 1977b). Similarly, the defense that may commonly be employed to ward off a frightening wish or feeling is likely to be, ironically enough, one of the major causal factors in keeping that wish or feeling a prominent (if not necessarily conscious) feature of the person's psychological life.

Consider, for example, the kind of individual who apears to the classical Freudian as someone who has developed a strong reaction-formation against deep-seated feelings of rage. From the classical perspective, the rage is viewed as "deeper" and "earlier"; it is more the cause of the reaction formation than vice versa (though, of course, it doesn't cause it directly—the arousal of anxiety and appraisal of danger, for example, are intermediate events). Inquiry is thus directed toward elucidating the historical origins of the rage, which is seen as having been there for a long time for reasons that have to do with the patient's childhood rather than primarily with what is currently going on. And, indeed, one can often discover events and situations in the person's childhood that do seem to be intimately related to the life pattern that still characterizes the person. Perhaps we can reconstruct that at a young age he harbored frightening violent urges toward his father, and that he desperately struggled to cover these up. The struggle in which he is engaged today may be sufficiently similar that it does not seem unreasonable to suggest that he is still defending against the same childhood wishes. Indeed, his dreams may suggest that the object of at least some of the hostile feelings with which he struggles may continue to be his father (even though such an idea is abhorrent to him), and other indications as well may point to warded-off rage involving his father.[2]

If one looks closely, however, at how he lives his life from day to day, one begins to entertain a rather different idea about why the pattern of excessive meekness and frightening, warded-off hostile urges characterizes his life. One sees that, however the pattern got started, it tends to keep itself going by the consequences it generates. The person's excessively unaggressive, cooperative, self-denying way of living is likely to lead him to continually accrue experiences in which he is taken advantage of, ignored, or overridden. He may manage to be well liked and positively regarded, but probably at the cost of subordinating his own real desires and interests to those with whom he ingratiates himself. Thus, he is likely to be continually confronted with the kinds of limitations and frustrations that tend to make people angry, and indeed if one looks closely at the dreams, fantasies, and private thoughts of such persons they frequently evidence signs of anger quite at odds with their manifest life-style and image.

---

2. See p. 75 for a different perspective from the "woolly mammoth" view of why people remain preoccupied with parental figures.

One can see this excessively unassertive and self-abnegating behavior as motivated by the need to cover up his strong aggressive urges, and this would be correct as far as it goes. But it is equally the case that such a life-style generates rage. Disavowed anger may be a continuing feature of his life from childhood, but the angry thoughts that disturb his dreams tonight can be understood by what he let happen to himself today.

Such a person is caught in a vicious circle. Having learned early to fear his angry feelings, he has built up overt patterns of behavior designed to squelch and hide them. Even the smallest assertion seems dangerous because he senses[3] an enormous reservoir of violence behind it. Yet, it is in just such excessive restriction upon his assertiveness that the conditions for further violent urges are created.

In one sense, he guards against his anger for good reason: As he is at any given moment, he *is* potentially explosive, he *is* resentful and full of hatred, he *would* be nasty and vindictive if he were not trying so hard to be otherwise. Ironically, if he were not so frequently bending over backward, if he could act with reasonable assertiveness and demand a fair return from others, he would discover that the underlying rage would diminish. But because at any given moment real aggressive inclinations and fantasies have accrued from his way of living, he is afraid to act assertively. So he once more squelches himself, thereby arousing the fierce resentment that will in turn motivate his further self-abnegation and lead once again to strong, if unacknowledged, resentment. In such fashion he perpetuates his personal myth that there resides within him an untouchable kernel of rage that is part of the essence of who he is. And to a substantial degree this myth may be subscribed to by his analyst as well, in the analyst's view that the anger is "in" the patient from the past, rather than a response to his life circumstances.

PERSPECTIVES ON PERSONALITY DEVELOPMENT

The perspective just described shares a good deal with traditional psychoanalytic theorizing. It attributes a substantial role to unconscious motives and fantasies, emphasizes conflict and defense, and stresses the strong hold that irrational anxieties can have on the

---

3. Here, as elsewhere in our discussion, the use of terms such as "sense," "believe," "fear," etc., does not necessarily imply a conscious experience. See Schafer's (1972) discussion of the false issue raised when such terms are taken to mean a concern only with what is conscious.

person's view of what is possible and desirable. It differs largely in that it assigns a far greater role to perceptual input in maintaining the seemingly irrational and inappropriate unconscious fears, wishes, and fantasies—and thereby a correspondingly diminished role in their maintenance to the effect of repression in cutting off aspects of the personality from further influence by such input (the "woolly mammoth" model).

In principle, there is nothing incompatible about examining the present feedback processes that maintain patterned sets of motives, expectations, and strategies of living and looking as well at the effects of repression and the dissociation of psychological systems in doing the same. (In fact, in my own clinical practice, I do look at both to some extent.) But, as I have discussed in detail elsewhere (Wachtel, 1977b), the two perspectives on psychological development point to different therapeutic strategies and lead the therapist to act in ways that will inevitably limit data relevant to evaluating and articulating one or the other view of the patient's dilemma. In emphasizing the interpersonal feedback perspective, I am making a heuristic choice, one based on an evaluation that the implications and potentials of the intrapsychic model have been more thoroughly examined and that new insights and new kinds of observations are more likely to be generated by the less thoroughly mined lode; and based, as well, on an analysis that suggests that the interpersonal version of psychodynamic thought lends itself more readily to an integration with such active-intervention approaches as behavior therapy and family therapy, an integration I believe to hold the brightest prospects for an advance in the field of psychotherapy as well as for advances in personality theory (see Wachtel, 1977a, and below).

In holding that the unconscious motives and fantasies and the debilitating conflicts that therapists can discern in their patients are not primarily a result of locked-in residues from the past, but rather are a function of how the person continues to live his life, one's view of the role of history in the therapeutic enterprise is likely to be modified. The painstaking unraveling of early experience does not seem as critical as it does from a classical Freudian perspective. In its place is likely to be an increased concern, as described below, with various active-intervention techniques that can break into the vicious circles that keep going both the maladaptive behavior and the motives, fantasies, and conflicts that can seem to underlie it.

Such a shift in therapeutic strategy may seem to some readers to imply an antidevelopmental point of view. For several reasons, however, this is not the case. First of all, there remain times when, even from the perspective offered here, it is useful for people to gain some insight into the events that have shaped their behavior patterns, both to facilitate discrimination between past and present contingencies (see Dollard & Miller, 1950) and to enable the patient to be relieved of guilt feelings stemming from an excessive sense of responsibility for his dilemma. Secondly, the therapist can often be helped by a knowledge of the patient's history to understand aspects of the patient's present difficulties and to be alerted to noticing subtle features of interaction that might otherwise pass him by (see Wachtel, 1977b, Chapter 7). Finally, as a theory of personality, the particular psychodynamic perspective described here must account for how various personality patterns develop, as well as how they are perpetuated. The model is primarily one of progressive or cumulative development, based on cyclical reconfirmation of anticipated experiences, rather than one emphasizing hierarchical structuring and the persisting effects of locked-in early tendencies—unlike Freudian theory, the model sees these early tendencies as continuing not despite what actually goes on in the person's daily adult living, but precisely because of what is going on (and is largely brought about by those very same tendencies). But the theory is indeed concerned with understanding development. While seeing such understanding as less relevant for bringing about change in the psychological problems of adults than does Freudian theory, the perspective offered here does concern itself with developmental issues for other reasons: e.g., for purposes of prevention of disorder or facilitation of personality growth; for purposes of guiding therapeutic work with children; and for providing a perspective on "human nature" that can guide efforts at social change and philosophical inquiry into value issues.

From the present point of view, then, understanding how adaptive and maladaptive personality patterns develop is of substantial concern. Indeed, even the critical role that psychoanalysis attributes to the very early years of life in determining later patterns does not distinguish it from an interpersonal or transactional psychodynamic perspective.[4] From the latter perspective, too, those early years are likely to be critical. The first few years of life are far more different from the rest of the life span for human beings than for any other creature. Humans have their view of the world and its possibilities shaped at a time when they are practically different organisms from

4. Providing a name for the present point of view is difficult. The terms "interpersonal" or "transactional" seem most descriptive, but it is not identical to Sullivan's interpersonal approach, and is quite unlike the transactional analysis of Berne. The reader will see obvious debts to the writings of Horney, Sullivan, and Erikson in particular, but especially as elaborated in Wachtel (1977b), it goes in directions rather distinct from any of these writers. Elsewhere (Wachtel, 1977a), I have used the term "cyclical psychodynamics."

what they will be later. In many respects, the caterpillar is far more like the butterfly than is the human toddler (much less infant) like the fully developed adult; and our ability to fulfill the potential that our later development should promise is often limited by our continuing, in important aspects of our living, to hold a world view that reflects that "previous existence." We start life in a position of extreme helplessness, largely at the mercy of giants whom we can barely comprehend and whom we love and hate with intensities that reflect both our intense neediness and our primitive cognitive development.

In those early years there is indeed reason to strive to be acceptable to those upon whom our very lives literally depend, as there is also good reason to fear that a fleeting idea or impulse will lead to action—and action whose consequences we hardly know how to comprehend or predict. The world is a dangerous and confusing place in the early years, and even if childhood can be a time of considerable joy and happiness, too—which I believe it can be and often is—it is a time when we necessarily learn a wide range of precautions and restrictions that we must subsequently unlearn or modify if we are not to be sadly limited adults. We must drastically modify those early precautions, or more generally the early view we have of what the world is and how it works, because in later years we are not (or need not be) such helpless creatures; we can afford to dare to chart our own course, to risk displeasing others, and to judge for ourselves what we want and what we can do. Moreover, we must make those changes because not only were our earlier views appropriate to a far different kind of organism than after 15 or 20 years we have become, but also they were formed by a mind that is only a pale shadow of that we now possess. Even as adults, we only approximate "reality" in our constructions of it, but those constructions exceed our early effort in both complexity and accuracy to such a degree that, as adults, we are amazed and fascinated when we observe the actual cognitive operations of the child's mind.

Yet, in many ways, or in many aspects of our living, we do not advance much beyond those early glimpses of what life holds. We continue to long for things that our present life circumstances would seem to largely render obsolete. We continue to fear saying, doing, or thinking things that perhaps were problematic for us as 2-year-olds or 4-year-olds but that are the key to full, rich living as adults. We continue to implicitly hold beliefs (say, about what happens when a penis enters a vagina, or when one says "no" or "I don't like that," or when one tries to be strong or tries to be weak) that if examined with our full powers of logic would appear absurd to us. And we do all of this, in many instances, without really being aware that we do so, often being aware instead of having headaches, or feeling depressed, or not feeling comfortable outside the house alone, or not staying very long with any one intimate partner.

It is such observations—or in many instances, inferences from observations—that have impressed psychoanalysts with the persistence of childishness in almost all adults. The interpersonal psychodynamic theorist (whose views are also shaped very largely by sympathetic listening to the intimate secrets of people desperate enough to try to stop hiding) similarly sees childishness implicit in much of adult living, and sees striking continuities between the feelings and fantasies of the early years and those (not necessarily conscious) of the adult. But his view of how the observed continuities are mediated is likely to be very different. Instead of stressing hierarchical layering of preserved residues, he instead examines how the early motives and fantasies are cyclically perpetuated by the kinds of behaviors they lead to and the responses that are then evoked in others—responses that, as illustrated below, are likely to create just the kind of experience that makes the original wish and the original view of the world still seem salient.

For example, the 2-year-old who has developed an engaging and playful manner is far more likely to evoke friendly interest and attention on the part of adults than is the child who is rather quiet and withdrawn. The latter will typically encounter a less rich interpersonal environment that will further decrease the likelihood that he will drastically change. Similarly, the former is likely to continually learn that other people are fun and are eager to interact with him, and his pattern too is likely to become more firmly fixed as he grows. Further, not only will the two children tend to evoke different behavior from others, they will also interpret differently the same reaction from another person. Thus, the playful child may experience a silent or grumpy response from another as a kind of game and may continue to interact until perhaps he does elicit an appreciative response. The quieter child, not used to much interaction, will readily accept the initial response as a signal to back off.

THE ROLE OF "ACCOMPLICES" IN DEVELOPMENT[5]

If we look at the two children as adults, we may perhaps find the difference between them still evident, one outgoing, cheerful, and expecting the best of people, the other rather shy and unsure anyone is interested. A childhood pattern has persisted into adulthood. Yet,

5. Portions of the next few sections are drawn from Wachtel (1977a).

we really don't understand the developmental process unless we see how, successively, teachers, playmates, girlfriends, and colleagues have been drawn in as "accomplices" in maintaining the persistent pattern. And, I would suggest, we don't understand the possibilities for change unless we realize that even now there are such "accomplices" and that if they stopped playing their role in the process, it would be likely to eventually alter.

It is important to recognize, however, that it is not that easy to get the accomplices to change. The signals we emit to other people constitute a powerful force field. The shy person does many sometimes almost invisible things to make it difficult for another person to stay open to him very long. Even a well-intentioned person is likely to eventually help confirm his view that others aren't really very interested.

Thus, from this perspective, the early pattern persists not despite changing conditions, but because the person's pattern of experiencing and interacting with others tends to continually recreate the old conditions again and again. In many cases, the effects are subtle and not readily apparent without careful scrutiny. But on close inspection, each person may be seen to rather regularly produce a particular skewing of responses from others that defines his idiosyncratic interpersonal world. Even in seemingly similar situations, we are each likely to encounter slightly different interpersonal cues, which may render the texture of the experience critically different. We then act (again) in a way that seems appropriate to this particular state of affairs, and create the conditions for others to again and again set the stage for the pattern to be repeated. Rather than having been locked in in the past by an intrapsychic structuring, then, the pattern seems from this perspective to be continually being formed, but generally in a way that keeps it quite consistent through the years. It may appear inappropriate because it is not well correlated with the adult's "average expectable environment," but it is quite a bit more closely attuned to the person's idiosyncratically skewed version of that environment.

TRANSFERENCE AND SCHEMATA

Emphasis on such a cyclical reaction of interpersonal events, and on the real behavior of "accomplices" in perpetuating characterological patterns, does not imply that the person is perceiving every situation "objectively." Most clinicians have seen abundant examples of patients' distortions of what is going on, particularly in transference phenomena. Such aspects of psychological functioning must be included in any viable account of how neurotic patterns are perpetuated. But rather than relying on the metaphors that analysts have traditionally employed in conceptualizing such phenomena, I prefer to think in terms of the Piagetian notion of schema; for such a notion implies that not only do we assimilate new experiences to older, more familiar ways of viewing things (as is implicit in the concept of transference), we also do eventually accommodate to what is actually going on.

Thus, as in transference phenomena, new people and new relationships tend to be approached in terms of their similarity to earlier ones; and frequently, particularly in the special conditions of the psychoanalytic situation, one sees what appear to be quite arbitrary assumptions and perceptions occurring. But in principle, I would suggest, accommodation is always proceeding apace and would, with nonreactive sources of stimulation, eventually lead to a fairly accurate picture of what one is encountering. The problem is that other people are not nonreactive. How they behave toward us is very much influenced by how we behave toward them, and hence by how we initially perceive them. Thus, our initial (in a sense distorted) picture of another person can end up being a fairly accurate predictor of how he will act toward us, because, based on our expectation that he will be hostile, or accepting, or sexual, we are likely to act in such a way as to eventually draw such behavior from the person and thus have our (initially inaccurate) perception "confirmed." Our tendency to enter the next relationship with the same assumption and perceptual bias is then strengthened and the whole process likely to be repeated again.

Such a perspective enables us to understand both continuity and change in the same terms. In a large number of cases, this process of "distorted" perception leading to a skewing of responses from others, and hence to a "confirmation" of the problematic way of experiencing, continues for years, and produces the phenomena so familiar to analytic observers. At times, however, a figure appears who, by virtue of his interpersonal history and personal force field, serves (with good or ill effect) to intervene in the developmental process rather than simply confirm present directions.[6] The patient's behavior may make this an unlikely process to persist, but if it does, it can be expected that he will eventually accommodate to this new input and show substantial change in an important aspect of his life. It is

6. Less dramatic instances of this sort in which each person changes a bit are common. Usually, however, the change is small, because each participant is free to leave rather than change. The more they are constrained to be together, the more each can alter the other.

likely that many of the "spontaneous" cures that make the controls in psychotherapy research so tricky are the result of such accommodative processes.[7]

TIES TO "EARLY OBJECTS"

In describing this view of development, there is one more issue it is important for us to consider at this point. Frequently psychoanalytic exploration reveals that, without awareness, the person remains tied in his fantasy life and in his secret striving to figures from his early past. Typically, discovery of such a tie is viewed as accounting for the inhibitions and symptoms of the adult. The pull from the past is regarded as the causal influence. We shall now consider an alternative way of understanding this common observation.

As but one example, let us consider still another set of interlocked influences our 2-year-old might encounter and then perpetuate. Suppose that he is not encouraged by his family to develop the skills that can help him gain greater independence from them. This need not take the form of outright prohibition or interference. Indeed, often the knot is tighter when not readily visible, as when an ambivalent parent gives explicit encouragement to the child's budding independence but in subtle ways undermines it. Perhaps mother, without noticing it, is more frequently warm and attentive when the child sweetly says, "I love you, mommy," than when he shows her something he has put together; or cuddles him when he stands apart from the other children ("to make him feel better, so he won't be afraid to play") instead of helping him to initiate play or joining in with the group of children until her child is comfortable there. There are many ways in which, through ignorance or unacknowledged intent, a mother or father can bind and cripple a child while thinking he is encouraging independence.

When such is the case there is likely to be a point where the child's fearful clinging is recognized as distinguishing him from his age-mates, and not infrequently the parental reaction is likely to be a nagging, complaining, or insulting one, motivated by parental anxiety, embarrassment, guilt, or desperation. Even if the parent does not come out with "What's wrong with you? Why can't you be like the other kids?" or some similar assault, simply continuing to encourage participation in age-appropriate activities, when not accom-

7. It is also a good part of the professional therapist's skill to be able to be a source of change in this way. As Wolf (1966) has described, however, this is often rather difficult for the therapist to do.

panied by effective efforts to help the child accomplish the transition, can be experienced as punishing and cause the child considerable pain.

A child caught in such a developmental tangle is likely to remain more tied to his parents than most children his age. Having fewer alternative sources of gratification and security, he is likely to feel more than most the need to be mommy or daddy's little boy. Not only is this likely to further impede the exploration and assertion needed to develop the skills that would get him out of this dilemma; it is also likely to make him quite fearful of expressing anger or disagreement toward his parents—and this in circumstances more likely than usual to arouse anger. So we see an unhappy little child, afraid to venture forth, clinging to mother in a way that angers her (even as it also may gratify), feeling frustrated and irritated and perhaps even, if it is the case, sensing the grasping intent in the mother's harmful cloistering, yet desperately trying to be loyal and a good boy to at least have *mother* securely; and in so doing, preventing himself from developing the independence and expansiveness that are necessary for him to be able to loosen his hold on mother or to feel able to cope with the complexity of his feeling toward her.

If the dilemma confronting this child is in the "neurotic" range, then he will continue to grow despite all these inhibitions. There are enough countervailing forces in innate developmental processes, as well as in the expectations and reward structure of the larger social order, and even in other aspects of their own parents' behavior, that millions of children with such a history grow up to become taxpayers, spouses, and parents and thus in a very general way functioning adults. It takes a rather extraordinary effort to inhibit cognitive and personality growth so completely that these rather minimal criteria of "normality" are not achieved.[8]

But the situation I have described takes its toll. He does not "make it" without pain and struggle, and usually he does not make it without a price. In many respects he may advance along the way more slowly than his age-mates, getting there eventually but always feeling a little bit behind or a little out of it, venturing less, mastering less, so again venturing less, etc. By gross criteria, he may function well, yet in the more private, subtle, and intimate aspects of his life he will show the scars of his early years. He may, for example, evidence reasonable social ease and competence in general, but be inhibited in making sexual advances. Or, he may be able to initiate

8. These criteria are meant simply to point to the *kind* of general achievements that tend to distinguish neurotic difficulties from more severe ones. It is in no sense meant to imply that individuals who do not marry, or do not have children, suffer from any personality disorder. My judgment on this would tend to be different, however, were the person completely lacking in human relationships.

sexual activity quite easily, and "perform" adequately, but may not experience complete sexual release and satisfaction. Or, perhaps the sexual aspect of sexual relationships is fully satisfying but does not seem linked to an intimate sharing of personal feelings.

Any of these limitations in living could, if found to occur in conjunction with evidence for disavowed ties to parental figures, be attributed to the effects of those ties. That has traditionally been the understanding of such observations by analysts; and the implication drawn has been that one must work on untangling those ties in order to increase the patient's freedom in living. But again, it makes equal sense to consider, for example, how longings for the ideal caretaker–beauty (mother) of childhood might be fostered by a current life style that excludes fully satisfying experiences of intimacy and sensual satisfaction.

The lure of the Oedipal imagery is strengthened each time the person has an encounter that proves to be frustrating or disappointing. Whatever role the vicissitudes of feeling for mother may have played in starting the person on a life course that is in some important respects restricted in freedom, concrete interactions with later figures tend to be significant in perpetuating it. If one is anxious or hesitant about sexuality or intimacy, one teaches one's partners to be similarly inclined. Satisfying sexuality and the experience of intimacy require a mutual trust and understanding. If an individual enters a new relationship in a hesitant way, the partner cannot long continue to be open with him, and he will find confirmed again and again throughout his life that his defensiveness in such situations is "justified," since he is inevitably disappointed and finds his partners tensing up or closing off in ways that hurt (and lead him to again be hesitant the next time and again evoke a complementary response from his partner).[9]

THERAPEUTIC IMPLICATIONS

The differences between the above version of psychodynamic thought and that of Freudian psychoanalysis have important bearing on how one approaches the conduct of psychotherapy.[10] The present

9. It should be clear that I am here describing something that does not necessarily go on consciously. Far from explicitly justifying a limited sex life on the basis of his partner's responses, the person may well extol both his partner and his sex life for quite a while. Only careful scrutiny may reveal the particular dissatisfaction or lack of freedom in the person's life.

10. See Wachtel (1977b) for further detailed examination and illustration of the implications for psychotherapy.

perspective, with its emphasis on self-perpetuating, cyclical processes (see also Wachtel, 1977a), points to a far more active role for
the therapist, who must use his psychodynamic understanding not
only to empathize with the patient and help him achieve insight, but
also to help the patient to break into the vicious circles that have
characterized his life. Intervention becomes a key focus of the therapist's efforts.

In much traditional psychodynamic writing on therapy, explicit
interventions by the therapist are discouraged both on ethical
grounds (see Wachtel, 1977b, Chapter 12) and on the assumption
that such intervention, or any "high-profile" activity by the therapist, makes it harder for the patient to recognize how much of his
reactions really have little to do with the current reality and reflect
instead the continuing influence of his past. The view that the
residues of past interactions have been internalized, and will remain
frozen (though active) in their original form unless a process of
uncovering reveals them and their inappropriateness to the critical
scrutiny of the patient's ego, has led to a de-emphasis on directly
intervening in troubling life patterns. A time-consuming, indirect
course appears, in this light, to be the only way to overcome the
effects of the past in any relatively thorough and extensive way (see
Wachtel, 1977b, Chapter 3).

From the present perspective, however, the effects of the past
are a result not of some primarily internal set of influences but of an
interlocking series of influences, both organismic and environmental
in nature, which can continue to bring about, in the present, conditions and reaction patterns that have characterized the person's life
for many years. Given such a view, the therapist is likely to be far
less hesitant to try to intervene in the patient's daily life patterns. He
will feel less of a need to do "nothing" in order to demonstrate that
the patient's reaction has little to do with him, both because he
recognizes that he cannot do "nothing" (that, for example, silence
from someone to whom one turns for help is striking and provocative, not neutral) and because he views the patient as always responsive to something, and wants to help the patient to understand the
total situation he tends to create (including both the responses he
evokes in others, including the therapist, and his idiosyncratic way of
interpreting what transpires) and not just how he sees what isn't
there.

The therapist operating from the perspective described here will
view the work of interpretation and elucidating unconscious processes as facilitated rather than impaired by providing aid in dealing
with life circumstances. If the intensity of unconscious desires or
fantasies can be diminished by helping to change exacerbating life

patterns, then those desires and fantasies can become less threatening and can be more readily recognized and controlled. Often, understanding or insight may be impeded by a pattern of behavior that intensifies frightening impulses to such a degree that only desperate defensive efforts seem permissible to the patient. Interpretive efforts are then bound to prove ineffective in helping the patient come to recognize the feelings and wishes that frighten him. Probably much failure of interpretive therapy is due to insufficient consideration of how the patient's neurotic behavior leads to intensification of forbidden impulses. We are too used to overemphasizing the other direction.

It has long been recognized that a particularly bad home situation can limit the effectiveness of analytic therapy, that the person's environment may undermine the gains of the analytic sessions. But the view of the neurotic process discussed above would suggest that in an important sense almost *all* patients live in growth-impeding environments. For one thing, the important figures in the person's life are usually engaged in a relationship with the patient in which the characterological features of the patient's neurosis are assumed. They have learned to come to terms with and have a stake in the old patterns of interchange, and frequently will exert considerable pressure to keep things as they were, even if mutually self-defeating. Resistance, then, is evident not only in the patient but also in his partners in important relationships. These figures have been chosen by the patient at least in part because they are willing and able to participate in the kinds of interaction that his character leads him to continually seek. Transference is manifested not only in perceptual distortions, that is, in seeing the past in the present when the present really is different. It also is manifested in creating old situations again, in really living with and relating to people who resemble figures from our past. Furthermore, not only do we choose people who fit our old categories and expectations; we also evoke a particular side of whomever we meet, and tend to elicit from others behavior that confirms old expectations.

Much of this goes on outside of awareness. The training that dynamically oriented therapists of all schools receive in discerning disavowed wishes and unacknowledged fantasies is critical in enabling the therapist to develop a full understanding of the life patterns that trouble the patient. The therapist must be sensitive to such unacknowledged organizing processes, and to the feelings evoked in him by being with the patient. But it is important to recognize that often understanding alone is not sufficient to help the patient change and grow in the face of the many conservative forces tending to keep things the same.

Frequently, for example, patients will report that in one situation or another they don't know what to say. Part of this "not knowing" is usually due to anxiety and defensive inhibition, and ceases to be a problem when the patient is less afraid of particular feelings or inclinations. But part is also frequently a result of a lifetime of cheating oneself out of opportunities to learn the effective behavior that most of us take for granted by the time we are adults. Children must go through a long process of learning how to effectively channel and express their feelings. Their initial efforts are quite crude, and would be readily discouraged were adults' standards of moderation and articulate expression applied to them. Fortunately, expectations are usually geared to the person's developmental stage, and in most respects we gradually learn how to express ourselves in ways that bring us satisfying interactions with other people.

But where neurotic inhibitions have prevented this gradual learning process the adult who is perhaps almost for the first time expressing a need rather than inhibiting it is likely to do so in rather ineffective or inappropriate fashion. As therapists, we are set to be sympathetic toward these initial expressions of honest feeling, and we respond empathically and encouragingly to behavior in our patients that we often would not tolerate in our friends. But I believe that when the poignant struggle we observe in our sessions does not lead to the kind of progress in the patient's way of living that we hope for, it is often because other figures in the patient's life are not nearly as encouraging of these first crude efforts as we are. In addition to having a stake in old ways, as discussed above, these figures also employ different standards in reacting to the patient's behavior, and in their reactions they again teach the patient that honesty is dangerous.

When one views the patient's problem not as something "in" him, but as a self-perpetuating pattern of transactions, maintained in the present by the way in which interpersonal consequences and (often unconscious) motives and fantasies generate each other, one sees a need both for interpretation and active intervention.

THE RELATION BETWEEN PSYCHOANALYSIS AND OTHER APPROACHES

As I have elaborated elsewhere (Wachtel, 1977a, 1977b), the cyclical psychodynamic conception described here can be integrated with the perspectives dominant in academic personality research far more readily than can the more predominantly intrapsychic model of

Freudian theory. As a psychodynamic model, it points to a great many process and content variables that have been largely ignored in academic research, but that, when framed in this way, are seen as complementary rather than contradictory to the academic conceptions. It is responsive to the influential contemporary critiques of psychodynamic thought that fault psychoanalysis for failing to recognize the degree to which human behavior must be understood as responsive to changing situational cues. Yet, it avoids the trap of "situationism" (Bowers, 1973), and attributes a robust and nonepiphenomenal role to the individual's motives, fantasies, and other organizing processes. Aspects of the perspective described here have contributed to critiques not only of the Freudian emphasis on history and intrapsychic structure, but also of traditional experimental methodology in personality research (Wachtel, 1973) and of much of the research on cognitive style (Wachtel, 1972).

The perspective offered here is "interactional," but can be distinguished from much work that goes under that label by its reluctance to treat "person variables" and "situation variables" as thoroughly independent. In much personality research, the interactionism comes in at the point of statistical analysis, when variables that are originally defined and conceptualized as very separate are combined additively and their statistical interaction viewed with interest. From the present perspective, however, it is hard to distinguish person variables and situation variables (or "internal" and "external" determinants). Aspects of the person and the situation he is in continuously interact. The appropriate mathematical representation for such interaction is not the statistical model of analysis of variance, but rather the model of the integral calculus. In most real-life situations, only for a diminishingly small instant is any person–effect manifested that is independent of the situation or does any situation unfold that is independent of the person who encounters (and changes) it.

5

On Some Complexities in the Application of Conflict Theory to Psychotherapy

Dollard and Miller's (1950) discussion of the role of conflict in the development of neurosis and in the process of psychotherapy is probably the most extensive and detailed available in the psychological literature. Although their effort to reconcile psychoanalytic and learning theory perspectives has been seriously criticized from both ends of the spectrum (e.g., Bandura & Walters, 1963; Rapaport, 1953), Dollard and Miller's formulations remain of interest as one of the few attempts to address phenomena of conflict in a learning theory approach to psychotherapy; behavior therapists have rather generally ignored conflict in their formulations, and this has been one of the most serious shortcomings in an otherwise extremely productive orientation (Wachtel, 1977b).

Ironically perhaps, the successful development of behavior therapy has been one of the prime factors responsible for what seems to be a relative decline of interest in Dollard and Miller's formulations in the recent literature. Although Dollard and Miller were among the pioneers in applying the findings of the learning laboratory to problems of neurosis, their analysis seemed at the time to provide support for continuing (although with some rather important modifications) to treat neurotic problems via psychodynamic, interpretive methods, and did not point directly to the development of the new learning-theory-based techniques which came into prominence a decade later. When such techniques did appear, their proponents

Reprinted by permission from the *Journal of Nervous and Mental Disease*, 1978, *166*(7), 457–471.

tended to view their success as a refutation of earlier psychodynamic theorizing (e.g., Bandura, 1969; Eysenck, 1959; Mischel, 1968; Wolpe, 1958); Dollard and Miller's formulations, which were in large measure based on such theorizing, were treated as both incorrect and superfluous.

In recent years, two important trends have developed which suggest that a reexamination of Dollard and Miller's formulations may be in order. A number of behavior therapists (e.g., Goldfried & Davison, 1976; Lazarus, 1971; Mahoney, 1974) have argued, on the basis of both clinical experience and empirical research, that a broader framework of theorizing seems needed than was implied in the writings of Eysenck, Wolpe, and other pioneers in the behavior therapy movement. These recent writers have emphasized cognitive formulations and/or considerations of interpersonal relations in ways that introduce considerably more complexity than was apparent in earlier efforts to relate specific problem behaviors to specific stimulus situations. Goldfried in particular (e.g., Goldfried & Davison, 1976; Goldfried & Merbaum, 1973) has suggested ways in which some of Dollard and Miller's conceptualizations may be useful to more cognitively oriented behavior therapists.

A second trend which suggests the value of a new look at Dollard and Miller's approach to conflict is reflected in the growing recognition that psychodynamic and behavioral approaches may not be as fundamentally irreconcilable as proponents of each have contended. Potential bases for convergence between the two approaches have been offered by an increasing number of clinicians and theorists (e.g., Alexander, 1963; Birk, 1970, 1974; Birk & Brinkley-Birk, 1974; Brady, 1967; Feather & Rhoads, 1972a, 1972b; Ferster, 1972, 1973; Greenspan, 1974, 1975; Marks & Gelder, 1966; Marmor, 1962, 1964, 1971; Rhoads & Feather, 1972, 1974; Sloane, 1969; Sollod, 1974; Sollod & Kaplan, 1976; Wolberg, 1974; Wolf, 1966).

Recently a more extended discussion has appeared of the theoretical and clinical issues which point toward a potentially fruitful integration of psychodynamic and behavioral approaches (Wachtel, 1977b). That volume makes considerable use of the theoretical analysis of Dollard and Miller, and indicates ways in which their contribution, while not having itself pointed directly to the development of behavior therapy, takes on new significance since that development. Rather than having been rendered incontestably obsolescent by the success of behavior therapy, Dollard and Miller's analysis can play a crucial role in providing a basis for considering phenomena of conflict in a way that is compatible with the thinking which underlies behavior therapy. As such, it can provide a sounder theoretical basis for much of the current innovation by behavior therapists as well as providing a way for those who think in psychodynamic terms to understand and make use of developments in behavior therapy.

The present chapter will consider a number of implications of Dollard and Miller's theoretical model which have not been sufficiently explicated heretofore and will examine their bearing on personality theory and theories of psychotherapy.

THE CENTRALITY OF FEAR IN DOLLARD AND MILLER'S ANALYSIS

In Dollard and Miller's conception of neurosis, fear is the most critical variable. Conflict is, of course, also a critically important concept in their analysis—and it more than anything else is what distinguishes their theoretical account from those of other learning-oriented writers (e.g., Bandura & Walters, 1963; Eysenck & Beech, 1971; Wolpe, 1958). However, in Dollard and Miller's account, fear may be seen as a more basic underlying concept than conflict. For one thing, in discussing traumatic neuroses, Dollard and Miller do make use of a straight fear-conditioning model of the sort argued for by Eysenck and Beech (1971). Unlike the particular psychoanalytic model criticized (only partly justifiably) by Mischel (1968) in his discussion of a traumatic war neurosis (pp. 264–272), Dollard and Miller's model does not require that all such cases be understood in relation to conflicts rooted in childhood. The analyses of particular cases of traumatic neurosis offered by Mischel and by Dollard and Miller (1950, pp. 157–195) converge to a striking degree.

Dollard and Miller do nonetheless argue that for a variety of reasons (see also Wachtel, 1977b), conflict is very central for most patients who come for psychotherapy. Even here, however, the role of fear is critical, since the kind of conflict which is likely to be protracted and lead to many complications is the approach–avoidance conflict, and the avoidance tendency in their analysis is most often a result of conditioned fear. The neurotic is highly motivated to approach some goal but is prevented from doing so because he also fears approaching the goal, and the degree of his fearfulness increases with increasing approach to the goal.

The centrality of fear in Dollard and Miller's analysis is made especially clear by their schematic diagram of the interaction of the various factors involved in neurosis (Figure 1). Close examination of Dollard and Miller's diagram makes it clear that in their view all of the major causal sequences can be seen as ultimately the result of fear. Tracing the arrows leading to symptoms, for example, reveals that in this model they are the result of fear, high drive, and

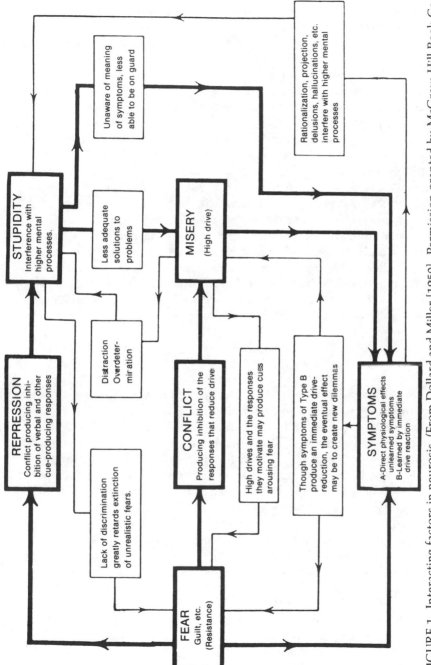

FIGURE 1. Interacting factors in neurosis. (From Dollard and Miller [1950]. Permission granted by McGraw-Hill Book Co.)

stupidity. They are behaviors which are reinforced by reducing to some extent the state of high drive created by conflict as well as by reducing fear. This is a learning theory translation of the traditional psychoanalytic view that symptoms are a compromise between impulse and defense.[1]

If we trace back still further the causal sequences leading to symptoms, we see that the stupidity which exacerbates symptoms and makes them more likely is a result of repression, which is in turn a consequence of fear, as we saw earlier. Similarly, the high drive which is also one of the motivators of symptoms is itself a result of two factors: (1) stupidity, which prevents the finding of effective solutions to problems which would be drive reducing (and which we just saw was ultimately derivable from fear); and (2) inhibition of the responses that reduce drive, which is in turn a consequence of fear. In fact, every heavy arrow in the diagram can be seen to be an extension of an arrow originating in the box marked fear, and only that box has heavy arrows which emanate only from it, none leading to it. (The "subsidiary" causal sequences in Dollard and Miller's diagram do feed back to increase or maintain fear. As discussed below and in Wachtel [1977b], such feedback processes may be more important in neurosis than is typically recognized.)

Some Complications with the Concept of Fear

In considering the role of fear in Dollard and Miller's theorizing, it is worth taking note of the fact that they essentially treat fear as a unitary concept, a "something" which can be learned and which has important consequences. This conceptual strategy has yielded much fruitful research and has helped to bring together a wide range of phenomena within a simple and consistent framework. It does present certain difficulties, however, which should be noted before proceeding with our discussion of conflict theory.

On the basis of a now classic study, Miller (1948) proposed that it is useful to conceptualize as an intervening variable a learned fear response which can be conditioned much as more overtly observable responses can be, and which follows the same set of laws. This hypothetical response has drive properties in that it produces strong

---

1. Dollard and Miller also note that some symptoms are not learned in this fashion, but are direct physiological effects of prolonged states of high drive and fear. Psychosomatic symptoms tend to be of this sort.

stimuli whose occurrence energizes behavior and whose reduction reinforces behavior, and cue properties in that its occurrence or nonoccurrence can differentially guide the direction of behavior.

Although postulating such a construct as fear is not entirely uncontroversial (cf. Skinner, 1953; Ullman & Krasner, 1969), the use of such a construct is rather widely accepted as having theoretical utility. Wolpe, for example, in an approach which has little sympathy for psychoanalysis, similarly relies on such a construct. Although its utility has been demonstrated in objective laboratory experiments, there is little doubt that a good portion of the interest in this construct, as well as the original impetus for its emphasis in theories of neurosis, derives both from psychoanalytic formulations, which from the 1920s on increasingly stressed the role of fear avoidance in neurosis and personality development, and from common subjective experience. We all are familiar with the experience of fear; we "know" that it is a real phenomenon and a powerful influence upon behavior.

What psychoanalysis added to such common knowledge was consideration of the variety of ways in which behavior can be a function of fear even when the subjective experience of fear does *not* occur. The psychoanalytic notion of "signal anxiety" (Freud, 1926/1959) has been replaced in much recent theorizing by less voluntaristic concepts such as "anxiety gradients," but there is rather wide consensus that avoidance behavior can occur which is based originally on experiences involving fear, but which currently is not accompanied by the usual obvious signs of fear (or presumably by the subjective experience) (cf. Seligman & Johnston, 1973; Solomon & Wynne, 1954; Wolpe, 1958, pp. 96–97). Clinically, even most behavior therapists would acknowledge that some important problematic behaviors are best conceptualized as fear-motivated avoidance behavior, even where the person reports no awareness of being afraid or avoidant (e.g., well-rationalized unassertiveness, or an excessive work load which "doesn't leave time" for sex).

At least partly because the role of fear in motivating behavior cannot always be reported accurately by the person manifesting the behavior, clinicians and researchers have sought a variety of indices of fear. These have ranged from increased defecation, "freezing," and cessation of consummatory behavior (in animal studies mostly), to such indices with humans as speech disturbances (Mahl, 1968) or long association times (Eriksen, 1952).

Increasingly, it has been recognized that the various indices of fear do not correlate very highly. Lang (1969, 1971), reviewing the literature on various indices, has referred to fear as a set of only partially coupled responses. Avoidance behavior may occur without physiological arousal, as may subjective reports of distress. Changes in any one component after therapy may occur somewhat independently of changes in the other components, and frequently, even where all change, one changes considerably in advance of the others (cf. Lang, 1971; Leitenberg, Agras, Butz, & Wincze, 1971; Rachman & Hodgson, 1974a, 1974b).

Thus, there are problems in postulating a unitary response called "fear." Fear does not seem to be one thing, but rather a *set* of behavioral phenomena which (partially) share some common antecedents and consequences ("partially" because a stimulus which elicits physiological signs of fearfulness may not elicit the subjective experience of being afraid, and vice versa). Detailed spelling out of the implications for conflict theory of a less unitary conception of fear would require a separate paper in itself, as well as a good deal more research. However, the reader should keep in mind in considering the issues addressed in this discussion that the simplifying assumption of a unitary fear response pervades theorizing on conflict, and that the possible implications for such theorizing of a "partially coupled set" conception remain to be rigorously worked out.

Varieties of Fear?

Apart from the issue of different indices of fear being only partially correlated, theorizing about fear is complicated by the occurrence of a variety of subjectively aversive states with (again) only partially overlapping functional relations. In both the psychoanalytic literature and the literature guided by one or another version of learning theory, there is a lack of clarity about the differing implications (if any) of such concepts as fear, anxiety, shame, guilt, and disgust.

Fear and Anxiety

Perhaps the most attention has been devoted to the distinction (or lack thereof) between fear and anxiety. Writers viewing the question from a learning theory perspective have tended to equate the two terms and/or to suggest that the distinction in when one or the other term is applied is not one of any theoretical importance (e.g., Dollard & Miller, 1950; Wolpe, 1958). Psychoanalytic writers have made more of the distinction, often reserving the term "anxiety" for instances where the fearful reaction is to an "internal danger" (roughly, in learning terms, to a response-produced cue) and/or where the source of the fearful reaction, or even its very occurrence, is not conscious; "fear," on the other hand, refers in such accounts to reactions to a consciously perceived external danger (Erikson, 1950). In some accounts (e.g., Freud, 1926/1959), "anxiety" seems to be used as the more generic term and the distinction is made among different *kinds* of anxiety (e.g., "objective anxiety" as the term for what is usually called fear; "superego anxiety" or "moral anxiety" as the term for guilt; and "neurotic anxiety" where the simple term "anxiety" is usually used). Other bases for distinguishing between fear and anxiety have been suggested: For example, I (Wachtel, 1968a) discussed the distinction between threats which could and could not be coped with, and Sarnoff and Zimbardo (1961) reported that subjects chose to be with others when in a state of fear but to be alone when experiencing anxiety.

Guilt and Shame

In most formulations, guilt and shame tend to play a similar role in the theoretical network as do fear and anxiety. They are terms denoting an aversive state which the individual is highly motivated to avoid, and which can be learned in relation to a variety of situations. Psychoanalytic formulations do assign a special role to guilt, in that it can motivate self-punitive behavior as well as the kinds of avoidance behaviors generally studied in relation to anxiety (i.e., the defense mechanisms). Some authors have stressed the distinction between guilt and shame, articulating the differing kinds of behavioral phenomena and functional relations which are denoted by these two terms and/or the different kinds of individuals in which one or the other tends to be salient (see, for example, Erikson, 1950; Lewis, 1965; Lynd, 1958; Piers & Singer, 1952).

Anxiety and Disgust

Another concept whose relation to anxiety is not quite clear is disgust. The term again refers to an aversive reaction which can be subjectively distressing, can at times be indexed physiologically, and can motivate avoidance reactions; and again it is not clear to what extent it should be distinguished from anxiety, be regarded as one of several alternative "forms" of anxiety, etc. A recent exploratory study (D'Zurilla, Wilson, & Nelson, 1973) suggests that the therapeutic procedures most effective with disgust reactions may be different than for the kinds of anxiety reactions which have been the focal concern of students of systematic desensitization.

WHY IS CONFLICT NOT SELF-RESOLVING?

Dollard and Miller's analysis of approach–avoidance conflicts suggests that because the avoidance gradient tends to be steeper than the approach gradient, the person in conflict will be trapped at some intermediate point where the approach–avoidance gradients cross, and will hover around the point of intersection (see Figure 2). He will be too afraid to approach further and achieve gratification, yet too attracted to leave altogether and achieve relief of fear; rather, he is caught in a conflict which can maintain both relatively high levels of unfulfilled desire and relatively high levels of anxiety at the same

FIGURE 2. Illustration of Dollard and Miller's representation of an approach–avoidance conflict. Since the Approach gradient is greater far from the goal, and the avoidance gradient (Avoidance 1) is greater near the goal, the individual should tend to stay in the region around point A1, where the two opposing directional gradients are equal. Since, however, he is exposed at point A1 to some of the cues associated with the feared goal, without untoward consequences, some of the anxiety should be extinguished and the avoidance gradient reduced to Avoidance 2. He should then tend to stay around closer point A2, be exposed to still more of the anxiety cues, undergo further extinction, etc. (Figure adapted, with variations, from Dollard and Miller [1950]. Permission granted by McGraw-Hill Book Co.)

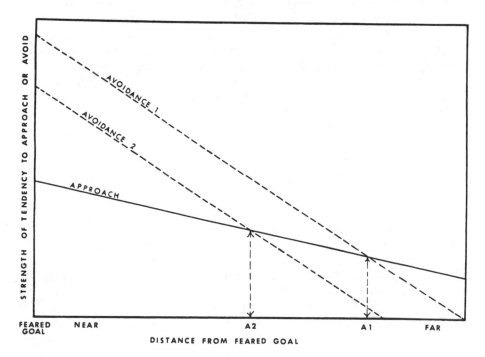

time. Dollard and Miller note that such a situation can be excruciating and that the help of a professional therapist may be needed to create conditions under which the anxiety can be extinguished and the individual can approach his goal without conflict. They describe in detail how this can be accomplished.

One may ask, however, why the anxiety is not in fact extinguished even without professional assistance. Explanations of the persistence of anxiety in neurosis often stress the subject's successful avoidance of the anxiety-provoking cues as a central factor in preventing him from learning they are not dangerous; since he is not exposed to those cues, he does not get to undergo any extinction trials. Dollard and Miller's account, however, differs from many others in its stress on *conflict* as well as fear. Their analysis—especially in its emphasis on anxiety attached to the person's own thoughts and affective reactions, rather than conditioned phobic reactions to external cues—suggests that the person often does *not* thoroughly avoid what he fears. Because he is in conflict, he also *approaches* the fear cues, and the point along the gradient where he tends to hover exposes him to some (although not all) of the cues which he fears (or to cues which are somewhat equivalent to the individual in terms of stimulus generalization). Why, then, does the individual who is hovering at point A1 (or, in line with Dollard and Miller's typical clinical extensions of the model, who is thinking A1-like thoughts) not show extinction of anxiety to the A1 cues? If his anxiety in the face of such cues is unrealistic and a result of earlier experiences which do not reflect the contingencies of his current life situation, he should be continually accruing extinction trials for his anxiety reactions to A1 cues. Then by generalization, one would expect a lowering of the entire anxiety gradient to the level of Avoidance 2, hence movement to closer point A2, then eventually extinction to the more direct cues of A2 and still further lowering of the gradient and subsequent further approach, etc.

To some extent, such a process probably does occur. The so-called "spontaneous remissions" of neurotic difficulties may be partly understood as a result of progressive extinction of this sort. For several reasons, however, this kind of "naturalistic therapy" is unlikely to put professional therapists out of business.

Conflict and Context

First of all, in the animal studies which are the prototype of Dollard and Miller's model, the animal is restricted to a confined area in which the cues associated with the approach and avoidance gradients are very salient; the animal cannot leave the runway, and while he is on it, he is in the presence of cues which have very powerful appetitive and aversive connotations. Human beings in their conditions of everyday living are not nearly as restricted.[2]

Conflict is manifested in a context. Particular cues may evoke strong tendencies to approach or avoid, and in their presence conflict can be acute. Other cues are much less relevant in terms of the conflict, and when we are in their presence acute conflict may not be evident. Even where the main cues which evoke anxiety are those associated with the person's own thoughts and feelings (as Dollard and Miller make clear is frequently the case in neurosis), contextual cues are still very relevant, for contextual cues may play a major role in evoking the thoughts and feelings which then lead to further associations and/or further anxiety and avoidance.

The shy young man whose combination of strong sex drive and considerable anxiety in approaching women put him in acute conflict and distress at parties may be quite comfortable in those daily situations where his conflict is not evoked. Although such situations are comfortable because they are situations in which his approach tendency is minimally evoked (as are consequent anxiety and avoidance tendencies), they are not really analogous to that of the animal who stays at the far end of the runway (point B in Figure 3) and experiences less anxiety and discomfort than the animal who is at point A; for in the runway situation, the animal will *not* stay far away. Since the tendency to approach is greater at point B than the tendency to avoid, he will move toward the goal rather than remaining there. Only when he reaches point A do the approach and avoidance tendencies cancel each other out and produce an equilibrium point. Point B is an unstable position, and the animal will advance to A.

Similarly, the young man, *when he is at a party*, finds it hard to resolve his conflict by simply avoiding. His conflict is intense precisely because—although it makes him anxious—he does approach to a point where he is acutely aware of both desire and anxiety. Not being at a party is not the same as being there and staying at a distance. When he is there, he *cannot* stay at a distance. The party is his "runway," and on it he is inexorably[3] drawn to a point of distress-

2. One of the few animal studies in this area which do not restrict the subject just to one straight-line runway is that of Murray and Berkun (1955). Their very interesting effort to combine Miller's conflict and displacement theories into one three-dimensional model has recently come to my attention, and seems quite relevant to further theorizing in this area.

3. I am here perhaps exaggerating the inexorability for purposes of exposition. His subjective experience may be of being irresistably drawn, but the question of whether a perspective of will or choice is appropriate as well is a complex one (see Wachtel, 1969; Wheelis, 1973).

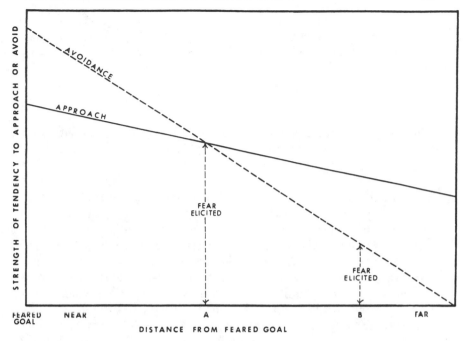

FIGURE 3. Illustration of the discomfort caused by conflict and the difficulty in avoiding it while one is "on the runway." The fear (height of
Avoidance gradient) elicited is considerably less at point B, far from the goal,
but the greater strength of the Approach gradient at that point draws the
person to point A, where both fear and longing are greater. (Adapted from
Dollard and Miller [1950]. Permission granted by McGraw-Hill Book Co.)

ing conflict. However, he *can* choose not to be on the runway altogether, by avoiding parties. This is a different kind of avoidance,
however, than the avoidance he partially tries to manifest—but cannot because of his simultaneous desire—at the party. It is essentially
"leaving the field," leaving the context in which the conflict is acutely
generated. In the animal studies, the animal is artificially *prevented*
from leaving the field; he is maintained in the situation which pulls
him in both directions. He leaves the field only when the experimenter removes him from the runway and places him back in his home
cage.

The restrictions of the experimental setup force the animal to be
positioned *somewhere* along the linear environment which has been
created, and so he ends up at the point of intersection of the two
gradients. This illuminates certain aspects of the psychological processes which are relevant but eliminates the possibility of others
being studied (e.g., leaving the field). Thus, as in other research, even
with humans, that is in the "implacable-experimenter" model (Wach-

tel, 1973b), the subject's choice or creation of environments is severely reduced, and one sees only the effect of his being presented with an externally imposed and restricted context.

Conflict and Metaconflict

Now, our hypothetical young man might *also* be conflicted about whether or not to go to parties at all. This is a related conflict, but a different one. Here it is the party itself which, because of the conflict it produces, has become an aversive situation, but which, for other reasons, the person is drawn to. His decision to go to the party may partly reflect movement along the original gradients (that is, when he is not in the presence of women—i.e., far away from the goal in terms of the original conflict—his approach tendency is greater than his avoidance tendency, and he decides to approach—only to begin moving back when he actually gets there and starts to talk to a woman). However, it is also a matter of movement along a *different* set of gradients, with the *party* rather than the *woman* as the object. One might refer to the conflict over the *party* as a "metaconflict," a conflict over whether to enter a situation in which a conflict will be acutely generated—in effect, a conflict over whether to "get on the runway."

Putting it that way clarifies one of the key roles that the therapist performs. The patient may sense in some way that if he does get on the metaphorical runway and stay there he indeed will experience the kind of "spontaneous remission" referred to above; but being on the runway is painful and so he is also motivated to avoid it altogether. The therapist, by keeping the patient focused on the issues about which he is in conflict, keeps nudging him back on the runway, where extinction of anxiety can occur.[4]

Such a perspective suggests that free association may be a rather inefficient means to achieve the goal of extinguishing the anxiety which sustains neurotic conflict. Were the patient to be restricted to the runway, then his free associations would be expected (because of his simultaneous attraction to thoughts which are feared and forbidden) to produce exposure to cues in the area of point A1 (Figure 2), and via exposure and extinction, and generalization, to lead eventually to the elimination of inappropriate anxiety and the attainment of the goal. However, since the patient may also evidence metaconflicts,

---

4. This is, of course, not all that the therapist does. There are many ways of viewing the therapist's role in facilitating change. Of particular relevance to the discussion below of Freudian and interpersonal perspectives is the therapist's role in helping the patient build social skills (see Wachtel, 1977b, Chapter 10).

and may leave the field by becoming preoccupied with an "off-the-runway" topic, free association which is not carefully directed by the therapist may be quite wasteful. The patient's associations may not necessarily lead in the direction required for therapeutic progress.

Dollard and Miller (1950) acknowledge that their analysis "is complicated by the fact that a number of different goals and subgoals are usually involved. At any given stage of the treatment the patient may be at different positions in a number of more or less related approach–avoidance conflicts" (p. 362). In principle, their theoretical analysis can be extended to include the therapist's role in keeping the patient in position to align himself along the gradient and accumulate extinction time. However, the main focus of their discussion seems to assume that the patient is already *on* the "runway" and describes what the analyst does to facilitate extinction of anxiety and movement along a straight and narrow path.

Interpersonal Feedback and Maintenance of Anxiety

Consideration of interpersonal feedback processes suggests some other important reasons why patients' anxiety is not automatically extinguished whenever there is conflict.[5] For one thing, conceiving of anxiety as a response suggests that all it takes is a rather occasional bad experience to maintain the anxiety at a high level. Responses on a schedule of intermittent reinforcement are extremely difficult to extinguish.

The occasional events reinforcing the anxiety seem to be primarily of two sorts. First, there will be times when the person is overtly and explicitly punished for expressing the conflicted tendency. He will be told that he should not get angry, that his sexual innuendo is disgusting, etc. Such occurrences seem unlikely to be strong enough to *originate* intense neurotic conflict, but may well serve to *maintain* an anxiety reaction which has already been strongly established. Further research along these lines seems clearly indicated.

The second kind of event which may be expected to prevent extinction of the anxiety by reinforcing it is the sort of pattern in which the patient's conflicted behavior induces a subtle disturbing reaction from others (e.g., the tensing of a sexual partner when the person approaches sexuality anxiously, or the disrespect accorded the person who puts his foot down in a hesitant fashion).

5. The discussion of Eysenck and Beech (1971) and Seligman and Johnston (1973) should also be read regarding processes which maintain maladaptive anxiety.

The extensive role of such interpersonal events in the perpetuation of neurotic anxiety is discussed elsewhere (Wachtel, 1977a; 1977b, Chapter 4). Because of the idiosyncratic interpersonal world which the person creates, and its effect on his ability to respond appropriately, his anxiety—inappropriate from one point of view—may be seen from another perspective as an understandable response to a particular set of repetitive interpersonal events. This is recognized by many behavior therapists, who view assertive training as appropriate in many instances where systematic desensitization was once preferred (e.g., Lazarus, 1971; Lazarus & Serber, 1968). It is also a central feature of Sullivan's (1953) interpersonal approach to psychodynamic theory.

Dollard and Miller's theoretical analysis does not strongly emphasize this aspect of how neurosis is maintained. Their psychodynamic perspective is primarily Freudian rather than interpersonal, and as I have discussed in some detail elsewhere (Wachtel, 1977b), one of the central features which distinguishes Freudian psychodynamic theorizing from interpersonal dynamic theories is the critical role the latter attribute to current feedback processes. Freudian theory assumes that repression prevents certain psychological processes from being modified by new experiences, whereas an interpersonal perspective suggests that *in principle* new experiences *can* lead to internal change, but that neurotic patterns of behavior tend in fact not to lead to such change-inducing experiences unless rather special circumstances occur (see Wachtel, 1977b, Chapters 3–5).

Dollard and Miller's analysis both clarifies and extends the Freudian position. Their analysis of repression as the response of not-thinking contributes substantially to an understanding of defenses not as barriers or dams but as something the person is *doing* (cf. Mischel, 1973; Schafer, 1976; Wachtel, 1973, 1977b). Further, their description of how repression contributes to limitations in the employment of higher mental processes enables us to understand the compounding effects of neurosis. The recent emphasis by behavior therapists on problem solving (Goldfried & Davison, 1976, Chapter 9) can be profitably combined with Dollard and Miller's account of factors (not usually considered by behavior therapists) which render problem solving inefficient and block potential solutions. Dollard and Miller's account of how the inhibition of verbal processes due to repression can limit our ability to profit from experience is an interesting one, and the research potential of Dollard and Miller's notion of "neurotic stupidity" has not yet been tapped.

As noted above, however, Dollard and Miller's analysis places major weight on the continuing effects of fear once it has been established. Although it is in some respects a model in which interacting effects continue to recreate the conditions under which the neurosis is maintained, Dollard and Miller's model does not emphasize the feedback processes which themselves keep the fear going (as they are in turn kept going by the fear—cf. Wachtel, 1977a). These processes are explicitly treated as subsidiary by Dollard and Miller, and receive relatively little attention in their book, notwithstanding the presence of an entire chapter on the importance of initiating new patterns of behavior in the patient's everyday living. Greater consideration of interpersonal feedback processes facilitates understanding of why severe neurotic conflicts can be maintained for years without the anxiety being extinguished; it also helps to account for the effectiveness of social training therapies such as Argyle's (Argyle, Trower, & Bryant, 1974) within a framework that also encompasses the observations and considerations of psychodynamic workers (cf. Wachtel, 1977b). Moreover, as will be clear shortly, it helps to clarify some confusing aspects of Dollard and Miller's approach with regard to the goals of therapy.

WHY DON'T PATIENTS SLEEP WITH THEIR MOTHERS AFTER THERAPY?

Consider the situation represented in Figure 4. It represents a schematic depiction of a patient in the midst of strong Oedipal conflict. In this illustration, the approach and avoidance gradients cross at a point (A) which permits the individual very little sexual gratification. In this sense, the aim of therapy would seem to be to enable the patient to move further along the dimension of increasingly sexual behavior (preferably by reducing the anxiety which inhibits his sexual behavior and motivates the avoidance behavior; see Dollard & Miller, 1950, pp. 355–363).

However, the situation depicted in Figure 4 differs from the situations which are the model for Dollard and Miller's conflict diagrams. Those diagrams are originally derived from experiments in which animals are shocked and fed at the same point. They are thus strongly inclined both to approach and avoid that point, and tend to hover around a point some distance from the feared but desired goal. The "therapeutic" aim in that instance, when the shocks are no longer to be given and hence the fears are "unrealistic," is to enable the animal to reach the goal, i.e., to be able again to eat.

Dollard and Miller (1950) argue, on both theoretical and empirical grounds, for the value of extending this paradigm to human behavior in which distance from the goal may be designated not only in spatial terms but more importantly along dimensions of "qualita-

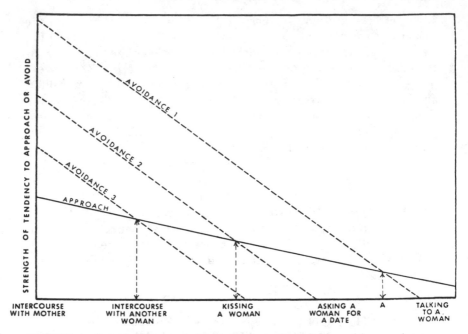

FIGURE 4. One depiction of the kind of conflict, discussed by psychoanalysts, in which the patient most desires, and most fears, sleeping with his mother, and in which related acts have lesser degrees of desire and anxiety associated with them. The patient initially tends to stay at point A, where approach and avoidance gradients intersect, and hence to have few opportunities for sexual intercourse. We must account for why further reduction in anxiety does not eventually lead to his having intercourse with his mother.

tive or culturally defined similarity of cues" (p. 355). This extension seems in some respects well justified and enables them to account well for a number of clinical phenomena (e.g., the relatively greater efficacy of reducing fears motivating avoidance rather than trying to increase motivation to approach; and the "negative therapeutic reaction" in which reducing the anxiety motivating repression may lead temporarily to an increase in distress and symptoms—pp. 355–363).

However, the situation depicted in Figure 4 is not really comparable to that of the animal afraid of the cues which also signal food. The aim of the therapy is presumably not for the patient to have intercourse with his mother! The simple diagrams presented by Dollard and Miller, while clarifying in some respects, are confusing with regard to the course of therapeutic change if one takes the notion of Oedipal conflict, and later sexual conflict as a generalization from it, at all seriously. Dollard and Miller, who have a good deal of respect for the observations of Freud and other analysts, do take such a view seriously.

In part, the difficulty can be dealt with by recognizing the limits of depicting only one dimension along which approach and avoidance can be measured, as in Figure 4. Dollard and Miller are quite aware of this problem. As quoted above, they note that in applying their model to psychotherapy, it is usually necessary to consider several different goals and subgoals, with the patient at different points along the various approach–avoidance gradients.

Thus, in the situation we have been discussing, one might distinguish a gradient of approach in thought from a gradient of approach in overt action. Then the difficulty is at least partially solved. The aim of undoing repression includes the ability to *think* anything. The aim of undoing inhibitions in action includes recognition that *not* all *actions* may be safely undertaken.

One difficulty with this solution is that there are few guidelines for just how to organize the multitudinous observations into a number of discrete dimensions of increasing closeness to the goal. One could, for example, imagine a dimension which included *both* thoughts and actions, and which embodied the observation that certain thoughts were more frightening than some actions (and of course, vice versa). Such a continuum might include, for example, the following (in descending order): having intercourse with another woman; kissing another woman; thinking of having intercourse with the woman; thinking of kissing her; etc.

Alternately (or complementarily), one might imagine one dimension in which approach was in terms of likeness to mother, another in which approach was in terms of similarity of the act, another in which the variable was degree of emotional involvement in whatever was engaged in, and/or any combination of these or others in either thought or actions. This difficulty in specifying in advance the dimension along which similarity (or approach and avoidance) varies was one of the major factors that led Bandura and Walters (1963) to question seriously the value of Miller's conflict paradigm. (However, see Wachtel, 1977b.)

Another difficulty with simply distinguishing a dimension of thoughts from a dimension of acts is that we are still left with our original dilemma regarding the acts. In the conflict depicted in Figure 4, if the patient's anxiety gradient is reduced to the point where he is able to enjoy intercourse with an "appropriate" woman without anxiety (reducing the avoidance gradient from Avoidance 1 to Avoidance 2 to Avoidance 3), why should not further reduction in anxiety lead to his then moving and going on to have intercourse with mother?

Here two considerations are relevant. First, the process of therapeutic change described by Dollard and Miller includes very centrally
not only extinction of anxiety, but also recovery of fuller use of
higher mental processes, as repression (or not-thinking behavior) is
diminished. Thus, the patient is better able to discriminate between
safe and unsafe situations and to plan and anticipate consequences.
The relevance of this to influencing differentially the inclination to
approach sexually either mother or "appropriate" sexual objects
should be obvious. These considerations are similar to those implied
by the traditional psychoanalytic terminology of integrating repressed wishes into the ego, and are related as well to Dewald's
(1972) emphasis on renunciation in therapeutic change, discussed in
Wachtel (1977b).

In considering this kind of solution to the conceptual problem
which has been pointed out, it should be clear that the simple picture
implied by the conflict diagrams is considerably altered. In light of
the above discussion, it seems necessary to stress that any particular
graphic representation of an approach–avoidance conflict is a depiction of the situation only at a given point in time. Whereas the simple
approach–avoidance situations of animals afraid of cues which also
signal food may be validly represented by one diagram for the entire
course of the animal's encounter with the conflict, the situation with
human neurotic conflicts tends to change with movement along the
original axis.[6] As new discriminations are fostered and new feedback
loops established, the dimensionality of the conflict tends to change.
That is, movement a certain distance along a particular dimension
may lead to events which, for example, make it necessary to depict
the original one dimension as two separate ones. This might occur
where the consequences of thoughts and actions are originally
poorly discriminated, and the patient's avoidances are describable
along a single dimension which includes both thoughts and actions
as on p. 99. As he proceeds along this dimension, and thinking
about forbidden things is restored, he can begin to make better
discriminations between thought and action, and the original global
dimension may no longer be a useful representation of his conflict.
Two *separate* conflict diagrams, one depicting approach in thought and
the other in action, might then be necessary instead. Thus, progress
along the single axis to a certain degree then makes that single axis
no longer a useful conceptual tool.

---

6. Although not germane to the particular point at issue here, it should be noted that
the individual's conflict will also vary at different times as a result of particular events
which influence self-esteem and/or imply greater permission or prohibition of particular kinds of acts.

A second consideration in understanding why the kind of situation depicted in Figure 4 does not imply intercourse with mother as its outcome is more directly related to the differing perspectives of Freudian and interpersonal approaches to understanding the fantasies and wishes which may be inferred from clinical data. As discussed in detail in Wachtel (1977b), in situations where Oedipal wishes and fears may reasonably be inferred, they need not be viewed as representing a simple perpetuation of a past situation, but can be understood as influenced by the patient's current way of living. Fantasies of sexual possession of an ideal woman, totally devoted not only to one's sensual desires but to the kind of total care provided only by a mother to a child, may be perpetuated and motivated by the current lack of satisfying and anxiety-free sexual experience. Rather than viewing the desire for mother as the "real" wish, of which more appropriate desires are derivatives or sublimations, such a view regards the Oedipal wish as itself a reaction to the current blockages in the person's adult living. Therefore, as the person comes to be able to engage in sensually satisfying and intimate relations with current sexual partners, the lure of the regressive object does not remain a constant. He is no longer particularly inclined to approach still "closer" to the "goal." The nature of the goal has changed as a result of what has ensued.

CONCLUDING COMMENTS

This chapter has focused largely on the difficulties with Dollard and Miller's formulations, on points where their analysis seems incomplete or potentially contradictory. It is a major asset of their approach that such difficulties can be discerned and subjected to theoretical analysis. The most common criticism of psychoanalytic theorizing is that it is not formulated clearly enough that points of difficulty can be readily identified. Miller's conflict paradigm is not similarly invulnerable; it is specifically designed to be amenable to careful critical scrutiny.

As convergence in the practice and theory of behavioral and nonbehavioral clinicians proceeds, formulations such as those of Dollard and Miller are likely to receive increasing reconsideration. If they are modified in the process, they will have fulfilled their purpose.

PSYCHOTHERAPY

Introduction to Part Two

The chapters in Part Two are in some respects the heart of this book. They spell out most directly the therapeutic implications of the point of view I have developed over the years, and they are most directly related to the title of the book. Although one of the chapters (Chapter 8) predates *Psychoanalysis and Behavior Therapy*, the rest of the chapters represent further developments in my thinking about psychotherapy since writing that book.

Chapter 6 originally appeared in a volume edited by Arkowitz and Messer (1984), which presented a variety of views on the question of whether integration of the psychotherapies is possible. An earlier version of it was presented at a symposium on the same topic at a meeting of the Association for the Advancement of Behavior Therapy in Chicago. At that symposium, some prominent psychoanalysts were invited, as well as commentators from a behavioral point of view. What became particularly clear to me at that meeting, and at a number of subsequent meetings and presentations at various locales, was that the nature of integration and the requirements for an integrative approach had been a matter of considerable misunderstanding among many of those who had considered it.

In attempting to clarify the nature of the integration that I have been proposing, the chapter first spells out what I take to be the most valuable and essential features of both the psychodynamic and the behavioral point of view. It takes issue with a number of characterizations of psychoanalysis (such as that it utilizes a medical model) that have been used to argue that there is a yawning gulf between psychodynamic and behavioral points of view. It then goes on to specify the most crucial elements from the psychodynamic perspective that enter into the approach I have subsequently called "integrative psychodynamic therapy" (Wachtel, 1985). These include an emphasis on unconscious processes, on conflict, on understanding the compromises the patient has (often unwittingly) made, on attending to the unusual or non-normative motives and fantasies that psychoanalysis alerts us to, and on the implicit rules of inference that guide clinical work and theorizing from a psychodynamic perspective.

From the behavioral realm, the properties discussed as entering into the integration include the use of active-intervention techniques, concern with the environmental context of behavior, a sharp focus on the patient's goals in the therapy, and the concerns of behavior therapists for empirical evidence for the efficacy of their methods.

The chapter then addresses in detail the critique of integration provided by Messer and Winokur (1980). Their arguments remain the most elaborate and sophisticated of the objections that have been raised to therapy integration.[1] As Chapter 6 points out, however, their objections stem primarily from a *comparative* orientation to the two approaches, rather than a consideration of true integration. Their characterizations of the modal attitudes of psychodynamic therapists and behavior therapists are, I believe, mostly useful and accurate. But they are largely irrelevant in considering the viability of an integration that takes elements from each approach and forges a new, third approach with its own characteristics. The quality of their critique pushed me to think through more clearly just what the nature of an integration in fact is, and enabled me to state more clearly than I previously had what sort of enterprise I was engaged in. This examination of the defining features of an integrative approach seemed the appropriate chapter with which to begin Part Two.

Chapter 7 is a much more clinical and practical paper. It is one of the papers for which I have received the most reprint requests since it was originally published, and I have found it especially useful in my teaching over the past few years. In some respects its guidelines and examples may seem "obvious," but considerable experience as a therapy supervisor makes it clear to me that at the very least it addresses issues that are not fully integrated into the practices of beginning therapists. I strongly suspect that even for experienced therapists the issues addressed in this chapter remain relevant in practice, even if in many instances they would be explicitly assented to in principle.

Chapter 8 is the only selection in Part Two that was published before *Psychoanalysis and Behavior Therapy*. It was my first published paper dealing with the integration of dynamic and behavioral ap-

---

1. See also their chapter in Arkowitz and Messer (1984) and their comments in that volume on the paper being discussed here, as well as my reply to both in the same volume.

proaches to therapy. My central aim was to raise questions about the common assumption among dynamic therapists that active-intervention methods interfere with deep exploration. The case discussed was not one of my own but that of a colleague who had described the case to me, and the paper was as concerned with what had not occurred as with what had. In this case, the therapist's not addressing sufficiently the ongoing sources of stress in the patient's daily life put an untenable burden on the transference relationship and interfered with the use of the transference as a vehicle for exploration. Ultimately, the case was a therapeutic failure.

I believe we are closer today than we were 10 years ago to answering the questions implicitly raised at the end of Chapter 8. Certainly there are now many models for how an integrative approach to therapy might be conducted, including not only the cases described in *Psychoanalysis and Behavior Therapy* and in this volume (see also Wachtel, 1985), but also those reported by the increasing number of therapists who describe themselves as integrative or eclectic in orientation.[2] It still remains to be determined, however, whether careful outcome data will demonstrate greater effectiveness for integrative approaches than for either dynamic or behavioral approaches alone.

Chapter 9 considers the question of integration from a reverse perspective—whether contributions from the psychodynamic end of the therapeutic spectrum can improve the therapeutic efficacy of behavior therapists. Because I was originally trained in the psychodynamic tradition, much of what I have written about integration addresses the concerns of that group and asks in one way or another what behavior therapy can contribute to a psychodynamic approach. This is the only chapter in which the primary focus is on the opposite question, though the question is strongly implicit in a number of other places. As might be expected, framing matters in a different way also helps to provide a useful perspective on earlier discussions; the chapter may well prove as useful to dynamically oriented therapists as to behavior therapists in understanding and evaluating the approach I advocate.

2. In my own writings, I do not use the terms "integrative" and "eclectic" interchangeably. To me, the term "eclectic" seems to imply a random mix rather than a synthesis that has been carefully thought out and examined in light of some coherent theoretical conception. Since the founding of the Society for the Exploration of Psychotherapy Integration (SEPI), however, I have become more aware of a wide range of approaches that are called "eclectic" by their proponents, and not all of them show the characteristics I have come to associate with that term. A fairly up-to-date bibliography of both integrative and eclectic approaches was compiled in a recent issue of the SEPI newsletter.

Chapters 10, 11, and 12 can be seen as closely related explorations, converging on questions of values in therapy and the stance of the therapist that is most helpful to the patient. The spectre of neutrality haunts all three chapters, as does the question of what kind of influence the therapist does and should have.

The starting point for Chapter 10 is the work of Carl Rogers, who has advocated a degree of nondirectiveness at least as stringent as the requirements of neutrality put forth by Freudian analysts. The chapter begins with a re-examination of a widely cited study by Truax that seemed to demonstrate that, based on tape recordings of Rogers's own therapy sessions, Rogers was not in fact nearly as noncontingent in his response to what his clients said as he claimed to be. A central concern of the chapter is to sort out just where it is and is not appropriate for therapists to indicate their views about choices their patients are making. The chapter attempts to distinguish between those (many) choices that the therapist must strive to understand but has no business trying to influence, and those that bear specifically on the work of the therapy and that the therapist has a responsibility to take up directly with the patient. The chapter comes to a somewhat surprising conclusion—that only by making clear judgments in some instances can one refrain effectively from communicating judgments when it is *not* appropriate. Unconditional positive regard for the patient as a person, it turns out, needs to be distinguished from a refusal to consider with the patient whether any particular choice he or she is making is a good idea.

Chapter 11 was originally presented as part of a panel on the concept of neutrality at the 40th anniversary celebration of the William Alanson White Institute in New York. In our field, there is perhaps no concept more confusing or—ironically—more fraught with emotion than neutrality. When discussions of therapeutic technique deteriorate into moralizing, it is likely that the idea of neutrality is close at hand. From my own perspective, neutrality is an extremely misleading and ultimately counterproductive notion. Chapter 11 states why I feel this way, and does so as well as I have been able to do thus far.

Chapter 12 was originally presented at a meeting of the Society for Psychotherapy and Philosophy of Science. Its major focus is on the ways in which the therapeutic goals of psychoanalysis have changed over the years without this really having been clearly and sharply noted. It addresses rather more directly than is typical the widely held assumption by psychoanalysts that psychoanalysis is a superior form of therapy, able to achieve results that are unattainable not only in nonpsychoanalytic therapies but in any other form of psychoanalytically oriented psychotherapy as well. In doing so, it clarifies the sense in which this position is frequently held even by practitioners who claim that for many patients psychoanalytic therapy rather than psychoanalysis is the treatment of choice.

The chapter looks at ways in which values find expression in the practice of psychoanalysis even when—or in some respects especially when—the analyst is aiming to be neutral. Neutrality itself is seen to be a highly value-laden notion, which has in fact contributed to changing the very goals to which the psychoanalytic process is devoted, and even to the downgrading of the therapeutic aims that still are the primary ones of those who seek the help of analysts.

6

On Theory, Practice, and the
Nature of Integration

It is really not very difficult to argue against an integration of psychodynamic and behavioral approaches. All one has to do is to define "psychodynamic" and "behavioral" in the right way, and they will indeed be incompatible. This the critics of integration have done, sometimes with flair and considerable sophistication. It will be the burden of this chapter to argue, however, that such criticisms do not really address the kind of integration I have proposed. They are, I suggest, articulate defenses of a less than satisfactory status quo, and they impede the creative fusion that I believe is necessary for a major advance in psychotherapeutic efficacy and in the theoretical understanding on which such enhanced efficacy must be based.

To some degree I myself have abetted the definitional confusion. For a variety of reasons, partly syntactic and aesthetic, partly having to do with the term "psychoanalysis" being more familiar and widely recognized, and partly, I confess, to arrest potential readers with a starker, more provocative challenge, I referred in the title of my book to psycho*analysis* and behavior therapy. It would have been less confusing to indicate (as I did do in the body of my book) that I was concerned with an integration of psycho*dynamic* and behavioral approaches. The term "psychodynamic" is a broader—and less jealously guarded—one that includes not only Freudian theory and those variations of it that have been included in what might be called the official psychoanalytic movement, but also points of view that, although originally rooted in Freudian thought, have presented direct challenges to certain assumptions still widely held by Freudians.

Reprinted by permission from H. Arkowitz & S. Messer (Eds.), *Psychoanalytic Therapy and Behavior Therapy: Is Integration Possible?* New York: Plenum, 1984.

It could reasonably be argued that "psychoanalysis" *is* the correct term for the points of view on which I rely. Horney and her followers did describe what they did as psychoanalysis, and many Sullivanians describe themselves as analysts. (Indeed, the journal of the William Alanson White Institute, the major Sullivanian training center, is called *Contemporary Psychoanalysis.*) Nonetheless, I do believe that it is more accurate—or at least less confusing—for someone like myself, who relies as much on Horney and Sullivan as on Freud, to describe my point of view as *psychodynamic* rather than specifically as psychoanalytic.

Freud himself varied on what he considered the essential defining features of psychoanalysis. In 1914 he said:

> Any line of investigation, *no matter what its direction*, which recognizes [the facts of transference and resistance] and takes them as the starting point of its work may call itself psycho-analysis, though it arrives at results other than my own. (Freud, 1914/1959, p. 298, italics mine)

A few years later a harder-line, more restrictive statement was offered—one that both upped the ante as to what a psychoanalyst must pay obeisance to and that was cast in a syntax of prohibition rather than of permission:

> The assumption that there are unconscious mental processes, the recognition of the theory of resistance and repression, the appreciation of the importance of sexuality and of the Oedipus complex— these constitute the principal subject-matter of psycho-analysis and the foundations of its theory. *No one who cannot accept them all* should count himself a psycho-analyst. (Freud, 1923/1959, p. 247, italics mine)

Freud's efforts to define the "sine qua nons" of the tradition he had launched were related to sectarian battles within the psychoanalytic movement. Fairly early, Freud was confronting the consequences of the extraordinarily stimulating effect his discoveries and theories produced; he spawned intellectual progeny he was eager to disown. He had, of course, every right to distinguish between his own theories and those of others whose ideas might be confused with his. I would largely agree with him that he is

> justified in maintaining that even to-day no one can know better than I what psycho-analysis is, how it differs from other ways of investigating the life of the mind, and precisely what should be called psycho-analysis and what would better be described by some other name. (Freud, 1914/1959, p. 287)

But if Freud could attempt with some justification to control what was to be called psychoanalysis, he had neither the right nor the power to control more generally how others were to reinterpret or selectively make use of his work. The more broadly psycho*dynamic* tradition consists of all those efforts to build a psychology starting from at least some of the central premises of Freudian thought, even if they diverged from Freud in substantial ways. After more than four decades of post-Freudian development, psychoanalysis itself— that is, modern Freudian orthodoxy—is hard to delineate precisely, and controversy (e.g., over whether Kohut's [1977] theorizing is properly Freudian psychoanalysis) abounds. The broader psycho*dynamic* umbrella is, of course, even harder to define. It is the essence of much of it that different proponents see different aspects of Freud's thought as the most crucial or most valuable. What is to one an unfortunate anachronism in Freud's otherwise brilliant work is to another the heart and soul of what makes psychoanalysis of continuing value.

Nonetheless, it is useful to delineate a broader psychodynamic point of view, many of whose proponents are steeped in Freud but are also critical of aspects of the Freudian mainstream. Despite the diversity of theoretical perspectives and of evaluations of Freud's own contribution, the notion of a psychodynamic tradition, encompassing Freudian psychoanalysis but including considerably more, is not really that vague. Agreement as to who would belong within such a category would be rather high. (And clearly, present-day behavior therapists would not fit within it.)

MISLEADING CHARACTERIZATIONS OF PSYCHODYNAMIC THOUGHT

There are certainly features of some versions of psychodynamic thought that would make an integration with behavior therapy rather difficult. Critics have seized upon these as if they were the essential defining features of a psychodynamic point of view. Some of these are almost totally red herrings. The contention, for example, that, unlike behavior therapy, psychoanalysis is a medical or disease model is thoroughly without merit. The close association of the official psychoanalytic organization in the United States with the medical profession was a matter of economics and guild protectionism and was counter both to the general policy of the International Psycho-Analytic Association and to Freud's (1926a/1959) own arguments. The psychoanalytic situation, in fact, was largely set up to *avoid* the kinds of interactions and expectations that are encountered in medicine. The psychoanalytic model is a psychological, not a medical model (Wachtel, 1977b).

More respectable, but still off the mark, is the contention that integration is impossible because psychoanalysis attributes causation to the past and because behavior therapy focuses on the present. It is certainly true that many analysts do contend that an exploration of the patient's past is essential for lasting and meaningful change. Such a view, however, though it was held by Freud, is not an essential characteristic of a psychodynamic point of view (Horney, 1939; Wachtel, 1977a).[1] Concern with unconscious motivation, with conflict—and even with the enormous shaping influence of early experience—can as readily be pursued via a model of cumulative skewing of development that gives great weight to present environmental input (Wachtel, 1973, 1977a, 1981b) as it can with a model that makes the influence of the past impervious to present realities. That is, one can trace how early experiences skew the kinds of later experiences one encounters, with the effect of maintaining the psychic structures previously existing. One can also trace how those psychic structures in turn lead to still further skewing of experience and to still further confirmation of existing structures in a continuing circle that at each point takes place in what is then the present. The mediational events in this continuing process can include unconscious conflicts and wishes, but they are always present wishes and conflicts, no matter however much they resemble those of the past.

A third objection is more interesting because it is based on a characterization that is indeed true for a very large majority of psychodynamic thinkers, whatever their specific persuasion. Franks (1978; Franks & Wilson, 1979) has described a methodological or epistemological difference between psychodynamic and behavioral thinkers. For the former, he suggests that "subjective data derived entirely from the clinical situation are typically regarded as valid" (Franks, 1978). The latter, he says, play by different rules.

The general picture this characterization presents of two groups of thinkers is largely accurate. Psychodynamic thinkers often do take as evidence for a particular formulation or general concept data that most behavior therapists do not find persuasive. As some analysts are beginning to articulate (e.g., Schafer, 1976), psychoanalysis is

---

1. Indeed, one can argue that even where a strong concern with the past does characterize a particular psychodynamic thinker's approach, that does not preclude the use of behavioral measures. It is only where a strong stance of nonintervention is taken in order to permit the transference to emerge or unfold that a concern with the past is problematic for the purposes of integration (Wachtel, 1977b, 1982c).

based on a methodology and epistemology that is more akin to that of history or literary studies than it is to that of the natural sciences. It seeks to explain by offering formulations that account for coherences in a diverse range of phenomena. It seeks also to show how the pictures offered by dreams, by slips of the tongue, by omissions and failures of memory, and by various otherwise puzzling behavioral patterns all converge—that is, to articulate unities behind the manifest diversity. The explanation is, to a large degree, one that *makes sense* out of the flux of events and that gives order and coherence. It is a latticework of evidence in which each strand supports the others and in which each piece of evidence *becomes* evidence only in the context of the other pieces.

The dream, for example, that gives weight to an interpretation that an overly solicitous son in fact harbors warded-off hostile feelings toward his mother might *not* be evidence for such a view if the other data (slips, "inadvertent" behavior patterns, particular trends in the sequence of associations, etc.) did not also point that way. Indeed, in another context, the same dream might be usable as evidence for a *different* line of interpretation. And the same holds, by and large, for *each* piece of evidence. To a very great degree, pieces of evidence gain meaning and evidential gravity *from each other*.

This does not mean that evidence is used arbitrarily, that you can use anything to prove anything. Unfortunately, there are more dynamically oriented clinicians than one would wish who do make of their formulations a procrustean bed in which any potentially disturbing observations are put to rest; and it is probably also true that the mode of evaluating evidence in psychodynamic work makes it easier to "cheat" or to fool oneself that one has proven what one has not than is the case for behavior therapists.[2] But there is a discipline available that helps to minimize such occurrences if it is properly used. There *are* pieces that do not fit, that serve a cautionary or disconfirming function. When the paradigm is properly applied, such new observations can—in the fashion suggested before—lend a different cast to all the data previously seen as supportive of one's first formulation and force a new formulation that provides a coherent picture of this newer, larger body of data.

Thus the "good" psychoanalyst discards prior hypotheses just as the experimenter does when new results require it. And among the followers of both methodological paradigms, there are those whose

2. It really does not take all that much ingenuity—or wrongheadedness—to cheat within the behavioral paradigm either. Behavior therapy, too, has begun to develop divergent schools with mutual bitterness and accusations of highly selective renderings and interpretations of data.

ideas show a remarkable immunity to new observations, and there are those who actually learn from what they do. But if one can make a case that the methodologies and epistemologies are equally defensible, they are nonetheless different. Indeed, I have at times been astounded at how refractory some behavior therapists can be to what I regard as solidly convincing configurational evidence.

There is thus something useful in Franks and Wilson's distinction between the methodological or epistemological orientation of psychoanalysts and behavior therapists. If you define the essence of the psychodynamic and behavioral approaches as they do, the case for integration does look shaky.

Even here, it should be noted, their distinction refers to something statistical rather than essential. That is, although it is true that *most* psychoanalytic thinkers have a different orientation to evidence than do *most* behavior therapists, there is at least a small minority in each group whose canons of evidence overlap considerably. There are, for example, a number of psychoanalysts who have felt a need to establish psychoanalytic concepts by experimental evidence as well as by the more common configurational kind of evidence (see, for example, Shevrin & Dickman, 1980; Silverman, 1976; Wolitzky & Wachtel, 1973). And, I suggest, in clinical practice many behavior therapists show at least some inclination to think configurationally rather than requiring anything like experimental confirmation before they regard a hypothesis as confirmed. (They are much more likely to require such confirmation with regard to general *principles*, but as I have noted elsewhere [Wachtel, 1982d], the relation between those general principles and their actual clinical functioning is far looser than is usually suggested.)

Now, of course, one could say that to the degree that they deviate from experimental canons of evidence they are not really behavior therapists. But this is winning the anti-integration argument by tautology. Or perhaps it would be fairer to say that Franks and Wilson argue against a different kind of integration than what I have advocated. Methodological or epistemological integration—that is, integration of ideas about evidence—may or may not be possible, but it is at the least very difficult. Certainly it is far more difficult than the kind of integration I have advocated.

Franks and Wilson suggest that at times it may be useful to attempt an integration at the level of clinical practice but not at a "conceptual" level. Even here they are rather skeptical and refer to this possibility as "technical opportunism," a term that could conceivably be defended as merely descriptive but whose connotation is hard to ignore. It is certainly true that there is yet scant evidence that an integration at the level of clinical practice will yield superior results. Though my own guess is obviously different, I regard as perfectly reasonable Franks and Wilson's hunch that in the long run advancement in clinical practice is more likely to follow from pursuing one of the presently established systems than from attempting an integration of techniques. But when they contrast their preferred scenario with "an indiscriminate deployment of what seems to work," I hope it is clear to the reader—and to them—that they are no longer referring to the kind of effort I have advocated.

My aim is not simply the practical application of a combination of clinical procedures, but rather to work toward a thorough conceptual integration. The particular way of proceeding clinically that I have developed out of my integrative efforts seems to me useful for now, but I am sure it will change. What seems more likely to be of enduring value is the construction of a frame of reference in which the ideas and the observations emanating from both[3] broad approaches can find a coherent place and in which the discoveries of each can push the other to expand. That frame of reference too is not a final or finished product; it continues and *must* continue to change and evolve in order to accommodate further observations and ideas. But, in my view, it is the development of a coherent way of thinking about clinical problems, a way open to input from a variety of sources, that will enable really effective clinical work at the practical level to proceed most expeditiously.

The development of a conceptual integration is, I think, usefully distinguished from a methodological or epistemological integration. Franks and Wilson conflate these two levels in arguing that a "conceptual" integration is impossible. They are quite right that "one's belief system" is hard to integrate with another that feels alien. Psychoanalysts and behavior therapists—to the degree that separate schools persist in coming years—will continue to hold different ideas about what constitutes "proof," as they will continue (at least as distinguishable statistical aggregates) to evidence different "visions" of life (see Messer & Winokur, 1980 . . .). But an integration at the conceptual—rather than the ideological or epistemological—level remains a useful and achievable goal. I will have more to say shortly about what such an integration is like, but first I would like to return to its constituents. I have said something about what I think are *not* the essential defining features of a psychodynamic or behavioral

---

3. Although the integration of psychodynamic and behavioral approaches in particular is both the focus of this chapter and the starting point of my integrative efforts, other perspectives, such as that of family therapists, of Piaget, or of gestalt therapists have also begun to be included in the integrative effort under discussion here and will probably continue to be to an increasing degree. (See, for example, Wachtel, 1981b.)

view and about what I think are misleading or irrelevant differences for present purposes. Let me now indicate, at least briefly, what I do take to be the most significant characteristics of each approach.

THE PSYCHODYNAMIC POINT OF VIEW

I have argued that a number of characteristics commonly claimed to be essential to the psychodynamic point of view are not really essential after all. The "medical model," the emphasis on the past, and (to a lesser degree) a particular epistemological orientation are, I suggest, misleading or unnecessarily constraining as defining properties of psychodynamic thought. To this negative list I would add such other candidates as the libido theory, Freud's mental geography, the requirement of neutrality or nonintervention by the therapist, and the insistence on insight as the primary source of psychological change (cf. Wachtel, 1977b, 1982d). Have I then succeeded in draining the term "psychodynamic" of all meaning and left just a hollow shell with no substance? I believe not. There remain a number of crucially important characteristics shared by all psychodynamic thinkers that clearly distinguish them from those in the behavioral tradition and represent, in my view, the most significant legacy of Freud's pioneering efforts.

Clearly, the single most essential defining property is a concern with unconscious processes. If anything is a sine qua non of the psychodynamic point of view, this is it. What Freud illuminated, more than anything else, was the degree to which we do not really know ourselves. Further, he points us to inquire into the *motives* for our self-deceptions and into their consequences: Our lack of awareness is not merely a failure to notice or to register. We *try* not to notice, and we *dare* not notice.[4] And, unfortunately, the immediate comfort this turning away brings us quite frequently has as its heir a disruption of our lives that is far out of proportion to the initial gain. The price of comfort is very high.

A second critical feature of the psychodynamic point of view is a focus upon *conflict*. What we want, it turns out, is not as simple as we would wish. In the prism of psychoanalysis our unitary actions or expressions of desire are resolved into components that, alone, would lead us in rather differing directions. Conceptions of conflict pervade the psychodynamic approach to motivation and, implicitly,

---

4. Sometimes, of course, simple failures to notice do occur. Freud distinguished between the dynamic and the descriptive unconscious. It is the former that plays such a key role in psychological difficulties and that Freud dedicated himself to illuminating.

suggest a quite different way of understanding what happens when a behavior therapist attempts to use reinforcements (Wachtel, 1977b, Chapter 11; 1982b). The psychodynamic conception of conflict is closely related to the concern with what is dynamically unconscious as well as to an increasing emphasis on the role of anxiety (Freud, 1926b/1959; Dollard & Miller, 1950). It need not, however, imply a strictly intrapsychic view of how conflict is generated or maintained (Wachtel, 1977b, 1982c).

A related feature of most psychodynamically oriented clinical work (though not as crucially defining a feature) is a concern with the *compromises* that conflict, anxiety, and self-deception lead to. From a psychodynamic perspective, even patterns of behavior or aspirations and guiding assumptions with which the person seems comfortable are likely to be called into question. This can at times be overdone, as behavior therapists have appropriately pointed out; the patient has a right to keep his goals and focus narrow, and some version of informed consent seems called for if the person's comfortable assumptions are to be systematically challenged. But if the analyst is attentive to the ethical complexities, this broader and deeper inquiry is one of the most valuable characteristics of the psychodynamic approach. Ignoring what the person is explicitly telling you is deplorable. But refusing to hear what cannot yet be put into words is unfortunate as well.

The psychodynamic perspective points not only to unconscious motives and to motivational conflict but to *unusual* and *non-normative* motives as well. Freud's researches have alerted us to the importance and the prevalence of wishes that differ substantially from what would conventionally be expected. Viewed psychodynamically, what people actually seek—as opposed to what they *say* they are seeking—can be rather surprising. Behavior therapists, in contrast, tend to assume that what people want is what they say they want and/or what is normatively expectable (Wachtel, 1977b, Chapter 7).

Finally, a crucial feature of the psychodynamic approach is the rules of inference whereby such nonobvious, non-normative motives can be identified. It is these rules that make claims regarding such motives not simply arbitrary assertions. Unfortunately, many of these rules have been passed along primarily by an oral tradition, and there is little good, explicit written material on the rules themselves. This has made it easy for opponents of psychoanalysis to view psychoanalytic claims about unconscious motives and thoughts as being essentially arbitrary. I have already indicated briefly some of the reasons why I think these inferences are *not* arbitrary. I hope before too long to complete a paper which examines this matter in more detail. For now, I simply wish to indicate that I regard such rules as essential contributions from the psychodynamic end to the synthesis under discussion in this chapter.

The reader will notice that such bellwether concepts as "transference" and "resistance"—the ideas Freud first designated as the essential defining characteristics of psychoanalysis—do not appear in the preceding list. Unlike "libido" or "neutrality," this is not because I think them faulty or inessential. In the case of resistance, it is merely that it is already subsumed under what has been outlined sketchily. Resistance is simply the manifestation in the therapy session of the conflict and motivated self-deception referred to previously (Wachtel, 1982b). The concept of transference—or at least the phenomena and concerns to which it refers—is certainly essential to address if one hopes to depict the psychodynamic point of view accurately. The term has, however, accumulated so much excess freight over the years and is so closely related to notions I do want to question, such as neutrality and nonintervention, that it cannot simply be listed without elaborate discussion. I have spelled out elsewhere alternative ways of understanding transference phenomena and how transference can be conceived so as to lend itself to the kind of integrative effort being discussed here (Wachtel, 1981b, 1982c).

THE BEHAVIORAL APPROACH

Indicating what I take to be the essential features of a behavioral approach is in some ways a more difficult task. As Franks and Wilson indicate, "there is much less of an abiding core to which all behavior therapists would subscribe." For present purposes, though, what is most important is to indicate those features of the behavioral approach that are central in the effort to achieve a psychodynamic and behavioral integration.

Perhaps most important in this regard is the emphasis on *active intervention.* Behavior therapists employ a wide variety of techniques to intervene in and alter maladaptive patterns of behavior. In their own way, so do analysts—both more and less than they think. They do more, in the sense that neutrality is a myth and influence is exerted in every choice to interpret, to remain silent, or to say, "Why do you ask?" They do less, in the sense that the clinical procedures of psychoanalysis are not nearly as powerful as one might hope and that they could be notably enhanced by the use of the intervention techniques developed by behavior therapists.

In psychoanalysis and in most psychodynamic therapy, the inquiry into the patient's difficulties and the intervention techniques are essentially the same. Understanding *is* the therapy. In behavior therapy, the understanding that is attained—by both patient and therapist—is *applied*. Explicit methods are utilized to assure that the patient garners the experiences that will enable him or her to change. These methods can also be used, I have argued, to make it more likely that the insights attained from a psychodynamic point of view in fact lead to the changes the patient is seeking (Wachtel, 1975, 1977b).[5]

A second feature of behavior therapy that is important in the present context is its concern with the environmental context of behavior, with relating the patient's behavior and experience to what is going on around him or her. Again, this is not something unique to behavior therapy. Even some versions of psychodynamic thought do this to a substantial degree (Wachtel, 1973), though usually not as thoroughly as behavior therapy. Family therapists, of course, are particularly concerned with relating behavior to context and have made valuable contributions in this regard that the present approach is still working to assimilate.

A third relevant feature is the emphasis by behavior therapists on an explicit contract between patient and therapist and a corresponding concern with specific target complaints. This leads, in conjunction with the emphasis on relating patients' difficulties to environmental events, to a kind of inquiry that has considerable merit both on ethical grounds and on practical ones. As discussed before, the articulation of a more explicit contract between patient and therapist need not exclude a concern with conflict or with examining the compromises and self-deceptions in the patient's life. But it does permit the patient to be a partner more fully in the therapeutic effort.

It is a common psychodynamic stereotype of behavior therapy that behavior therapists are authoritarian and manipulative and that they *work upon* the patient. Actually, in many respects the behavior therapist is *less* guilty of such an orientation. The emphasis by many dynamic therapists on therapeutic anonymity, the frequency with which questions are not explicitly answered, and other related features of most psychodynamic approaches contribute to an atmo-

5. One can, of course, define psychodynamic therapy so as to include as an essential feature the presently common one of the therapist's striving for neutrality and/or an exclusively interpretive approach. To do so would, of course, make the use of active interventions incompatible with anything psychodynamic. Clearly, that is not the notion of psychodynamic therapy under discussion here. I regard the prevalent emphasis on neutrality as unfortunate and in no way required by the logic of the psychodynamic point of view per se (Wachtel, 1977b, 1982c).

sphere in which the patient is in a childlike, one-down position. Behavior therapists, by and large, rather than dynamic therapists, are the ones who share explicitly with the patient what the rationale is for each thing that is being done and who concern themselves most explicitly with whether the work is moving in a direction that is consonant with the patient's own aims. Once anonymity and the idea that the transference should "emerge" or "unfold" without interference from the therapist are excluded as defining features of a psychodynamic approach (Wachtel, 1982c), it becomes possible to be similarly collaborative with the patient while maintaining a recognition of the important role of unconscious processes and motivational conflict.

As I noted earlier, I think it is misleading to identify a greater concern for evidence as an essential defining feature of behavior therapy, though I would agree that, as a group, behavior therapists are probably more alert to the need for, and pitfalls in gathering, such evidence. The characteristics of behavior therapy just noted, however—the effort to specify very clearly and precisely what changes the patient wants to achieve, and the effort to relate particular patterns of behavior to particular environmental contexts—do facilitate the evaluation of therapeutic efficacy. The effort to discuss patients' difficulties and the goals of the work in terms at least potentially amenable to evaluation—although sometimes leading to excessive narrowness or unwillingness to address what cannot be immediately measured—is a valuable feature of the behavioral approach that is capable of being incorporated into an integrated model. The goals of psychodynamic therapy are often discussed in such terms as "autonomy," "structural change," or "resolution" of conflicts or of the transference—notions that are notoriously hard to evaluate (See Chapter 12).

MESSER AND WINOKUR'S OBJECTIONS

The most interesting and sophisticated objection that has yet been made to the integration of psychodynamic and behavioral approaches has been offered by Messer and Winokur (1980). I believe that their objection can be effectively answered and that it really reflects a *comparative* orientation to psychodynamic and behavioral therapies, rather than one that fully takes into account the selective and emergent properties of a true integration. That is, they look at similarities and (especially) differences between psychodynamic and behavioral approaches, but do not as explicitly address how an integration—as a new, third orientation—might yield conceptions that reconcile those differences that presently exist. Nonetheless, their argument is an important one that must be addressed by any proponent of integration.

Messer and Winokur attempt to show that the values and the grounding vision that characterize psychoanalysts and behavior therapists are basically different. Even between the most ego- and reality-oriented analysts and the most cognitive or broad-spectrum behavior therapists, there is, they suggest, a "nagging breach" that is based on different conceptions of what is important in human life and what is possible. They pursue their comparative analysis by considering how an analytically and a behaviorally oriented therapist would pursue the same case as well as by a more general consideration of the basic orientation of each approach. Their descriptions seem to me, for the most part, to be fair-minded and accurate, and they do reveal some very significant differences. In some respects I have sensed similar differences myself in my own interactions with proponents of these two broad schools of thought. There are, however, a few points at which I would question their characterization, and I would like to address these before going on to consider my main objection to their line of argument—that differences *between* approaches do not necessarily preclude an integration *of* them.

In depicting the difference between the psychoanalytic and the behavioral vision, Messer and Winokur rely on a paper by Schafer (1976) that uses Northrup Frye's categories of mythic forms (Frye, 1957). Schafer argues that psychoanalysis can be seen as being characterized by four complementary visions of reality—the romantic, the ironic, the tragic, and the comic—and he elaborates the nature of each. This mode of characterization is useful in conveying various aspects of the psychoanalytic world view per se. But when it is employed by Messer and Winokur in an effort to compare the psychoanalytic vision with that of the behavior therapist, it is far less satisfactory. For *this* purpose, this set of categories has some insurmountable problems.

To begin with, the choices offered by this particular fourfold scheme lead to the vision of the behavior therapist being characterized as "comic." Messer and Winokur state explicitly that in this context the term is not meant to connote "funny," "in a light vein," or "not serious." But surely, as analysts they must recognize that connotations are not so easily dispelled. Whatever verbal disavowal may be offered, to characterize an entire approach to human problems simply as comic cannot fail to detract from any sense that that approach has something profound or serious to offer. Yes, Shakespeare's comedies can indeed be viewed as both profound *and* serious, but what Shakespearean scholar, writing commentaries on those plays, would be pleased at having his or her *own* work described simply as comic?

Moreover, even Messer and Winokur's explicit definition of "comic," meant to dispel the aforementioned connotation, is really a loaded one. In the comic vision, they say, conflict "can be eliminated by effective manipulative action or via the power of positive thinking." Why do they speak of effective *manipulative* action? Why do they not say effective action only? This is a small point perhaps but is not the word "manipulative" here both unnecessary and possessed of a possibly negative connotation? Similarly, "the power of positive thinking" is, after all, the title of a book that is not a scholarly work but a bit of pop preachiness for the *Reader's Digest* set—and, moreover, it is a book written by one of the favorite preachers of our most disgraced president, the man who presided over the wedding of Julie Nixon. In a paragraph devoted to dispelling the idea that comic implies a lack of seriousness or profundity, was there not a phrase with more scholarly associations that could have conveyed the same idea?

Further, Messer and Winokur go on to say about the comic vision that "endings are happy ones free from guilt and anxiety." This may be a more or less accurate picture of the structure of dramatic comedy. But does not the term "happy endings" nonetheless evoke the superficiality of Hollywood at its worst, where even films not intended as comedies have foolish, hard-to-take-seriously happy endings? And does this really—as it seems to by the associative link they develop—characterize not just the comic vision but the world view of behavior therapists as well? By and large, behavior therapists do seem to be more optimistic in their outlook. They are less certain that tragedy and the involution of desire must haunt our days. But do they really expect simply happy endings, and do they really claim that after therapy patients are completely free from guilt and anxiety?

Finally, we come to a more subtle bias that is introduced as a consequence of the scheme Messer and Winokur use to analyze the competing visions. As an artifact of how they choose to slice the pie, it appears that psychoanalysis has *four* separate visions, whereas behavior therapy has but one. That alone, it seems, would make psychoanalysis far more comprehensive. Behavior therapy, with its single vision, seems superficial just by virtue of that. Of course, a vision of reality is not a "thing." It makes no sense to count visions or add them up. Yet, there is something initially compelling about seeing that the vision that guides behavior therapy is but one of the four visions guiding psychoanalysis.[6]

The problem, of course, lies in the terms in which the comparison is framed. The psychoanalytic world view is neatly dissected by this scheme, and the multiplicity of its perspectives is revealed. But the various facets of the behavioral vision are not similarly captured by this particular way of slicing things, so it is left with just "one" vision. In fact, the comic view of behavior therapists is a quite different one from the comic view of the analyst. Whereas for analysts this concept of Frye's intersects with but a small portion of their total world view, it is forced, within the constraints of this scheme, to cover the totality of the behavior therapist's vision. The behavior therapist's comic vision, however—being coterminous with the behavior therapist's vision per se—is (not surprisingly therefore) more complex. There is a sense, in fact, in which it can be said to be the container for the behavior therapist's sense of tragedy, of irony, and of romance. His or her vision is not totally devoid of these elements. Rather, they are organized differently; they are subsumed under a general orientation toward meliorating suffering rather than enduring it and under a basically optimistic (but not necessarily Pollyannaish) view of human possibilities.

Consider, for example, Messer and Winokur's discussion in their paper of the psychodynamic approach to a hypothetical patient, Mrs. J.

> When the dynamic therapist allows Mrs. J. to experience grief, mourn her losses, see the death of her father and loss of her husband in their tragic grimness, the thrust is to help her change by facing the loss, reexperiencing it and working it through, with all the pain involved. Only rarely, the dynamic therapist would say, does growth in therapy, as in childhood, take place without some suffering. In all this, the tragic element in life is recognized. (p. 824)

This certainly is a different picture than one would expect from a behavior therapist. Yet the gulf is not as thoroughly unbridgeable as it first might seem. After all, it is the essence of many behavioral measures to enable the patient to expose himself or herself to the experiences and situations he or she has previously avoided. Often,

---

6. I do not mean to imply here that Messer and Winokur themselves count visions and argue on that basis. They do not. Rather, the point is that the scheme they use is likely to lead the *reader* to be struck by the seeming fact that the behavior therapist's vision is but one of the four visions of the analyst and to be led, perhaps without even recognizing it, to perceive behavior therapy in a way that introduces a negative bias.

as in systematic desensitization, the attempt is made to minimize the pain, but some pain is almost inevitable and in certain techniques, such as flooding, things are arranged so that the pain is considerable. Behavior therapy is not predicated on avoidance of the painful but on confrontation and mastery.

WHAT IS AN INTEGRATION?

My point is not to deny the differences between the psychoanalytic and behavioral visions; the differences are real and in some ways substantial. My preceding objections notwithstanding, I regard Messer and Winokur's characterizations as largely accurate and in essence to be fair-minded. I do not think that the instances of bias I have pointed out were conscious efforts to mislead. They reflect, rather, an almost inevitable influence on our language of the passionate convictions that sustain any good work. I discussed them both to attempt a corrective and to indicate that the gap is not thoroughly beyond the reach of any conceivable effort at bridge building. At this point, however, I wish to approach the issue from a different angle. Let me alert the reader to the fact that it is in the following paragraphs that the most important part of my argument can be found.

Arguments showing that psychoanalysis and behavior therapy are *different* do not really bear on the question of whether they can be integrated. Indeed, were they not rather different, there would be little point in an integration. It is the very fact that each stresses certain things that the other does not that makes an integration more useful than either separately. And, of course, it is their differences that make an effort at integration interesting and challenging. It is no feat to put together what seems compatible and alike to everyone.

As I conceive it, an integration is not just a hodgepodge of eclecticism, a salad with a little of this and a little of that tossed in. The goal, rather, is the development of a new coherent structure, an internally consistent approach both to technical intervention and to the construction of theory. An integrative or synthetic effort is built on both an admiring and a critical attitude toward each separate approach. It is admiring in the sense that each has something useful and important to contribute, and it is critical in the sense that each is seen as *omitting* something useful and important (for the most part, something that is part of what is valuable about the other approach).

Messer and Winokur (1980), for example, capture well some of what I find valuable in psychoanalysis and somewhat missing in behavior therapy. They indicate, for example, that they could not approve of any approach that "denies complexity, ambiguity, and the ubiquity of conflict in human affairs" (p. 825). Neither could I.[7]

But I have come to feel that an approach that fails to appreciate the enormous significance of present contextual cues and contingencies, that fails to consider the therapist's responsibility to help the patient systematically to apply the lessons learned in the sessions to his or her daily life, that underestimates the factors that make it difficult for the patient to make that application spontaneously, or that has a deep-rooted bias against active intervention by the therapist is also unacceptable. As things stand now, we have the choice of embracing one set of follies (and of course strengths) or the other. The aim of an integration is to build upon the strengths of each without the limiting blinders. This can seem a grandiose aim (and in Messer and Winokur's terms it is comic—an effort to transcend the limitations, to take only the good). But one need not feel that the millennium is around the corner to strive for something better than we have or to expect some tangible gain from an integrative effort.

It is important to be clear that one can value the unique contributions of each approach without endorsing each and every feature of either. As a proponent of integration, I am frequently in the position of trying to persuade my behavioral colleagues of the virtues of a psychodynamic point of view, and vice versa. In this task I am at times embarrassed by things that are written by representatives of one or the other school. But that embarrassment stems from tactical rather than logical considerations. That is, it stems from a recognition that foolish excesses from either side make it harder to get people from the other side to see or hear what really is useful, and thus they play into an attitude of "See, I told you that stuff is worthless." But these embarrassing impediments to the *practical* task of persuading people on either side of the great divide are not necessarily impediments to the *theoretical* task of devising a new synthesis that incorporates the best of both. I agree with my psychoanalytic colleagues about many of the things they find objectionable in behavior therapy, and vice versa with regard to my behavioral colleagues. My charge as an integrationist is not to defend everything that analysts or behavior therapists say or do, but rather to show

7. I wish to make it clear that I do not endorse the implicit message that behavior therapists deny all complexity and ambiguity. Messer and Winokur's specific way of stating their point here seems to me a bit unfair. But I do agree that there are complexities to which behavior therapists give *insufficient* attention, and my own inclinations are closer to those of Messer and Winokur. With regard to conflict in particular, a more categorical criticism of most behavior therapists does seem in order (cf. Wachtel, 1977b).

that each side contributes *something* useful that the other omits or plays down and to show how these *selected* features can be put together in a logically coherent fashion.

The total package that presently constitutes behavior therapy is indeed incompatible with the total package that is called psychoanalysis. One cannot be a psychoanalyst *and* a behavior therapist—at least not simultaneously. Messer and Winokur have helped to clarify further the nature of the differences. But one can take *elements* of each and combine them into a new synthesis that is still a *third* package, as it were.

The fallacy in most arguments against integration is a failure to appreciate that a synthesis is a different entity than either of its constituents. It is a clinical and theoretical approach with its own structure. It can be selective in what aspects of each approach it incorporates, drawing upon what seems potentially useful in constructing a new synergistic strategy, rather than upon what proponents of each as *separate* therapies regard as most important. The major constraint is that the elements must not be incompatible in the context of the new structure.[8]

Messer and Winokur state that behavior therapists are primarily interested in the external reality of their patients' lives and that psychoanalytic therapists are primarily interested in (conscious and unconscious) subjectivity. Representatives of each school might object to this, pointing to ways in which they do manifest the opposite perspective. But, as a broad characterization of emphasis, it is probably accurate. In the integrative approach discussed here, *both* perspectives are given substantial weight. This occurs not by striving for a balance by doing a little of this, a little of that—a kind of one-perspective–one-vote rule—but through the utilization of a conceptual structure that unites the two perspectives and reconciles their differences. That conceptual structure, for me, has centered on an effort to describe people's difficulties in terms of vicious circles, in which neither impulse nor defense and neither internal state nor external situation is primary; they are continually determining each other in a series of repeated transactions. I have described that

8. What makes the approach described in this chapter an integration rather than a third approach is, first of all, the fact that its elements come primarily from the approaches being integrated rather than being original to it; what is unique is how they are put together. Secondly, this approach, rather than being a new "school," is founded on the conviction that schools have become more limiting than facilitating at this point. Finally, this approach is based upon respect for the earlier approaches rather than opposition to them.

conceptual structure as one of "cyclical psychodynamics" (Wachtel, 1982c, 1985) and have tried to show how it makes possible the reconciliation of what seem like opposing viewpoints (see also Wachtel, 1973b, 1977a, 1977b).

When the sharp dichotomy between "inner" and "outer" is challenged, one can see how even the deepest levels of subjectivity reflect, frequently in a symbolic way, the person's life situation. Thus, one patient began to dream of melting into his girlfriend and of being swallowed by her. Such fears and experiences of merger and boundary dissolution are frequently described by analysts as "deep" or "early" and are attributed to the intrapsychic residue of early experiences with mothering. The experiences the patient reported, however, could also be understood as symbolizing his present way of life: He was very inhibited and unassertive and felt unable to say no to his girlfriend or to spend any evenings alone or with friends if she wanted to see him. As he became more able to do so, he felt less swallowed up by her, and his sense of ego boundaries became firmer. Regardless of the origins of the experience he reported, it was not a purely intrapsychic event but a function as well of manifest events in his daily life.

At the same time, the situations one finds oneself in can often be understood not as thoroughly external events but as products of one's subjective particularities. That is, the events do not simply "happen" to us but are a predictable consequence of our internal state and the behavior it leads to. The stark impassiveness of a dominating husband, for example, both contributes to the wife's fear of assertiveness and stems from it. One woman I worked with was stunned to discover how much of a "pushover" her husband was once she started asserting herself. As she spontaneously put it, "I thought he was the situation I faced, but he was the situation I *made*."

Recently, the social learning formulations that have provided the theoretical background for much of the work in behavior therapy have stressed similar circular causal chains under the rubric of "reciprocal determinism" (Bandura, 1978). This seems to reflect an incorporation of earlier criticisms of social learning theory (Wachtel, 1973) and of earlier formulations of "social behaviorism," which Staats has argued—in a paper with extraordinary claims and an even more extraordinary history—have systematically preceded similar, more frequently cited formulations by Bandura (Staats, 1983).

Messer and Winokur note that "where the behavioral approach, consonant with the comic view, leads to action, the psychoanalytic approach, following the tragic view, leads to reflection and inquiry." For an integrative approach, *both* action and reflection are central.

Messer and Winokur suggest this combination may be difficult to effect because of "the radical shift in perspective and vision involved" (1980). I would agree: It *is* difficult. My own efforts thus far, though encouraging, still remain far from the fully integrated ideal toward which I strive. But the difficulty is not so much the seemingly intractable one of irreconcilable visions as it is a practical one of finding just what is the best way to proceed (a difficult, painstaking task, but one that it is reasonable to expect might yield to continued effort). After all, by Messer and Winokur's own account, psychoanalysis has managed to contain and integrate four rather different visions of reality. As a synthesis of several visions, psychoanalysis is itself evidence that a powerful overarching vision can reconcile polarities among its constituent elements.

The challenge is to achieve a new sustaining vision of sufficient breadth and power. That task has only begun. I am optimistic about the possibilities of a synthesis rooted in the study of vicious circles, of how defensive efforts contribute to the very wishes and feelings they defend against, of how significant people in the present serve as "accomplices" in maintaining neurotic patterns, of how recognition of this can enable a conception of skewing of development to replace earlier notions of fixation and developmental arrest, of how such a perspective permits a transcendence of the dichotomy between an inner world and outer reality, of how conceptions of transference are altered by the application of Piagetian notions of "schema," "assimilation," and "accommodation," and finally, of how all of these conceptual modifications point to a greater variety of ways to intervene in the processes that produce neurotic misery.

The references cited in this chapter point to some of my own efforts in this direction. These efforts have been preceded and paralleled (and greatly aided) by important work on the part of a relative handful of innovative theorists and clinicians (see Goldfried & Padawer [1982] for a good review of this body of work). There are indications now of interest in the possibilities of integration on the part of a larger number of people. This greatly increases the likelihood of significant advances. The challenge will soon have to be faced of how to coordinate and bring together these various efforts. Working between rather than within established traditions is difficult, personally as well as intellectually. A support group that provided workers on the interface with a shared identity would be very useful. Both a journal and an organization could help to give this work a home, to attract young researchers and clinicians to this effort, and to enable a wider audience to become aware of the work and of new developments in it. But there are dangers as well. It would be unfortunate if integrative psychotherapy were to become a new "school," with gradually encrusting borders. Its strength lies precisely in its continued openness to the work of others. Devising the proper organizational framework to represent such a multi-faceted and open-ended effort may be as important a challenge as is the development of the ideas and techniques themselves.[9]

9. Shortly after the completion of this chapter, the Society for the Exploration of Psychotherapy Integration (SEPI) was founded.

7

What Should We Say to Our Patients?: On the Wording of Therapists' Comments

Surprisingly little has been written about just how therapists should word their comments to patients. The assumption seems to be widespread that if the therapist understands his patient sufficiently, and if countertransference factors do not interfere, then the right way of communicating his understanding to the patient will follow more or less automatically. The present chapter takes the position that, as with the timing of interpretations—where technical considerations have been more commonly discussed—there are questions of technique with regard to the selection, focus, and wording of therapists' comments that are important to consider in their own right. In particular, the chapter will examine in some detail the likely impact (perhaps we might say the "average expectable transference") that might be associated with particular ways of phrasing an attempt to convey to the patient something about himself.

THEME AND VARIATIONS IN THE WORDING OF A THERAPIST'S COMMENTS

Interpretations sometimes have the tone or implication of "You're hiding something," and even occasionally of "and that's not a good thing to do." Recently, in a supervisory group I was conducting, a therapist reported a session in which the patient, a painfully shy young woman, sat for a long time in an uncomfortable silence,

Reprinted by permission from *Psychotherapy: Theory, Research and Practice*, 1980, 17(2), 183–188.

occasionally adding that she just didn't have anything to say. Finally, at one point the therapist said to her, "I think you're silent because you're trying to hide a lot of anger." We had been discussing in the group for several weeks the issues addressed in this chapter, and the therapist herself raised the question in the group discussion of whether this had been the best way to make the interpretation. She recalled being unhappy with her comment even at the time, but for a variety of reasons she felt that some comment was called for to break the impasse, could think of no other way to phrase it, and felt that what she had to say was basically accurate (the entire group, including myself, concurred on this latter point).

In the group, a number of alternative ways of conveying the interpretive message to the patient were suggested. Interestingly, the first few that were put forth were not very different in spirit. They all omitted the implicitly accusatory word "hide," but had the same tone to at least some degree. One softened the comment somewhat by substituting for the word "hide" the phrase "keep from yourself." Other suggestions included: "I think you're feeling very angry at me and the boredom is a cover." "Behind your silence is a great deal of anger." "I think you're really very angry." "You're denying how angry you are."

Contrast those versions with the following two: "I have the sense that you're angry but feel you're not supposed to be." "I wonder if you're staying silent because you feel you had better not say anything if what you're feeling is anger." These latter two statements carry a much clearer implication that it's all right to be angry. They emphasize not hiding or denying, but rather the patient's fear, and they carry the message that maybe the fear is unnecessary. Interpretations phrased this way, I would suggest, get across to the patient what is needed with far less damage to his self-esteem, and permit the patient to pick up on them without reacting as defensively.

A version of the same message that is even less threatening would be for the therapist to say: "I find that sometimes when I have nothing to say, after a while I realize it's because I'm angry." Such a statement by the therapist, of course, reduces his anonymity, and thus would be an unlikely one for an approach closely resembling the classical psychoanalytic model. A detailed discussion of when and why one might choose to limit one's concern with anonymity, and of the price that is paid either way, is beyond the scope of this discussion (see Wachtel, 1977). There are, however, several things which are accomplished by such a statement to the patient, which are worth noting here. For one thing, such a comment does not set the therapist apart from the patient, does not implicitly communicate that such experiences are part of being a "patient" and that the therapist has, in effect, only encountered such reactions from textbooks or from watching impaired others. Moreover, in this last version, the therapist is acknowledging not only that he gets angry, but also *that he is sometimes unable to acknowledge it at the time.* Thus, the patient's *defenses* do not set him apart any more than his anger does, and he is more able to examine both without a great loss of self-esteem.

At the same time, such a comment by the therapist conveys to the patient that it is possible to cope with and overcome such conflicts. The therapist presents to the patient a coping model (Bandura, 1969; Meichenbaum, 1977). He has been in the situation and has emerged from it intact and comfortable about discussing it. Moreover, the therapist's describing his reaction as one in which the anger was at first not experienced, but was later recognized as such, enables him to engage the patient's interest even if the patient is not at the moment feeling that he is angry. Even if the patient's immediate experience remains the (presumably) defensive one of simply having nothing to say, he is encouraged not to consider the matter closed, and perhaps to examine with interest and curiosity the marginal thoughts and associations which may well lead him to a clearer sense of both sides of his conflict.

FINDING THE FEELING

In the example just discussed, we considered the situation in which the patient claims not to be experiencing what the therapist infers is operative at some level. At times, especially with obsessional and schizoid patients, one encounters the claim that the patient does not feel *anything at all.* I have found that frequently it is useful to say something like "I think that you have some idea of what you *should* be feeling, and because you're not feeling *that*, you register it as not feeling anything." I then might say (depending on the exact nature of the case—i.e., just what I did think the patient was experiencing) something like "Indifference is a feeling too. It's not that you're not feeling anything. You're feeling indifference. In fact, you're feeling a *great deal* of indifference." This slight recasting of the patient's experience has served on a number of occasions to break an impasse and enable the patient to resume therapeutic work in a fresh way, with a greater sense of self-esteem and of feeling in touch with himself.

Several patients have reported that this emphasis on the fact that they do have some kind of experience enabled them to avoid the discouragement and the battles that occurred in previous therapies, where they felt the therapist was criticizing them for holding back or that he was telling them that they were less than human. (One patient said he felt "like a reptile, cold-blooded and scaly," when his former therapist kept hammering away at how he ran from his feelings. "I didn't know what to do, how to satisfy him. I just kept feeling more and more inadequate, unworthy, inhuman.")

In one instance, a patient reported that his father died, and said he had no feelings. He felt we should talk about his father's death but didn't know how to because he didn't feel anything about it. From clues in the interview and from what I already knew about him, I suggested that it wasn't true that he didn't have feelings about it. He just wasn't feeling *grief* at the moment. Instead he was feeling a sense of relief at his father's being gone and a defiant feeling of "I don't care." The patient broke into a nervous laugh and said, "Yes, that's right! But is that a feeling?" He began to reflect that maybe he wasn't "good," but he was a "real person" after all. A variety of meaningful and affect-laden associations began to occur to him and, interestingly, later in the session he did directly experience feelings of grief and loss. It seems likely to me that had I focused upon his defensive way of warding off feelings (however "accurate" my interpretations), he would have had considerably more difficulty getting in touch with the range of feelings that the death stirred in him.

BUILDING ON VARIATIONS IN THE PATIENT'S FUNCTIONING

Therapy is a process of change. When it is working as it should, any description of the patient is a description of a person in transition. Often, one of the major problems which must be overcome is the patient's tendency to think of himself in static terms, and it is one of the important functions of the therapist to help the patient see himself as changing and/or as able to change (Frank, 1973).

Therapists' comments can facilitate or impede the patient's sense that change is possible. Variant ways of communicating what is largely the same message can either contribute to the patient's feeling of being "stuck" or encourage him to project himself into a variety of alternate futures. For example, a supervisee recently said to a patient who was frequently silent, "You seem to have difficulty talking." The therapist's comment was essentially accurate, but I raised a question about it in the supervisory session. It seemed to me that this way of phrasing it contributed to a self-attribution by the patient of "I am a person who has difficulty talking," and that its static ring could be discouraging.

In contrast, I suggested that it would be more useful in the future to say something like "Sometimes you talk more easily than at other times." Such a way of putting it has the advantage of including a recognition that there are times when the patient *does* talk readily. It conveys that there is something to build on, that not-talking is not some kind of fixed attribute of the patient, which he must simply accept as "what I am like." There are times when he is quite capable of talking, and this too is part of who he is. Further, it encourages the patient (and the therapist) to try to understand *why* he has difficulty talking some times and not others, to examine when (or to whom) he talks readily and when he has difficulty.

In principle, few if any therapists are not interested in such questions. But by thinking of patients as silent patients, or as patients with poor reality testing (rather than as patients whose reality testing is impaired in certain circumstances), or as seductive, or hostile, or unassertive, or masochistic, the therapist can lose track of the variations and the search for what accounts for them. When, in addition, such static characterizations are conveyed to the patient in the phrasing of interpretations, the process of search and change is further impeded.

A different perspective on how building on variations in the patient's functioning can be helpful is provided by the following case. A behavior therapist described to me a case of his in which the patient had great difficulty in being open, direct, or expressive. He wanted to make some kind of interpretive comment about it, but felt, on the basis of his knowledge of the patient, that she would take any comment along these lines as critical, and would get angry and upset and perhaps would leave therapy. He felt quite pessimistic about the case.

I suggested that he address this issue by making use of the variations that existed in this pattern. I recommended that he wait until a point when she was being more open than she usually was, then comment on the fact that she was being so and wonder what enabled her to do so on this occasion. Such a comment addresses the same issue, but does so in a less threatening and challenging way. It enables her to reflect on the question of being more open or closed without pinning the label of "closed" on her or pointing to where she is falling short. It catches her at a point where she is likely to be more receptive. When the therapist shows he is attentive to positive change in her, she may be able to hear what he is saying without becoming as defensive. Such a comment conveys hope. It indicates that she *can* be more open, and makes the examination of when or why she is sometimes (even frequently) uncommunicative one that can be faced with greater courage and confidence. We are usually far better able to face difficult issues at moments when we feel stronger than when we are fearfully hiding. Yet that is often just when the therapist is calling attention to such matters. In the version suggested here, the therapist can address a delicate issue without hitting the patient when she is down.

ACKNOWLEDGING THE PATIENT'S BELIEFS WHILE CHALLENGING THEM

A common impediment to exploration of important issues in the patient's life is the patient's justification of his behavior on the grounds of deeply held values or religious convictions. What complicates such a situation frequently is that the religious belief may in a sense be sincerely held and yet be a rationalization in this particular instance. That is, without a good deal of anxiety or conflict, the patient might well act in specific ways that contradict the tenets of his belief and, importantly, might experience a good deal less distress and conflict than when following the letter of the law.

Particularly in matters of sexual behavior, people to whom church-going and membership in an organized religion are important can nonetheless proceed in certain forbidden behaviors, secure in the knowledge that most of the others in the church behave similarly. When a patient is *not* able to do this, it is frequently a sign of anxiety and conflict at a very different level than that of the explicit ethic the patient avows. Yet at the same time, the therapist's perception of the issue in terms of anxiety and conflict is likely to reflect not only his technical training but his own values and beliefs. The complex ethical and epistemological issues associated with such a situation are beyond the scope of this discussion. What I would like to address here is the technical matter of how, given that the therapist does see the issue as largely one of irrational anxiety, the therapist might address the patient on this matter.

A supervisee reported such a case, in which the patient, a young Hispanic woman, was in considerable conflict with her boyfriend because of her unwillingness to engage in intercourse. Her claim that the reason for this was her religious beliefs seemed to her therapist, for a variety of reasons, to be a rationalization. The therapist, however, did not know how to present this to the patient and felt stymied. She sensed that a head-on confrontation with the patient's avowed beliefs would be unproductive, but could not think of how to say it in a way that had a chance of being heard and considered.

The following comment was suggested: "It sounds like certainly one of the reasons you're reluctant to have intercourse is because you feel sex before marriage is bad; but I have the impression you're also beginning to sense that you have a lot of anxiety about having sex with a man."

This particular way of phrasing it was chosen for a number of reasons. First of all, it acknowledges the patient's belief as a factor in her decision, instead of dismissing it. Thus it refrains from attacking something important to her, and thereby eliciting excessive resistance and counter arguments. It invites the patient to consider the possibility that anxiety is also involved—but in a way that is less threatening. Further, it is worded so as to attribute *to the patient* the idea of anxiety as a factor in her attitude. It gives the *patient* credit for sensing the anxiety, rather than implicitly saying "*You* think you're doing this for religious reasons, but *really* it's because you're afraid." In this respect, this example dovetails with the earlier discussion of not accusing the patient of hiding things.[1]

EMPATHIC AND CONFRONTATIONAL PRESENTATIONS

The next example illustrates the utility of highlighting the patient's *conflict* as a way of presenting the therapist's observation in a less threatening manner. A very argumentative patient was continually chiding his therapist for not going deeply enough, but launched into elaborate intellectual arguments or changed the subject whenever the therapist tried to address aspects of his experiences which were not fully manifest. The therapist, when he addressed this issue, tended to say things like, "You say you want to go more deeply, but when I try to do it with you, you don't want to."

Consider instead the following alternative, "You want to go deeper into your experiences, but it's frightening; so you hesitate and change the subject even though you also want to stay with it." Such a way of putting it highlights the patient's anxiety and conflict rather than simply his resistance. It acknowledges that the patient's desire to go deeper is also real, and it sides with the patient much more than the first version.

---

1. In order for this sort of comment to be effective—and honest—it must be *true* that the patient has, to at least some extent, sensed that anxiety too is involved. But then, it is only in such circumstances that *any* comment along these lines is likely to be useful. And it is certainly possible—I would suggest it is in fact common—for the therapist, even when the patient does sense it, to fail to include this attributional emphasis in his wording of the interpretation.

PERMISSION, REPRIMAND, AND REINFORCEMENT

A central assumption of the above discussion is that—apart from issues of transference and countertransference—the actual structure of the therapist's comment is likely to make a substantial difference. The wording and tone of an interpretation can communicate an encouraging sense that the patient has permission to experience more fully and directly things he has previously avoided as forbidden—or alternatively, a sense of reprimand for being dishonest, unfeeling, or in some way defensive or weak. Much of such meaning is, of course, read into the statement by the patient in idiosyncratic fashion; but recognition of this should not distract us from examining the nature of the comment itself.

Interpretations of defenses, for example, frequently can convey to the patient that he is doing something wrong or falling short of what is expected. This may be especially problematic with obsessional patients, who already labor under severe superego demands and a constant sense of falling short of expected perfectionistic standards. To point out to such a patient that he is hedging, that his meticulous phrasing keeps him out of touch with the affective heart of what he is saying, or that his focus on details serves to distract him from what really is at issue can be to confront him with another failure. Many patients with this defensive style are well aware that they have trouble getting in touch with their feelings; often they experience considerable frustration and lowering of self-esteem in this regard. Interpretations which call attention to this "shortcoming" can be painful and discouraging.

At times, of course, such interpretations are necessary. Deeply entrenched defensive patterns must be dealt with, or they will render the therapeutic process lifeless and ineffective. But recognition of the way in which interpretations tend to function also as rewards and punishments enables one to see some surprising, and useful, parallels between traditional clinical considerations and the perspective provided by research on operant learning. Elsewhere (Wachtel, 1977, Chapter 11) I have discussed how such a perspective sheds light on questions of just when to focus one's interpretations primarily on the defensive aspects of the patient's behavior and when to attend to what is (however haltingly) being expressed and carried forward.

Frank recognition of the way in which therapists' comments convey permission or reproach, and willingness to make use of such effects strategically in the therapy, clash with the emphasis on neutrality that is prevalent in many views on psychotherapy. Many analysts argue, for example, that when the analyst resists the temptation to influence the patient in the desired direction, the patient is enabled to find the authority for his actions within himself, and thus can achieve a measure of autonomy and a depth of change which is otherwise unattainable. Discussion of the reasons for being skeptical that the degree of neutrality posited by analysts is really attainable, or that it is in fact most helpful to the patient, is beyond the scope of this chapter (Wachtel, 1977, 1979).

To be sure, it is very important that the therapist not simply take over for the patient in such a way that he temporarily feels better, but without having achieved the ability to later master things himself. The concern of many analysts that "structural change" be achieved is, in that sense, appropriate and important. But I do not believe that change of this sort is always best accomplished by seeking to minimize the therapist's role as giver of directions, permission, or encouragement. Often it is argued that the therapy should not serve as a "crutch." It should be noted, however, that crutches are not always employed as a permanent supportive device; often crutches are used as a temporary way of enabling a healing process to proceed in such a way that crutches will no longer be necessary. It is in this spirit that I advocate the therapist's bearing more of the burden of change than has been traditional in therapies that seek to promote insight.

The therapist temporarily does some of the things the patient must eventually do for himself in order to help the patient gain sufficient strength to be able to do it well without him. The dependent tie to the therapist is "resolved" not so much through insight into its childhood roots as by the patient's developing effective and gratifying patterns of living (through skillfully structured therapeutic experiences) that make further dependency unnecessary. Dependent ties are then replaced (as they are in all successful therapies) by feelings of warmth and gratitude—ties compatible with freedom and independence.

THE ISSUE OF COUNTERTRANSFERENCE

I have not had much to say in this chapter about countertransference. This is not because it is a topic of little importance, but rather, almost for the opposite reason. Countertransference is a topic of such major importance for understanding (and improving) the therapeutic enterprise that discussion of countertransference tends to be far more common than discussion of the kinds of matters addressed here. If the therapist says something to the patient that does not seem helpful, supervisory sessions are far more likely to focus upon what the therapist was feeling toward the patient than upon any principles of how to put comments to patients. And appropriately so—up to a point. It is essential that the therapist learn to understand how his own reactions play a role in the therapeutic process, and how to be continuously alert to the role of the emotional interplay between the participants. Indeed, *very often* when the therapist cannot think of a facilitative way of presenting an idea to a patient, it is due to the interference of his own conflicted intentions and feelings with regard to the patient far more than to any lack of "knowledge" about how one "should" say things.

But, I would contend, one of the ways in which potentially disruptive effects of countertransference can be modulated is by having a firm sense of the structure of therapeutic statements. As the literature on perceptual defense and need-in-perception has shown (Wolitzky & Wachtel, 1973), a person's emotional state is far more likely to affect his behavior in situations where ambiguity predominates over structure. When the therapist does not have a firmly held sense of how to word what he says to his patients, his comments are far more likely to drift in the direction of the countertransference. It is my hope that attention to the issues addressed in this chapter can provide a rudder which can help keep the work of the therapy on course.

8

Behavior Therapy and the Facilitation of Psychoanalytic Exploration

Limits of time, money, patients' frustration tolerance, etc., frequently lead psychoanalytically oriented therapists to rely considerably on kinds of interventions other than interpretations, which are the preferred therapeutic interventions from the psychoanalytic point of view. It is generally acknowledged in the psychoanalytic literature that such extrainterpretive interventions often provide considerable help to patients, and that for many patients only by altering standard psychoanalytic procedures in this way can useful therapeutic aid be provided. But such divergences from purely interpretive therapy are frequently discussed as a kind of necessary compromise, which, though often of substantial value, nonetheless limit the depth of treatment and cannot produce as extensive and permanent personality change (e.g., Luborsky & Schimek, 1964).

The therapeutic interventions developed by behavior therapists tend to be particularly eschewed by dynamically oriented practitioners. These methods have arisen out of a tradition which not only does not stress exploration of unconscious motives and conflicts, but is in many respects self-consciously *opposed* to the psychodynamic point of view. Not surprisingly, use of behavioral techniques is regarded by many analysts as strongly antithetical to the psychoanalytic method and as seriously interfering with the kind of exploration analysts view as essential to major personality reorganization.

A number of trends in psychodynamic thought, however, seem to suggest that efforts to directly alter certain problematic behavior

Reprinted by permission from *Psychotherapy: Theory, Research and Practice*, 1975, 12(1), 68–72.

need not be antithetical to the fuller development of insight and self-confrontation. Alexander, among others, has suggested that insight might well follow behavioral change, and many of the writings in the interpersonal psychodynamic tradition, following the lead of thinkers such as Horney and Sullivan, also point to the ways in which our actual day-to-day behaviors, and the responses they evoke from others, help to maintain and perpetuate the neurotic conflicts which are evident in character neuroses. Much of the writing in psychoanalytic ego psychology also considers the reciprocal interaction between behavior and its consequences on the one hand and intrapsychic structures on the other.

It will nonetheless be clear to the reader familiar with current writings in the interpersonal and ego-psychological literature that even here explicit or implicit opposition to the use of behavioral methods is the rule. To fully consider all the objections which have been raised would require a rather extensive examination of the history of psychodynamic thought, its necessary and non-necessary assumptions, alternative interpretations of psychoanalytic data, etc. Such an examination is currently being undertaken. The present contribution, however, will limit itself to an illustration of how behavioral intervention might facilitate psychodynamic exploration in a particular case.

ILLUSTRATIVE CASE MATERIAL

The patient to be discussed was not someone in treatment with me, but rather a young man whose case I heard presented at a case conference, and about whom I conferred with his therapist several times for purposes of this chapter. He was a student who lived at school all week and returned home to his mother on weekends. The time he spent at school was fraught with anxiety. He was extremely isolated, avoiding contact as much as possible because of the considerable anxiety he felt whenever he was with another person, whether the janitor, his classmates, his teachers, or anyone else he might encounter. He went right from class to his room, ate alone, and would walk considerably out of his way to avoid seeing anyone he might have to say hello to.

Being home with mother on the weekends, while not particularly joyful either, was nonetheless rather a reprieve for him. He was relatively free from anxiety at home, and relaxed most of the day, often in front of the TV set. His relationship with his mother was described as involving seductive behavior on her part, but rejection when he got too close.

Much of the therapist's efforts were directed toward elucidating the patient's strong erotic and symbiotic ties to his mother. It was expected that resolution of his core conflicts regarding parental figures

would be a central means of creating the change necessary for improvement in the other relationships in his life and a reduction of his intense
anxiety at school. The patient's strong and conflicted tie to his mother
was viewed primarily as an independent variable, changes in which
would lead to changes in the other troubling aspects of his life.

While I would agree that this patient's particular ties and conflicts with his mother were probably *historically* primary (i.e., earlier),
the relationship he had with his mother at the time he began therapy
may be seen as a *product* of how he was living his life away from her as
much as a *cause*. The cumulative effect of his developmental history
found him at a point where, for all the conflict he experienced
regarding her, his mother was by then the only person he could
relate to with even a modicum of gratification and freedom from
anxiety. Because of this, attempts to clarify the irrational and inappropriate aspects of the patient's relationship to his mother might be
expected to be made difficult by her current *real* importance. Like a
child, he was turning to mother for safety from a world both bewildering and frightening. His anxiety when he was away at school
(whatever the original reasons for it) prevented him from forming
any alternative ties which could serve as a base for leaving mother in
any sense. For this reason it seemed to me that unless early direct
efforts were made to reduce his daily burden of anxiety, and facilitate interaction with others at school, exploration of the patient's
feelings toward his mother was likely to be limited.

The Therapy Relationship and the Problem of
Intense Demands

To some extent one might expect that his dilemma could be mit-
igated, without the introduction of behavioral methods, by the development of a strong relationship with the therapist. By providing the
patient with an *alternative* to the mother as an important object, the
therapist could help make the relationship with the mother less
urgent, and thereby make it more possible for the patient to experience "forbidden" feelings toward her which he didn't dare experience when she was all he had.

Additionally, in this new relationship with the therapist, feelings
similar to those experienced toward the mother might be expected to
arise, but this time in an atmosphere in which their exploration and
fuller understanding could occur. By responding differently to the
patient's expression of feelings than the parents originally did, and
by aiding the patient to recognize the differences between his helpless position as a child and his present situation of *self*-created depen-

dency, the therapist could create conditions in which the patient could establish new and more growth-facilitating patterns.

These latter considerations tend to buttress the traditional strategy of focusing on the development of the patient–therapist relationship and regarding improvement in his day-to-day behavior as a more distal consequence of the therapeutic interaction. But if the alleviation of the misery and emptiness in the daily life of a man such as this is viewed as an ultimate outcome rather than a more immediate and direct goal, the therapeutic relationship itself may not develop in an optimally useful way; for to the degree that the patient's needs go unmet in his daily living, his demands on the therapist are likely to be more intense, and extremely intense demandingness by the patient poses a number of problems for the therapist.

Now, of course, intense demands by patients are not unfamiliar to analytic therapists. At the height of the transference neurosis in a classical analysis, the demands made by the patient are often remarkably intense and primitive. In the face of such demands, the therapist must be very skillful to avoid either confirming infantile and neurotic patterns or being rejecting in response to them. Wolf (1966) has described vividly how therapists may at times intensify the patient's difficulties by responding in ways evoked by the patient's neurotic behavior. It is in large measure to prevent such an occurrence that the guidelines have developed which limit contact with patients outside of therapy hours and also place limits on full mutuality within the sessions. The technical guidelines help the therapist to be able to *interpret* instead of *acting* on the patient's demands. But it has been increasingly recognized that the stance of emotional neutrality which the analyst takes can be experienced by the patient as cold and rejecting, and if not tempered by sufficient indications of warmth and interest may limit the patient's ability to usefully participate in a process of therapeutic change (Greenson, 1967; Stone, 1961).

When the patient's neurotic demands are especially intense and persistent, it is difficult to maintain a useful balance of neutrality and empathic engagement. To avoid falling into countertransference traps, the therapist may have to distance himself more than usual from the patient, with the danger of aloofness and lessened responsiveness to the patient's emotional communications. Such distancing is also problematic by virtue of being even more *different* from ordinary social intercourse, and hence exacerbating the always troubling issue of whether whatever change does occur in the therapy sessions will generalize to the patient's life situation.

> Problems deriving from intense demands did arise in the case under discussion. For the first few months of therapy, the therapist was pleased with the progress being made. In the early spring, the patient

took a leave from school and felt somewhat better, seeing some old friends occasionally and experiencing less of the overwhelming anxiety he had felt when at school. But he still was never really relaxed with others and couldn't maintain a conversation. The main improvement evident was in his relationship with the therapist, where greater trust was clearly evident. The therapy continued to focus largely on the transference relationship.

After the therapist's vacation, the treatment began to unravel. Rather early in treatment the patient had become very attached to his therapist, and had revealed wishes to live with him, follow him around and learn from him, etc. These had been within manageable bounds, however, and seemed to the therapist to provide fruitful areas for exploration. After the vacation these desires and fantasies became so intense that they were disruptive. The patient would plead with the therapist to "take me home and teach me how to live." He would tell the therapist that he was the only nice person in the world, literally the only one worth being with, and would combine this with strong complaints that the therapist wasn't helping enough, wasn't giving enough. The therapist began to feel flooded by the patient's demands, and frustrated by the patient's *complete unwillingness to reflect upon what he was expressing.*

The patient's behavior became increasingly bizarre. He exhibited strange obsessions and depersonalized experiences, frequently checking and feeling himself to see if he was still there. His fantasies of incorporating the therapist became more overt and literal and more destructive. He made biting grimaces in the sessions and said he wanted to eat the therapist's head, swallow him up, etc. All the while he would continue to demand that he be taken into the therapist's home and be with him all day, and to bitterly complain that the therapist was holding out on him by not doing so. Eventually, the patient left the therapist and checked himself into a psychiatric day hospital.

Considering Behavioral Interventions

Such an unsuccessful course of therapy can be understood in many ways. Questions about the therapist's countertransference reaction to the patient's demands are appropriate, as are considerations of the most skillful and effective way to handle the situation within a traditional mode of therapeutic interaction. But the considerations advanced earlier suggest it may also be fruitful to ask whether an exploratory mode of therapy was impeded by the degree of anxiety and inhibition which were manifest in the patient's everyday life, and whether efforts to directly intervene in his day-to-day problems might have increased his freedom to explore and reflect upon those inclinations which he had been finding too frightening to face. One might anticipate a number of positive synergistic cycles following upon assistance in interacting more comfortably with the people he saw during the day: (1) The more success with people, the less anxiety, the more further success, etc. (2) The better his relationship to others, the less desperate and irrational the ties to mother and to therapist, the better his relationships to others, etc. (3) The less pressured the ties to mother and to therapist, the greater the possibility of *exploring* feelings regarding them, the greater the freeing from those ties, etc.

One approach to intervention might be to attempt to reduce his extremely intense anxiety about being with people via systematic desensitization. In considering how one might go about constructing a hierarchy for desensitization with such a man, it is interesting to note that the layering of inclinations, fears, and avoidances which is familar to the analytic therapist may be perceived in this context as well. Early in the therapy, while he was still in school, the patient first indicated his anxiety whenever he saw others in the hall. It intensified as the other person approached, especially if it were someone the patient knew, who might attempt to engage him in a conversation. The patient would try to avoid such an encounter, because he was even more afraid that a conversation might start and that he wouldn't be able to think of anything to say. He imagined himself standing there feeling awkward and immobilized, yet unable to either leave or talk, and he felt very anxious at the thought that he would then seem very odd to the other person. Further probing by the therapist revealed that the patient would be silent in such situations because he was afraid he would have to tell the other person he was "full of shit," that they were just making small talk, and he didn't believe the other person was really interested in him.

Several alternatives for desensitization seem possible here. On the one hand, one might proceed via scenes of increasing approach of the other person, or greater familiarity with the person approaching, increasing the likelihood he would stop and talk and the anticipated embarrassment at appearing foolish. Images of standing there with nothing to say would be very high on the hierarchy. On the other hand, one might proceed in the manner of Feather and Rhoads (1972), emphasizing conflict over aggressively accusing the other person, and encouraging the person to combine muscular relaxation with imagery of acting out his most frightening fantasies.

An additional aid in helping the patient to reduce the social anxieties which plagued him might be provided by role playing or behavior rehearsal. Providing the patient with opportunities for modeling and practice in conducting small talk would enable him to develop skills which his life history had inhibited his acquiring. It would also enable his early trial-and-error efforts to occur with the *therapist*, where there would be far less damaging consequences, and an opportunity to "take it from the top" when something seemed to go wrong. In everyday social intercourse, such awkwardness would not be as likely to meet with a sympathetic response, and he could readily have his anxieties confirmed and intensified instead of diminished. It is likely that a good deal of undermining and failure in psychotherapy is due to the retraumatizing effect of trying out new behavior patterns with others before they have been developed to the point where they are likely to lead to a rewarding interaction.

ANTITHESIS OR COMPLEMENT?

Such efforts to directly assist in the change of specific troubling life patterns are typically viewed as an *alternative* to the exploratory and interpretive methods of psychodynamic therapists. It is held by many analytic therapists that such methods are manipulative and that they necessarily limit the possibilities of exploration and of resolution of underlying core conflicts. On the other hand, much of the behavior therapy literature argues for the *exclusive* use of such direct change methods and sees the events of the psychoanalytic interview as merely prescientific mumbo-jumbo, or at best inadvertent and inefficient behavior therapy.

It is recognized by most clinicians, regardless of theoretical orientation, that anxiety is strongly implicated in a wide range of maladaptive behavior patterns, and that avoidances, including alterations of attentional focus, can readily obscure the source of anxiety and prevent opportunities for its extinction. The interpretation of defenses in analytically oriented therapies is designed to reveal those avoidances and help the patient attend to the real source of his anxieties. To the extent that anxiety gradients persist and remain undetected, they can continue to motivate avoidances and restrict the range of possible adaptive behaviors. In such circumstances, recurrences or new instances of neurotic behavior are likely. Reports by behavior therapists that their direct interventions into specific maladaptive behavior patterns do not frequently lead to symptom substitution or recurrence of the troubling behavior suggest that a larger range of maladaptive behavior may be independent of underlying unconscious conflict than was originally assumed by psychodynamic theorists. Apparently, the opportunity to experience new contingencies in one's day-to-day life is often sufficient to maintain new patterns, regardless of the origins of the patient's problems. The question of whether such gain is at the expense of subtle and undetected negative characterological change, or of intensification of childlike fantasies of protection by powerful authorities, is an important one which cannot be considered in this brief presentation. The observations of behavior therapists thus far have suggested that there are *positive* changes in other aspects of the patient's daily living. Whether more subtle probing will reveal opposite tendencies remains to be seen.

But even strong proponents of exclusively behavioral approaches to therapy have acknowledged that the success of such efforts is considerably greater with a limited range of isolated phobias or the fears of volunteer college students than with the more pervasive and intense difficulties of most psychiatric patients (e.g., Eysenck & Beech, 1971). And Lazarus's (1971) recent reports regarding relapse in behavior therapy patients suggest that behavior therapists have tended in the past to underestimate the importance of underlying characterological features in the generation and perpetuation of neurotic patterns.

Much further investigation is needed to determine how readily psychodynamic inquiry into hidden aspects of patients' adaptational dilemmas can be combined with direct efforts to relieve specific troubling behaviors and how much each approach can enhance the effectiveness of the other. The case discussed here is one that analysts would be unlikely to regard as a "good analytic case," and thus the question is also raised as to whether, even if helpful with cases such as these, behavioral methods would also facilitate work with the kind of patients now in classical analysis. Psychoanalytic writers have stressed the ways in which direct intervention can limit the scope and depth of exploration. But as illustrated above, there are barriers to exploration stemming from *not* intervening as well. The development by behavior therapists in the past decade of useful specific interventions requires a rethinking of the rationale for the traditional psychodynamic stress on nonintervention in light of the countervailing considerations which have been discussed.

9

What Can Dynamic Therapies Contribute to Behavior Therapy?

The topic of this chapter is a more difficult one to address now than it would have been 10 or 15 years ago. The boundaries between approaches have blurred as behavior therapists have broadened both the range of patients and problems seen and the range of techniques and concepts employed (e.g., Goldfried & Davison, 1976; Lazarus, 1976; Mahoney, 1974, 1980; Meichenbaum, 1977). Thus, some of what used to be the exclusive province of more traditional therapists is now securely within behavior therapy, and demonstrating a unique and additional contribution that ought still to be called psychodynamic is more difficult. Nonetheless, I think it can be shown that there are still many features of the psychodynamic approach that are clinically valuable and that have not yet been incorporated into the work of even the most open-minded and sophisticated group of behavior therapists. Moreover, the aforementioned blurring of boundaries can aid, as well as hinder, the line of argument presented here, for it helps in countering the contention that psychodynamic and behavioral approaches are so fundamentally incompatible that no integration effort can be successful.

MISCONCEPTIONS ABOUT PSYCHOANALYSIS

Part of the skepticism shown by behavior therapists toward ideas of integration of approaches is due to a misunderstanding of what the essential features of the psychoanalytic approach really are. Changes that have occurred through the years have modified some of the

Reprinted by permission from *Behavior Therapy*, 1982, *13*, 594–609. Copyright © 1982 by the Association for Advancement of Behavior Therapy.

characteristics behavior therapists are likely to be most troubled by, and have made the possibilities for integration considerably more interesting. Psychoanalysis is no longer deep in the heart of cathexis.

Ego Psychology and Environmental Influences

For some time, psychoanalytic formulations tended to focus one-sidedly on the structure and dynamics of internal states, virtually to the exclusion of environmental influences upon behavior. Perhaps because Freud's earliest formulations—those regarding specific infantile traumas—were concerned with the consequences of real events, and because to his embarrassment they had to be retracted, he seemed for many years to show strong avoidances when it came to considering the role of the environment (cf. Rapaport, 1959). But beginning in the 1920s, this imbalance began to be corrected, and classic works by Hartmann (1939/1958) and Erikson (1950) gave a powerful impetus to psychoanalytic efforts to address the much-neglected role of the perception of environmental events in the generation and maintenance of troubling patterns of behavior. To be sure, even today most analysts are insufficiently aware of the environmental contingencies that help shape their patients' behavior, but the basic structure of the theory is now one which in principle can readily incorporate and direct attention to such contingencies.

Decline of the Energy Model

One of the weak points in psychoanalytic theorizing, leading to reifications and circular reasoning, and giving the entire enterprise a somewhat archaic air, has been the propositions about psychic energy. The effort to build a model of the mind out of concepts better suited to hydraulic engineering—libido being dammed up, diverted, threatening to break through, etc.—was for many years a central feature of psychoanalytic formulations. In recent years, however, a number of critics from within the psychoanalytic movement have recognized clearly the shortcomings of such an approach and have demonstrated that it is in no way essential to the psychoanalytic enterprise (e.g., Gill, 1976; Holt, 1967, 1976; Klein, 1970, 1976; Schafer, 1976). Among Freudians, this critical point of view may still be a minority one, but it is a rapidly developing trend, and the authors just cited are among the most respected of modern Freudians. Among non-Freudian psychodynamic thinkers, this rejection of the energy model is very much the modal view.

Psychoanalysis and Action Language

Schafer (1976) has been critical not only of the energy notions in particular, but of much else in the way psychoanalytic ideas are formulated. A distinguished psychoanalyst, Schafer remains committed to the basic ideas and observations on which psychoanalysis is based, but he has attempted to recast them in a way that is clearer and avoids reification. In particular, he has proposed an "action language" in which nouns and adjectives are replaced by verbs and adverbs. Thus, instead of referring to egos, ids, impulses, or barriers, Schafer refers in a rich variety of ways to the actions of persons. He shows in great detail how psychoanalytic accounts can be cast into this less reified discourse.

In such an emphasis, the formulations of psychoanalysis are seen to be about *behaviors*, about what the person is doing, not about hypothetical entities and energies. That some of these behaviors are neither overt nor acknowledged by the person engaging in them, and that some of them are pinpointed by a process of inference rather different from that engaged in by most behavior therapists, are certainly important to note. But behavioral theories, too, have included nonobservable hypothetical constructs, and Schafer's pruning of obscure language, along with his demonstration that, ultimately, psychoanalysis is not about egos and ids or energies and dams but about behaviors, is one more indication that the building of bridges between approaches is not as impossible as it has been believed by many on either side of the ideological chasm.[1]

Varieties of Psychodynamic Theories

Finally, it is important to recognize that the psychodynamic point of view is not monolithic. There are a number of different ways of conceptualizing the basic observations on which Freud's theory was founded and the subsequent observations from which psychoanalytic thought has evolved. All psychodynamic theories emphasize unconscious motivation, motivational conflict, and varieties of motivated forgetting, inattention, or cognitive distortion. But in other respects—and even in how these particular phenomena are addressed—they differ substantially.

1. It should be noted clearly that Schafer himself has not offered his recasting of psychoanalytic propositions with an eye toward a reconciliation with behavioral theories. The implications I draw from his work are not the same as his.

Perhaps the best-known area of controversy regards Freud's instinct theory, which is by no means accepted by all psychodynamic thinkers. But for present purposes, another line of cleavage is even more important: In Freudian theory, the seemingly infantile ideas and wishes that become apparent in the course of an analysis are understood to have remained infantile because they have become impervious to influence by environmental input. This model of development—really of nondevelopment—is the most serious substantive obstacle to the reconciliation of psychoanalytic and behavioral points of view.

But an alternative psychodynamic understanding of the same set of observations (Wachtel, 1977b) has very different implications. In its description of how past experiences have shaped present personality, the classical Freudian emphasis on fixation and developmental arrest is replaced by an account stressing the cumulative skewing of experiences through the course of development (Wachtel, 1977a). These experiences lead to patterns which, whatever their origins in the person's history, are maintained in the present by their present consequences.[2] This account is compatible in many ways with contemporary cognitive perspectives in behavior therapy and is fully consonant with a strategy of using present-centered, active-intervention methods. It helps to reconcile psychoanalytic observations regarding continuities between past and present behavior and behavioral research demonstrating the responsiveness of behavior to variations in present contingencies (cf. Mischel, 1968; Wachtel, 1973a, 1973b).

THE CLINICAL CONTRIBUTION OF THE PSYCHODYNAMIC PERSPECTIVE

I have argued that the view that a psychodynamic perspective is fundamentally incompatible with behavior therapy is based on a number of misunderstandings. This is not to say that there are no differences between dynamic and behavioral approaches as they are currently practiced. Indeed, there would be no point in attempting an integration if they overlapped completely. Each approach has included features which can contribute to the clinical repertoire of practitioners from the other orientation.

2. Those consequences, it is important to note, must be understood not as "objectively" given, but as they are given meaning by the person's intentions, assumptions, and perceptual biases.

I will begin my illustration of this with a common feature of behavioral therapies, the use of praise as a reinforcer for client behavior that is consistent with the goals of the therapy. Such a use of praise is consistent both with learning theory and with everyday common sense. And frequently, it is helpful and effective. But it is precisely in the reliance on the culture's common sense that the potential limits of present behavioral approaches—and the potential contribution of the psychodynamic perspective—begin to be evident.

Behavior therapy is based on theories that are essentially content-free, theories concerned with basic processes, with *how* but not particularly with *what* is learned or thought or found reinforcing. Consequently, since these theories do not guide them in this respect, behavior therapists have tended to base their content assumptions on general cultural assumptions. That praise is a positively experienced event is just such an assumption.

Psychoanalysts, on the other hand, have been very much concerned with content questions. Moreover, in assuming that the effective reinforcers in people's lives are often other than what they report or consciously assume,[3] psychoanalysts open to study a wide variety of unusual and non-normative motives. The complexity and diversity of human motivations has been much more a subject of study for dynamic than for behavioral therapists.

Praise, to the dynamically oriented clinician, can mean any number of things, from the simple positive experience that the culture generally assumes it to be, to a demand for still more, to a subtle trick or manipulation, to a covert accusation that the person has tried to outdo his betters. In principle, this can be discerned by the behavior therapist too. The behavior therapist is committed to an empirical orientation which investigates the individualized variables relevant in any particular case. If such are the meanings of praise, the behavior therapist might well say, let them be demonstrated; let observations, not theory, be the key. But in practice, I submit, this is not the case. Both my reading of behavioral journals and my observations of behavior therapists in action suggest that behavior therapists rely very largely on culturally normative assumptions about what people want. Behavior therapists do have a means of investigating whether praise might have a different meaning, but they are unlikely to assume that such an investigation is worth undertaking. The number of potential lines of investigation in any case is almost infinite, and one must have some guidelines for what to assume and what to question actively. When one is operating from a theoretical

---

3. I am obviously translating here into other than the original terms.

orientation concerned rather exclusively with process, the content assumptions tend to come from the culture at large.

Now many psychoanalysts do tend to play fast and loose with their inferences, and the behavioral clinician may view many of the content assumptions of the psychoanalyst as, to put it kindly, rather creative. How do we know that praise is experienced as a demand by a particular client? The very large question of the nature of clinical inference in dynamic and behavioral therapies cannot be addressed here, but two points are worth making. First, in deciding on the proper level or degree of inference to be made, the clinician faces a problem comparable to that of dealing with Type I and Type II errors in statistical inference. In the clinical instance as in the statistical, too great an effort to guard against one kind of error automatically increases the risk of the other. As compared to dynamic therapists, behavior therapists have been far more concerned with avoiding the clinical equivalent of Type I errors (that is, not with incorrectly rejecting a null hypothesis per se, but with avoiding drawing incorrect inferences about meanings or causal connections).[4] Consequently, the likelihood of "Type II" errors—of falsely accepting the null hypothesis, as it were, by failing to draw *sufficient* inferences—has been very high.

Secondly, it is important to recognize that the relation between "modern learning theory" or "experimentally verified principles" and actual clinical practice is not as clear as is sometimes suggested (cf. Breger & McGaugh, 1965). Indeed, it may be said that the relation between the practice of behavior therapy and the laws of learning is much like the relation between behavior therapy and the laws of physics: Behavior therapists' work is consistent with both—behavior therapists cannot defy gravity nor can they abrogate laws of extinction or generalization; but they could no more conduct therapy just knowing the laws of learning than they could just knowing that $F = ma$. For his or her actual clinical decisions, the behavior therapist inevitably brings to bear a host of other assumptions about meanings, intentions, and subjective experience.

When one is working from common cultural assumptions, praise is frequently not just viewed as invariably positive, it is also frequently administered in the spirit of the more (and the more intense)

---

4. It is important to note that "meanings" have taken on increased importance for more cognitively oriented behavior therapists (see, for example, Kendall, 1982). But the description here and below of the psychodynamic approach to meaning should make it clear that there are still substantial differences both with regard to how inferences are made and how much they rely on culturally normative assumptions.

the better. Behavior therapists, in my experience, are often too effusive in their praise. When every little step by the client is met with "beautiful" (or "BEAUTIFUL!"), praise itself begins to lose its value and/or the therapist can begin to be experienced as insincere. Moreover, if the therapist's criteria for praise are not reasonably close to the client's, praise can be noxious. To be told you have done something worthwhile when you regard it as a meager step can lead to feeling that the therapist is insulting or doesn't understand you. It is still possible to reinforce with praise in such circumstances, but only if the person's own subjective standards are grasped and acknowledged with statements of the sort: "This doesn't seem like much to you, but I think it was a valuable and worthwhile step." Such a comment is more likely to be heard or accepted, since it does not fly in the face of the person's experience.

Sometimes therapeutic work is aided by a consideration of meanings of praise differing still further from the simple positive meaning that is prescribed by everyday common sense—say, as a demand, as a manipulation, or (still more exotically and occasionally) as an indication that the therapist cannot bear to face how bad or damaged the client is. Such meanings are, to be sure, harder both to verify and to guess at in the first place. Behavior therapists are generally unpracticed in generating or evaluating such sorts of inferences; they have been trained to work on more familiar ground.

GENERATION AND EVALUATION OF INFERENCES

How then, might one come up with such hypotheses about idiosyncratic meanings, and how might they be brought under some reasonable constraints of evidence? To begin with, one needs to supplement the linear logic of independent and dependent variables with a concern for patterns and consistencies. Second, one must entertain the notion that events frequently have meanings to individuals which differ both from the familiar meanings that are culturally prescribed and sanctioned and from what the person himself can report. Then one must look for coherences in the person's early life and present behavior that suggest speculations about why the client has not responded to more straightforward interventions in the expected way.

In seeking coherence, one assumes that perceptions have been shaped or biased by early experiences. The person whose father is discovered to be a harsh taskmaster may be more likely, for example, to hear subtle demands in your praise than one who has been indulged (who may be more likely to feel you are being "nice" but not "realistic"). Such assumptions on the therapist's part are not held to steadfastly, but are employed tentatively, as a heuristic which may be retained or not in a given instance, depending on what one finds.

One looks as well at how the person seems to act and construct meanings in relation to the therapist. I refer, of course, to the concept analysts term "transference." The notion of transference is much akin to that of generalization. For those of a more cognitive persuasion, a recent examination of the concept has suggested it can best be understood in terms of the Piagetian notion of schemas, in this case as pointing to schemas where assimilation predominates over accommodation (Wachtel, 1981). New perceptual input is interpreted in terms of existing cognitive structures and when—as in the (crucial) realm of feelings and of interpersonal attitudes and intentions—there is considerable ambiguity, those structures can perpetuate error for a long time.

As an instance of how one detects such structures and brings together one's understanding of the client's past and present, consider the following clinical vignette: The client was a doctoral student in chemistry who had delayed for several years completing his dissertation. A brilliant student, he had been working for some time as a lab technician and was afraid that his inhibitions would lead to this ending up as his career. Moreover, even in this role, he assumed a considerably more menial stance than was required. In his social relations, too, he was inhibited and unassertive. Though nice-looking and capable of being rather charming, he had difficulty maintaining relationships with women and experienced considerable anxiety and inhibition in sex.

His difficulties were initially addressed largely within the paradigm of assertiveness problems, but progress was not impressive. As the work proceeded, it became clear that in many ways his parents had covertly communicated the message that only bad people get ahead in this world and that if he wished to be a good person, and to retain their support, he had better keep himself in check. In a recurring dream, he and his whole family had their noses pressed against the window of a bakery, panting with hunger as marvelous aromas wafted out to where they were so pitifully stationed. His first association to this Dickensian image was "Well, at least we're together," and indeed that turned out to be a crucial conflict for him—whether to succeed, to make it inside, and lose the sense of solidarity and goodness, or to stay on the outside, starve, and remain loyal. The conflict was further complicated (as conflicts tend to be) by the fact that in living life as an outsider, a loser—and, he vaguely sensed, a self-imposed loser—he continually had to struggle with the anger generated by such a state of affairs. This anger and resentment felt like proof he really was bad, and so he had to try even harder to counter it by failing—failure being the family currency—thereby again intensifying both his frustration and his resentment and keeping himself in a continuing bind.

As this pattern was clarified, and he began to understand better why he was sometimes moved to sabotage efforts to do better, assertiveness training began to be more effective. We noticed that the times he got into trouble tended to be shortly after having done particularly well, and he began to be able to immunize himself against these lapses by being alert to them and reminding himself of the cost—and the ultimate futility—of seeking to be good in the terms of the familial model.

On one occasion—the particular illustration I want to concentrate on here—he came in complaining about his girlfriend's behavior with him in bed. He was talking about what *she* did wrong, but I began to surmise—partly cued by the kinds of things just described—that an important piece of his report of this experience was the implicit message "See, I was doing well and I got my comeuppance." I didn't say anything about it at that point but shortly thereafter, I noticed that while he was talking, he was rubbing the stainless steel arm of the chair over and over, wiping out the smudges that sweat and fingerprints can make on such a surface. I said to him, "I think maybe you are afraid you were being offensive with Sara, and that she acted as she did because of that." He recognized at once (though it had not occurred to him before) that that indeed was what was eating him, and there followed a careful examination of what had actually ensued, which led to a strengthened conviction on his part that his strength and sexuality really were okay. He reported in the next session that they had had particularly gratifying sex the next night, and that, encouraged by this, he discussed with her the events of the previous night; they both realized that she had been turned off not by his strong sexuality but the opposite—by his pulling back, which he did because, without realizing it, he had become frightened of how potent and masculine he was feeling.

My hunch that he had felt "offensive" in bed with Sara was not simply an ineffable intuition, nor, I would insist, was it just a wild-eyed piece of psychoanalytic mythologizing. It was an hypothesis based on a considerable amount of data—what I knew about his past and the proscriptions that surrounded really succeeding; our mutual identification of numerous instances in the present when he got particularly anxious after doing well; my observation that he was suddenly concerned he had dirtied my chair; my knowledge that he had feelings about sex and the body being smelly and dirty (the reason, together with the chair observation, that I said "offensive" instead of "too powerful" or "too successful" as I might have in a slightly different context).

When the therapist begins to orient the therapy around meanings or experiences that depart from the manifest and from the culture's common-sense notions, or that vary from the client's report of his conscious experience, it is essential to be cautious; one must keep clearly in mind the difference between a tentative hypothesis and a proven fact. But such hypotheses are not mere flights of fancy; they can derive instead from the very effort to take seriously the clinical data. And in many instances, willingness to consider such kinds of hypotheses—and to learn how to generate them—can substantially facilitate one's clinical work.

NORMATIVE AND NON-NORMATIVE ASSUMPTIONS

Clearly, as the above illustration shows, it is not just in understanding praise—our initial starting point—that it is useful to go beyond the culturally normative assumptions that tend to guide behavioral work. The psychodynamic viewpoint can be useful to the behavior therapist with regard to a wide range of non-normative motives and ideas, particularly those which the client cannot readily report. Ironically, part of what enables the therapist employing a psychodynamic perspective to be effective in this regard is a greater attention to the person's actual behavior at certain crucial points. Behavior therapists, in their distaste for the way some analysts have abused the notion of unconscious motivation, frequently bend over backward to avoid such notions and thereby accept at face value their clients' reports of their intentions and reasons. In so doing, they end up employing a naive introspectionism which is quite at odds with their other philosophical commitments.[5]

Analysts' inferences about unconscious motivations or cognitive processes are based in large measure on careful attention to regularities in the client's behavior, along with the question, "What would he or she have to want or think in order to behave that way so frequently?" Whether it be observations of rubbing on a chair, of the occasions when the client talks self-deprecatingly or acts in a self-defeating way, or of such behaviors—and they of course *are* behav-

5. This is less true of those in the Skinnerian wing of the behavior therapy movement, but they pay a price for their consistency in "Type II" errors.

iors—as slips of the tongue, it is in their linking of inferences to observations of behavior that dynamic therapists best exemplify their paradigm.

In the therapy session itself, concern with non-normative and unreportable motives can aid the behavior therapist in providing effective reinforcement for desirable behaviors. Not only may praise have idiosyncratic meanings for the client, but so too can such things as the therapist's tone of voice, silence, questions, or way of phrasing comments. For one client, gentle, carefully measured statements may be reinforcing; for another the same kind of therapist behavior may be aversive (a sign the client must be treated with kid gloves; a sign the therapist is not clear about what should be done, etc.). Moreover, some therapist behaviors may interact with others in determining the reinforcing properties of particular acts. For some clients, if the therapist is willing to make frequent appointment changes, it shows he or she "cares" or is "sincere," and praise from the therapist then can serve as a positive reinforcer. For others, such behavior shows you are "weak" and "manipulable," and thus words of praise from you count for little; had you instead shown you were "tough" and "savvy" by not agreeing to the appointment change, *then* your praise would be worthwhile.

It is of course not possible to keep track of *all* possible meanings and implications of the myriad choices of strategy, of tone, or of style that the therapist (wittingly and unwittingly) displays. But greater attention to the complexities of motivation, and greater skepticism toward the normative assumptions which usually characterize the client's account of his aims and difficulties, are frequently useful.

The same perspective is useful as well in attempting to understand the relevant contingencies *outside* the therapy sessions that help determine the client's difficulties. Here too, sometimes the socially expectable relationships are evident—they would not, after all, have *become* socially expectable if they did not have some fairly regular influence—but frequently, a rather different set of relationships can be found to be relevant if the therapist is set to notice them.

On several occasions, for example, student therapists whom I was supervising presented cases of undergraduates with difficulty studying or completing papers or other assignments on time. The basic (and reasonable) assumption of both client and therapist was that the client wanted to succeed and was being hampered by excessive anxiety and/or poor planning, study habits, etc. The therapists in these cases tried a number of straightforward interventions—e.g., desensitization; contingency contracting for doing a certain amount of studying or writing; teaching the clients to attempt to do a reasonable amount of work and then stop instead of demanding an awesome, open-ended amount of work and then quickly retreating from this impossible task; and so forth. These measures, it is important to make clear, had been successful for these therapists with other clients. But in some cases these, and similar straightforward interventions, did not work. Either the clients would try them but report little progress, or would seem in a variety of ways to misunderstand, to forget, or otherwise to undermine the therapeutic effort.

In the supervision, I raised with the therapists the possibility of conflicting (and unconscious) motivations which interfered with the clients' ability to engage in the therapy wholeheartedly—anger at parents that made them not want to give them the satisfaction of having a successful son or daughter; a desire to outshine the parents which felt forbidden and required efforts to undo any success; a fear that success would evoke hostility from others or untoward demands; etc. I stressed that these were tentative hypotheses to be explored with the clients and/or raised in the context of an observation that might be suggestive.

One therapist began to see his client differently after noting an "oddly glowing" expression on his client's face when reporting how disappointed his father would be if he failed. Another pointed out to a client that she seemed frequently to refer "in passing" to news stories of people who were successful and met tragic fates, and elicited thereby the client's recollection of a dream in which the client was growing bigger and bigger and a buzz saw was suspended from the ceiling, in position to decapitate her if she got any bigger, and then of another dream in which she was going broke because she constantly had to buy new pants as she grew. Her surprised and spontaneous association was "Oh my God, I guess I'm afraid of getting too big for my breeches."

As this latter client began to realize that she was avoiding completing assignments or studying hard because she was afraid of the consequences of doing too well, she began to explore the powerful but unstated assumptions in her family and her role in the family constellation, as well as to question from a fresh, rational viewpoint the implicit assumptions that had guided her behavior. The therapist then introduced desensitization around a hierarchy of images of success and envy from others.

In the first case (the "odd glow"), the client became more aware of his use of failure at school to get back at his father. Some effort was made to help him identify what irritated him about his father, and assertiveness training was introduced with regard to some of these issues. He was also aided to find other ways of expressing the

residual anger he felt that did not have such serious negative consequences for his own life.

Importantly, in the present context, in both cases the therapists
eventually returned to the original behavioral measures introduced
to deal with the school difficulties. The dynamic exploration had
aided these clients substantially in other ways and had seemed to
help some in reducing the presenting problem, but not completely.
This time, the clients cooperated fully in the behavioral interventions, and improvement was substantial.

"RESISTANCE" IN BEHAVIOR THERAPY

The foregoing examples can also be seen as illustrating the phenomenon of "resistance" in behavior therapy. Such occurrences as the
client "forgetting" to do assignments, "misunderstanding" the instructions again and again, missing sessions, or coming late at key
times, etc., are not really uncommon in behavior therapy and represent one of the chief places where a dynamic perspective can prove
useful.

Consideration of such a thing as "resistance" by behavior therapists used to be almost unthinkable. Partly this was because the
concept was understood—really misunderstood—as simply a way of
saying that lack of progress in therapy was the client's fault or that
the client was being willfully uncooperative. In fact, it refers primarily to the way in which the very anxieties that led to the client's
problems also can interfere with his effective participation in the
effort to change them.

A number of prominent behavior therapists have recently discussed, in an edited volume on "resistance," how such interferences
can occur in behavior therapy and how they can be dealt with
(Goldfried, 1982; Lazarus & Fay, 1982; Meichenbaum & Gilmore,
1982; Turkat & Meyer, 1982). Increasingly, behavior therapists are
recognizing that their behavior analysis must point not only to what
therapeutic techniques would, in principle, lead to change, but also to
methods of assuring that the client actually does participate in those
techniques in an effective and meaningful way.

Here traditional behavioral strategies such as shaping or graded
structure (Lazarus, 1968) are relevant, as are strategies deriving
from social psychology research, such as the "foot-in-the-door" approach (Freedman & Fraser, 1966; Goldfried & Davison, 1976). But
here is also where the perspective of the psychodynamicist may be
particularly relevant. Understanding idiosyncratic sources of reinforcement, as discussed above, can be very helpful in clarifying why a

client does not make use of help in the expected way. And understanding of motivational *conflict* (to be discussed next) can be particularly useful in such instances.

THE ROLE OF CONFLICT

Writings on behavior therapy tend to include very little about conflict. This is unfortunate, not only because conflict is very frequently an important feature of psychological difficulties, but also because the analysis of conflict is perfectly consistent with behavioral principles (Dollard & Miller, 1950; Miller, 1959).

Of particular relevance to the difficulties which lead people to seek psychotherapy are approach–avoidance conflicts, in which the avoidance tendency typically is a function of anxiety. When anxiety has come to be associated with cues that are part of an expressive or appetitive sequence, not only is there distress and/or disruption of adaptive behavior patterns and seeking after satisfactions; there is also a strong tendency to avoid thinking (Dollard & Miller, 1950) or perceiving (Wolitzky & Wachtel, 1973) those things associated with the frightening cues. This leads to difficulties in thinking through the dilemmas and complexities that life presents, and also to an inability to sense alternatives. When one looks beyond the specific symptoms on which behavior therapy originally cut its teeth, to the broader kinds of complaints more frequently encountered today, it is particularly the inability to grasp alternatives that is problematic. Part and parcel of this is the inability to be clear even about what it is that one wants and is blocked in pursuing. And since the client cannot name what will bring him satisfaction (since in his present condition it will also bring him anxiety), the therapist cannot know it if he sticks only to the client's verbal report as a designation of what the client wants.

As Miller's (1959) analysis of approach–avoidance conflicts shows, it is in the nature of such conflicts that what one wants when one is far away from a desired but frightening goal is different from what one wants after one has approached. From a distance, a whole cluster of related goals, activities, or experiences seem appealing because the approach gradient for them is higher than the avoidance gradient. But if one approaches past the point of intersection of the two gradients—and a wide variety of stimulus and response variables make it common for this to happen, rather than stopping precisely at the point of intersection—then a different cluster of goals, activities, and experiences begins to look attractive. These are given their new lustre, as it were, by being other than what was previously sought (and feared), but they are often not experienced simply as escapes: They are goals in their own right, enhanced in attractiveness by being escapes but sought for other reasons as well. Indeed, frequently they are themselves implicated in other approach–avoidance conflicts such that further pursuit of them creates a strengthened desire for something "other" with regard to them (which—together with the enhanced attractiveness of the first cluster due to retreating to a point where its approach gradient is again higher than the avoidance—may lead to a rekindling of interest in those things which just previously had lost their lustre). To be sure, the simple schematic of the single approach–avoidance conflict is usually very much oversimplified (Wachtel, 1978b)—but much less so than the monomotivational situation of the starved animal, which forms the paradigm for so much of the experimental research on reinforcement.

One important clinical virtue of the conflict paradigm is that it can help give some unity and coherence to the bewildering array of goals that clients can present from session to session. Attempting to track them along hypothetical approach and avoidance gradients can help provide orientation in cases where the client is unable to follow through because what seems desirable or important to him keeps changing.

Dealing with the client's conflicts does not mean limiting oneself to facilitating "insight" about them. Certainly a clearer understanding of what he or she wants or fears—and how the latter shapes the former—is part of what a client can benefit from in therapy; but the behavior therapist has other measures for dealing with conflict as well, once conflict is accepted as a focus of therapy. Approach–avoidance conflicts are, after all, a function of anxiety, and behavior therapy has a number of effective ways of reducing anxiety. Combining those methods with the methods for identifying sources of anxiety that the psychodynamic perspective offers can yield a synergistic combination that is very powerful (Wachtel, 1977b).

THE THERAPEUTIC CONTRACT

One of the most salutary features of behavior therapy has been its concern with making the therapeutic contract more explicit than had been true with other therapies. Although the notion of a contract between the participants had been introduced in psychoanalytic therapy also (Menninger, 1958), nowhere does it approach the explicitness it does in behavior therapy.

But there are important features of the psychoanalytic contract that it would be unfortunate to dismiss completely. Behavior therapists have noted the abuses that can occur when analysts redefine the goals of therapy in terms other than the client has presented. These abuses are all too real at times, but they are not as universal or essential as sometimes seems to be implied. In addition to addressing the goals the client initially feels he or she wants to pursue, a therapist can help by raising questions about the goals themselves, can try to determine if they are in fact what the client wholeheartedly wants, or if they instead reflect a compromise based on unrealistic fears. Such a compromise may not really represent the best that life has to offer the client. There is nothing unethical about raising this possibility at the beginning of the treatment, so long as the therapist is explicit about it, and so long as the choice of pursuing the client's original aims is not disparaged.

In many instances, an attitude of examining compromises can be extremely helpful to the client. Not all phobias are reported or even experienced. Many are covered by rationalizations. The man who fears intimacy may feel that his problem is simply that he isn't meeting the right women; this one isn't pretty enough, this one not intelligent enough, this one too aggressive, etc. The youth who fears surpassing his father may convince himself he has dropped out of school to become a sandal-maker solely because he is not materialistic. The therapist must take the client's conscious aims seriously, but it is not disrespectful to also raise with the client whether more might be involved. Here is perhaps the place in therapy where tact and skill in the wording of comments to clients is most required, but there are guidelines available in this regard that can help the therapist to communicate in a way that is helpful rather than confrontational (Wachtel, 1980).

CONCLUDING COMMENTS

In the psychoanalytic tradition, virtually all of the influential writers were active clinicians. In the behavior therapy movement, this has not always been the case; some of the most frequently cited books and papers are by individuals who have little or no clinical experience or who have not practiced very much for years. Interestingly, these tend to be among the most vociferously antipsychoanalytic works in the behavioral literature. When theory and general viewpoint are so substantially shaped by experimental laboratory researchers rather than clinicians, what is likely to be produced is theory that is very neat but not as close to clinical reality as one might hope. Some of the differences, for example, between social learning theory and the psychodynamic viewpoint are attributable to the former's grounding in laboratory phenomena, rather than in those phenomena that most intrigue and challenge the clinician (Wachtel, 1973a, 1973b).

Increasingly, it is the clinicians in the behavior therapy movement who are becoming the models for young students. This—together with the increasing recognition by dynamic therapists that there are valuable things to be learned from their behavioral colleagues—should lead to a greater openness toward the integration of varying perspectives on clinical problems and to a more comprehensive and satisfactory therapeutic approach.

10

Contingent and Noncontingent Therapist Response

Is therapeutic change best viewed as an interpersonal influence process, in which the therapist differentially reinforces certain patient behaviors in order to bring about desirable change? Or is it the therapist's uniquely noncontingent, accepting attitude that produces change? The latter position is of course advocated by Rogerian therapists, and in slightly different form by psychoanalytic writers stressing the growth of autonomy as a therapeutic goal (e.g., Paul, 1974). Social learning theorists such as Bandura (1969), on the other hand, argue that "[s]trict adherence to the position that therapists should be unconditionally accepting is virtually impossible" and that even were it possible it would not effectively help people to change. Bandura further argues that a therapist's interpretations are likely to lead to the patient's conversion to the therapist's point of view rather than to self-discovery and greater inner freedom.

The present chapter seeks to look more closely at the question of just when the therapist does (and when the therapist should) respond contingently to the patient's behavior. It attempts to consider aspects of the therapist's influence which have not been sufficiently considered previously.

Since the publication of Truax's (1966) widely cited study, it has been difficult to maintain that the therapist can realistically expect to be thoroughly unconditional or noncontingent in his response to the patient's varying behavior in the office and in his life outside. Truax's demonstration that Rogers, the archproponent of unconditional positive regard, in fact responded quite differently to different patient

Reprinted by permission from *Psychotherapy: Theory, Research and Practice*, 1979, 16(1), 30–35.

behaviors was dramatic and persuasive. Let us, however, take a close second look at Truax's findings, for they have important implications for the topic at hand.[1]

The classes of behavior to which Rogers was found to behave selectively were (1) similarity of patient style of expression to that of the therapist, (2) patient learning of discriminations about self and feelings, (3) clarity in the patient's expressions, (4) expressions of insight, and (5) a problem orientation in what the patient said. With the exception of the first of these, these classes of behavior are both broad and (relatively) uncontroversial with regard to value issues. That is, what was reported as influenced was not a specific choice of spouse or job, whether to divorce, or spank the children, or lie to the boss, or take a day off from studying. Rather, influence was suggested upon a rather general direction to behavior, along the lines of the patient's gaining a clearer picture of himself and his life situation. Few therapists would contend that they don't even try to explicitly bring that about. The controversy regards the more specific choices, for which a broadly accepted set of values is not readily at hand.

We do not know from the report of the Truax study whether Rogers also differentially encouraged certain specific life choices of the patient. Because only certain categories were examined for their correlation with therapist response, the data do not tell us whether Rogers was more accepting and empathic when the patient chose a girlfriend Rogers thought was "good" for him, or a job Rogers thought suited him better, or a nicer way of talking to his mother. It may well be that further research will reveal that these kinds of things too are encouraged or discouraged to some extent by therapists who don't think they do so. But it is important to recognize that differential response of this second sort presents rather different kinds of issues, and was not demonstrated in the Truax study.

Further, it should be noted that the role of the therapist's contingent response in the behavior change which occurred was not as clear-cut as some who cite the study seem to imply. For obvious reasons, the A-B-A design which is common in case studies focusing on the effects of reinforcement was not utilized.

To be sure, the behaviors which increased in frequency were those that were differentially followed by empathy or acceptance, and behaviors not subject to contingencies in this regard did not change in frequency over time. But it was also the case that the

---

1. It could, of course, be argued that Rogers himself is not able to be noncontingent but that other therapists can, or that this particular case represented a deviation from Rogers's usual therapeutic behavior. I am not aware, however, of any public presentations of such an argument.

behaviors which received contingent responses and increased (patient similarity to therapist in expressive style, learning of discriminations about self and feelings, patient's insight, and problem orientation) were those which might be expected to increase with therapeutic success regardless of the process accounting for the success, and those which did not increase (blocking, anxiety, and expression of negative feelings) were those which would not be expected to increase if therapy were successful. Interestingly, the one behavior which increased in frequency through time though it was not contingently rewarded was "catharsis," which, if it were scored whenever an intense emotional expression occurred, could also be viewed as a success indicator, related to reduced defensiveness and emotional constriction.

Thus, though Rogers did clearly respond differentially, it is not as clear that this differential response was the reason that some behaviors changed and others did not. If a study were to be done in which the therapist reinforced some "desirable" behaviors and not others (e.g., one therapist reinforcing insight but not positive feeling, and another therapist doing just the opposite), and the contingencies were shown to relate to just what changed, the case would be much stronger. Truax's findings are suggestive of a reinforcement process (and clear regarding Rogers's contingent behavior), but they are not conclusive with regard to the process of change in the case.

REINFORCEMENT AND CHOICE

I raise such considerations not to imply that reinforcement is not an important part of what happens in psychotherapy—I devoted a whole chapter of my book (Wachtel, 1977) to discussing the importance of reinforcement considerations even in the wording of interpretations—but rather to point out that the precise role of reinforcement considerations on the one hand, and what might be called "traditional" considerations in therapy on the other, is still far from clear. Following the lead of Skinner, many therapists claim that we are always being controlled, and so the therapist might as well attempt to exert his control of the patient in a thorough and carefully planned way that is consistent with the goals of the therapy. The implication seems to be that any view which stresses the role of the patient as an active chooser or organizer, and which treats the therapist's contribution as one which fosters an atmosphere in which the person can more clearly make his own choices, is naive and no longer tenable. Issues of control, determinism, and choice, however, are far from finally resolved in one direction. Indeed, determinism and genuine choice are not even empirically separable explanations of behavior (Wachtel, 1969; Wheelis, 1973).

Studies such as Truax's do not rule out an important role in psychotherapy for unconditional "acceptance" on the part of the therapist. Such research does suggest, however, that the therapist's effort to be unconditional might perhaps better be limited to substantive life decisions, rather than as open-ended as Rogers and others have sometimes suggested. It is probably difficult to be thoroughly neutral and accepting even in this realm (i.e., whom to marry, whether to divorce, whether to strive or devote more time to leisure, etc.). Therapists have values, and they are hard to keep out of the therapy room. But it is especially hard to be neutral about the values which constitute the therapy process itself—not to care, for example, if the patient does or doesn't engage in self-exploration or make an effort to express his feelings more clearly and directly. What Truax's study showed most clearly is that in this latter realm, even the therapist with a very strong commitment to facilitating the patient's undirected self-exploration is likely to respond differentially to the patient's efforts. Indeed, one might well expect that it is particularly therapists with such a commitment who would respond contingently in this realm; the therapist with less of a commitment to self-exploration and more of a "behavior control" perspective might well be much more noncontingent in his response to patients' efforts in this regard (though he would likely be more thoroughly contingent in response to a variety of other patient behaviors).

NONCONTINGENT ACCEPTANCE AND VALUE ISSUES

Where, then, does this leave the role of noncontingent acceptance? To begin with, almost all therapists would agree that there are matters about which the therapist must strive to be neutral and accepting, even though he might quite vociferously express his opinion about them in other relationships. In general, such matters as the patient's political views, his or her views on abortion or divorce, whether to live in the city or the suburbs, whether to buy expensive clothes or spend one's money on theater-going or vacations, etc., are all topics about which the therapist might hold strong personal opinions, and might try to influence his friends about, but with regard to which he should not try to exert his influence upon his patients. To withhold his opinion about such matters or keep them as far in the background as possible is not to be ungenuine or secretive. Not all self-disclosure facilitates therapeutic change or trust on the part of the patient. The therapist must recognize that some things are, in this context, "none of his business."

Often, however, the guidelines regarding what is or is not the therapist's business are not clear. What does one do if one senses that the patient's ethical commitment to the sanctity of the family is largely based on an unrealistic (and perhaps not conscious) fear that if he is divorced everyone will spurn him and he will live out his life alone, or if his commitment to the value of hard work and his working through the night to get ahead seem largely a function of sexual fears and fear of intimacy? Should the fact that the therapist's own values do or do not coincide with the patient's be taken into account in deciding how to proceed? Most would probably agree that the therapist should be continuously alert to the possibility that he sees psychopathology lurking behind patients' choices which are discrepant from the therapist's own values and sees as healthier and less conflict-derived those choices which are closer to his own ethical, aesthetic, or life-style preferences. But beyond this homiletic recommendation, hard choices are faced in concrete instances.

Bandura (1969) is correct, I believe, in suggesting that dilemmas of this sort are particularly acute for dynamically oriented therapists, who tend to see much more of the patient's life as relevant to any particular problem than do more behaviorally oriented therapists, and who view wide-ranging exploration of all of the patient's choices as an important part of the therapeutic process. When this is the therapist's orientation, he is indeed obligated to inform the patient of this very early in the treatment, so that the patient can decide whether he wants so much of his life subjected to critical scrutiny. Whether such scrutiny is necessary, however, is quite a separate issue from whether it raises ethical dangers. It is interesting to note that in recent years behavior therapists have increasingly seen a need for understanding patients' problems in a broader context than was originally the case (Goldfried & Davison, 1976; Lazarus, 1971, 1976).

REACTIONS TO PATIENTS' CONSEQUENTIAL CHOICES

Thus far I have discussed areas where almost all therapists strive to be noncontingent and have moved to the gray area where there is a blurred border between value choices which are none of the therapist's business and choices which are closely tied to the patient's conflicts and difficulties. There is another class of choices by the patient which most therapists, whatever their orientation, would see as related to the patient's chances of improving. It does make a difference in a person's life whom he marries, for example, and some potential partners seem obviously poor choices; persistently unassertive behavior, whether well or poorly rationalized, is likely to take its toll on the person's chances for full and gratifying living; the choice of a career for which a young person seems particularly poorly suited, and which he reluctantly pursues because of parental pressure, is likely to make a substantive difference in his sense of well-being. In these and other matters, different therapists are likely to make somewhat different judgments about just what is obviously a choice which will have unpleasant consequences or is at odds with the person's own deeper or more genuine inclinations—this is what makes our field such a difficult one to develop as a science, and what leads some therapists to try to eschew interpretive statements and others to eschew reinforcements—but almost all therapists are likely to agree that it is not rare to encounter situations where they are personally rather certain that the patient is making a mistake.

Therapists do differ, however, in whether they feel they should tell the patient where they think he is making a mistake and where they think he is making a good choice. It is my expectation that further research on the model of the Truax study will reveal that in such situations statements by client-centered or analytic therapists designed to "clarify" the issues for the patient, and/or expand his awareness of the full range of his feelings about the matter, will be shown to function as contingent rewards. In my own view, not only is it difficult to be genuinely noncontingently accepting in such circumstances, but, given the cumulative effects of feedback processes upon future choices and future opportunities for further feedback, it is not even desirable (Wachtel, 1977b).

Nonetheless, despite the wide range of ways in which the therapist can be found inadvertently to contingently reinforce his patient's behavior, and the not infrequent occasions when it is important that he take responsibility for guiding the patient in directions more likely to get him what he wants, there remains a substantial range of therapeutic interactions where a noncontingent, accepting attitude seems desirable and is likely to be feasible. One reason I hold to this is that, like many therapists, I view people as striving for a considerably wider range of aims than just those they consciously acknowledge, and it seems to me important in many instances to hold in abeyance judgments about whether any particular step by a patient is likely to further his aims until one has a clearer sense of what his aims are.

The patient whose fear of assertion has inhibited the expression of expansive and ambitious longings might be consciously pleased to have chosen a girl who believes in "fitting in," "not rocking the boat," and accepting a simple life rather than striving for excellence and success. For some people, such a choice may be a good one, and may reflect the attainment of an inner peace and rejection of externally imposed performance demands. But for the person whose ambitious aims and fantasies have been repressed, such a choice may be a self-betrayal, seemingly consonant with what he really wants, but in fact expressing only a portion of his true aims—and perhaps that portion most due to unrealistic fears and constraints. In such a case, to encourage the patient to take the step consonant with his professed aim may be counterproductive; an attitude of suspending judgment about his decision and focusing instead simply on understanding may be much more helpful.

Suspending judgment and focusing on understanding are therapeutically useful also because they render the later effort to explicitly influence the patient's choices more effective. Transference notwithstanding, the therapist's own behavior will make a difference in how much the patient values his opinion and approval. The patient does not automatically do whatever the therapist suggests. Sometimes the therapist's influence can be rather minimal. In some respects this is fortunate. It can prevent to some extent the therapist's (conscious or unconscious) abuse of his position by pushing his own values; and it limits the danger—real, but often exaggerated—of directiveness by the therapist leading to a passive, dependent attitude on the part of the patient. But if one views as a legitimate source of therapeutic gain the therapist's advice as to which courses of action are likely to further the patient's real interests—and I do view such advice as frequently legitimate—then the ability of the therapist to create circumstances in which what he says will be considered seriously is an important part of the therapist's skills. In this regard, the therapist's maintenance for a period of time of an unconditionally accepting attitude is likely to facilitate the patient's responsiveness to his communications. When the patient feels that the therapist is on "his side," and understands him, he is likely to be more ready to follow the therapist's recommendations.

A somewhat similar consideration was discussed by Truax in the paper referred to earlier. Truax argued that the view that reinforcement is a very important factor in therapeutic change did not reduce the significance of the (also empirically established) role of therapist's warmth and empathy. He suggested that such therapist qualities correlated with success because therapists high on these qualities had more valuable reinforcers to dispense. Truax was, however, limiting his discussion to the contingent application of these valuable humanistic supplies. I am suggesting as well that another determinant of the value of the therapist's contingent responses may be his noncontingent listening and commenting at another time in the therapy.

HOW DO WE STAY NONCONTINGENT?

Precisely how the therapist can maintain an attitude of unconditional positive regard, even to a limited extent, is a matter requiring a good deal of research. Though perhaps, as Truax has shown, it is difficult to attain an ideal of perfectly noncontingent responsiveness to the patient, it does seem that therapists can at least do a good deal more in their practices than in the rest of their lives. It certainly seems to me that I can suspend judgment with my patients to a substantially greater extent than I can with my wife, children, or friends, and I daily accept behavior from patients I would not dream of tolerating from my friends.

Partly this seems a matter of set, of giving oneself a continuing directive to look at how things seem through the patient's eyes. But this is far from a fully satisfactory explanation. We need to know much more about how we do this and when we succeed and fail at it. It seems to me likely that one way in which we are likely to produce failure at the task is to place too great a strain upon ourselves, to expect that we will never make judgments or be directive. It may be easier to be nonjudgmental and nondirective for a time if one's approach to therapy does allow active intervention at some point in the process and/or if one permits directiveness at least around the issue of exploration and therapeutic work itself. All therapists are directive to at least this extent, I am quite certain, but I am aware of many therapists—especially students—who feel guilty at any divergence from an ideal of nondirectiveness. From what we know about the effects of guilt and of driving oneself to standards which cannot be met, this is not likely to facilitate therapeutic functioning.

Even when responding contingently to the patient's behavior, it is possible to have unconditional positive regard for him as a person. For the therapist to provide direction is not to alternately love and reject, or even necessarily to reward and punish. Recent views of reinforcement have emphasized the informative function of the events which have been labeled as reinforcers (Bandura, 1974; Wachtel, 1977). The therapist's ability to maintain a continuing regard and respect for the patient, despite the many things he may do that are annoying, foolish, or self-defeating, is not necessarily strengthened by a therapeutic superego which sets off an alarm each time the therapist makes a judgment about something the patient does or says. Genuine regard for the patient is likely to be strengthened by not viewing such regard as antithetical to contingent response to specific actions.

11

You Can't Go Far in Neutral: On the Limits of Therapeutic Neutrality

The therapeutic stance that is referred to as "neutral" is designed to protect the patient and the therapeutic situation. It is an effort to structure into the therapeutic process a benignly nonjudgmental frame of mind. It is also an epistemological stance, one designed to permit "deep" material to come forth undistorted by the analyst's input. On both counts, it is certainly true that our own reactions as analysts or therapists can be problematic. I sympathize with the aims that have led to the precept of neutrality. But I believe that the ideas and practices associated with so-called "neutrality" are deeply flawed, and that we would do well to relinquish our ties to that particular attempted solution to the hazards of doing therapy.

My dissatisfactions with the idea of neutrality derive largely from Sullivan's implicit recasting of the central premises of psychoanalytic thought. Indeed, it is remarkable to me that so many decades after Sullivan, and after Heisenberg, we should still find neutrality so prominently discussed among analysts.

The stance of neutrality is designed to assure that we do not muddy the waters of transference, or, to use another commonly used and related metaphor, that we do not contaminate the field. But Sullivan made it clear that one *can't* stay outside the field; one *can't* not influence what one is observing. We are always observing something that occurs in relation to us—and not just to us as screens or phantoms, but to us as specific flesh-and-blood human beings sitting there in the room.

Paper presented at the 40th anniversary celebration of the William Alanson White Institute, New York, 1983.

To be sure, what transpires doesn't *only* have to do with the person of the analyst. Some of what the patient experiences, he would probably experience in roughly similar fashion whoever was sitting in the analyst's chair; and any particular analyst certainly evokes different reactions in different patients. It is essential that the analyst address the unique individuality of the patient (and it is unfortunate that Sullivan, in countering the prevailing atomistic bias, was moved to rhetorical excesses that seemed to link his systematic ideas to a denial of individuality). But the person's individuality is not something stored up inside him that just "emerges" or "unfolds" if the analyst just gets out of the way (Wachtel, 1982c). Rather, we express and exhibit our individuality as living, responsive beings—assimilating new experiences to old psychological structures, to be sure, but also (inevitably) accommodating those structures to the ongoing events of our lives (Wachtel, 1981b). We exist and give meaning to our lives in relation to the significant events *of* our lives, and if the interaction with the analyst is not one of those events, then the analyst should not be charging a fee.

How long will it take us to realize that if we are silent we see one aspect of the patient, and if we criticize, praise, give advice, laugh at a joke (or don't laugh at a joke) we see other (equally significant) aspects? As family therapists are fond of saying, one can never "not communicate." The effort to do so is itself a communication—indeed, a very powerful one.

RELATIVE NEUTRALITY

Such arguments have by now become familiar enough that few analysts really claim to be neutral in any thorough-going sense. Usually the influence of the analyst is recognized and acknowledged by advocates of neutrality, but the claim is made that one can—and should—strive to minimize that influence as much as possible. Thus, while strict neutrality is admitted to be impossible, *relative* neutrality is put forth as a valid and salutary ideal. This seemingly sophisticated and realistic position seems to me much like describing someone as a little bit pregnant. "Neutral" is not something you can be a little bit of or a lot. It involves a basic epistemological stance: Either one recognizes the contextual nature of what one observes in analysis and understands that it is inevitably a product of both live organisms in the room, or one contends that—even if one slips some of the time (even *much* of the time)—when one *doesn't* slip one has removed oneself from the picture (except as a projection screen). The latter position does not make sense to me.

Although one cannot be neutral in any epistemologically sensible way, one can certainly *behave* in the ways that have traditionally been associated with neutrality. One can, for example, be silent much of the time, or titrate the overt expression of one's reactions to the patient. But relative silence is not the same as relative neutrality. Relative silence per se does not imply an epistemological position. It is a way of acting, an interpersonal tactic. Sometimes such a way of interacting with the patient has a useful impact on the therapeutic process (it always has *some* impact). But its value is limited, and often it can be counterproductive.

The reason for the limitations of the interactional stance usually assumed by proponents of neutrality again goes back to Sullivan, at least indirectly. Implicit in an interpersonal point of view, I believe, is a vision of personality that stresses repetitive circular processes or interaction cycles (Wachtel, 1977a, 1982c). The difficulties the patient finds himself in are not simply the product of early experiences, or defensive efforts that have achieved some sort of structuralization. The patient requires "accomplices" to maintain his neurosis (Wachtel, 1977b). Without the continuing participation of other people, the pattern cannot sustain itself. Therefore, it is essential to understand how the patient induces others to act in ways that keep the maladaptive pattern going. It is essential as well that the patient understand this too. Self-knowledge, from an interpersonal perspective, is knowledge not just of one's warded-off wishes, thoughts, and feelings, but of the interpersonal situations that give rise to such psychological events. It includes very centrally understanding not only of the impact that particular interactions have on one's own psychological state, but of one's impact on others (which in turn feeds back, through their behavior in relation to oneself, to affect one's own sense of self—usually in a way that again keeps the entire pattern going).

Given such a view, it is easy to see why the stance usually associated with "neutrality" is unsatisfactory. What one wants the patient to understand in relation to the analyst is not simply that he has seen the analyst incorrectly as resembling an important figure from the past (an aim for which it can be useful for the analyst to appear to have done nothing to merit the patient's attribution). Rather, one wants to use the transference in a different way: as an exemplification of the way the patient sets up a relationship in such a fashion that old patterns are actually repeated. From such a perspective, it is to be expected that the analyst will in fact act like significant figures from the patient's past (and, if the pattern is really one worthy of therapeutic attention, from the patient's present as well). It is to be hoped that the analyst will not participate as an "accomplice" in quite the way that others in the patient's life do; that would hardly be an improvement. But even if the analyst's participation is more modulated, modified by his being a participant–*observer*, it is almost inevitable that he will in some way replicate the experience others have with the patient (cf. Wolf, 1966). But this is not as unfortunate as it may sound at first. For it is in the very act of participating that the analyst learns what it is most important to know about the patient. And it is in coming to see their joint partici- pation in what is for him a familiar pattern—but a joint participation, with the crucial difference of reflectiveness—that the patient too learns what he must in order to begin the process of change.

If the analyst adopts the pose of neutrality, this crucial aspect of therapeutically useful insight is short-circuited. It is precisely in pointing out how the patient's reactions are *not* simply a distortion, in examining (through the microscope of the transference, as it were) just how the patient has evoked a familiar reaction (first internal, then overt) from the analyst, that the most therapeutically valuable aspect of the work is achieved.

What is being addressed here is the mirror image of what Alex- ander (e.g., Alexander & French, 1946) described as the "corrective emotional experience"; the virtue of the analytic interaction lies in how it both replicates *and* deviates from other significant interactions in the patient's life. Such a combination of replication and deviation need not be approached in an artificial or manipulative way. It happens inevitably, whether one intends it to or not; the force field of the patient's emotional pull on the one hand, and the effects of training and self-reflection on the other, see to that.

The replication aspect, of course, is not likely to be immediately fully recognized by the patient. Part of why he is in analysis is precisely because he does not see how he brings about the same set of circumstances over and over. In this sense, what transpires in the analysis is at first not experienced as nearly as familiar as it really is. But in pointing out what has transpired between them, the analyst can help the patient to recognize a pattern to his personal relations and to see how this pattern relates to the more private states that are also a central concern of analysis. A stance of seeming neutrality excludes much discussion of what happens *between* the two people in the room, focusing the analysis almost exclusively on the private states themselves, rather than on how they are a part of a context of evolving relationship. This has, of course, been the traditional focus of analysis. But it should not be one's exclusive or preponderant focus if one takes the insights of the interpersonal point of view seriously.

What is at issue is not simply a matter of the analyst's using his own reactions as a clue *for himself* about what is going on in the patient. Such a use of countertransference feelings as a private guide to empathic understanding is already part of standard psychoanalytic methodology. It is certainly useful and important, but it is not enough. Usually it accompanies, in a classical approach, a concerted focus on the patient alone. There is rarely if ever a confirmation of the patient's experience, even where it is correctly apprehended. So long as the analyst hides behind a "neutral" self-presentation, so long as his own participation in the session's events does not become part of the focus of what he discusses with the patient, it is difficult for the patient to understand not just his own experience but how he goes about creating and recreating it in his daily life.

DOES THE PATIENT REVEAL MORE
IF THE ANALYST REVEALS LESS?

A central concern of proponents of the concept of neutrality is that any other stance will interfere with full exploration of the patient's conflicting inclinations. As Schafer (1983) puts it, "the analyst who remains neutral is attempting to allow all of the conflictual material to be fully represented, interpreted, and worked through" (p. 6). To side with any particular view or inclination of the patient can seem to mean standing *against* another, since conflict is so pervasive a characteristic of psychic life. What the analyst strives to create, says Schafer, is an "atmosphere of safety" in which the analysand feels it is safe to reveal *any* aspect of himself.

There is an important kernel of truth in this position. It is essential that the analyst continually keep in mind the ubiquity of conflict and be aware of the various subjective meanings that even apparent approval can have to the patient. But several considerations suggest that "neutrality" is not the best way to deal with this issue.

Schafer's reference to the "atmosphere of safety" is part of a general line of argument that shows far greater appreciation than most analysts have of the crucial clinical implications of Freud's theoretical reformulations in *Inhibitions, Symptoms and Anxiety* (Freud, 1926/1959). But Schafer does not go quite far enough. The new centrality of anxiety in clinical theory points to the critical importance of helping the patient most of all to overcome his fears and inhibitions. Given the intensity of the infantile fears that generate neurotic patterns, and of the continuing anxieties that help keep them going, neutrality is simply too weak a stance to do the job in many cases. A more positively affirmative stance is required. In this sense, Rogers's term "unconditional positive regard" is a better one than "neutrality." But Rogers and his followers tend to exhibit the same confusion that has characterized psychoanalytic discussions on the topic—a confusion between regard for the *person* and regard for any particular act or idea. It is the former that is crucial for the patient to experience.

In their excessive concern that approval of one line of thought or action implies disapproval of those that conflict, some analysts seem to exhibit the same kind of thinking they should be helping their patients to overcome! What the patient needs very much to learn is that disapproval of something he does is not the same as rejection of him as a person. If the analyst runs scared—if he organizes his whole therapeutic effort around avoiding anything that could smack of disapproval of any thought or act, rather than concerning himself simply with maintaining an overall affirmative attitude toward the patient as a person—he ends up depriving the patient of a crucial learning experience. Being able to acknowledge that "Yes, my encouragement of your taking an assertive step in the face of your anxieties does mean I prefer your doing that to your opting to hold back, as you sometimes also feel like doing" can be combined with pointing out "But you experience it as if I would be utterly disgusted with you and totally reject you if you did something I didn't approve of." And one could add (if one adopted throughout the stance recommended here instead of one of neutrality), "You've seen me not like a particular choice you made in the past. Did it in fact lead to the kind of total rift you fear?"

Even apart from the observations above, there is reason to question whether refraining from making overt judgments actually facilitates the patient's feeling safer and freer to express a wider range of his thoughts and feelings. There is reason to think that the analyst's stance of ambiguity can at times *increase* the patient's anxiety, making it more pervasive. Without clear indications of how the analyst is reacting, the anxious patient can sense potential disapproval over *everything* he says. When the analyst is less covert about his reactions to what the patient says, it can help reassure the patient that when the analyst *doesn't* express a negative reaction, he really means it.

When the analyst is consistently ambiguous, the patient's proclivities to experience disapproval are given free reign. This may be useful for the purpose of exploring those proclivities themselves (and occasional technical use of ambiguity and silence—*followed at some point by clarification of what one's reaction really was*—can be of considerable value). But it is certainly not a reassuring stance for many patients, for whom the atmosphere of safety is diminished by the lack of feedback. The patient then learns a lot about his resistance (and unfortunately can come to view himself as very resistant), but has less opportunity to explore those aspects of himself he has heretofore fearfully avoided, as he continues to experience self-revelation as dangerous.

For some patients, the stance of neutrality can contribute to their tendency to invalidate their own perceptions and even to doubt their own sanity. Early in life, parents serve as mediators of reality for the child, helping him to organize his perceptions and to give meaning to events. Perhaps most important of all in this development is learning to read and understand the emotions of other people. For a variety of reasons, parents frequently (and often unconsciously) distort this development in their children by being unclear about their own motives and emotions toward their children— saying they are doing something to be helpful when they are really angry, indicating they are not upset about something when they really are, and so forth. Indeed, a good portion of our practices can be traced to such experiences.

By hiding behind the stance of "neutrality," the analyst can interfere with the patient's efforts to overcome the effects of such an upbringing. I have found patients all too ready to "explore" the associations, early memories, or recent life events that might hold a clue to a disturbed feeling in the session or in the period between sessions, only to flounder until I indicated that perhaps they were reacting to the fact that I had been sleepy or annoyed or inattentive. Such comments brought enormous relief and a genuine "Ah ha!" experience. The patients had dimly sensed my state, but had years of experience in "not noticing" such things. They were all too ready to attribute to arcane recesses of their psyches what were primarily reactions to what I had done right in front of them. It would have been easy to "get away with" a continuing posture of neutrality, but it would have been a disservice to the patients. Since analysts are human, occurrences of this sort are not at all rare. They are in fact opportunities for significant corrective experiences for the patients, but if an analyst's ideology makes such frank revelation of his experience unseemly, they can instead be countertherapeutic.

This is not to say that the analyst should simply "let it all hang out." Irresponsibility is hardly an improvement over neutrality. Just as neutrality is a myth at one end of the spectrum, so too is symmetry at the other. Although in one sense patient and therapist are assuredly equals—both are "more simply human than otherwise" and equally deserving of respect and human dignity—the relation is nonetheless asymmetrical. One is asking the other for help. Sometimes (as we all know), the help *seeker* is the healthier of the two. Often (as we also know), the helper gets a good deal himself from the process. But the asymmetry still stands. The roles and responsibilities of the two parties are different. The patterns of one person's life are the focus of both. Consequently, where one of the two people (the patient) is free to say and reveal whatever he wants, the other (the therapist or analyst) does so only judiciously, when he thinks it will be helpful.

I wish there were very clear rules as to just when such revelations *are* helpful. Unfortunately there are not, and those with a great need for certainty are likely to prefer a set of premises that give at least the appearance of consistency. This is unfortunate, because the therapist's reactions cannot really be eliminated or hidden. They can only be removed as a topic to address explicitly. In this way, rather than serving as a focus for clarification of the interpersonal patterns the patient gets involved in, they remain vague and unarticulated and become instead a further source of mystification.

This goes for interpretations as well. No less than advice, encouragement, self-disclosure, or technical recommendations, interpretations inevitably convey an attitudinal metamessage as well as the explicit content intended. In addition to illuminating the meaning of some thought or experience of the patient, interpretations, depending on how they are couched, tend to be either invitations or admonitions. The prevailing emphasis on neutrality has led to insufficient attention to the impact of alternative ways of conveying to the patient information about what he is warding off. Consequently, interpretations are often unwittingly cast in a manner that is therapeutically counterproductive (Wachtel, 1980; see also the excellent discussions by Wile [1982, 1984] in this regard).

THE CONSEQUENCES OF LANGUAGE

It is easy for proponents of neutrality to feel that critics are attacking a straw man. It is certainly true that modern defenses of neutrality do not suggest that the analyst really can or should be a blank screen, or advocate the cold, surgeon-like attitude that Freud's metaphors led some incorrectly to assume was appropriate. Writers such as Stone (1961) and Greenson (1967) have presented a far more flexible and humane vision of the analyst's stance. Schafer (1983) notes that "there is always room in analytic work for courtesy, cordiality, gentleness, sincere empathic participation and comment, and other such personal, though not socially intimate, modes of relationship" (p. 9). He later adds a "respectful affirmative attitude" and an attitude of "appreciation" (p. 9).

Thus, over the years, much that is humane and sensible has

accrued to the account of neutrality. We have indeed reached the point where the best of analysts now really advocate what might best be called a non-neutral neutrality. In the many efforts to clarify that "neutral" does not mean "cold," "distant," "uncaring," "stiff," "impersonal," and so forth, advocates of neutrality are at the same time demonstrating the difficulties with the idea of neutrality itself. For what they are saying is that the usual meanings of "neutral" are misleading, and that they mean "neutral" in a way that is in many ways quite at odds with how the term can be expected to be taken.

To be sure, they are also pointing to a specific, technical meaning of the term that, if well understood, can be far more useful than a naive sense of what the word should mean in the analytic context. But our language has consequences. Even the most advanced and sophisticated of analysts, I contend, are constrained by the necessity to show that they are in at least some way "neutral." The dangers such constraint prevents are, in my view, outweighed by the opportunities for creative intervention that are foregone.

BUT IS IT ANALYSIS?

The reader will probably notice that I have not been concerned with drawing a sharp distinction between psychoanalysis and psychotherapy. This is no oversight, but a very conscious intention. It is my belief that all too often the questions "Is it analysis?" or "Is it analytic?" have taken precedence over "Is it good for the patient?" Psychoanalysis is, after all, but a form of psychotherapy. Freud himself believed that psychoanalysis as a theory of mind would stand long after the specific therapeutic *technique* called psychoanalysis—a technique not altered terribly much since early in this century—had become obsolete. Excessive concern with distinguishing psychoanalysis from all other psychotherapies—even among interpersonalists—has exerted a powerful conservative constraint on the development of a more effective psychotherapy, informed by psychoanalytic insights but free to evolve in ways that go beyond our present ability to be helpful.

12

The Philosophic and the Therapeutic: Considerations Regarding the Goals of Psychoanalysis and Other Therapies

One of the greatest sources of confusion in attempting a comparative analysis (or possible synthesis) of differing approaches to psychotherapy is the difficulty in sorting out what are differences in the empirical substance of what is done or predicted and what are differences in the goals that it is hoped will be achieved. Do two theorists or therapists disagree about how best to arrive at the desired destination, or is their disagreement about what destination is to be sought? And if it is the latter, do they differ because of their assessment of how much and what kind of change is a practical possibility, or because of different views of what psychotherapy should be concerned with, what are good and bad ends in human relationships, what constitutes ideal human development, whether the very notion of "ideal human development" is an instance of hubris, and so on?

The present chapter is concerned more with questions of goals than with theories of how change is achieved. But it is of necessity also concerned with at least some aspects of the latter. For I would contend that one cannot appropriately address one without considering the other. Much of the debate about which therapeutic approaches are more effective, or about how to bring about the maximum degree of change, is obscured by the protagonists' having different ideas of what genuine or meaningful change really is. And, in turn, alternative visions of what psychotherapy should attempt to accomplish are rooted in assumptions about what kinds of changes

Paper presented at the meeting of the Society for Psychotherapy and Philosophy of Science, New York, 1977.

185

are indeed possible to achieve and about how the therapeutic process can bring such changes about.

My aim in the present contribution is particularly to explicate the assumptions underlying the view—still the prevailing one among psychoanalytically trained therapists—that of all the various "psychoanalytic psychotherapies" spawned by Freud's work, none can (with a patient who is potentially "analyzable") achieve quite the results of psychoanalysis proper. Some of the basis for this view lies in substantive theoretical considerations having to do with the necessity for a full regressive transference neurosis, and linked to the idea that repression seals off certain early psychological experiences and structures from further influence by reality events. I have discussed these substantive theoretical issues in some detail elsewhere (Wachtel, 1977), and I do not address them here to any substantial degree. Rather, I focus instead on a number of considerations that seem to belong more in the realm of value choices and preferences, and that I think also contribute substantially to the view regarding the superiority of psychoanalysis proper over all other psychotherapies.

First, though, it may be necessary to clarify what I mean by the assumption of the superiority of psychoanalysis proper.[1] Many of those whom I would include as holders of this assumption would argue that they do *not* hold such an assumption—that they apply the appropriate technique for the appropriate patient, and that for many patients psychoanalytic psychotherapy is a better technique than psychoanalysis (indeed, that for many patients psychoanalysis is counterindicated). Clinically, of course, this is the case. But if one looks closely at *why* psychoanalysis is viewed as counterindicated, in almost every case the reason lies with something that is ultimately a deficit in the patient: The patient lacks ego strength; he is latently psychotic; he has poor impulse control; he is unable to tolerate the regression or the frustration. Sometimes the limitations are less *inherent* in the patient, but lie in his current situation: He lacks the money to pay for a full-blown analysis, or perhaps he must leave the city in a year. Nonetheless, it is some limit in his ability to participate fully in the experience of a psychoanalysis that leads to the decision that—for him—psychoanalytic psychotherapy, rather than psychoanalysis proper, would be best.

---

1. Throughout this chapter, I often use the phrase "psychoanalysis proper" when I wish to distinguish between psychoanalysis as a technique and those variants usually referred to as psychoanalytic psychotherapy. The term "psychoanalysis," used without modification, has so many different meanings and connotations in different contexts that it can often be unclear to just what it refers.

In still other instances, the limit is of a different sort, and these instances may be the most interesting in discussing the issue of the role of values in these seemingly neutral clinical judgments. Some patients simply don't *want* what analysis has to offer. They indicate clearly that they have only a limited interest in insight, and that they are primarily interested in as rapid relief as possible from a disturbing symptom. If they are particularly adamant, the analytically trained therapist may conclude that even psychoanalytic psychotherapy is not appropriate, and might, in this day and age, refer the patient to a behavior therapist or to someone whose orientation is psychopharmacological. But with many such patients, the problems will not seem insurmountable, and they will be accepted for psychoanalytic psychotherapy (but not psychoanalysis).

In such an instance, the analytically trained therapist might well point to his acceptance of the patient's definition of what he wants as an illustration of his not imposing his values on patients. In one sense it is; it is also good clinical judgment (and, of course, the patient may change his mind as the process proceeds). But what is of concern to me in this chapter is the therapist's thought (which I think it will be agreed is a not uncommon one) that if only the patient were sufficiently motivated for a real analysis, how much more could be accomplished.

Now the "limitations" or "deficits" just described in various kinds of patients are quite heterogeneous; it may be argued that they are merely descriptions of the "indications" for analysis or for psychoanalytic psychotherapy, and that the designation of them as deficits or limitations is in the eyes of the beholder—in this case, my own. To this I can only request that the reader reflect on whether criteria such as ego strength, impulse control, frustration tolerance, or even interest in achieving insight (as opposed to merely wanting relief) are really free of an evaluative component. This reflection may be aided by asking oneself which end of the spectrum one would rather occupy—and, moreover, which end one would wish to be viewed as inhabiting by one's colleagues.

Although many clinicians practice psychoanalytic psychotherapy with the sense that, for the patients they are seeing, they are giving their patients the very best treatment available to them, they nonetheless—and this is the crucial point I wish to explore here—regard psychoanalysis proper as more than just the particular kind of psychotherapy indicated for a particular subset of patients. Rather, they regard it as the queen of the psychotherapies, as the apex, as an experience that (if the person is "analyzable") is unmatched in the depth and breadth of positive change it can yield.

Why do I think this is an issue of such importance, especially when psychoanalysis proper constitutes such a small percentage of the treatments actually being administered today? The answer is threefold. First, I think, along with Frank (1973), that therapeutic optimism on the part of both patient and therapist is a very important factor in all therapies. To the degree that the work being done is regarded as a deviation from some ideal standard, to the degree that either patient or therapist thinks of it as "only psychotherapy" or as a "compromise," its effectiveness is likely to be impaired.

Second, I think that the reverence for psychoanalysis proper as a therapeutic modality can have an untoward effect on the practice of psychoanalytic psychotherapy. It can lead to an effort to conduct the psychotherapy as much as possible like an analysis—to make only those "deviations" or "compromises" that are absolutely *required* by the characteristics of the patient, the setting, or the therapeutic contract. And it can thus limit the effort to apply the insights of psychoanalytic *theory* in completely different kinds of *techniques*.

Finally (and relatedly), I am quite skeptical as to whether psychoanalysis proper—at least as it is described in the literature (including the writings of the most "modern" or "flexible" analysts)—is in fact the treatment of choice even for "analyzable" patients. I believe it is a false ideal, and that hewing to it has had constraining effects on the development of psychoanalytic theory and practice. In the eyes of some readers, this skepticism may lead me to be perceived as antipsychoanalytic. The condensation of terminology whereby the term "psychoanalysis" has come to mean both a particular treatment technique and the entire psychoanalytic approach to understanding psychological phenomena makes this more likely. My aim, however, is to examine what we have made of Freud's discoveries—not for the purpose of casting them aside, but to aid in the process of sorting out what remains useful and what is a poor foundation on which to build a growing and developing psychoanalytic point of view. Commitment to psychoanalysis as a way of understanding human behavior and experience—a way that stresses the importance of unconscious motivation, of conflict, of defensive distortion of experience, etc.—need not imply commitment to the particular therapeutic application of those ideas that we have also called (in contradistinction to all other psychoanalytic psychotherapies) "psychoanalysis."

THE CHANGING GOALS OF PSYCHOANALYSIS

It is interesting to note that the therapeutic goal in Freud's early work was essentially *symptom relief*. Patients came with complaints such as pains, paralyses, disturbing sensations, or intrusive affects, and Freud in effect contracted with them to help them move their arms or legs, gain relief from the pain or sensation, etc.

Initially (in his prepsychoanalytic days), Freud thought he could achieve these goals without knowing his patients well as people. He would be a doctor dispensing various technical procedures (e.g., warm baths, massage, electrical stimulation). And when these procedures were initially rejected by him, they were rejected on the ground that they *didn't work*—didn't work in the sense that the symptoms didn't go away, or came back, or were replaced by other symptoms.

Even when he began to explore the possibilities that he sensed in Breuer's work with Anna O, Freud did not quite grasp yet the degree to which he would be treating his patients' personalities rather than their symptoms. As he moved from suggestive to abreactive techniques, he began to see the need for an expansion of his patients' awareness, for them to become conscious of things they had put out of their minds. But the things conceived of as kept out were, to begin with, memories of isolated, traumatic experiences. Although almost from the beginning he saw the role of associated experiences as part of the complex to be explored and recovered (and thus had some sense of following the thread of unconscious mental processes through the person's life), he nonetheless defined his task as one in which he dealt with unusual experiences, not with the typical. The logic of the theory he labeled his "neurotica" (Freud, 1896/1962) required that he be a doctor, concerned with the effects of certain specific unfortunate accidents, rather than a psychologist concerned with general phenomena of human development (Wachtel, 1977, Chapter 2).

This limitation was overcome when Freud was forced to reject his theory of infantile trauma and arrived instead at a theory of psychosexual development and conflict (Freud, 1905/1953/1954; Wachtel, 1977, Chapter 2). This reconceptualization led eventually to an understanding of the way in which his patients' symptomatic complaints were in essence an expression of the key issues in their lives. Permanent relief of symptoms, it was recognized, could not be achieved simply by achieving (even with considerable struggle and with full affective intensity) the recollection of one or several key incidents. Increasingly, the goal of symptom relief came to be linked inseparably with that of deep and genuine self-understanding.

Concomitantly, the nature of the symptoms—or, more broadly, the presenting complaints or targets of the therapeutic work— evolved as well. Today, patients frequently come to therapy with a variety of vague yet painful discontents. Symptoms in the old sense may still be part of the picture, but in large measure what many patients are seeking is the good life—richer, fuller, warmer, and more meaningful interactions with others, and a sense of wholeness, aliveness, and expansiveness in oneself. Psychoanalysis (and later all therapies) came to be seen as the last best hope of many who suffered not from anything even quasi-medical in nature (such as obsessive thoughts or attacks of anxiety), but from a general malaise, inharmonious personal relations, a sense of stagnation in one's career, etc.

Now it is worth reminding ourselves that no one would have been likely to consult Sigmund Freud, neurologist, for such problems in the 1880s or 1890s. These were not the kind of problems Freud was originally trying to deal with. Only gradually did psychoanalysis come to be seen, both by its patients and by its practitioners, as a method relevant to the quest for meaning in one's life and aiming for an examination of the basic grounding of one's values, ethics, and sense of self. For many years now, this has been so central a part of what the analyst does that it is easy to lose track of this evolution. But it is important not to, for in the change from a primarily medical to a primarily philosophical inquiry, many confusions were introduced that can perhaps best be understood by taking this evolution into account.

SAFEGUARDS AND PERILS IN
THE PSYCHOANALYTIC METHOD

This evolution in the nature of the psychoanalytic enterprise presented certain dangers. The matters with which analysts now had to deal went far beyond isolated symptoms or anything that could remotely be thought of as medical. The analyst had inevitably to be concerned with delicate life choices and with all of the subtleties and ambiguities of human feeling and moral decisions. Patients came to analysts to discuss whether to leave their wives for other women; to devote time to work or to their children; to maintain the social ideals of their youth or pursue wealth and opportunity. They came to work out for themselves how much sadistic activity in their sex lives was morally acceptable or to what extent denial of such yearnings was making them feel deprived and embittered. They came to work out how much allegiance they owed to their mothers and how much right they had to hurt or disappoint their parents in the pursuit of their own gratification and ideals. They came on the verge of breaking up a relationship to sort out whether they were wisely avoiding a potentially unhappy union or again avoiding commitment and intimacy. In short, they came looking for answers to age-old dilemmas, and turned to the analyst as a source of wisdom who could settle these matters once and for all.

The temptation, and the danger, are obvious, and Freud was alert to them. He saw clearly the potential for abuse when the analyst took the position of one who knows how others should live, and he recommended that the analyst be neutral with regard to a patient's choices. The analyst was not to try to remake patients in his or her own image, or to bring patients to any "truths" other than those of their own inner nature. Moreover, psychoanalysis as a science was to remain free of value prescriptions; it was not to become a *Weltanschauung*.

Freud was also modest about the goals toward which psychoanalysis as a therapy should strive. He anticipated and opposed quite early the view that psychoanalysis had ushered in a millenium. Instead, he suggested that psychoanalysis simply sought to turn neurotic misery into everyday unhappiness. Later, after psychoanalytic exploration had shed light on the pervasive role of unresolved early conflicts in limiting satisfaction and personal effectiveness, Freud suggested that the outcome of a successful psychoanalysis would be that the patient could love and work—again, an appealingly simple and modest proposal (though, of course, neither "love" nor "work" is a very simple term upon reflection).

Freud's cautions were cogent and important, and have helped to shape some of the most valuable features of the psychoanalytic process. Patients in analysis, and in many of the variety of therapies that have directly or indirectly been spawned by Freud's approach, often do get to experience (to a degree that is rare in our culture) the concern and attention of someone who is listening to *them*—an interested, but putatively neutral listener who is able to hear and see them because he has put aside in this context the expression of his own point of view. Analysands get considerable opportunity to present themselves without being manifestly judged or corrected, and this can facilitate their getting in touch with aspects of themselves that they have heretofore had to keep hidden.

Nonetheless, despite these salutary features of the classical psychoanalytic approach, Freud's recommendations about neutrality present two serious problems. The first has to do with the degree to which such neutrality by the analyst is actually achievable. Analysts have recognized from the beginning that neutrality is difficult to attain—indeed, that only *relative* neutrality can reasonably be striven for. This caution notwithstanding, however, I believe that most analysts have seriously underestimated just how much deviation from neutrality actually characterizes the psychoanalytic process. Sullivan's (1953) model of the participant–observer acknowledges far more frankly and clearly the therapist's substantial role in determining what goes on in the sessions, though its full implications are often ignored by many presumably interpersonally oriented therapists—as they were at times by Sullivan himself.[2] From the viewpoint of this model, the classical analyst's belief in neutrality can be seen, ironically and unintentionally, actually to *increase* his influence upon the patient and to make it *more* difficult for the patient to sort out what are genuinely his own inclinations and what is the result of the analyst's subtle but powerful prodding (Wachtel, 1977).

The second difficulty with the safeguards Freud suggested against intrusions of the analyst's values into the analytic process is that the safeguards have themselves become values that intrude. The emphasis by analysts on the fostering of the patient's autonomy as a primary goal of analysis is not a value-free one. Nor is the stress on the patient's achieving whatever gains are attained by a process of self-understanding that fosters freer and more rational choices. For such an approach can mean that the pain of symptoms and maladaptive behavior is borne longer by the patient, who may (and frequently does) feel at that point that he'd rather feel better than understand himself more deeply.

EMPIRICAL REQUIREMENTS FOR CHANGE, OR PSYCHOANALYTIC VALUES?

For much of the history of psychoanalysis, the degree to which value choices were implied in the goals of psychoanalysis was obscured. It appeared to be the case that unless the efforts at change were approached in the way developed by psychoanalysts, the patient's improvement was unlikely to be enduring. There seemed to be an empirical link between the depth of the patient's insight and the degree and permanence of change achieved. Since substantial and durable relief from suffering seemed to depend upon self-understanding and upon the evocation of the buried past in the analytic hours, one could hardly pit insight against symptom relief and see to which one was more committed; the emphasis on insight appeared to be not a value choice, but an empirical requirement for attaining what the patient requested.

Presently, there are a great many alternatives to psychoanalysis for treating psychological problems. At the time Freud began considering these matters, however, there was essentially just one: Prior to the development of psychoanalysis, suggestion (or various physical

2. See Wachtel (1977) for an examination of Sullivan's varying stances regarding the degree of guidance and direction the therapist should provide, as well as a discussion of some of the observations which recommend the participant–observer model over that of the neutral analyst for describing what actually ensues in an analysis.

treatments which can now readily be viewed as primarily having had their effect via suggestion or placebo) was about all that was available to the physician for dealing with psychogenic complaints. Throughout his career, Freud continued to think of suggestion when he discussed alternatives to psychoanalysis. Even when, late in his career, he could imagine diluting the "pure gold" of analysis by alloying it with a base metal, the base metal envisaged was suggestion.

Freud was certainly correct that the gross way in which suggestion was used in the days before psychoanalysis did yield improvement that was neither as deep nor as broad as that produced by psychoanalysis, and doubtless the improvement resulting from suggestion was frequently transient. Simple admonitions that a symptom will disappear do not address any of the underlying causes of the symptom, and it is not surprising that when, as is common, those causes persist, the symptom is likely to return or another to appear in its stead.[3]

This negative evaluation must be modified somewhat if one considers suggestions directed not toward the disappearance of a specific symptom, but toward a more general sense of being able to cope and worthy of succeeding. Such general "ego-strengthening" or reassuring suggestions have been an implicit or explicit part of almost all treatments through the years, and probably account as well for much of the "spontaneous remission" of neurotic problems without formal treatment. The value of general reassuring or coping suggestions is limited, however, when not based on a sound understanding of the basis for the patient's difficulties. Thus again, suggestion can legitimately be seen as inferior to analysis.

Due largely to Freud's own influence, however, such sorts of suggestion are no longer the only alternative to classical psychoanalysis. The understanding of neurotic phenomena brought about by Freud's work has led to a wide range of scientifically based therapeutic approaches, many of which incorporate the findings of psychoanalysis but employ them in a very different way than Freud did. It makes little sense today simply to distinguish between psychoanalytic and suggestive approaches. The range of processes relevant to change even in analytically based therapies is now recognized as

3. When, as is sometimes the case, the symptom has become an anomaly no longer serving any function (other than perhaps to maintain the pride of the patient, who would be ashamed to acknowledge he could give it up when it became convenient to do so), then a symptom-oriented suggestion, or any placebo that provides a rationale for one's saying he has been "cured" of the symptom rather than having decided to cut it out, can achieve a permanent result (see Blanchard & Hersen, 1976).

considerably greater (see, e.g., Bibring, 1954; Frank, 1973; Greenson, 1967; Kohut, 1984). Moreover, even with regard to suggestion per se, it can now be used in combination with psychoanalytic understanding in order to help make the suggestion (or any use of the therapist's personal influence) more precise. More movement can be achieved when leverage is exerted in the right place.

Freud himself saw some place for suggestion-like processes in psychoanalysis. Although his emphasis was clearly on interpretation, he recognized that interpretation alone was not likely to be able to overcome the strong emotional forces working against change. He felt that the leverage provided by the suggestive influence of the analyst's authority, rooted in the positive transference, was essential to overcome the patient's resistance, and he recommended interpreting the positive transference only when it clearly became itself a source of resistance.

Thus, Freud was willing to temper his strong emphasis on change through understanding and on psychoanalysis as an investigative endeavor (see below) in order to achieve certain practical gains for the patient. In 1914, psychoanalysis—for all its already rather substantial development toward a philosophical system—remained very closely concerned with practical therapeutic gain, and was seen by its practitioners as essentially the only way to achieve such gains in a reliable way. Its concrete goals were important enough to induce some compromise of the purity of its method. If something (like suggestion) that was not strictly "psychoanalytic" was seen as possibly enhancing the effectiveness of the procedure in achieving those goals, it was viewed as appropriate and even essential. The contemporary emphasis on the "therapeutic alliance" seems essentially in the same spirit.

There has been another trend over the years, however, which has increasingly emphasized the purity and self-sufficiency of the classical psychoanalytic method and those aspects of it that are unique to or derive rather exclusively from psychoanalysis. Brenner (e.g., 1969) is a good example of this trend.

Brenner (1969) argues that it is an error for analysts to continue to follow Freud's 1914 recommendation of using the leverage provided by the positive transference. Such an approach, he says, does not take into account the understanding later achieved by Freud and other analysts of the activities of the ego in defense and resistance. According to Brenner, this newer knowledge enables analysts to approach the task of analysis in a purely interpretive way, without using the positive transference in the way Freud suggested. His vision seems to be one of change that is not contaminated by any suggestive influence or moral force exerted by the analyst—change in which the emotional forces that have led to neurosis can be conquered purely by the patient's insights, by the elaborate and persistent application of autonomous rationality.

It is particularly interesting to note Brenner's discussion of Freud's recommendation that at a certain point in analysis the phobic patient must be told to confront the object of his fear. Unlike the issue of when to interpret the positive transference—on which there are many views, and Brenner's is a not uncommon one—here Brenner does seem to be relatively alone, the purest of the pure in avoiding any "nonanalytic" intervention. Freud's recommendation regarding phobias is still very commonly cited by analysts, and is used, interestingly, to argue that what is of value in behavior therapy has been the property of analysts for years, though as only part of a broader and richer treatment. Brenner contends, however, that "[i]f a patient maintains that he understands a phobia perfectly, that it has been well analyzed, but still continues to avoid the activity that he claims to fear no longer, it would seem to be *less analytic* to urge him to do something, i.e., to give up his symptom,[4] than to point out to him that he is deceiving himself, and that there must be more to analyze" (p. 349). The italics have been added by me, to highlight Brenner's emphasis on what is "analytic" as essentially equivalent to what is good. Presumably Brenner has achieved some good therapeutic results with phobics by "analyzing" instead of urging as Freud did. But the reasons for his good results are anything but definitively explained by the notion of pure insight, and the empirical utility of Brenner's approach as compared to Freud's has not been systematically assessed.

Such a comparison may well be beside the point, however. Where one's main concern is with how "analytic" the process is, overcoming the phobia recedes as a criterion.

VARIETIES OF APPLICATIONS OF FREUD'S DISCOVERIES

The recommendations of Freud that are problematic to such analysts as Brenner were themselves still predicated on the primacy of insight; noninterpretive methods were seen by Freud as essential to enable interpretation to be an effective therapeutic tool, but their function was most basically to promote the conditions for fuller attainment of insight. It is possible, however, to use differently the

---

4. Brenner's assumption that all that is involved here is asking the patient to "give up" his symptom is open to serious question. An important part of *treating* the symptom involves providing a structure for the patient to *expose himself* to what he fears, so that he may re-evaluate the fear (see Wachtel, 1977b, Chapters 8, 9, and, 12).

new knowledge of motivational conflicts and neurotic patterns provided by Freud: One can use the new understanding to help guide
the patient toward new behavior patterns that can reverse the vicious circles of neurosis. This was to some extent what Franz Alexander and his colleagues did (Alexander, French, et al., 1946),[5] and
the reaction of the psychoanalytic community to their work helps to
highlight the degree to which psychoanalysis had come to be the
embodiment of a particular set of values, rather than a more strictly
therapeutic endeavor.

Alexander himself was not fully consistent on this matter
(which is not surprising, when one considers the extraordinarily
negative reception his work received and the degree to which his
claim to legitimacy as a psychoanalyst was challenged). Thus, he
claimed in response to his critics that his use of the corrective
emotional experience was designed only to further the patient's
understanding of his dependency (Alexander, 1956). Yet he also claimed
(quite correctly, I would suggest) that insight was often not the
central generator of the change process but a useful by-product,
which followed upon behavior change as frequently as it caused it.
Implicit in his method was the idea that the knowledge gleaned from
clinical work in the modality of classical analysis was now substantial
enough that it could be used to generate *new* treatment methods.
Alexander respected Freud's contribution sufficiently to believe that
it could be a foundation for continued innovation, that its potential
applicability to changing troubled lives was not tied to the limits of a
method developed decades earlier. That method was not just a historical accident—there were many good reasons why psychoanalytic
technique evolved as it did, and many valuable features of the so-
called classical method—but in Alexander's (and my own) view, excessive reverence for that method had prevented psychoanalytic
technique from evolving as fully and creatively as it might have.

To his critics, however, Alexander's approach was not genuinely
"psychoanalytic." In perhaps the harshest and most biased critique of
Alexander's work, Eissler (1950) contended that Alexander practiced
"magic" and that only the classical psychoanalytic method was "rational." Alternative rational strategies in psychotherapy were ruled
out because "there is usually only one road open to structural
changes" (p. 118). Eissler admitted that "even with the greatest of
caution it is a very difficult clinical task to ascertain a structural

---

5. It is also the basic premise of my own work, which takes off from the view of
Freud's that it was his *observations* more than anything else that were of permanent
value. I start from the premise that understanding of psychodynamics can lead to a
wider range of intervention procedures than has been typical of analytically oriented
therapists.

change and it may happen more frequently than not that an assumed structural change turns out later to have been a change of content only," and that, moreover, "it is easier to determine in negative terms rather than in positive what theoretically a structural change is" (pp. 117–118). Eissler seemed undaunted by this, however, and proceeded to construct on this flimsy foundation an elaborate edifice of condemnation of Alexander's approach.

Eissler defined structural change as "an internal change which leads to mastery. It is a change performed in and on the ego in respect to extending its area of capacity mainly by the elimination of certain defense mechanisms" (p. 117). This seems precisely what Alexander aimed at. As he discussed in numerous publications, his procedure was designed to facilitate mastery of impulses that were experienced in childhood as too much to cope with except by such emergency measures as repression. One can argue over whether Alexander's approach achieves this aim as well as the classical method—though the argument is rather hampered by the almost complete absence of data that are not thoroughly mixed with opinion and subjective judgment—but to imply that Alexander did not aim for mastery and an extension of the ego's range and capacity is very seriously to distort his arguments. Eissler's distinction between the classical technique, where there are no secrets between analyst and patient, and the technique of Alexander, which Eissler characterized as "always secretive," was not only a gross and misleading oversimplification; it was also completely beside the point, for it failed to confront Alexander's arguments for how his technical variations ("secretive" or not) promote the very mastery and expansion of the ego's range that Eissler prized, as well as Alexander's arguments for why such mastery can be achieved more readily with his method than with the classical method. Alexander's arguments were not refuted; they were ignored. And in their stead Eissler battled with a phantom approach that seeks only symptom relief and social adaptation, obtained by bolstering repressions instead of undoing them.

To be sure, both symptom relief and social adaptation seemed to be valued far more by Alexander than by Eissler. In large measure this was because Alexander saw them as far less antagonistic to what Eissler called structural change than Eissler did. Eissler derided Alexander's view that "[t]here is no more powerful therapeutic factor than the performance of activities which were formerly neurotically impaired" (Eissler, 1950). To Eissler, such views were the "empty reverberations of a society overly concerned with utilitarian values." As discussed below, the image of psychoanalysis as the champion of true values in a debased, philistine society has played an important role in maintaining the commitment of psychoanalysts to their method.

THE PERSISTING FAITH IN
PSYCHOANALYTIC SUPERIORITY

The supposed superiority of the classical technique to that of Alexander, or to other versions of psychoanalytically oriented psychotherapy, is not a view supported by solid observational data. Though analysts might claim that in their own clinical experience they have achieved more substantial results with the classical technique (when the patient is "analyzable") than with variant methods derived from psychodynamic premises, this view seems to me far more an article of faith than one based on careful evaluation. This is how things "should" be, and therefore how they *must* be.

In recent years the most serious challenges to psychoanalysis have come not from deviationists within the movement, but from clinicians whose work departs more substantially from psychoanalytic premises (or, more accurately in many instances, begins with rather different premises). Behavior therapists in particular present a challenge to psychoanalysis that differs significantly from earlier challenges. Rather than basing their arguments strictly or primarily on theoretical grounds or on their own clinical impressions, they have emphasized from the beginning systematic, controlled empirical validation and comparison of effectiveness. To be sure, the empirical demonstrations of the superiority of behavior therapy—or even of its effectiveness altogether with most serious clinical problems— are far from conclusive. (I have myself presented arguments questioning some of the research in this regard; see Wachtel, 1977, Chapter 8.) Nonetheless, the accumulating clinical reports and controlled studies do, as a body, seem substantial (even if not definitive), and certainly the evidence is at least as solid as for psychoanalysis in terms of any criteria that are defined in terms of readily observable changes in functioning. Symptom substitution has not turned out to be evident to any substantial degree following competent behavioral treatment, and behavior therapists are increasingly concerning themselves with (and being evaluated with regard to) a broad range of areas of personal satisfaction and social effectiveness (see, e.g., Sloane, Staples, Cristol, Yorkston, & Whipple, 1975).[6]

---

6. Sloane et al.'s study was concerned with the comparative effectiveness of behavior therapy and brief (40-session) psychoanalytically oriented psychotherapy, *not* with psychoanalysis per se. That behavior therapy essentially equaled (and in certain limited respects surpassed) the effectiveness of the analytic therapy in areas other than the target symptom may thus seem irrelevant to the committed psychoanalyst. It is important to note, however, that there is no strong evidence from controlled research that formal psychoanalysis produces more substantial changes than were demonstrated for *either* kind of therapy in the Sloane et al. study.

It has become more and more difficult to argue the superiority of psychoanalysis on the grounds of superiority either in eliminating the presenting complaints or in improving readily measurable aspects of social functioning or object relations. To a substantial degree, the arguments for the superiority of the classical psychoanalytic method have shifted toward an emphasis on criteria that are difficult (if not impossible) to assess in an objective, empirical way. At least implicitly, the message has increasingly become that it *doesn't matter* whether other approaches are equal (or even superior) to psychoanalysis in treating symptoms, or even in improving overt social functioning. I have indicated this earlier in discussing Eissler's criticisms of Alexander's work, and it is even more true today, when the dominance of the traditional psychoanalytic approach is being challenged to a far greater extent. The superiority of psychoanalysis is being argued today very largely in terms of such criteria as "inner freedom," "autonomy," or "the growth of the ego." The grounds of the argument have very largely shifted from empirical considerations to considerations having more to do with ethical or value issues.

PSYCHOANALYTIC GOALS AND PSYCHOANALYTIC VALUES

The basic values that underlie psychoanalytic work are perhaps clearer now than they were originally, when they were hard to separate from empirical propositions regarding what enables patients to recover. As other means have been developed and refined, psychoanalysts have had a more difficult time arguing that they do what they do because it is the only way that enduring change can occur. It has become increasingly clear that analysts seek certain *kinds* of changes more than others, seek changes achieved in certain *ways* (rather than whatever "works"), and base their work on certain philosophical premises that guide their clinical choices at least as much as do the professed goals of the patient.[7] Freud's contention that psychoanalysis is not a *Weltanschauung* does not turn out to be fully supportable.

7. I am not contending here that psychoanalysts are unique in this respect. Therapists from other orientations are similarly guided by grounding assumptions. It is simply that I am focusing primarily on the assumptions of psychoanalysts in the present context, and on the assertion that psychoanalysts have been particularly prone to deny the role of their own values in their work.

Rational Conquest of the Irrational

One of the most important basic features of psychoanalytic thought is its strong emphasis on the value of rationality, understanding, and self-knowledge. Originally, self-understanding was discussed largely as a means to an end: It was essential for the patient to gain understanding of himself in order to be free of whatever distress he came to analysis to alleviate. By now, however, what was originally a means has become an end in itself. Methods that might more directly achieve the original ends (i.e., ends such as symptom relief) are eschewed on the grounds that they limit the attainment of insight.

Not only is the ultimate achievement of understanding regarded as crucial (as *the* crucial criterion in many cases), but the *process* must be via understanding as well. In a true analysis, change is to be brought about primarily, if not exclusively, via interpretations. Other kinds of interventions mobilize forces other than understanding, and are therefore undesirable. Recall in this connection the earlier discussion of Brenner's paper.[8]

Psychoanalysis has at times been viewed by its opponents as a libertine philosophy. In fact, it is almost the opposite. The preoccupation of psychoanalysis with the sensual and irrational has largely been for the purpose of its conquest. Conquest of the irrational by rationality is a dominant image in psychoanalysis. The extrapolations of Brown (1959) or Marcuse (1955) from psychoanalysis stray far from the intent that was clear in Freud's work. Freud wanted to know more about the id, but he did not welcome or trust it. Indeed, Freud's effort to make the unconscious conscious

> had more the quality of a search and destroy mission than an effort to liberate. Freud was essentially a sophisticated conservative who knew that, like a village that flies the flag but harbors guerillas, the civilized psyche could not be secure, and certainly could not prosper, until the enemy within was brought to light. Once out of hiding, it could be better controlled or perhaps reformed. "Where id was, let ego be" is clearly not a formula for expanding the territory of the id. It points rather to a repatriation program. (Wachtel, 1983a, p. 216)

The emphasis on rational control of the irrational is tightly woven into the classical psychoanalytic method and plays a central role in the persistence of that technique. For many analysts, follow-

---

8. Some recognition that such an approach to generating therapeutic change is (at the very least) sometimes problematic is reflected in the concept of "parameters" (Eissler, 1958). An extended discussion of the difficulties with the way in which this notion has been used is, however, beyond the scope of this chapter.

ing one thread of Freud's thought, an essential feature of change in psychoanalysis is the conscious repudiation of impulses that previously were repressed and therefore repudiated automatically and without the participation of the rational portions of the ego.[9] Such an emphasis on conscious and rational renunciation plays a role in maintaining resistance to procedures whose chief focus is on alleviating patients' difficulties via reducing their anxiety about their impulses, an approach that is at once more emotional and more permissive.

As noted elsewhere (Wachtel, 1982c), Freud's (1926/1959) revised theory of anxiety could have been taken to imply that therapeutic change has less to do with creating the conditions for rational and conscious choice than with overcoming anxieties and inhibitions that are no longer (and perhaps never were) necessary. Such a line of development points to the utilization of a variety of anxiety-reducing procedures and to a rather different perspective even in making interpretations than does the classical psychoanalytic orientation, and it implies as well a rather different understanding of human "irrationality" (cf. Alexander et al., 1946; Wachtel, 1977b; Wile, 1981, 1984).

Freud stated in *The Ego and the Id* that "the task of psychoanalysis cannot be to make pathological reactions impossible but to give the patient's ego the freedom to choose one way *or the other*" (1923/1961, italics added). The first half of that sentence is unobjectionable—no treatment can absolutely guarantee health—but the second half seems to make little sense. Who, if he or she were *really* free to choose, would choose pathology?[10] The sentence can only be understood if one recognizes it as an ideological or value statement indicating Freud's strong commitment to the idea that psychoanalysis promotes rational choice, a commitment that has had a fateful effect on psychoanalytic technique through the years.[11]

---

9. For a particularly clear illustration of this, see Dewald (1972). Dewald's presentation also has the advantage of illustrating this orientation to the process of change within the context of describing almost verbatim a complete case—a rare occurrence in the psychoanalytic literature, and one that enables the reader to see clearly how predilections and procedures interact.

10. To be sure, if one's vision were still clouded and/or one's conflicts still unresolved, one might choose in a pathological direction (e.g., if under the sway of strong masochistic trends or a harsh superego). But the "freedom to choose" that psychoanalysis is intended to bring about surely includes a freedom from such influences at the point where the choice is made.

11. It is interesting to note that *Free to Choose* is the title of one of the most influential of recent defenses of capitalism. A number of considerations suggest that this consonance may not be simply a coincidence (see, e.g., Wachtel, 1983a, 1983b).

Psychoanalysis as a Research Method and the Value of Exploration

Related issues are raised by the strong emphasis in psychoanalysis upon the psychoanalytic method as a research tool as well as a therapeutic one. I would suggest that the relatively limited degree of improvement and modernization of the technique of psychoanalysis proper over the past 70 years—and the continuing insistence that this method, if at all applicable, be regarded as the absolutely pre-ferred one—is partly a function of the method's having been the major source of data for developing the science of psychoanalysis. Freud described himself as rather lacking in therapeutic zeal, and much of the motivation for his work had to do with his research interests. Unlike the subjects of most psychological research—but in common with many subjects of medical research—the subjects of the investigations of Freud and his followers were not paid for their participation, but in fact paid rather substantial fees for the privilege of participating in these unique experiments. Psychoanalysis as a science has been financed not primarily by foundation or govern-ment grants, but by the very subjects it has studied. It is thus not surprising that there should be a strong emphasis in psychoanalytic thought on the profound benefits of participating as a subject in this research.

Although I do believe that many have benefited quite consider-ably from being patients in psychoanalysis, it is necessary to note that there is little hard evidence that these benefits have been greater or more profound than those of all other forms of therapy (including the various "psychoanalytically oriented" therapies that are based on similar premises). The fortunate coincidence that the very way in which Freud chose to conduct his research should turn out also to be precisely what would most benefit the subjects of the research seems to me unsubstantiated. I would suggest in fact that the therapeutic value of psychoanalysis has been seriously comprom-ised by the need to accommodate to the research goals of the enter-prise (Wachtel, 1977b).

Freud's earliest research was histological. As a psychoanalyst he could not place still tissue under a microscope; however, he managed to devise an analytic tool that could magnify the phenomena he was interested in observing and, to the extent possible, hold them still so they could be studied. Freud's deepest interest was in discovering and charting the most hidden recesses of mental functioning, not simply in producing therapeutic change. His research goal was an ambitious and difficult one, and it would have been undermined to some extent if the things he was trying so hard to observe were to change too rapidly. The psychoanalytic method cast a light on these hidden recesses, and did so in a way that enabled Freud to study their contents systematically and thoroughly. Too rapid change would have prevented such scrutiny, as would the development of methods of change for which such thorough plumbing of the depths was not necessary.

The expectation that meaningful change must come slowly and that it requires painstaking exploration of the intricacies of unconscious mental processes and of their origins in the patient's early history helped avert a potential clash between the goals of therapeutic change and the goals of psychoanalytic research. In recent years, considerable evidence has accumulated to show that psychoanalytically oriented therapies that are quite brief by traditional standards can achieve degrees of change far more extensive than would have been expected under the usual assumptions of psychoanalytic thought (e.g., Malan, 1976; Strupp & Binder, 1984). Moreover, there is virtually no solid evidence that a full-scale analysis can achieve any greater degree of relief from distress or change in troubling life patterns than can these modern brief therapies. Only if exploration and discovery are understood as values in their own right—quite apart from change or improvement in the complaints that brought the patient into analysis—can the powerful insistence on the classical method be understood.

THE BLURRING OF FINAL AND TECHNICAL GOALS

What much of the discussion thus far comes down to is that over the years there has been a tendency for processes and perspectives that were seen as necessary *precursors* of desired change gradually to come to be viewed as ends in themselves, and as essential desiderata for the therapeutic process. Thus what might be called *technical* goals or *empirical* goals—occurrences that are to be sought, so long as they can be shown empirically to lead to the outcome for which therapy was originally sought (the *final* goal)—came to be regarded as themselves part of what analysis should aim for and be judged by. That is, technical goals became final goals.

Originally, for example, making the unconscious conscious was a technical goal. Freud found that empirically it led to symptom reduction, which was what the patients came for, and what he regarded as the criterion for whether his efforts were successful. Over the years, however, this former technical goal has come to be itself a criterion of whether the analysis has been a success. Reduction or elimination of symptoms without a concomitant increase in a patient's understanding of previously unconscious aspects of his personality is regarded by many analysts as an outcome with relatively little merit. In part, this is because of theoretical predilections suggesting that symptom change of that sort is not likely to be permanent. But for many analysts, even apart from the issue of permanence (which is increasingly recognized as not always very predictable by the degree of insight achieved), change without insight is not viewed as a desirable outcome.

To some extent, this reflects the change noted earlier in the complaints brought by patients. Where symptoms constitute only a minor part of what the patient wishes were different, and where increased self-understanding and getting more in touch with one's feelings are what the patient seeks, then making such goals primary is legitimate. But often the primacy of insight and self-exploration can be more a concern of the analyst than of the patient.

The issue is complicated, because one of the things that frequently occurs in analysis—and is in fact of considerable value to the patient—is that the nature of his goals is itself examined, and some of them are seen as resulting from defensive distortion of his deeper aspirations. Even where this happens in a beneficial way, however, it is necessary to consider whether this examination of his goals was originally conceived of by the patient as part of what would happen and was clearly understood by him as part of the contract between him and the analyst. I think it is safe to say that there are still a substantial number of patients entering analysis for whom self-exploration is not, at least to begin with, an aim in itself, but is at most a technical goal in the service of some other kind of change. For the analyst, on the other hand, it is likely to be at the very heart of what he hopes to accomplish.

A somewhat similar issue may be seen with regard to the transference neurosis and its resolution through interpretation. Originally, the development of the transference neurosis was an unexpected occurrence that had to be coped with. As Freud began to work with the phenomenon, he reached the conclusion that it created opportunities for a more immediate experience of some of the developmental issues that needed to be mastered by the patient, and found interpretation a useful tool for accomplishing his aims. Interpretation of the transference neurosis was originally a technical procedure for facilitating the patient's ridding himself of the painful symptoms.

Over the years, however, a subtle shift has occurred. The development of the transference neurosis, and its resolution via interpretation alone, came to be viewed as the criteria for deeper, more extensive, essentially "superior" treatment. The full flowering of the transference neurosis, and the avoidance of interventions other than interpretations, began to take on a quasi-ethical quality; treatments that did not proceed this way were "manipulative" (surely a term that, however technically it is defined, has connotations that are intended as derogatory). It *did not matter* if by "superficial" (i.e., readily observable) criteria, some other (more "limited") approach than classical analysis seemed to yield equally beneficial results. The criteria that really mattered were increasingly interiorized and made subtle beyond measurement—or at least beyond measurement by anyone but the analyst himself, for another aspect of this trend has been to place more and more emphasis on criteria and phenomena intrinsic to the method itself, rather than on observations and/or concepts that are in the general domain.

The evolution I have depicted suggests a shift from an enterprise concerned mainly with symptoms or specific and identifiable distresses to one concerned mainly with the way the person is leading his life and with the degree to which his choices are autonomously directed or unwittingly perpetuate the unequal relations of power between parent and child. It is thus, in a sense, a shift from a (primarily) therapeutic to a (primarily) philosophical undertaking. The therapeutic aspect of psychoanalysis proper has receded, I believe, to a far greater degree than is generally recognized. Perhaps this is why the strange linguistic habit has persisted so long in psychoanalytic circles of distinguishing "psychotherapy" from "psychoanalysis" rather than referring to psychoanalysis as a form of psychotherapy.[12] It is also why psychoanalytic critiques of therapies like behavior therapy are so readily misunderstood—both by behavior therapists and by analysts themselves.

It is not just a matter of the different therapies' having different goals (in the sense of one seeking just symptom change and the other seeking change in the underlying basis of the symptom). Such differences exist, of course, though to a far lesser extent than was once the case; behavior therapists today are far less exclusively focused on symptoms than they once were. More basically, I think, the attitude of many analysts toward behavior therapy—and even, to some extent, toward psychoanalytically oriented psychotherapy—is one of ambivalence *to therapy per se*. It is implicitly a contention that such

12. All analysts would acknowledge, of course, that the term "psychotherapy" is in fact logically the broader, more generic term, but in common usage one frequently reads or hears sentences such as "That was not analysis; it was just psychotherapy."

activities are, in a sense, *merely therapies*, and a recognition that psychoanalysis has become to a substantial degree another kind of activity altogether. For this reason, *any* kind of comparison or contest waged on the field of "therapeutic results," however they are "measured," may be beside the point. That is not really what analysis is mainly about any longer.

STRATEGIES AND TACTICS OF CLINICAL RESEARCH

Introduction to Part Three

The four chapters in this section were written over a considerable span of time and have different foci. What unites them is an interest in the process by which we come to learn more about personality and psychopathology.

Chapter 13 represented an important turning point in my work and remains in my view one of the most important papers I have written. It was my first effort to reconcile some of the seeming differences between the psychodynamic and behavioral points of view. In this case, the effort centered around understanding how different strategies of investigation can lead to different theoretical conceptions (which in turn lead to further reliance on the same strategies of investigation once again).

The chapter takes as its starting point the criticisms of psychodynamic theories by Walter Mischel (1968). Although the paper became part of a "debate" with Mischel in the pages of the *Journal of Abnormal Psychology*, it reflects as well the considerable impact that reading Mischel's critiques of the psychodynamic approach had upon my work. Reading Mischel made much clearer to me what had led me to favor a more interpersonal emphasis in my approach to psychoanalytic theory and practice. Mischel's book highlighted for me the enormous variability that each person shows in behavior and experience, and the importance of considering how that variability is related to the ongoing events in people's lives. When I reflected on Mischel's arguments, it seemed to me that such concern with the importance of context was not exclusive to social learning theories, but was characteristic of interpersonal psychodynamic theories as well—or, at the very least, it was *potentially* characteristic of such theories. As I interpreted the writings of Erikson, Horney, and Sullivan, they seemed to me quite capable of addressing the variability that Mischel had highlighted, and of doing so in a way that dealt better with the complexities of real-life behavior than did social learning theory. Mischel's arguments, however, alerted me to ways of drawing on those dynamic theorists' conceptions in a fresh fashion. Moreover, they led me to rethink many of my assumptions about what was important and what was possible in conducting psychotherapy.

Perhaps most important for me in the process of coming to terms with Mischel's criticisms of psychodynamic theories was the spur to understand how intelligent observers could so easily find either consistency or variability in behavior, depending largely on their initial orientation. The key to understanding this was a recognition that variability is highlighted in situations in which the person has little control over what he or she encounters and where there is relatively little ambiguity. In contrast, a fair degree of consistency in behavior is evident when (1) the situational demands are ambiguous, thereby giving the person's assimilative proclivities wider latitude, or (2) the situation is not fully independent of the characteristics of the person being observed.

Both of these latter properties are endemic to the affective and interpersonal events that are at the heart of the psychodynamic therapist's concerns. When people interact with others, the main situational variable is the behavior of the other person. But the other person's behavior is not really an "independent variable"; it depends very largely on the first person's behavior. Thus the relevant environment for much of our most significant behavior is largely self-created. Herein lies perhaps the primary source of the consistency of personality that has been evident to so many observers. That such consistency can coexist, as it were, with the variability observed by many experimentally oriented observers is a function of most observers' (of either orientation) choosing to examine only a portion of what is in fact a circular causal network. That circularity is, of course, one of the central themes of this book.

Chapter 14 was originally an invited contribution to a conference on interactional psychology in Stockholm, Sweden, in June 1975. The chapter follows up on some of the key themes in Chapter 13, but this time puts forth a positive recommendation for a research strategy to overcome the limits of the "implacable-experimenter" model—namely, the utilization of observational methods that take as their basic unit neither a stimulus situation nor a response, but rather the *circle* of situation and response that repeats itself over and over in a person's life. Such an observational unit, the chapter suggests, captures many of the key dynamics with which the personality psychologist is concerned and provides the possibility of transcending piecemeal approaches that lead to fruitless debates about the relative weight of person and situation variables. As the chapter describes, efforts to put things back together by examining interactions in the *statistical* sense, after having artificially created a context in which the usual back-and-forth interchanges between people are prevented, are unlikely to take us very far.

By the time I began work on my presentation in Stockholm, I was already hard at work on *Psychoanalysis and Behavior Therapy*, and the larger set of issues discussed in that book forms the background for Chapter 14 as presented here. The particular focus of the chapter is on how the concept of "self-perpetuating interaction cycles" can lead us to research strategies that capture more satisfactorily the complexities of causation and motivation in interpersonal behavior. In the light of the analysis the chapter provides, a number of influential lines of research are seen to be "truncated," in the sense of illuminating only a segment of the circular causal sequence. Proponents of particular lines of truncated research tend to see as primary the particular portion of the causal network their own paradigm reveals, and to be unaware of or dismissive toward the rest of the pattern of coherence that can be revealed by a broader inquiry.

Chapter 15 seemed to be a paper that touched a raw nerve in our field. I have received more reprint requests for it and more letters about it than for almost anything else I have writen. One feature that seems to have captured people's interest is that it addresses forthrightly something that many students of personality recognize but that is frequently avoided—the lack of significant progress over the years. Clearly some progress has been made, and if one measures in decades rather than years, there are certainly things we have come to understand better. But all in all, if one is honest with oneself, the yield of countless research studies has been less than overwhelming. The chapter seeks to examine some of the characteristics common in psychological research that may account for the unimpressive results. The proposals made in the chapter have largely gone unheeded, but I was pleased that several correspondents indicated that it gave them the courage to pursue more directly their interests in theory, and that a number of others informed me that some of the specific suggestions were brought to bear in tenure and promotional decisions in their departments.

On a personal level, the chapter also provided an opportunity to reflect on what had become my dominant mode of intellectual work, and to provide a clear rationale and defense of what is in the overall context an unusual pattern for a psychologist in the academic world. My convictions about the importance of facilitating people's working in modes consistent with their talents and interests derived not only from my own experience. Over the years, I had also been struck by how extraordinarily talented and inquiring were the individuals entering the clinical psychology programs in which I was teaching, and by the very low percentage of them who made real contributions to the literature after they graduated. There are many explanations for this, including very centrally the monetary rewards and intellectual challenges of clinical practice. But I became convinced that part of the problem also lay in clinical students' conceptions of what research was. Many of them were simply not temperamentally suited for doing experiments or other kinds of traditional research studies. Since they felt that such studies were synonymous with "research," they concluded that research was not for them. In recent years I have been vociferous in trying to persuade the students in our clinical program at the City University of New York that case studies and theoretical inquiries (of the sort to be found in this book, for example) are also "research." Other faculty members have been supportive of this view, providing the students with real options to do a variety of kinds of dissertations, from experiments and other empirical studies to more conceptual kinds of efforts; it is my impression that the result has been a higher percentage of students in recent years who become contributors to the literature after they graduate. (Perhaps one of the more empirically minded students may even do a study to determine if this impression of greater contribution to the literature is in fact correct, and, if so, whether it is due to the factors I think it is.)

The final chapter in this section was written much earlier than most of what appears in this book. It is included as a sample of how painstaking systematic observation can yield a recognition of regularities that are not visible to "the naked eye." The use of videotape recording has increased enormously since the time Chapter 16 was written, but its full potential remains largely untapped.

13

Psychodynamics, Behavior Therapy, and the Implacable Experimenter: An Inquiry into the Consistency of Personality

One of the central points of contention between behavior therapists and those theorists and clinicians with a psychodynamic viewpoint is the degree of consistency and generality evident in personality functioning. Dynamic therapists tend to view personality as an organized system. Many diverse events are viewed as functionally related, and the person's individuality is expected to show itself in a wide variety of situations. Even where seemingly inconsistent behaviors appear, the viewpoint of most psychodynamic thinkers points toward a search for underlying organizational principles that can account for the phenotypic behavioral differences in terms of a genotypic description of that person's psychic structure.

Such a characterization of psychodynamic approaches as seeking coherence in people's behavior may at first glance seem inconsistent with the strong emphasis of psychodynamicists on conflict. But an examination of the explanatory role of conflict in most psychodynamic theories reveals that often *conflict itself* is the organizing princi-

Reprinted by permission from the *Journal of Abnormal Psychology*, 1973, *82*(2), 324–334.

Much of the work on this chapter was accomplished while I was at the Research Center for Mental Health at New York University and was supported by Grant 5-P01-MH17545 from the National Institute of Mental Health. Discussions with many colleagues have helped to clarify the ideas expressed below. It is a particular pleasure to acknowledge the contribution of my wife, Ellen F. Wachtel, whose critical comments at all stages of the writing played an essential role.

ple providing coherence in the seeming diversity of everyday behavior. For example, excessive timidity in one context and extreme aggressiveness in another may both be seen as manifestations of a strong conflict over aggression. Both kinds of behavior may be seen as bearing the stamp of the person who is readily aroused to act hostilely and who is also afraid of this tendency in himself. Such divergent extremes are viewed from a psychodynamic perspective, especially one that emphasizes the analysis of character, with an eye toward finding underlying unities, though these unities lie in the organizing role of conflict or apparent disunity.

In contrast, the theoretical underpinnings of behavior therapy have tended to stress specificity in behavior and the relative independence of an individual's various response dispositions. Little emphasis is placed on the relation among the responses made by a person in different situations or between these responses and any organizing personality structure. As Mischel (1968) pointed out, low response–response correlations are expected by social behavior theory, and the focus of investigation by workers in this framework is on how particular behaviors are independently related to particular stimulus situations. Mischel's influential brief for a social behaviorist approach to personality assessment and therapy begins with and is largely based upon a critical examination of the research on consistency of personality. The meager yield of efforts to demonstrate consistency is one of the central issues in Mischel's argument against the psychodynamic approach.

Mischel's arguments are cogent and his analysis thoughtful and perceptive. But before psychodynamic concepts are forever consigned to that scientific Valhalla flowing bountifully with phlogiston, ether, and the four humors, it may be of value to take another look both at the kind of consistency in fact predicted by psychodynamic theories and the kind of studies that have supported the case for specificity. The present chapter argues (1) that modern psychodynamic theories are far more able to deal with the facts of man's responsiveness to variations in stimulus conditions than the model of psychoanalysis typically described by proponents of behavior therapy; and (2) that the particular way of framing questions in much experimental personality research tends to underestimate the degree of consistency that does exist in the everyday behavior of individuals. Consequently, there is far more possibility of convergence between the theories and techniques of behavior therapists and dynamic therapists than is generally recognized. The worker from either perspective who dismisses the work of the "opposing" approach risks diminishing his efficacy in aiding men of flesh and blood for the pleasures of slaying men of straw.

VARIETIES OF PSYCHODYNAMIC APPROACHES

Typically, when proponents of behavioral approaches discuss psychodynamic theories, it is Freudian psychoanalysis of the early 20th century that is their focus. Little attention is paid to the later developments in Freud's own work, much less to those contributions of later writers within the psychoanalytic and interpersonal traditions. For example, Bandura and Walters (1963) stated:

> The psychodynamic "disease" model thus leads one to seek determinants of deviant behavior in terms of relatively autonomous internal agents and processes in the form of "unconscious psychic forces," "dammed-up energies," "cathexes," "countercathexes," "defenses," "complexes," and other hypothetical conditions or states having only a tenuous relationship to the social stimuli that precede them or even to the behavioral "symptoms" or "symbols" that they supposedly explain. (p. 30)

In a later volume, Bandura (1969) again suggested that psychodynamic theories posit "an organism that is impelled from within but is relatively insensitive to environmental stimuli or to the immediate consequences of its actions" (p. 19).

Were such characterizations written before World War I, they might have been cogent and important. For a variety of reasons, discussed elsewhere, Freud did for a time emphasize internal, "instinctual" processes almost to the exclusion of environmental and learning factors. Even in his later writings, despite the introduction of important conceptual changes pointing toward concern with environmental events (e.g., Freud, 1923/1961, 1926/1959), Freud's theorizing showed an imbalance in favor of the inner and automatic. And it is unfortunately the case that many psychodynamic thinkers continue to operate on the basis of this inadequate early model.

But more sophisticated modern varieties of psychodynamic thinking are quite different from this early model. An important example of the development in psychodynamic models is provided by recent psychoanalytic discussions of the energy concepts in psychoanalysis. Critics of psychoanalysis have often, with considerable cogency, pointed particularly to the circular and pseudoscientific way in which terms and concepts such as "cathexis," "countercathexis," and "dammed-up libido" are used. Within the psychoanalytic community as well, such criticisms were at times voiced (e.g., Kubie, 1947), and Erikson (1950), in his highly influential *Childhood and Society*, commented that Freud's use of the thermodynamic language of his day, with its emphasis on the conservation and transformation of energy, was an analogy or working hypothesis that "appeared to be making concrete claims which neither observation nor experiment could even attempt to substantiate" (p. 59). But despite Erikson's clear illustration by example that the important insights of psychoanalysis could be expressed more clearly without resort to the confusing and vulnerable energy formulations, such "metapsychological" theorizing continued to abound in psychoanalytic writing.

Within the past few years, however, a number of authors writing from a perspective within the psychoanalytic point of view have provided not only serious criticism of the energy constructs but demonstrations that *such constructs are not at all essential to the main points of psychoanalysis* (e.g., Holt, 1967; Klein, 1966, 1969; Loevinger, 1966; Schafer, 1970; Wachtel, 1969). Thus criticisms of psychoanalysis as positing a closed energy system within which blind energies build up and discharge, oblivious to the world outside, address themselves to an outmoded and inessential feature of the psychoanalytic approach.

Other developments in psychoanalytic theory in recent years also distinguish it from the model usually discussed by behavior therapists, and render it more able to handle the data indicative of behavioral specificity. Although earlier versions of psychoanalytic theory paid inadequate attention to adaptation and response to real situations, the psychoanalytic ego psychology that has developed from the work of Hartmann (1939/1958), Erikson (1950), and others has led to a far greater concern with how the developing human being learns to adapt to the real demands, opportunities, and dangers that his ever-widening world presents to him. To be sure, psychoanalytic workers do attribute greater organization and consistency to personality than stimulus–response theorists, and posit greater residual influence of psychic structures formed by the early interaction of biological givens with environmental contingencies. But these integrating structures are not independent entities driving people to predetermined behaviors regardless of the stimulus conditions that prevail. They are, rather, persistent proclivities to perceive particular classes of stimulus configurations in a particular idiosyncratic fashion, and to behave in accordance with these perceptions.

Accordingly, selectivity of perception has become a central concern of modern psychoanalytic researchers, who, far from being indifferent to how stimuli influence and guide our behavior, have intensively studied precisely how we do register, interpret, and respond to environmental stimulation. Thus psychoanalytically oriented researchers have in recent years been studying processes of selective attention and inattention (Luborsky, Blinder, & Schimek, 1965; Shapiro, 1965; Wachtel, 1967), styles of perceiving and thinking (e.g., Gardner, Holzman, Klein, Linton, & Spence, 1959), the effects of weak or ambiguous stimuli (Pine, 1964), and the effects of the *absence* of environmental stimulation (e.g., Goldberger, 1966;

Holt, 1965). Psychoanalytic thinkers guided by such models would hardly be embarrassed by observations of different behavior in different situations.

Even more explicitly attentive to situational influences and the occurrence of different behavior in different situations is the interpersonal school of psychodynamic thought (e.g., Sullivan, 1953). Sullivan has in fact questioned the very concept of a "personality" as an entity independent of the interpersonal situations in which a person exists. In place of the older, more static model of the analyst as a blank screen upon which the patient's transference distortions are projected, Sullivan emphasized the analyst's role as a *participant-observer*. The blank-screen model did stem largely from a conception of personality that paid little attention to stimulus determinants of a person's thoughts, feelings, and actions. The underlying structure was sought in a way that implied it could be described independently of the situations in which the person found himself. In the absence of external distractions, the true personality was expected to be revealed. In contrast, the model of the participant–observer implies not only that the analyst cannot be a blank screen (after all, a person upon whom one is relying for relief from suffering, who does not permit himself to be looked at, rarely answers questions, and requests a good portion of one's income is hardly a "neutral" stimulus), but also that to even attempt to observe the "personality" free from the "distorting" effects of one's own influence upon the person's behavior is to seek after an illusion. For the person is always responding to some situation, and a silent, unresponsive analyst is no less "real" a stimulus than a warm, energetic, or humorous one.[1]

The contrast between the "blank-screen" and "participant-observer" models raises a number of therapeutic issues that cannot be discussed in detail in this presentation. Among them are (1) the importance of the therapist knowing clearly what kind of stimulus he in fact is (the "myth of therapist homogeneity" is apparent not only in outcome research, where Kiesler [1966] first labeled it, but also in much theoretical writing on technique in the psychoanalytic literature); (2) the advisability of the therapist *intentionally* being a different stimulus at different times (cf. Alexander, 1956; Wolf, 1966); (3) the role of group therapy in eliciting a wider range of the patient's responses to various interpersonal situations; and (4) the

---

1. It should be clear, however, that when the therapist does not reveal his reactions to the patient's behavior, he makes more likely the observation of hidden assumptions and strivings which might not emerge were clearer clues as to "expected" or "appropriate" behavior to homogenize patient response. Stone (1961) and Greenson (1967) have presented sophisticated discussions of these issues from a Freudian point of view. My differences from their view center on the degree to which psychodynamic descriptions can and should consider evoking situations.

relation between interpersonal assessments and behavioral assessments as ways of sampling response to a variety of situations (cf. below and Goldfried & Kent, 1972).

It may also be noted that in some sense experimenters are now going through a reorientation similar to that which occurred in psychoanalysis. The work of writers such as Rosenthal (1966) and Orne (1962) points to the limits of a "blank-screen" conception of the experimenter, and the importance of recognizing that the experimenter too is a *participant*–observer. Parts of the discussion below suggest that, rather than being merely a nuisance to be corrected for, the experimenter's influence as a participating human other may be an untapped source of richer knowledge of personality functioning.

FRAMING OF QUESTIONS BY
ANALYSTS AND EXPERIMENTERS

It should now be clear that the picture of psychodynamic theories as necessarily describing people as moved solely by inner urges and as inattentive to environmental demands is a portrait in straw. The mere fact that behavior varies from situation to situation is in no way a refutation of the psychodynamic approach. Equally fallacious is the view, held by many dynamic thinkers, that all behavior therapists are unaware of individual differences, blind to the role of language and cognition, and uninterested in how a person's history has led to idiosyncratic patterns of equating situations and developing preferences (see, e.g., Mischel, 1968, or Bandura, 1969). Tenable theories converge as their range of inquiry begins to expand and overlap. Nonetheless, it hardly needs to be pointed out that Mischel's conclusions from the data he cited do differ considerably from the view of man evident in the writings of even modern psychodynamic thinkers. This chapter now considers how in some respects both views may be seen as correct, as a step toward guidelines for theoretical integration and practical innovation.

"Neurotics" and "Normals"

Psychodynamic theories developed originally to account for primarily maladaptive behavior. Learning theories, in contrast, have tended to start with observations of successful alteration of behavior in response to situational demands. (Learning curves are typically monotonically increasing.) Though both broad theoretical perspec-

tives have subsequently developed to encompass detailed consideration of both adaptive and maladaptive behavior, each still bears the
stamp of its origin. Learning theorists prefer to examine how even
behavior that is troublesome is in some way in tune with current
environmental contingencies. Dynamically oriented thinkers, on the
other hand, frequently are most interested in how a person's behavior is *out of touch* with the current situation, how he *fails* to adapt to
changing situations.

In a sense, the defining property of neurotic behavior is its
rigidity, its inflexibility in the face of changed conditions. Psychodynamic theories, which originated as theories of neurosis, heavily
emphasize concepts that account for lack of change and are particularly designed to describe the persistence of past patterns into the
present. Among the most prominent of these concepts is that of
transference, the tendency to react to persons in the present as
though they were important figures from one's past.[2] Transference
is viewed by psychodynamic thinkers as a phenomenon evident in all
people, but one whose influence may be expected to be greater in
more severely neurotic persons than in the general population.
When one considers the difference between the population of severe
neurotics who constitute the observational base for psychodynamic
theories, and the less psychologically handicapped groups who form
the population for most of the studies Mischel cited as evidence for
specificity, at least some of the difference in theoretical perspective
becomes understandable.[3] It is likely that the neurotic patients seen
by psychoanalysts are considerably less able to alter their behavior
appropriately from situation to situation and person to person than a
typical group of children or adults. That inability is a major reason
why the former are in therapy.

Ambiguity and Affect

Mischel noted in passing, but did not emphasize, that when stimulus
conditions are ambiguous, individual differences arising from past

2. Here again it should be clear that transference need not be viewed as a completely
autonomous inner disposition, but rather as a particular way of organizing new
stimulus input, biased but not completely unresponsive to the actual situation (cf.
Alexander, 1956; Sullivan, 1953; Wolf, 1966).

3. Alker (1972) has made a similar point in an important recent paper that may be
seen as complementing the present contribution. Several sections which appeared in
earlier drafts of this chapter have been shortened or omitted because they are excel-
lently dealt with by Alker.

history are more noticeable. Here lies another important source of difference in the observations and theorizing of analysts and social behaviorist researchers. In addition to focusing their efforts on somewhat different populations, workers from these differing orientations also concentrate on different phenomena.

The data generated and examined by most behaviorally oriented students of normal and abnormal behavior involve changes in clearly denotable behaviors in response to clear, unambiguous changes in environmental events. The subject, or the model in some studies, is given money or has it taken away; he is shocked or he escapes from shock; he is allowed privileges or they are denied him; etc. Under such circumstances, a kind of lawfulness tends to emerge in which the complicated formulations of psychodynamic theorists seem very much beside the point. Behavior varies closely with changes in environmental events. The individual's "learning history with similar stimuli" is, of course, relevant, but one hardly needs to conceptualize complex personality structures with considerable cross-situational application. Change the situation and you change the behavior.

To the analyst, however, such studies are likely to seem irrelevant to the phenomena of interest to him. The data he observes consist largely of statements such as: "I feel angry at my girlfriend because she smiled in a condescending way. She said it was a warm smile, but it didn't feel that way to me." Or, "My boss criticized me for being so insistent with him, but I could tell from his tone of voice he was really proud of my assertiveness, and I had a good feeling that he supports me." Or, "It seemed to me you were more silent this hour. I felt you were angry with me because I complained about the fee, and I was afraid you'd say we should stop therapy. I know you'll think I'm the angry one, and I want to stop, but I think you're wrong, and I resent your distortion of my feelings."

Such reports do describe behavior in response to environmental events. In principle, a girlfriend's smile, a boss's tone of voice, or an analyst's silence are events that can be observed, just like the administration of a food pellet to a rat or a token to a back-ward patient. But whereas the latter two events are specifically chosen to be clear and unequivocal, the interpersonal events scrutinized by the analyst are often exceedingly ambiguous. The experimenter, no less than the subject, must judge on largely idiosyncratic grounds whether a smile is warm or condescending, and observer reliability regarding a tone of voice is unlikely to be impressive. Views may and do differ as to whether it is a wise *strategy* to study such ambiguous events at this point in the development of our discipline, but it must be acknowledged that we all spend a good portion of each day responding more or less adequately to just such ambiguous "stimuli."

The events focused on by analysts, then, tend to be those in which their patients' ability to discriminate is most challenged. Finely articulated alteration of response with stimulus changes, evident in studies where environmental events are readily discriminable, is not so evident where affective, interpersonal events are concerned. In the latter realm, early global and generalized predispositions may less readily become differentiated, and assumptions and reaction tendencies may apply to a wider range of situations. In Piagetian terms, analysts are likely observing phenomena where difficulties in perceptual discrimination make assimilation predominant, whereas Mischel's emphasis on specificity applies to situations where a greater degree of accommodation and differentiation is possible.

It should also be noted that in the examples of psychoanalytic data noted above, the patient's *response* is complicated and ambiguous, as well as the situation to which the response is made. The man who claimed his analyst was more silent during the hour stressed that he (the patient) was not angry, that it was the analyst who was angry at him. But he ended up saying he *resented* the analyst's distortion, and he earlier *complained* about the fee. One may well wonder whether this man was in fact angry; or, framed differently, at what point in the session he first became angry; or, from a slightly different perspective, which situations evoke in him a tendency to attack or hurt and which to experience and label his response as "anger." However one wishes to frame the question, it would seem that how best to conceptualize and describe his affective response to the situation he perceived is exceedingly difficult, and that a great deal of interpretation and inference is necessary to decide fully just how he did respond.

Many researchers, faced with such ambiguity, have decided it is best to study simply the overt behaviors that can be reliably and consistently identified and that to worry about whether or not the patient is really "angry" is a fruitless endeavor. Such a strategy does yield clearer curves and a greater sense of having discerned a repeatable pattern. But it must also be noted that the dilemma faced by the researcher is also faced by each of us in our everyday lives. We are all frequently faced with the task of understanding and identifying our own affective responses to the events of our lives, and as Dollard and Miller (1950) have pointed out, failure to label accurately one's own drive states has very serious consequences. Further, the personal experience of feeling and wishing, no matter how difficult to study, remains an exceedingly important psychological phenomenon, and changes in experienced feeling states are often the implicit hidden criteria of avowedly behavioral programs of therapy (Locke, 1971).

The difficulty in accurately identifying ambiguous affective and motivational phenomena renders perception of these events, whether one's own feelings and wishes or those of others, peculiarly susceptible to the distorting effects of anxiety; hence the particular emphasis on anxiety and defense by psychoanalytic authors. In attempting to study defensive processes experimentally, researchers have frequently focused on distortions of perception of *external* stimuli and have been forced to introduce ambiguity through artificial means, such as tachistoscopic presentation. Such procedures correctly take into account that the concept of defensive distortion depends on ambiguity and does not imply an arbitrary and unchecked intrusion upon perception of clearly discriminable events. The study of defense via perceptual experiments has, however, typically involved a number of other difficulties (Wachtel, 1972a, Wolitzky & Wachtel, 1973). Psychodynamic concepts of defense are concerned primarily with phenomena of *self*-perception, particularly perception of one's own affective and motivational states. As with other aspects of psychoanalytic thinking, defensive phenomena too are now seen as responsive to environmental, as well as organismic, events, but their relation to environmental occurrences is seen as far more complex than is the case with the behavioral phenomena typically studied in social learning experiments (see Silverman, 1972, for an interesting and lucid discussion of clinical and experimental data bearing on the psychoanalytic conceptualization of this relationship).

The preference of behaviorally oriented investigators for seeking simple stimulus–response relationships, and for focusing on clearly discernible events, may lead to an underestimation of the importance of complex anxiety-distorted mediating processes. In turn, the particularly strong interest of psychoanalytic investigators in the murky subtleties of wish and feeling has likely led to an underestimation of how directly their patients might respond to environmental contingencies when they are up off the couch and taking clearly visible steps. Results of efforts to alter directly psychotic behaviors (e.g., Ayllon & Azrin, 1968; Ullmann & Krasner, 1966) or particular behavioral deficits in children (e.g., Allen, Hart, Buell, Harris, & Wolf, 1964) suggest that this may be the case. As Davison (1969) has pointed out, however, such alterations of overt behavior do not necessarily imply an alteration of the ideas and feelings that accompany them.

The "Implacable Experimenter"

Still another way in which differing strategies of investigation may lead dynamic and behavioral investigators to differing conclusions is illuminated by an interpersonal perspective on human behavior. If each person's behavior is largely a function of the interpersonal situation in which he is engaged, then when two or more people interact, they are each not only influenced by the behavior of the other (in the familiar sense of a response to a stimulus); each also influences the behavior of the other, by virtue of the stimulus properties of his own behavior. Person A responds to the stimulus properties of person B, but person B in turn is responsive to the behavior of person A, which he has in part determined. Further, these are both continuous adaptations, not simply sequential. From such a systems orientation, the understanding of any one person's behavior in an interpersonal situation solely in terms of the stimuli *presented to* him gives only a partial and misleading picture. For, to a very large extent, these stimuli are *created by* him. They are responses to his own behaviors, events he has played a role in bringing about, rather than occurrences independent of who he is and over which he has no control. The seductive, hysterical woman who is annoyed at having to face the aggressive amorous advances of numbers of men has much to learn about the origin of the stimuli she complains she must cope with. So too does the man who complains about the problems in dealing with his wife's nagging, but fails to understand how this situation, which presents itself to him, derives in turn from his own procrastinating, unresponsible behavior.

From the above considerations we may see that the postulation of consistency of personality need not be incompatible with the view that people may be acutely sensitive to changes in the stimulus situation. For consistency need not be the result of a static structure that moves from situation to situation and pays no heed to stimuli. Much of the rigidity and persistence of human behavior can be accounted for without conceiving of an id, cut off from the perceiving, adapting aspect of the personality; and the striking tendency, observed by Freud and many others, for human beings to persist in beating their heads against countless proverbial walls does not require the postulation of a repetition compulsion (Freud, 1920/1955). Rather, one can in many cases view consistency as a result of being in particular situations frequently, but situations largely of one's own making and themselves describable as a characteristic of one's personality.[4]

These considerations suggest that the finding in many experiments of rather minimal consistency in behavior from situation to situation (Mischel, 1968) may be in part an artifact of the conceptual model and research strategy that has typically guided American

4. Millon (1969, Chapter 5) has also pointed to ways in which the principles of social learning theory may be consistent with the expectation of considerable generality in important aspects of personality.

personality research. Mischel noted the discrepancy between these research findings and the persistent impression that people are characterizable by their typical way of acting. He attributed the discrepancy largely to a documented tendency for observers to *falsely* construe consistency when diversity is the fact. But genuine consistency may also occur in most life situations and yet not be evident in the laboratory. For the typical experiment, with its emphasis on standardized independent variables as antecedents of the behavior to be studied, may short-circuit the mutual influence process described above, which is importantly involved in the generation of consistency.

In most experiments, some stimulus event is designated as the independent variable, and every effort is made to assure that this independent variable is presented to each subject in the same fashion. Research assistants are trained to behave similarly with each subject, and if they do vary their behavior in response to some feature of the subject's interpersonal style, this is generally viewed as a failure of the experimental method; the "independent variable" is supposed to be standardized. Such a model of research, with the behavior of the experimenter preprogrammed to occur independently of the myriad interpersonal cues of the subject, may be designated as the model of the "implacable experimenter."[5]

Such a model is well suited for testing the isolated effect of a particular independent variable, for it assures, if proper controls are included, that that variable is what accounts for the differing behaviors in the various experimental groups. Mischel's survey suggests that in experiments conducted in this fashion, the behavior of individuals will vary considerably when the "independent variable" is varied (subject, of course, to the limiting parameters discussed above—e.g., degree of psychopathology and ambiguity of the situation encountered).

But let us note what such a research procedure does *not* examine. Although the highly practiced and routinized behavior of the experimenter does not rule out all opportunity for observing individual differences in the subjects of the study—differences in perception or interpretation of events, or in response to the same situation, may be noted—it does effectively prevent the subject from recreating familiar stimulus situations by evoking typical complementary behavior by the experimenter in response to the subject's behavior. In most

5. Of course, some behavior of the experimenter may be *contingent* on the subject's behavior, but it should be clear that this is a far cry from the kind of interpersonal processes discussed in this section. See Carson (1969) for descriptions of research that comes closer to the model discussed here; see also Laing, Phillipson, & Lee (1966).

life situations, whether someone is nice to us or nasty, attentive or bored, seductive or straight-laced is in good part a function of our own behavior. But in the typical experiment the subject has little control over the interpersonal situation he encounters. It has been determined even before he enters the room. Borrowing the language of the existentialists, such experiments reveal a person in his "thrownness," but do not make clear his responsibility for his situation.

Mischel (1968) suggested that the impression of identity or constancy in personality may be reinforced by regularities in the environmental contexts in which a person is observed. Mischel's focus is on the occasions when the regularity is a function of the conditions of observation rather than of the person's life, as when we only see someone in a particular context, though he in fact operates in a wide variety of situations. But what if the person is *usually* in a particular situation? In such a case it may be true that his behavior is describable as a function of his situation, and perhaps also that he could act differently if the situation were different. But then we must ask why for some people the situation is so rarely different. How do we understand the man who is constantly in the presence of overbearing women, or constantly immersed in his work, or constantly with weaker men who are cowed by him but offer little honest feedback? Further, how do we understand the man who seems to bring out the bitchy side of *whatever* woman he encounters, or ends up turning almost all social encounters into work sessions, or intimidates even men who usually are honest and direct?

Certainly we need a good deal more data before we are sure just how general such phenomena are, how characterizable people are by the situations they "just happen" to run into. What should be clear, however, is that piecemeal observation of "stimuli" and "responses" or "independent" and "dependent" variables, divorced from the temporal context of mutually influencing events, can shed little light on these questions. If experiments in the implacable-experimenter model are the central source of data for one's view of man, it is understandable that conceptions of man as constructing his life or his world, or of personality as a self-maintaining system, would have little appeal.

Bem (1972), in a recent defense of Mischel's critique, has argued that the burden of proof lies with those who would posit considerable consistency in personality to demonstrate it empirically. But empirical studies may get different answers, depending on how they ask their questions. A conceptual understanding of the limits of the implacable-experimenter model, as well as of the other issues discussed above, may prevent a premature judgment of failure.

CONCLUDING COMMENTS

To ask whether behavior is best describable in terms of global traits or as responses to particular situations is to misleadingly dichotomize a very complex and important question. We have seen that modern psychodynamic thinkers do indeed consider how an individual responds to the situations he encounters. The difference between psychodynamic and social behaviorist positions lies not in whether the role of environmental events is considered, but rather in the nature of the relationship between environmental and behavioral events. To the psychodynamic theorist, this relationship is more complex and less direct than it tends to be in social learning accounts. Psychodynamic investigators have been particularly impressed with the complicating effects of anxiety and efforts learned to avoid it. The protracted helplessness of the human young, his need to rely on seemingly all-powerful giants for many years, and his almost inevitable fear of displeasing these enigmatic authorities are seen by psychodynamic thinkers as making anxiety and defense a regularly important feature in the development of personality and psychopathology.

It follows from the considerations advanced in this chapter that recent efforts to invalidate the psychodynamic viewpoint on the basis of currently available data on specificity and generality are based on misconceptions both of what modern psychodynamic theories are like and of the bearing of most research studies on the critical issues addressed by psychodynamic thinkers. The present arguments do not imply, however, that this is a time for psychodynamic workers to breathe easy and conduct business as usual. Mischel, for example, has based his case against psychodynamic theories not only on the observations of behavioral variability considered above, but also on what he views as a failure of psychodynamic clinicians to demonstrate the utility of their judgments. In his more recent writings (e.g., Mischel, 1971), this issue has become the central focus of Mischel's critique of the psychodynamic approach, and his earlier work (Mischel, 1968), like that of Meehl (1954), Sawyer (1966), and others, reviews considerable evidence that may be construed as casting doubt on the utility of psychodynamically derived assessment methods. Holt's (1970) recent paper is in many respects a cogent and effective reply to such critiques; but it is consistent with the arguments of the present chapter, and with Holt's paper as well, to suggest that psychodynamic theories might well benefit from further consideration of specificity in human behavior, and to consider as well ways in which clinical assessment methods may have lagged behind the theoretical developments in psychodynamic theory discussed earlier.

Psychodynamic theories are still based largely on a body of clinical observation. Work such as that of Chapman and Chapman (1967), which illustrates the pitfalls in such observational methods, presents another serious challenge to psychodynamic workers. Whether psychodynamic ideas can or should be examined by strictly experimental methods is a controversial question.[6] Although a great many experiments have been inspired by psychoanalytic concepts, the bearing of experimental findings on psychoanalytic theory is far from clear (cf. Hilgard, 1968; Horwitz, 1963; Rapaport, 1959). The present discussion has pointed to ways in which current experimental studies tend to focus on different phenomena than those traditionally of central interest to psychoanalytic investigators. Unless experiments can be devised that adequately deal with the problem of man's behavior as both chosen and caused (Wachtel, 1969), with disavowed intentionality (Schafer, 1973) with freedom and inhibition of affective experience, and with the perpetuation of old patterns and expectations by the evocation of "countertransferential" behavior (cf. Laing et al., 1966; Wolf, 1966), some form of naturalistic clinical observation will probably continue to be an important means of exploring key psychological questions. The need for such efforts to be more systematic (e.g., by examination of tape-recorded clinical data, open to alternative interpretations and checks of reliability) is obvious. Some of the work reviewed by Luborsky and Spence (1971, especially pp. 423-430) represents important steps in this direction. It is likely that some of Freud's more baroque formulations will prove casualties of such refined observation. But the conviction of many social behaviorist writers that almost all of psychodynamic thought will prove to be merely a time-wasting detour on the road to a purely situational theory (see Bowers, 1973) seems to me to be a product of the failure to recognize that psychodynamic theories have developed from observations of phenomena that experimentally derived theories have hardly considered.

Developments in behavior therapy are likely to prove a corrective to the zealots of both dynamic and behavioral persuasion. Already, the impressive results reported by behavior therapists are forcing psychodynamic thinkers to reconsider a number of their basic premises and their limitations. On the other hand, contact with

6. The too ready assumption by many psychologists that the experimental method is the only path to truth has been critically examined by Bowers (1973) in a valuable paper that is in many respects complementary to the present one.

the more complex problems of neurosis and "real-life" joy and suffering is likely to bring more to the fore the phenomena that until
now behavioral theories have dealt with only by analogy. In observations of behavior therapists at work, I have noted a good deal more
interviewing and efforts to grasp ambiguous occurrences interpre-
tively than one would expect from the literature (see also Klein,
Dittman, Parloff, & Gill, 1969). Recent writings by practicing behavior therapists (e.g., Lazarus, 1971) have stressed the primacy of
careful clinical observation over strict adherence to a stimulus–
response faith. In future communications, guidelines for the integration of dynamic and behavioral approaches will be examined in detail.
It is hoped that the present contribution will aid in diminishing the
resistance to such efforts.

14

Interaction Cycles, Unconscious Processes, and the Person–Situation Issue

Few modern personality researchers, theorists, or clinicians are likely to disagree that behavior is jointly determined by environmental events and person variables. Yet, beyond agreement on this broad, almost platitudinous level, there is considerable ambiguity and disagreement regarding precisely *how* person variables and situational variables jointly bring about the events that psychologists study. To evaluate the contributions from various theoretical perspectives, or even to determine where they differ in substance and where only in semantics or in allegiance to different men and different historical traditions, is no easy matter.

In this chapter I take the position that much of the current debate in personality theory derives from the utilization—by theorists of a variety of persuasions—of conceptual strategies and units of observation which have been too narrow or restricted. It is my contention that it is possible to discern a level of orderliness in how people live their lives that can encompass the seemingly contradictory views and findings of psychoanalytic observers and of researchers guided by social learning theory. On this level of coherence—the self-perpetuating cycle of interaction—it is possible to integrate the roles played by unconscious processes and by perception of current environmental events and, importantly, to gain some understanding of how these interact. The rejection by social learning theorists of conceptions of unconscious motivation and conflict, and by psychoanalytic thinkers of efforts at direct intervention into troubling life patterns, is thereby put in a new light.

Reprinted by permission from D. Magnusson & N. Endler (Eds.), *Personality at the Crossroads: Current Issues in Interactional Psychology*. Hillsdale, N.J.: Erlbaum, 1977.

SELF-PERPETUATING INTERACTION CYCLES

Let me at this point indicate very concretely what I have in mind when I suggest that the self-perpetuating cycle is an extremely useful unit for the study of personality. Consider a man who may be described by a psychoanalyst as evidencing reaction formations against intense and frightening rage. We may notice that he frequently acts in an excessively and inappropriately[1] meek, helpful, or cooperative manner. We would probably see some ways in which he suffers from this pattern of behavior, either directly or indirectly (e.g., depression, low self-esteem, psychosomatic symptoms). Moreover, we would be likely to see some evidence that very angry, destructive behavior is being actively held back (perhaps in his dreams, in slips of the tongue, in "accidental" or "unintended" consequences of his actions, in the degree to which his excessive niceness is greatest when anger or assertion would seem most likely, etc.). Patterns such as this have been understood, with some justification, as reflecting the persisting influence of intrapsychic conflict.

However, let us step back and examine such a life with a wider lens. We might then be struck by some other aspects of this man's excessive meekness and niceness. Looking at how others react to the social cues embodied in his behavior, we would be likely to find that this pattern of behavior leads to a variety of ways in which he gets taken advantage of, dismissed, deprived, and frustrated.

Living that way is likely to be infuriating. Yet fury, indeed even annoyance, is not part of his self-image nor of the pattern of behavior he finds permissible. His social adaptation and sense of being acceptable has emphasized being "nice" to an extreme, and arousal of anger is frightening; so he tries even harder to inhibit the feelings and incipient behaviors aroused and emphasizes again cooperative, mild-mannered habits of thought and action. Instead of solving his dilemma, however, this (far from completely conscious) strategy again leads to experiences that generate angry feelings and hence (given his particular adaptive strategy) the need to defend against them. Thus, although his defensive behavior may be understood as in response to conflict over angry impulses, the impulses themselves can be seen as a function of the defense against them: Were he not acting in such a way that he constantly stifled himself and invited others to do so, he would not be so full of rage. On the other hand,

---

1. It is important to recognize that not *any* nonaggressive behavior can be taken as evidence for a defense against aggressive tendencies. As discussed below, the rules for making such inferences are not as explicit as we may hope, but they are far from as arbitrary as is sometimes implied.

were he not so full of rage, so ready to do very hostile and destructive things, he would not be so afraid of giving up the desperate defensive efforts. Impulse leads to defense, defense leads to impulse, and the cycle keeps maintaining itself.

Let me give a second brief example and then elaborate how I think the cyclical view differs from the traditional psychoanalytic one. Suppose one sees in a particular patient evidence for strong Oedipal conflict—longing for sexual union with the pure, chaste, care-giving mother, and anxiety as a result of such forbidden longing. Suppose also, as is commonly the case, one sees difficulties in the patient's sex life (whether gross, as in impotence or acute inability to make advances to the opposite sex, or more subtle, as in being able to feel lustful only with women he does not like, or functioning as a sexual athlete but not really being able to make an emotional commitment to the partner). One *could* understand his sexual problem as a function of his Oedipal conflict, and this would, I believe, often be justified. It is only part of the story, however.

Again expanding our view, we can see how the signals the patient gives off as a result of his conflict—that is, his actual overt (although sometimes subtle) interpersonal actions and messages— lead to consequences that feed back in such a way as to intensify his longing for a fantasied figure who is pure, all-giving, all-protecting, nurturant, and larger than life. (Here it is important to recognize that the figure longed for *is* a fantasy. The word "mother" obscures. He does not long for the *real* mother. Alexander Portnoy does not long for the Sophie he describes to us in such repulsively accurate terms. He longs for a *fantasy* figure, who has become enmeshed with his concept of "mother.")

Now, in traditional psychoanalytic accounts, such fantasy figures, as well as the various conflicted impulses the patient is struggling with (e.g., the rage in the first example, the desire to wallow in mess or disorder in an obsessive, etc.) tend to be viewed as *preservations of the past*, as fantasies and wishes from *childhood*, which have remained unchanged since then. The processes of defense are viewed as creating a split of psychological functioning that renders certain psychological processes and events not susceptible to the influence of new perceptions of reality or newer, more sophisticated cognitive developments that alter the person's understanding of how the world works. In the language of ego psychology, perception and organization are characteristic of the ego, and the id, which is split off from it, is not influenced very much by perceptual processes and does not show the kind of organization or pressures toward logic and consistency that are seen in ego processes.

This model stresses that the surprising wishes and fantasies which become evident in the course of psychoanalytic exploration have been preserved in their original form, essentially uninfluenced by what has come later (i.e., we want childish things and maintain childish fantasies *in spite of* our adult reality). To return to our hypothetical Oedipally conflicted individual, for example, he is seen as suffering from a piece of his childhood which influences his present without being influenced by it, and the persistence of which has to do with an intrapsychic state of affairs (the defenses which keep it "id" instead of allowing it to be integrated into the ego and hence made reasonable). The cyclical view, in contrast, sees his Oedipal longings not as a direct preservation of childhood, and not as persisting in spite of how he currently lives, but as a result of precisely how he is currently living and what feedback he is currently receiving. In this view, early childhood fantasies and fears play an important role in *starting* the patient on a life course in which restrictions and inhibitions are characteristic of his sexual encounters. Once the pattern is started, however, both self-initiated restrictions and the disturbing or disappointing response of partners to anxious, constricted, or insensitive actions by the patient begin to have effects on the process, confirming his apprehension and conflict about sexual experiences and hence leading him to again approach sex fearfully and once more induce the experiences that confirm his anxieties still again. The early fantasies that have been so major in initiating his repeated pattern are also likely to be maintained by the feedback that is generated: If one already has a tendency to long for the figure who once nurtured, soothed, and caressed one's body without the performance demands of adult sexuality, such a tendency is likely to be strengthened by repeated experiences of unsatisfying sex in adulthood, even as it arouses anxiety which helps to keep those adult experiences unsatisfying.

CYCLICAL PSYCHODYNAMICS AND SOCIAL LEARNING THEORY

The cyclical view described here shares much with the Freudian model but differs in important ways. Both, for example, emphasize the importance of unconscious processes and suggest that early experiences are likely to have a major role in shaping later personality. In the cyclical view, however, seemingly irrational and anachronistic wishes and fantasies are not just remnants of the past, but are understood in terms of the kind of experiences the person continues to have (largely because of the influence and consequences of those very wishes and fantasies); and the critical role of childhood is understood in terms of the way in which the particular patterns of behavior one develops skew the kinds of later experiences one is likely to encounter, and hence create an idiosyncratic environment of a sort likely to maintain the very pattern which produced that kind of environment in the first place.

Perhaps most importantly, the two models differ in their implications for how personality changes. Elsewhere, in a more extended presentation (Wachtel, 1977), I have tried to show how the cyclical psychodynamic model lends itself to an integration of psychodynamic methods with those of behavior therapy and have argued for the value of such an integration both in clinical practice and in personality theory.

To many proponents of social learning theory, such an integration seems unlikely, if not impossible. It has been claimed that psychodynamic and social learning approaches are "fundamentally different" (Lazarus, 1973; Mischel, 1971). In its current state, social learning theory does seem to differ rather substantially in some respects from psychodynamic approaches. Perhaps most crucially, writers in the social learning tradition have tended to more or less explicitly disavow any interest in conflict, as well as the necessity for inferring motives and expectancies of which the individual is not aware. Mischel (1971) asserts that "social behavior assessments do not . . . infer [the individual's] conflicts and motives" (p. 77). Bandura's (1969) large and influential volume does not have a single reference to conflict in its 27-page index. Brody (1972), moreover, whose text is strongly in the camp of social learning theory, explicitly acknowledges that such findings as those of Epstein and Fenz, which are based on a conflict model, "do not appear to be amenable to an analysis in social learning terms" (p. 333) (although he then goes on to endorse social learning theory with no further mention of Epstein and Fenz's work, adding that social learning theory may be fruitfully integrated with Eysenck's theory because it shares such "ideological presuppositions" as being "antipsychoanalytic").

Brody's statement in particular reveals that the disavowal of interest in conflict and unconscious processes (which Dollard and Miller showed long ago can be readily conceptualized in learning theory terms) is not a logical necessity but an ideological commitment. Instead of being viewed as an *alternative* to the concepts of social learning theory, psychodynamic concepts can readily be seen as complementary concepts that, among other things, fill in some of the details in the open-ended, content-free skeleton provided by social learning theory (cf. Pepitone, 1974).

The importance of reinforcement per se is not being questioned, for example, if one looks for possible reinforcers of individuals' behavior of which they are not aware and which they may even vehemently deny are in fact reinforcing their behavior (nor, in such instances, if one understands further that their denial of the role of such reinforcers is itself reinforced by reduction of the anxiety generated by thoughts such as "I enjoy hurting my mother" or "I feel better when I can get someone else to take care of me"). Similarly, the concept of expectancy is extended but certainly not challenged by considering that individuals may anticipate outcomes to certain actions that are quite idiosyncratic and that, again, they do not recognize as the expectancies which guide their behavior (i.e., "unconscious fantasies").

Part of the opposition to concepts of unconscious motivation, conflict, or fantasy seems to derive from insufficient knowledge and understanding of recent trends in psychodynamic thought. Formulations in terms of energies, libidinal cathexes, etc., are indeed problematic, but these problems have been recognized by a number of psychodynamic thinkers as well, and it has been clearly demonstrated that such formulations are not at all essential to the main points of psychoanalysis (e.g., Klein, 1967; Loevinger, 1966; Schafer, 1972, 1973; Wachtel, 1969). In particular, Klein's effort to recast psychoanalytic thinking in feedback terms, and Schafer's development of an "action language" for psychoanalysis, in which all thing-like entities are eliminated and the full range of psychoanalytic ideas is expressed in terms of what the person is doing, go far toward reducing the gap between psychoanalytic thought and academic psychology and are "must" reading for anyone who purports to understand the potential contribution of psychoanalysis. Schafer's approach in particular is strikingly congruent with Mischel's (1973b) emphasis on considering what a person *does* rather than what he or she *has*.

Mischel's (1973a) contention that "[t]he psychodynamic approach [*sic*] . . . shares with the trait approach a disinterest in behaviors except as they serve as signs—albeit more indirect signs—of generalized dispositions" (p. 254) lumps all psychodynamic approaches together. It should be clear that the cyclical psychodynamic view described here is in fact crucially concerned with the person's behavior—indeed, even the persistence of unconscious motives and fantasies is understood in terms of the consequences of what the person actually does in his daily life. However, if not *exclusively* concerned with behavior as providing clues to cognitive and motivational processes, this approach certainly does view behavior in this way as well. The data with which one is confronted in doing intensive psychotherapy seem to many to require inferring motivational tendencies and cognitive constructions which are influential in the person's life, although not readily accessible to awareness.

Social learning theory has been derived primarily from a data base of experimental research, and, accounting for the data they encounter, social learning theorists have not seen a need to make such inferences. The experimental method is, of course, an enormously important tool of scientific investigation, but as a rather exclusive data base for theorizing about personality, experiments can be limiting and can lead to misleading conclusions regarding what kinds of concepts are necessary. I have previously discussed, for example (Wachtel, 1973b), how experiments frequently fail to address the way in which we generate the stimuli we encounter, and thereby lead to overlooking an important way in which consistency characterizes a human life, even if in principle behavior may vary considerably when the situation is different.

Even more importantly, perhaps, experiments frequently fail to examine the *kinds* of behaviors and situations in which the concepts of psychodynamic theories seem necessary. The need for standardization, among other things, has led to the investigation of a restricted range of behaviors in response to a restricted range of situations. Not only are independent variables chosen that can be presented in a preprogrammed way, but both independent and dependent variables tend to be chosen that can be identified, labeled, or categorized quickly and with high reliability. The advantages of such a choice are obvious; the difficulties both in conducting and in interpreting research not so designed are drummed into every graduate student very early in his or her career.

What is less frequently noted, however, is the price that is paid for these gifts that the wry god of methodology has bestowed upon us. To gain the advantages just noted, investigators are often required to investigate the phenomena of interest to them only by approximation or analogy. The assumption (and the hope) is that the variables are the same in the laboratory situations and those of everyday life. However, there is good reason to be skeptical that this is indeed the case. Particularly with regard to the role of unconscious motives, fantasies, and conflicts, such experiments may be misleading. In having chosen stimuli and responses of minimal ambiguity, many studies are set up in precisely the way that most effectively minimizes the role of unconscious organizing processes, and theories primarily derived from such studies indeed find little need for conceptualizing such processes. In the kinds of situations investigated in the laboratory, behavior seems to vary smoothly with changes in stimulation, with no need to conceptualize more complicated mediators that require a good deal of inference (see Wachtel, 1973a, 1973b for a fuller discussion of the issue of ambiguity and unconscious processes).

The Relevance of Behavior Therapy

It may be objected, with some justification, that social learning theory has not been limited in its concerns exclusively to the results of experiments, and that in some respects its most important source of support is the success of the therapeutic efforts with real-life problems that have derived from this point of view. Here several considerations are relevant. First of all, as social learning writers themselves frequently point out, the success of therapeutic efforts is by no means a clear indication of the correctness of the theory that underlies them. The factors that account for the efficacy of systematic desensitization, for example, are by no means clearly established, and explanations of this therapeutic method have stressed psychodynamic, Hullian, Guthrian, cognitive, operant, and other concepts (cf. Davison & Wilson, 1973; Feather & Rhoads, 1972a, 1972b; Goldfried, 1971; Leitenberg, Agras, Barlow, & Oliveau, 1969; Wachtel, 1977, Chapter 8; Weitzman, 1967; Wilkins, 1971; Wilson & Davison, 1971; Wolpe, 1958).

Second, it may be noted that the interaction between social learning theory and clinical practice has not been bidirectional, as has been the case in psychoanalysis. Psychoanalytic theory has not only been the theoretical foundation for particular kinds of clinical practices, but has also been extensively influenced in turn by the observations deriving from these practices. Freud revised his conceptions extensively on a number of occasions as a result of what he observed in his clinical work. There are few comparable instances in which social learning theory has been similarly influenced by observations in the clinic. The concepts one sees represented in the texts on social learning theory are almost exclusively derived from laboratory experiments. The creative innovations and clinical observations reported by behavioral practitioners have had little impact on how social learning writers tell students to conceive of personality. Their role in the textbooks has been almost exclusively to demonstrate the sufficiency of these laboratory-derived concepts. (The recent increase of interest by social learning theorists in "self-control" seems to be a noteworthy exception, and a very positive sign.)

It must also be noted that the effectiveness of behavior therapy with the broad range of problems people bring to the clinic has by no means been clearly established, nor has its superiority over traditional psychotherapeutic approaches. The clearest demonstrations of efficacy have been in reducing a number of quite specific fears and in instituting a number of basic social behaviors, such as minimal language or orderly ward behavior in autistic, retarded, and schizophrenic individuals. These demonstrations are not unimpressive, especially where they have established behavior that others have felt was impossible to institute, and they are bolstered by a large number of case studies which provide more or less impressive circumstantial evidence for the efficacy of these principles with more complex and subtle problems of human intimacy, despair, identity, and self-fulfillment. In these latter realms, however, the evidence for behavior therapy is on very much the same footing as that for psychodynamic therapies, which can also present case studies with more or less impressive documentation. It is simply not the case that therapeutic efforts which have eschewed the notion of unconscious motives, thoughts, and conflicts have been proved clearly superior to those which do utilize such concepts. (For a fuller discussion of the relative evidence for the two approaches to therapy, see Wachtel, 1977, Chapter 8.)

Furthermore, in practice, the behavior therapists I have observed do seem to infer motives and conflicts that the patient does not report, although they do not do so as frequently as dynamically oriented therapists. Published case reports and writings on theory by behaviorally oriented psychologists, however, tend to explicitly rule out the role of such events. This has the effect of making an important part of clinical practice an "underground" which, because it is inexplicit and hidden, cannot be fully developed or examined. It also leads to unnecessary restrictions in theory. Much of what goes on in behavior therapy is consistent with the laws of learning in the same sense that it is consistent with the laws of physics. It does not contradict these laws, but those laws alone hardly account for what goes on or give the therapist much guidance as to what to do next.

Evidence, Experimental and Not

In evaluating statements about the evidential status of psychodynamic concepts, it is important to recognize how frequently the question of whether there is sufficient evidence is treated as equivalent to whether there is *experimental* evidence, as if other contexts for observation have no relevance. Much of the evidence for psychodynamic concepts involves discerning coherences in complex events that bring some order to what otherwise may appear to be a bewildering collage of unrelated occurrences. As an increasing number of sophisticated psychoanalytic thinkers have begun to recognize, the rules of evidence and logic of inquiry relevant here are in many respects more akin to those of such disciplines as history or literary criticism than to those of laboratory science. Psychodynamic hypotheses tend to be formulated from and verified by a network of converging observations that are capable of confirming or disconfirming hypotheses, or leading to their alteration or refinement.

Unfortunately, the rules for evaluating these converging observations tend to be implicit rather than explicit, and to be taught primarily via an oral tradition rather than through a literature accessible to all. It is frequently suggested by critics who seem unfamiliar with the actual interpretive activities of good clinicians that analysts view occurrences that are the opposite of what they expected as evidence equally confirmatory of their hypotheses, and therefore that their formulations are impervious to empirical disconfirmation. Students who find themselves in the hands of skilled supervisors, however, soon find they cannot get away with such nonsense. If the student is to support his or her formulation by the patient's denial of it, the denial must be shown to have rather special properties. The denial, or the manifestation of opposite behavior, might be extremely, perhaps inappropriately, intense; or the opposite behavior might be evident particularly when its antonym would be strongly expected; or the consequences of the one kind of behavior might quite regularly, and "surprisingly," turn out to be those one would expect from the trend the therapist postulates. In instances where several of these sorts of considerations converge with what is occurring in the patient's dreams, his or her slips of the tongue, and the experiences gained with similar kinds of patients, *then* the confirmation by opposites begins to look more substantial.

The explication of the rules of evidence and inference in psychodynamic thought is a major need, long overdue. There are rich lodes of insight here, which have directed observers to notice things that the laboratory investigator would never have thought to see or connect. However, there is also much fool's gold, for which a high price has been paid. Combined with the utilization of tape recordings of therapeutic sessions and other interactions to replace the recollections that have had to suffice as data in the psychoanalytic literature heretofore, such explication can be of major importance. Inquiry into the logic of psychoanalytic inference and the development of ways of investigating coherences in recorded psychoanalytic data (e.g., Dahl, 1972; Luborsky & Auerbach, 1969) should help to clarify and solidify the kinds of evidence and inferences that have played such a major role in psychodynamic thought and may help to establish such "converging network" kind of evidence as an accepted complement to the yes–no hypothesis testing of the laboratory.

Experimental Evidence

My argument for the legitimacy of nonexperimental evidence for such concepts as unconscious conflict or defense should not be taken to imply that the experimental evidence is all negative. In fact, there is some rather strong support for these concepts from experimental research. In a previous review of the research on "perceptual defense," for example (Wolitzky & Wachtel, 1973), I have indicated how this research is more consistent with psychodynamic conceptions than most recent discussions of it have acknowledged. The work of Silverman and his colleagues (e.g., Silverman, 1971, 1972) provides particularly striking experimental evidence for the importance of conceptualizing unconscious processes. In a large number of studies, some of which have been independently replicated, Silverman has found that stimuli presented tachistoscopically, of which the subject has been unaware, have increased or reduced particular psychopathological reactions in ways consistent with predictions from psychoanalytic theory, and that these effects have *not* been manifested when the subject has perceived the same stimuli at speeds where they can be registered consciously. Space precludes detailing here the variety of striking findings reported by Silverman or indicating why experimenter-bias explanations or earlier criticisms of tachistoscopic studies, such as those of Eriksen, do not seem relevant to Silverman's studies.

It is perhaps understandable that this work has been largely ignored so far by antipsychoanalytic writers (Silverman's findings are startling and in some respects puzzling even to a psychodynamically inclined psychologist, such as myself, and are reported in a matter-of-fact way as if they are perfectly expectable), but they can no longer be responsibly ignored by writers who claim no role for unconscious processes. This is hardly the only evidence in experimental work that supports psychodynamic assumptions, but it is perhaps the most dramatic, and it represents a strong challenge to theorists who exclude concepts of unconscious processes. Particular studies in the series, or particular details, can be seen as vulnerable, but the entire body of findings has achieved a critical mass that requires a response.

UNCONSCIOUS PROCESSES AND PERSON-SITUATION INTERACTIONS

The question of whether it is necessary to conceptualize unconscious processes and emphasize multiple and conflicting motivations is the kind of issue that is very much at the heart of the current ferment in the study of personality regarding the person–situation issue. For the real debate among proponents of differing views is not over whether behavior varies from situation to situation or whether stable individual differences can be identified—almost everyone can agree that both are true—but rather over *how much* of the variance is attributable to persons, to situations, and to their interactions; and, more importantly, over *how* the variability and stability occur, that is, over the *processes* that are necessary to conceptualize in order to account for what is observed and to intervene effectively.

Much of the work that Ekehammar (1974), in his review of interactional psychology, labels as interactionist is concerned with the first of these two issues. That is, it is concerned with *statistical* interaction and emphasizes that in analysis-of-variance designs the interaction between person and situation variables tends to account for more of the variance than does either of the main effects. Some of the limitations of this approach have been concisely stated by Ekehammar (1974, p. 1041). I should like to elaborate briefly on a few in terms of their relation to what has been presented in this chapter and to try to clarify thereby in what respect the present approach is an interactional one.

For one thing, as Ekehammar notes, "the relative magnitude of the main components can be manipulated in a favored direction through a selective sampling of persons and situations" (p. 1041). Ekehammar (1974) gives relatively little weight to this consideration, for he feels that in the studies he has reviewed "there seems to be no reason to believe that the selection of persons and situations has been biased in order to sustain a certain hypothesis" (p. 1041). The discussion of methodological issues in traditional research noted earlier in this chapter (see also Wachtel, 1973a, 1973b) suggests, however, that there may be more skewing than has been recognized; for not only is the selection of a particular sample of people or contexts of concern, so too is the sample of *behaviors*. One may get quite a different picture if one asks children whether they prefer bad food now or terrible food later, or tallies the frequency of talking or smoking or drinking, than if one is concerned with the determinants of genuinely intimate sharing of feelings, the experience of a coherent identity, or the maintenance of a feeling of ease in conversation with a shy partner. The latter kinds of behaviors are harder to study and to reliably categorize, but certainly no less important.

Additionally, totaling up variance components tells us little about how or why things happen as they do, only what factors seem to be weighty. An understanding of the *process* can lead to a refining of our model so that we ask better questions, which may yield quite a different set of numbers.[2]

The conceptualization of self-perpetuating cycles discussed here represents one way of trying to address person–situation interactions in terms of process. Like many other psychologists whose views have been shaped by experiences doing psychotherapy, I have felt a need to include as part of the process some conception of unconscious motivation and fantasy and of conflict. Perhaps because of this emphasis on unconscious processes, Ekehammar (1974) has categorized my position as one of "personologism," depicted as "advocating stable intraorganismic constructs . . . as the main determinants of behavioral variation" and has implicitly treated my position as de-emphasizing the role of environmental events. As I have tried to show in this chapter (see Wachtel, 1977, for a more detailed presentation) however, there is a substantial difference between psychodynamic views which postulate that many of the most important processes influencing our current personality are sealed off from influence by current environmental input, and those psychodynamic views, such as that presented here, which treat the unconscious processes as part of a set of interlocking events in which what is currently going on plays a very crucial role.

The perspective presented here seems to me a more thoroughly interactional one than many that are so labeled. In the present view, persons and situations can in fact hardly be separated, for it is stressed that in some of the most important aspects of our lives the situations we encounter depend on who we are, as who we are depends on what we encounter. Unconscious motives and fantasies, in this view, are not structures or properties carried around by a person, but ways of coming to terms with continuing experiences in daily living, even as they influence those very experiences and help shape and select them.

SELF-PERPETUATING CYCLES AND TRUNCATED RESEARCH

From the perspective of the cyclical view presented here, a great many lines of research, from a variety of theoretical viewpoints, may be seen as truncated, in the sense of providing a picture of only a

---

2. A similar point has been made by Holt (1970) in a different context, in a paper which also confronts and challenges the oft-voiced conclusion that clinical modes of personality assessment have been shown to be without value.

portion of the cyclical processes that determine (or constitute) be-havior. When explicitly recognized as such, studies of this sort can be of considerable value in providing a detailed picture of one aspect of the network of influences and outcomes in psychological phenom-ena; it is hard to study everything at once. However, when there is not explicit recognition of truncation, misleading or unproductive research is likely.

I have recently, for example, discussed in some detail the prob-lems and limitations of cognitive-style research as it is typically conducted (Wachtel, 1972b; Wolitzky & Wachtel, 1973). One prob-lem with this work is that it seems to promise something very exciting and glamorous—picking up real "personality" characteristics with just a few simple, objective laboratory tests—yet in fact in most cases it is directly assessing only abilities, which may or may not form the basis for a particular personal style, depending on a host of other variables. The relation between scores on such tests as the rod and frame or embedded figures and the matters that have tradition-ally fascinated students of personality are far more complicated and indirect than the literature in this area tends to suggest. This confu-sion is caused in substantial measure by an empirical and conceptual strategy that implicitly treats people as static things or structures,[3] instead of viewing man as dynamically interacting with and respon-sive to events. Environmental stimulation, in most cognitive-style research, is primarily of interest as a way of revealing what structure the person carries around with him or her.

The conception that originally sparked much of the research on cognitive style (e.g., Klein, 1958) was potentially a much more inte-grative and useful one. It could have led to examination of how particular modes of organizing thought and perceptual input led to actions and adaptations that eventually fed back to stabilize and perpetuate those very modes (at least in a particular class of per-ceived situations). Shapiro (1965) did do this to some extent, treating cognition as much more part of a sequence of adaptive efforts than was true in most of the cognitive-style work, although presenting an excessively and unnecessarily typological picture. In most of the laboratory research on cognitive style, however, a rather static ap-proach has been employed, which instead of viewing cognition as

---

3. The literature on field dependence does, of course, discuss change in amount of field dependence with increasing age, and even how different kinds of child rearing make the amount of increase and final level achieved greater or lesser. It should be clear, however, that this has not been discussed in fully interactional terms (although it can be) and has been treated primarily in terms of factors that influence the parameters of the structure.

part of a sequence of adaptional efforts and perceived consequences, studies the cognitive activity just in itself or for purposes of categorizing the individual (see Wachtel, 1972a).

This kind of problem—treating a cognitive product as an end point instead of as a part of a process that leads to further events which feed back and influence subsequent (although instantaneous, in the sense of an integral calculus) cognitions—is apparent as well in the tachistoscopic research on perceptual defense mentioned earlier and is one of the main reasons I have suggested that such research is more relevant to students of microscopic perceptual processes than to personality theorists (Wolitzky & Wachtel, 1973). It is similarly apparent in much of the research—still potentially of considerable importance—relating aspects of attention deployment to personality and psychopathology. In re-examining recently one of my own contributions in this area (Wachtel, 1967), I became aware of ways in which the implications of the *actions* that flow from cognitions, and their perceived consequences, had not been fully considered. That paper had been concerned with clarifying the variety of ways in which concepts of breadth and narrowness of attention have been used to elucidate phenomena related to cognitive style, arousal, anxiety, and schizophrenia. Although the paper still seemed to me in retrospect to contribute toward elucidating how variations in cognitive activity mediated personality phenomena, I was equally impressed by what I had left out. In reviewing my discussion, for example, of the various ways in which anxiety infuences the deployment of attention, it seemed to me that I did not consider sufficiently how focus on a restricted range of cues, or inability to synthesize and coordinate enough stimulation, can hamper adaptation, leading to further anxiety, still further restriction, etc. I would now highlight such momentum-generating sequences to a far greater degree and would be dissatisfied with any formulation that did not include a focus broad enough to encompass such a cyclical process and/or describe how the cycle came to an equilibrium or was interrupted or reversed. (There has not been very much emphasis in this chapter on this latter, and crucial, aspect of a cyclical psychology—why cycles do not repeat themselves indefinitely. The issue, which is particularly crucial in devising strategies and conceptions of psychotherapy, is discussed in various ways in Wachtel, 1977b.)

Many more considerations are obvious implications of the views presented here but must await future communications to be spelled out. For one thing, we obviously need far more observational research on meaningful interpersonal behavior in ecologically relevant contexts. Far too large a proportion of psychology's research activity has been concerned with laboratory analogues. It should be clear that the conception stressed here points particularly to the importance of naturalistic observation.

Second, the conception presented here has obvious implications for the notion of "stimulus control" of behavior and suggests that there are empirical as well as philosophical problems with conceiving of stimulus control as the basic reality behind an illusory sense that the person himself or herself is responsible for what he or she does. I have presented arguments elsewhere (Wachtel, 1969) for the view that conceiving of behavior as determined is no more or less sensible or useful than conceiving of it as genuinely chosen. The considerations presented here point to observations and perspectives that further highlight the stimulus-control conception as but one way of organizing the data, which if relied on exclusively can have serious distorting effects (see also de Charms, 1968; Wheelis, 1973).

Finally, the views presented here clearly imply that a far more complex view of motivation is required than is typically found in nondynamic theories. I have shown that psychodynamic theorizing about unconscious motives need not be characterized by a depiction of thing-like entities possessed by a person and locked into him or her early in childhood; a dynamic view can be wholly consistent with all we know about environmental infuences. In fact, the model presented here seems to me to be one of the few genuinely interactional accounts of motivation of which I am aware. Far from being viewed as structured residues of childhood, motivational processes are depicted here as very much a function of how the person is currently leading his or her life and what happens to him or her, both as a result of his or her own actions and as a result of more extrinsic factors; yet the organizing effects of motivational variables are treated as real and powerful, leading to particular behavioral choices in response to stimulus conditions, to selectivity in what stimulus conditions are encountered, and to particular ways of construing what is encountered so that the very term "stimulus" begins to look vague or anachronistic.

In the laboratory, it is (relatively) safe to assume that certain common and obvious motives are operative, or to define motivational variables in terms of simple, discrete operations of deprivation or stimulation. In most real social situations this is simply not the case. It is necessary to "infer conflicts and motives," and the choice is between doing so naively and/or through the eyes of the society's normative expectations, versus doing so in a way that utilizes the guidelines for observations and inference which have accrued from decades of clinical focus on motivational variables in particular (see Wachtel, 1977, Chapters 6 and 7, for a much fuller discussion of this issue and of the importance of motivational conflicts).

There have been, to be sure, enormous difficulties with psycho-dynamic methodology and theorizing. But one can be nourished by a body of work without swallowing it whole. Perhaps what is needed is a concerted effort by dynamic and nondynamic observers to examine the same (real-life) material and to determine what concepts and inferences each seems to need and what each leaves out that the other insists on noticing. If this chapter should kindle interest in such a collaborative research effort, its purpose will have been achieved.

15

Investigation and Its Discontents: Some Constraints on Progress in Psychological Research

Physicists, I am told, rarely read their journals. By the time a study appears in a journal, it is already obsolete. New discoveries have moved the field to another point by then. Unless one is in personal touch with those who are generating the vanguard data, one is hopelessly out of date.

Whether such a view of physics (or chemistry, or molecular biology, or other "hard" sciences) is an outsider's romantic exaggeration or not, it certainly seems that (to put it kindly) our studies in psychology tend to be of more enduring interest. A good 1950s study in the area of personality, for example, could, I contend, get published readily today (with appropriate disguise, of course) as an interesting new finding. Our rate of obsolescence is rather low.

This is not to suggest that no progress has been made. In certain areas of psychology, the progress has indeed been substantial, and even in those areas where cyclical fashions seem more common than a straight trajectory, some new elements are injected each time around. Nonetheless, the state of our field seems to me to leave much room for discontent. In what follows, I will examine some prevalent assumptions and ways of proceeding that I think have limited progress in our discipline, and will suggest some alternatives.

In one way or another, the issues I will address concern the reward structure of our field. I will look at what is encouraged or discouraged, either explicitly or covertly, and perhaps inadvertently. I will examine first the rather pervasive biases that weigh against the

Reprinted by permission from *American Psychologist*, 1980, 35(5), 399–408.

full-time pursuit of theoretical inquiry. I will then turn to some consequences of the stress on "productivity" and its quantitative assessment, and of the way in which research is funded by grants. Though these are somewhat separable concerns, a common thread runs through them: A number of interlocking influences in the academic world have had the effect of encouraging *activity* at the expense of *thought*. At least as much as to problems with any particular theory or paradigm, the limited progress in certain areas of psychology can be attributed to pressures to *do* more and more and to factors—ranging from attitudes toward theorizing to the need to be productive—that discourage reflection. While psychologists debate about paradigms, the higher order metaparadigm, as it were, discussed in this article may represent the most critical issue.

TEMPERAMENT, TALENTS, AND STYLE OF INQUIRY

Some time ago, I commiserated with a colleague who was having difficulty "debugging" an experiment. His study required complicated equipment, and day after day something was not working right and had to be attended to. As we discussed the experience, I was surprised to discover that although he would have preferred that everything go smoothly, he did enjoy the *process* of tracking down equipment failures or procedural difficulties and whipping things into shape—that was part of the "fun" of doing research. He, in turn, was surprised at my surprise, and at my assumption that what he found fun was just a painful nuisance. As we talked further, he was even more surprised when I confessed to a similar kind of experience, but at the stage of *writing up* the study; I too would prefer (I suppose) that the writing go completely smoothly, but had to acknowledge that "debugging" pages or paragraphs did for me what debugging equipment did for him—it was part of the fun, part of the craft. For him, however, this aspect of the work was sheer drudgery, unredeemed by any sense of pleasurable challenge.

This incident came at a time when I was re-examining the kind of research I wanted to do, and it played a role in influencing my choice of a course somewhat away from the mainstream style of academic inquiry. It also suggested to me that the typical model of psychological research and of research training in psychology tends to be far too monolithic. We need, I believe, to take into account far more than we do the variations in talent and temperament of individuals who are in a position to contribute to progress in our field.

The person who is able to identify significant theoretical issues, who can synthesize diverse findings into a coherent conceptual framework, or who is quick to notice ambiguities and methodological flaws in data that have been generally accepted is not necessarily the person who can devise an ingenious experimental manipulation, who possesses the skills to administer and implement a study once it is designed, or who has the temperament to do the painstaking detail work that can make the difference between a sloppy experiment and one that really advances knowledge.

To be sure, there are some fortunate individuals who seem to be well endowed with both sorts of talents. It is interesting that it is these individuals who tend to be recognized as having made "theoretical" contributions to the field. In almost every instance—one reviewer of an earlier version of this chapter suggested the names of Ulric Neisser, Paul Meehl, Daryl Bem, Martin Orne, James and Eleanor Gibson, and Jean Piaget—the individuals who have achieved a reputation as theorists have also done substantial empirical work. They are really theorist–experimenters, not theorists per se. We do not encourage those whose bent is more exclusively theoretical. There are precious few examples of successful psychologists who pursue theoretical inquiry as a full-time occupation. Our theorists are expected to do empirical work as well. Yet, as Mitroff and Kilmann (1978) have shown, the fact is that scientists do tend to have highly differentiated talents and preferred styles of inquiry, and those talented in conceptual inquiry may not be particularly well suited to design and conduct experiments.

Those who can also do a decent job as experimenters survive. But we may be losing potentially important contributors who either do not enjoy or do not feel they are good at devising experiments. Since such individuals receive little encouragement to pursue purely theoretical efforts, they are likely to drop out of the academic world altogether or to end up at institutions where they have little time to pursue research—which in their case, ideally, would mean spending their time pursuing theory. They are victims of our unwillingness to recognize that talents can be specific and that someone who, for reasons of temperament, talent, or both, is unlikely to make important contributions in the experiments he or she designs may well be a potentially important contributor to theory.

Ironically, in physics—which, appropriately or not, is for so many psychologists the model put forth to emulate—this differentiation of talents is clearly recognized. Physicists can and do, of course, move back and forth between theory and empirical research; but it is noteworthy that the categories "experimental physicist" and "theoretical physicist" are familiar and prominent ones. There is no real equivalent in psychology. We certainly have experimental psychologists, but do we have a recognizable category of theoretical psychologists?

Throughout the history of physics, there have been important figures who were primarily or exclusively theoreticians. To be a theoretical physicist is a prestigious calling. I know physicists who boast that their only equipment is their head and a pencil. Dare one say that in a psychology department? More important, dare students seek to do strictly theoretical dissertations, in which they themselves do not collect or generate any new data of their own?

In many graduate programs in psychology such dissertations are simply not permitted. Careful theoretical analysis is, of course, valued, it is contended, but the work is incomplete if it does not include an empirical component. In discussing the issue of strictly theoretical dissertations with colleagues from various universities, I have heard (on more than one occasion) the claim that such dissertations do not merit a degree in psychology, since such work belongs in the realm of philosophy. Not only does such a view rigidify the boundaries between disciplines to a debilitating degree, but it seems to overlook as well that the degree awarded is, after all, a "doctor of philosophy."[1] Moreover, the tone of indignation at the suggestion that a doctorate should be awarded for work that does not include data collection seems to overlook the fact that universities regularly grant doctorates in areas (e.g., philosophy, English, music) in which empirical contributions are certainly the exception, or, again, that theoretical dissertations are often quite acceptable in physics departments.

There are, it should be said, some conditions which distinguish the state of physics and of psychology that may influence the potential contribution of theoretical work in the two disciplines. By and large, there is greater agreement in physics on what are appropriate measures of concepts, and it is thus easier to determine whether a finding is or is not consistent with the predictions of a theory. Thus (although physics is itself far from lacking in controversy in this regard), it is probably the case that theoretical statements in physics are more likely to be "empirically responsible" in the sense that—at least implicitly—they are tied to empirical operations that can be generally agreed on as appropriate tests of the theory. In addition, theoretical work in physics is often of a highly mathematical nature

---

1. In those places where a "doctor of psychology" degree has either been instituted or is being considered, it has not, to my knowledge, ever been requested by proponents of mandatory empiricism as the degree *they* would prefer so that they would not be confused with mere doctors of "philosophy."

and rather closely tied to data points generated by experiments—even if others' experiments. Such work often takes the form of finding a mathematical function that will fit a curve to the data already generated and will predict new data points for experiments with somewhat different procedures or boundary conditions. Thus, theorizing in physics is often more "technical," appears less to be "armchair speculation," or, put differently, tends to *look like* physics, not like philosophy or like "common sense," as does much psychological theorizing.

Theorizing in psychology is frequently of a quite different sort, but it is no less essential. Perhaps we have failed to appreciate its importance because of a kind of intellectual Gresham's law, in which bad theorizing has driven out the good. To be sure, a great many pronouncements, utterly untestable either in practice or in principle, have been put forth under the guise of "theory"; and, alas, these have been most prominent in my own area of clinical psychology and personality theory. It is these easy and irresponsible forms of theorizing that have received the most frequent attention from the general public, and of which freshmen and sophomores in introductory courses have had to be disabused. Perhaps as a consequence, psychologists in the academic world have become suspicious of theorizing altogether, especially when the theorist has not proved his or her mettle as a scientist by also conducting experiments.

But there is another kind of theorizing as well, which resembles neither the mathematically precise equations of theoretical physicists nor the wholly speculative spinning of yarns by certain kinds of clinicians and would-be gurus. It is the careful, tentatively speculative forming of hypotheses by individuals who have immersed themselves in the data currently available and have tried to find some coherence in the varying outcomes under varying conditions of observation. It involves both a talent for synthesis and an eye for contradictions and inconsistencies, often of a subtle or hidden sort. To see not only where the findings in an area do not hang together but with what set of changed assumptions and concepts they might is a challenging task.

There is room (and need) for a great deal of theoretical inquiry that is not necessarily mathematical or in the mode of contemporary physics. Increasingly, we are realizing how theory-laden our facts are, how much they depend on the particular way we ask our questions and on the assumptions (often unarticulated) that lie behind our choice of methods. Teasing out those assumptions, asking how things would look if we started with different assumptions or if we posed our questions slightly differently—that, too, is theoretical work. Davis (1971) has spelled out a whole range of questions that point to reconceptualizations of familiar phenomena, to new perspectives and new gestalts that open up inquiry to fresh empirical assaults. Looking for unity in seemingly diverse phenomena, seeing diversity and distinctions among phenomena thought to be similar in nature—these and other such reversals of accepted explanations and descriptions are what Davis is pointing to in his discussion of what makes for interesting theoretical work.

One likely reason that the importance of this kind of effort is underplayed in psychology is that, in principle, it is just this kind of thinking that precedes the conduct of any experiment. One likes to think that an experimenter does not design an experiment unless he or she thinks that it will answer a question that is worth asking, that it addresses a problem that he or she has identified as a significant one. In practice, however, this is often not the case. As Gergen (1978), McGuire (1973), and others have pointed out, most graduate programs provide precious little training in constructing theory or generating hypotheses. The emphasis is on devising techniques to test ideas, not on generating interesting ideas to test. This has led one respected observer, in commenting on the state of social psychology, to remark that "social psychologists have done no more than to operationalize questions and answers which were imagined elsewhere," and to characterize that work as "not the work of scientific analysis but that of engineering" (Moscovici, 1972, p. 32).

I share Moscovici's concern about the lack of fresh and original research, but not his disparagement of the value of experimental ingenuity per se. It is precisely because I think that the design of an experiment that really gets at a theoretical idea—even if it is someone else's theoretical idea—is a challenging and creative endeavor that I am advocating a greater specialization of function in psychological research. Just as those who are good experimenters may not be so good as theoreticians, so too may the reverse be true. At an important point in my own career, when I had been working for some time in the area of attention and cognitive style, I concluded that the quality of my conceptual inquiries in that area (e.g., Wachtel, 1967, 1972b) was higher than that of my empirical work, and I decided to concentrate primarily on the former, leaving the designing of studies to test these ideas to others whose talents lay primarily in that direction (talents that are very much part of the task of scientific analysis and not merely engineering). The research reported by Mitroff and Kilmann (1978) suggests that scientists who are talented as experimenters and those who are noted as conceptualizers may have rather different characteristics. In expecting psychologists to be jacks-of-all-trades, we may be failing to exploit fully the differentiated talents of members of our discipline.

The argument that such differentiation would not work in psychology because our theories are less mathematical and harder to test does not hold up. The possibility of spinning theory that is self-contained and unresponsive to observations does not eliminate the need for *good* theorizing. Indeed, if generating good theory—theory rooted in the observations accrued thus far, pointing to interesting new observations, and at least in principle testable by those observations—is hard to do in psychology, that difficulty points even more urgently to the need to encourage those who have talent in this realm to pursue it full-time and not also design experiments unless they are equally good at that activity (which in many instances is likely not to be the case).

All this is not to say that conceptual analysis is good and empirical research is not. It would disturb me as much to find psychology departments pushing everyone toward conceptual analysis as it does to see them now pushing everyone toward data collection. It should be clear from what I have said thus far that good theoretical work depends on the development of new methods of empirical inquiry and on the generation of new data every bit as much as the latter endeavors depend on good theoretical and conceptual analysis. Empirical work and theoretical work go hand in hand. The error is simply in insisting they must always be the two hands of the same person.

THE PERILS OF PRODUCTIVITY

The second constraint on the quality of psychological research that I wish to discuss—that associated with the push for productivity—is not unique to psychology. But its consequences are, I think, more severe for psychology than for many other disciplines. This is particularly the case because the stress on productivity interacts with the tendencies discussed in the first section of this chapter to place further emphasis on going out and "doing" studies rather than taking the time to think about the issues.

"Productivity" is a frequent term in the academic world these days, and when used by administrators, its overtones are often ominous. But well before the present crisis in funds for higher education and for research, academics were describing admired colleagues as "productive." As many of us have begun to be asked to account for exact numbers of student-contact hours and the like, we have reacted to the crassness of an industrial model of intellectual endeavor. Yet the quantitative measuring of output, along with the emphasis on sheer numbers (of articles, of dollars in grants, or whatever), has long been prevalent in academic circles.

One reason that this kind of thinking is particularly problematic in psychology is that psychology is about the easiest and also about the hardest discipline to do research in. It is easy in that studies can be run (and can be published) just by, for example, giving a class of undergraduates a few tasks or questionnaires that have not previously been correlated in public, writing a page of introduction and a page of discussion, and sending it off. Relatively little work is required, and most of that is the clerical work done by graduate or undergraduate research assistants. True, the very best journals have high rejection rates, but the study will probably end up in some journal—and hence on a vita.

Not all research, of course, is approached so cynically or so superficially (though I am afraid that a distressing percentage is). But the more typical, and more sincere, effort also usually entails some very serious compromises, and here is where the *difficulty* in doing psychological research is relevant. To do really good research in psychology, research that really breaks new ground or gives definitive answers to important questions (as opposed to research that simply makes it into journals), is exceedingly difficult. Our subject matter is extremely complex and ambiguous, and the boundary conditions are often critical for determining whether the study is generalizable to important real-life situations. To conduct really adequate studies requires enormous resources of time and money. In the face of this, researchers frequently bow to "reality" or "realism," and studies appear in which, by the end, one has almost as many questions as one began with (and not really new and different questions). One then reads a discussion section that states directly or implies that "practical limitations" prevented the implementation of the kind of study that really could answer the questions.[2] What seems to be left unsaid or not noticed is that in many cases these same researchers have done several such studies each year! If they had simply done fewer studies, they would have had the resources to do properly those they did do.

Some degree of compromise is, of course, essential in any human endeavor, and certainly is in research. Indeed, one of the main skills we teach students when we provide them with research training is how to choose compromises judiciously. What the research apprenticeship adds to the texts on experimental design is in very large measure the development of some intuitive wisdom regarding how to accommodate the complexities and limitations of reality without trivializing the study. But the reinforcement contin-

---

2. I think this is particularly true of psychotherapy research, but it is true of research in a great many other areas as well.

gencies that operate in the university make the task far more difficult than it otherwise might be.

The push for productivity, defined as regular and frequent publication, is not just an issue for the untenured or the still-to-be-
promoted. As a tenured full professor, I still can anticipate anxiety
and shame if the sheet my university sends around each year for
listing new publications and achievements were to be sent back
naked. There is no honorable space for indicating the time and effort
spent thinking things through this year so that what gets listed next
year (or maybe not until 3 years from now) will be of higher quality,
or for the papers *withheld* from publication so that they could be more
complete and of greater value when they did appear. The pressures
are greater and have more concrete consequences early in one's
career, but the desire for the respect of one's colleagues remains
later as a motivator; one doesn't want to be viewed as "deadwood."
Moreover, the habits of inquiry developed in one's early years are
likely to persist, since that is what one has gotten good at. "Short and
sweet" and plentiful frequently describe the necessary characteristics for research conducted in the vulnerable years of one's career,
and often those are characteristics of the work of seasoned researchers as well.

I have wondered at times whether granting agencies might be
induced to pay researchers not to publish in certain years, as farmers
are paid not to grow crops. This suggestion, while unconventional, at
least has the merit of being lucrative. Another proposal—which this
time I mean in all seriousness—is likely to sound just as peculiar at
first, without the saving grace of either pecuniary advantage or
(intended) humor. I would like seriously to suggest that in matters of
hiring, tenure, and promotion, psychology departments (and equivalent research and/or service organizations)[3] discard the present form
of the curriculum vita, with its complete listing of all the candidate's
publications (or, in the case of some especially senior or productive
individuals, who have further refined one-upmanship, a list of "selected" or "recent" publications, carefully chosen both to choke a
small-sized horse and at the same time to convey quite clearly that
were one not so genteel, a large-sized horse would not stand a
chance either). Instead of such a listing, I would propose that we
require the individual being judged to submit *no more than* three

3. Obviously, much of what I am suggesting here is relevant to other academic
disciplines as well, and there is no reason whatever why this would not be a useful
suggestion for them, too. Indeed, for department decisions that are reached this way
to be affirmed and ratified by appropriate committees, deans, or other officials, it
would probably be necessary for psychologists to proselytize for this scheme.

published works, to be judged on their merits. While in many cases one could not really expect the search committee or the tenure or promotion committee to be completely blind regarding the actual number of publications the candidate has, at the very least the ground rules would be clearly established that it was quality and not quantity that was being weighed.[4]

Such a way of proceeding would have several valuable consequences. For one thing, it would force applicants to searchingly ask themselves just what their most significant contributions have actually been. Critical self-reflection of this sort can be of substantial value to persons being judged in helping them sort out just what they have really been trying to accomplish and where they have and have not succeeded. Furthermore, if such a system began to be used fairly widely, it could be expected to be a force for change not only at the point where those being evaluated look back on what they have done, but also in terms of the very products they have to look back on. From the beginning of their careers, ambitious individuals, instead of striving for many publications, could strive to produce a few really outstanding contributions. How different our journals might look if the leaders of our discipline began to develop a rhythm of producing three top-notch publications, say, every 5 years!

Such a system would not be likely to lead people to work less hard. In fact, one could make a good case that it would lead people to work even harder, for they would know that the results of several years' work would be judged not just in terms of whether they managed to get something out, but rather on whether they really managed to accomplish something worthwhile. It is important to recognize that by three publications I do not necessarily mean three studies. Indeed, I would think it would be rather perilous to base one's tenure or promotion on just three of the single-experiment publications that are now so prevalent.

As things stand now, it is often hard to distinguish one publication of a particular researcher from another without a scorecard. One must look carefully to discover that of ten publications, one was a "preliminary report" of a study described in another paper with a larger n; one was a replication of that study with women instead of men; one was another version using a slightly different questionnaire; and so on. How much more useful it would be if it were typical

4. As a practical matter, it might be arranged that for hiring or tenure decisions, any three publications might be submitted, but for promotion, only publications that have appeared since appointment or since the last promotion. Or, some departments might want only work of the last 5 years for any decision, looking for the quality of the person's relatively current work, rather than of work done a long time ago.

to have the whole series of studies concisely described in one paper so that their overall implications and limitations could be more readily grasped (and of course more economically presented). Such programmatic reports do appear even under present contingencies, but they are hardly the mode.

Such a publication pattern would enable both researchers and readers to put into perspective and better understand false leads and artifactual findings. Single reports that are published as soon as the data are in permit such Trojan horses to stand as independent archival contributions, which are subsequently modified for readers only if they happen also to read an author's later report 3 years hence (and perhaps in a different journal).[5] And researchers themselves, under such circumstances, are likely to be at least somewhat in the position of continuing to defend their initial reports, which they did after all choose to publish as independent findings under their own names. A system that more strongly encouraged delay of publication until a programmatic report could be developed would not only benefit readers, but also free researchers to put their ongoing work into context. Under the present system, it is likely that people will be prematurely identified with and hence frozen into positions that they would not want to defend and pursue had they not committed themselves in public.

The proposed system would also be likely to discourage the all-too-frequent studies in which the sample is too small for meaningful inferences to be made. If researchers were encouraged to concentrate their resources in a smaller number of higher-quality studies, what we have learned about power analysis (Cohen, 1969) could be more generally incorporated into research strategies.

Quality control is, of course, not entirely lacking in the present system. Publication in American Psychological Association journals tends to count more than publication in journals less rigorously refereed, and increasingly, such measures as citation indexes are used as at least an approximate assessment of whether a publication has actually made a contribution to the field. Moreover—radical as it might seem—evaluating committees have been known to actually *read* some of a candidate's publications, not just count them.

Nonetheless, the emphasis on sheer number of publications, on "productivity" per se, is still too widespread to require documentation. We are far from the day when academics would not instantly recognize the phrase "You can get a paper out of it," or when even

5. There is, of course, a substantial publication lag in many of our journals, but the delay holds equally for later publications which modify earlier ones.

seasoned researchers might be entirely immune from this siren call. And inevitably, in pursuing the quick and the "do-able," the nature of inquiry is altered in highly significant ways.

THE DISTORTING EFFECTS OF GRANTS

Research grants must also be understood as playing a role in determining the kind of inquiry that takes place and as responsible for some of the limitations on progress in our field. As I will try to show, the influence of grants and granting agencies is in important respects complementary and/or parallel to the other influences discussed so far. In many institutions, faculty members can be under considerable pressure to apply for grants, for reasons rather extraneous to the requirements of the questions they wish to pursue. One factor in this, of course, is simply the prestige value—for the individual and the institution—that comes with receipt of a large research grant. But another, whose consequences are insufficiently addressed, is the role of grants in the support of universities. Through payments for indirect or "overhead" costs that are funneled to the institution where the research takes place, a good deal of financial support is provided to universities, and it is well known that when the amount of grant support began to be reduced, many universities found themselves in serious financial difficulty

In principle, providing support to the parent institution is an eminently reasonable idea. If a faculty member requires an extra room for purposes of his or her study, or is keeping the lights on longer hours while working at research, or needs the services of a guard on a Saturday to open a door that would otherwise be locked, or requires a portion of the building to be heated to protect animals for a research project, the university may reasonably regard the presence of the project as an expense and expect to be reimbursed. But the overhead costs charged by universities tend to be well beyond the actual increment in expense the study brings. When one recognizes that—even without the grant-supported study—the faculty member would still require his or her own office,[6] which would

6. In principle, of course, there could be a good deal of sharing of offices, since apart from time spent working on research, the "official" working hours of faculty members (meeting with students, etc.) are short. Some schools do in fact require a good deal of office sharing by faculty. But—completely apart from grants—high-quality institutions provide conditions in which faculty can engage in serious intellectual endeavor, and those that do not suffer in the quest for top-quality faculty. Even in today's depressed academic job market, some schools continue to attract stronger faculties than others.

still need to be lighted, heated, and cleaned, and that maintenance and security forces and a library would still be required, then the actual extra costs to the university are hardly what are charged. Indeed, were this not the case, universities would not be pressing so hard to have grants come in, nor would they have been hit so hard when the grants diminished. If the grants really just covered the increment in expense brought about by the faculty members' using university facilities, then the university would only be breaking even on the grant and would neither have a stake in an influx of grants nor suffer a loss at their reduction.

All this, of course, is hardly news. All parties wink with regard to these circumstances because in fact research grants have come to serve a secondary purpose in addition to supporting specific research projects: They are a means of indirectly providing support for our universities. Now, in my view, supporting universities is a fine idea. Universities are a valuable resource to a society, and providing external financial support for them—so that tuition costs do not have to be prohibitive (or faculty salaries prohibitive in a different sense)—is a very worthwhile end. Indeed, even in terms of the somewhat narrower aims of an agency interested in promoting high-quality research, and hence in keeping healthy the institutions from which such research emanates, there is some sense in supporting universities.[7] The problem arises because the support is indirect and because this indirect support has a distorting effect on the research that is conducted.

This kind of situation is not unique to universities and research grants. Indirect support of desirable social goals is very common in this country, where remnants of a frontier ethic make it hard to openly advocate government support of needed services. Much as the need to support our universities is covertly met, in part, by research grants, so too is the need for government support for housing covertly met by manipulation of the tax laws rather than by direct government subsidy. The depreciation provisions with regard to real estate in our income tax laws are far more elaborate and creative fictions than the overhead charges of universities administering grants. And they, too, are social-engineering subterfuges to achieve useful social ends that the public would be likely not to accept on an explicit basis. Moreover, they, too, tend to have a distorting effect that might be eliminated were support more open and direct (Nessen, 1977).

7. To a greater or lesser degree, most of what here refers to universities is applicable as well to other institutions that provide the facilities and auspices for research and benefit from grants (e.g., private research institutions, museums, etc.).

The distorting effect of grants takes several forms. One of them is to exacerbate the already problematic position of theoretical work noted above. Theoretical work is relatively inexpensive. It requires the time of (usually) a solitary thinker, some books and journals, paper and pens, and not much else. In contrast, empirical research requires all of the above, plus often a good deal of equipment, money for subjects, a corps of research assistants, and so on. Now one might expect that as a consequence theoretical work would appear to be rather a bargain and might therefore be encouraged.[8] In fact, however, the low cost of theoretical work may actually work to its disadvantage. Since theorists do not need to apply for large sums of outside grant support, they are neither in a position to brag about the big grants they have received nor, more practically, in a position to bring in much overhead profit[9] that could support the salary of an administrator or the cleaning of a lavatory. Indeed, so far as I can tell, there is relatively little provision in the budgets of granting agencies for *any* kind of purely theoretical or conceptual inquiry in psychology, and thus even the small costs that theoretical work does entail are likely to be paid for out of the department's budget or the individual's pocket; and though theorists are as likely as their empirically oriented colleagues to be working on their research during the summer, such perquisites as the standard two-ninths summer salary are unlikely to come their way.

These factors do not exactly strengthen the already rather fragile position of theoretical inquiry in psychology.

The role of grants in the research process also structures the kind of inquiry conducted by psychologists in another way. Grants tend to be awarded more frequently for well-articulated hypothesis-testing experiments than for exploratory work. The latter is by its very nature likely to be less crisp and neat, and also more risky. With an experiment, the granting agency knows what it is buying. Indeed, it often knows the likely *outcome* of the study as well, and although (fortunately) experiments sometimes do not come out as expected, by and large psychological research is—and is in a sense encouraged to be—rather predictable. Researchers who have been conditioned to think in terms of grant support are likely to short-circuit the explor-

---

8. For the empirically minded reader who might be hesitant to infer inner states without systematic readings of the position of my tongue and cheek, I must hasten to add that I am not suggesting that we adopt cost-benefit analysis as the prime criterion for evaluating an intellectual endeavor (though I do think it more irreverent than irrelevant to consider whether the result of a very expensive study will really be worth the expenditure).

9. I use the term "profit" advisedly.

atory and observational stages of research and to leap quickly into saleable designs.

It is a commonplace by now (to which we have, unfortunately, become rather desensitized) that researchers often "go where the money is." It is important to recognize, however, that this is true not just in terms of what topics are studied, but also with regard to method. The modal practices of granting agencies have contributed to a severe truncation of open-ended exploration in psychological research. In the history of science, there have, of course, been important new ideas introduced by unexpected occurrences during an experiment—whether these be a surprising discomfirmation of anticipated outcome or the kind of serendipitous event we associate with names like Fleming. One can, I suppose, proceed on the assumption that "accidents will happen" and go on formulating highly controlled experiments first thing after breakfast. But a little *planning* for new ideas, an *intentional* creating of circumstances in which new observations are made more likely, seems a not unreasonable alternative.

LIMITATIONS OF THE EXPERIMENTAL METHOD

The preponderant emphasis on the experimental method—fostered both by the prevailing ideology in the field and by the exigencies of the grant process—not only has the effect of stressing confirmation of hypotheses over generation of hypotheses, but creates problems of a substantive nature as well, yielding misleading findings and one-sided conceptualizations. The merits of the experimental method are, of course, substantial and certainly do not require any elaboration here. Nothing in what follows should be taken as suggesting we abandon the experimental method. But I do wish to highlight certain very important distortions that arise when experiments become too exclusively relied on to supply new ideas and even to confirm ideas already conceived.

Certain lines of criticism of experimental methodology have been very prominent in recent years. The work of Orne and of Rosenthal in particular (e.g., Orne, 1962, 1969; Rosenthal, 1966; Rosenthal & Rosnow, 1969) has brought to light subtle biasing factors in experiments, long overlooked or minimized by experimenters. The point of these critiques was not to rule out experiments altogether (indeed, the critics continue to conduct experiments themselves, even in investigating the very topic of experimenter bias). Rather, it was to enable us to conduct and evaluate experiments in a more sophisticated manner and thereby make them a more useful investigative tool.

Essentially, these critiques point to ways in which experiments in fact fail to conform fully to the ideal model of the experiment presented in textbooks of methodology. They do not argue that experiments are more likely than other methods to reflect the biases or demand characteristics of the experimenter, but only that even experiments may not completely rule such biases out. Thus they point not to problems that are unique to experiments, but to sources of error that are even more massive in other methods—but which we have overoptimistically assumed to be eliminated by the experimental method. A more recent critique of experimental research in personality (Wachtel, 1973a, 1973b) has complemented the by now classic criticisms of Orne and Rosenthal by taking a different tack—focusing on problems that are *particularly* acute with experiments and that are a function of the *successful* implementation of experimental controls (to the degree that this can be attained).

The answers one gets in research depend on the questions one asks. The way of asking questions in most experiments places subjects in a standardized situation in order to investigate its effects on their behavior. The experimenter is trained not to vary from subject to subject; he or she must treat all the subjects in any group the same. This is difficult to do in any kind of fairly complex interpersonal transaction, and that is one of the reasons that the situations and behaviors in most experimental studies are so impoverished (Wachtel, 1973a). But to the degree that the experimenter does accomplish standardization from subject to subject, another kind of difficulty is introduced: The subjects then enter a situation that has been completely determined in advance and that is minimally influenced by and novel to them. While such situations are unfortunately quite common in the modern world, as Kafka portrayed so well, there does remain a large domain in which the situations we encounter are not simply independent variables but are in large measure a function of our own behavior. This is particularly true in the realm of intimate, affectively meaningful interactions with other persons, and it is in this realm above all that the typical experimental paradigm can yield misleading results. Research conducted in this "implacable-experimenter" model has led to formulations that seriously overestimate and oversimplify the role of situations in determining our behavior (Bowers, 1973; Wachtel, 1972a, 1973b).

The imbalances in social learning theory that the implacable-experimenter critique was originally designed to address have begun to be corrected. Indeed, Bandura (1978b) has recently advocated a model of "reciprocal determinism," which seems to have adopted almost totally the theoretical core of the critiques of earlier versions of social learning theory—the idea that behavior and environmental events influence *each other* and that both also interact reciprocally with the person's internal state (Wachtel, 1972a, 1973b, 1977a, 1977b). For Bandura, however, despite this evolving direction of his theoretical position (see also Bandura, 1974), the experimental method remains the *via reggia* to progress in psychology (Bandura, 1978a). In contrast, I have suggested (Wachtel, 1977a) that a recognition of the cyclical and reciprocal nature of personality processes points to an important role for observational research.[10]

Both greater emphasis on observation—a riskier enterprise than experimenting, but one more likely to yield new ideas—and greater attention to detailed, critical, and thoughtful theorizing seem to me essential if we are to move past proving the obvious and on to the accelerating curve of discovery shown by other sciences. The influences noted in this chapter—the insistence that theorists also be experimenters, whether or not that is where their greatest talents lie; the emphasis on productivity and its encouragement of quickly doing, at the expense of reflecting on what one does and determining the resources needed to do the job well; the effects of grants in exacerbating both these tendencies; and the often exclusive reliance on experiments as the sole means of empirical inquiry—all interact to produce a pattern of research activity that has limited progress in our field. If we are to reach the point at which we, too, can regard old journals as ancient history, we must re-examine these interlocking social and ideological forces, retaining the many valuable features of our present approach but opening the door to a greater diversity of method and mode of thought.

---

10. Social learning theory and cyclical or transactional psychodynamic theory (e.g., Wachtel, 1977a, 1977b) still differ in important respects beyond research strategy. Although the latter approach has benefited substantially from the work of social learning theorists, it places much greater emphasis, for example, on conflict and on the need to make inferences commensurate with the complexity of human motivation (Wachtel, 1977b).

16

An Approach to the Study of
Body Language in Psychotherapy

It can hardly be denied that the movements and positions of the body communicate a great deal about what a person is like and how he is feeling. Everyday phrases like "keep your chin up," "down in the mouth," or "walking on air" reflect the degree to which we all assess others' moods by bodily cues. The sexy woman and the West Point graduate tell us much about themselves by their walks.

It is also clear, however, that our ability to understand the language of the body is rather limited. We have difficulty understanding the nonverbal communications of people of other cultures (Hall, 1959), and we probably make many more such errors amongst our own people than we realize. Birdwhistell and his coworkers (Birdwhistell, 1952, 1963; Scheflen, 1964, 1965) have demonstrated nonverbal patterns of interaction with very little awareness by the participants. The success or failure of an interaction may well depend on such unconscious behavior. Observation of video tapes of psychotherapy sessions played without the sound reveals a remarkable amount of activity which, if understood, should be of considerable use to the therapist in his efforts to deepen his understanding of his patient. The present discussion describes one approach to the clinical evaluation of nonverbal behavior which has led to some provocative observations.

The raw data for this work were videotape recordings of therapy interviews. Using the audio portion of the tape, 5- to 10-minute segments were selected which seemed to express the patient's symptoms most clearly. The patient's posture and movements in the

Reprinted by permission from *Psychotherapy: Theory, Research and Practice*, 1967, 4(3), 97–100.

segment were then studied intensively, regarding them in a fashion similar to responses to a Rorschach card or free associations in analysis. Each movement or position was conceived of as having adaptive, expressive, and defensive functions, some conscious and some unconscious. Each body adjustment was seen as being responsive to the patient's intrapsychic state, the real social stimuli, the transference perceptions of the situation, and (an additional variable in this sphere which must be considered) the physical forces acting on the body, such as gravity. A thorough clinical evaluation of the significance of the patient's use of his body was sought.

In making the analysis I did not limit myself to the body material alone; the tapes were viewed with the sound on, and the interpretation took the verbal material into account. Again an analogy to the Rorschach is appropriate. As compared to blind analysis, knowledge about the patient's history and life situation modifies and clarifies our interpretation of his responses, while at the same time the test data shed new light on the biographical material. In the present context, I was interested not so much in what is communicated by the body alone, but in how addition of the body observations to the verbal data provided richer understanding of what was happening in the interview. A brief illustration may be helpful at this point.

In a paranoid patient, to be discussed in greater detail below, it was noted that paranoid ideation was generally preceded by an increase in the amount of gesturing. However, two instances of paranoid ideation were not preceded by such gesturing. I then looked more carefully at the verbalization in these two instances. With this key it was noted for the first time that in these two instances the patient prefaced her statement by attributing it to another doctor, something she did not do at any other time. An observation about the patient's gesture brought to light an important distinction occurring entirely in the verbal realm.

Thus, one way in which the body and verbal material enrich each other is in pointing out where to look more carefully. The differences in expression were theoretically noticeable just from listening to the words. In fact, however, they were missed in listening, as many important features always will be.

There is another way in which concomitant concern with both verbal and bodily data may be mutually enriching. Not only may new observations be made, but new interpretations of those observations as well. Noting, for example, a pattern of movements associated with aggressive comments and then observing a similar pattern occurring when person A's name was mentioned might lead to the hypothesis that the patient had aggressive feelings toward person A. Clearly, one must be cautious in this type of interpretation, but its potential seems considerable.

Observations of Mrs. L

I shall consider here some observations of a particularly fascinating patient. Mrs. L was a paranoid patient whose intake interview at the clinic was recorded on videotape.[1] Much could be surmised about her from the unusual posture she assumed during the interview. Her chair faced the therapist, but the lower part of her body did not. Her legs were pointed at about a 30° angle to the left of the therapist, thus requiring her, in order to face the therapist, either to turn her torso at an angle to her legs (creating torsion at the waist) or turn her neck at an angle to her torso. She did both of these at times, and the effect was to prevent complete relaxation and to give her body somewhat the quality of a coiled spring. She always leaned to the left side of the chair, the side away from the therapist. Her posture allowed her considerable movement and enabled her to be in a continued state of readiness even when leaning back. In addition, in this posture she also presented less body area to the therapist, as in the sideways stance of a fencer, and indeed one has the impression from the entire interview that part of her personal definition of the relationship was as a kind of duel in which she must protect herself and be alert at all times. Many of her hand movements as she talked had a quality of struggling with or warding off.

Along with this defensive definition of the interview, however, Mrs. L also showed a strong tendency to reveal to the therapist what was bothering her. She openly expressed much delusional material, though expressed in a tentative, embarrassed way. She seemed aware that the thoughts bothering her were strange and while wanting some clarification and guidance from the therapist, she also seemed ready to withdraw her account if it were to provoke a negative reaction. Her extremely frequent shifts in position from leaning back to leaning forward and then back again seemed a bodily expression of this ambivalence about expression of her thoughts. When leaning forward she gestured more, her face was more expressive, and she expressed more delusional thoughts. Leaning back, she was less expressive facially and gesturally, and her conversation was more likely to be hesitant, neutral, or the modifying of an earlier assertion.

Many of Mrs. L's movements and gestures showed considerable literalness and concreteness. At one point she described how a date seemed to flash spontaneously across the paper as she was typing, and as she described this she moved her open palm in a horizontal flashing motion indicative of the occurrence described. Similarly, when she mentioned an incident when a plane flew by overhead, she looked up as if the plane were present. This degree of literalness seemed related to her paranoid symptoms, for it occurred only when she was expressing delusional material. Perhaps when she began to discuss this material she became immersed in it in a very concrete fashion. This interpretation must be viewed cautiously, however, because the extent of delu-

1. Especially with paranoid patients, such recording has important implications. I shall not, however, go into them here.

sional material in this segment was considerable, increasing the likelihood that any observed behavior would occur primarily while she was expressing such thoughts. Also, it was when she was forward that she both gestured more and related more delusional material, and with increased gesturing in general, concrete and literal gestures would be more likely.

The most striking observation concerned a pattern of verbal statements, postural adjustments, and hand movements which appeared quite frequently and seemed an expression of the conflict between expressive and defensive efforts. The general form of this pattern consisted of leaning forward, facing the therapist intently, and increased gesturing, followed by a verbal expression of delusional material and then an embarrassed laugh, turning her head to the left, burying or hiding it in her shoulder in ostrich-like fashion, and then leaning back.

Having said something which she was aware was a bit odd (this patient was an outpatient with sufficient reality testing to realize that her delusional thoughts were strange and inconsistent with everyday logic; her confusion and perplexity at what she was thinking was quite evident in her verbal statements), she became anxious and dealt with this by laughing at what she had just said and by turning away from the therapist and hiding her face from him. The bodily cues here give important indications that at some level much of her anxiety is shame-anxiety. This gives clues about the nature of the conflict and her underlying character structure. Her laughter gives the message "Isn't this silly?" It also suggests an effort to prevent further threatening thoughts from being expressed by cutting off stimuli which are helping to elicit them. The head-hiding, as well as the leaning back, would be seen in that context as efforts to disrupt the expressive pattern.

Though the general pattern described above was readily apparent, each occurrence was unique, with its own variations on the general theme. Thus, on one occasion, after burying her head in her shoulder she did not immediately lean back. She remained forward while making a statement which modified her comment and disavowed some of its implications, at the same time putting up her hands in a gesture of blocking or warding off an attack. Then she again told of the words flashing across her paper, made a literal gesture describing this, and then buried her head in her shoulder without laughing. At the end of this complete expression–defense event, she finally leaned back.

Close examination of the succession of variations in the pattern revealed important progressions and shifts in the relative strength of expressive and defensive tendencies as the interview proceeded. Toward the end of the interview segment under discussion, the therapist asked the patient a probing question and she responded by leaning further back into her chair. (Recall that all expressions of delusional ideas took place while she was leaning forward.) Silence accompanied this postural expression of resistance. The therapist then said reassuringly, "You can tell me," whereupon she began to look around, turning her head somewhat from side to side, then leaned forward and began to speak. She expressed the content of a delusional idea (significantly, this was the first of the two statements, noted above, which were attributed to another doctor), then laughed, buried her head in her shoulder, and retreated back to the chair. Her initial leaning into the chair, her seemingly suspicious glancing around before the expression of her thought, and the attribution of her idea to another doctor all suggest heightening defensive effort at this point.

Shortly after the above sequence, she began to lean forward and gesture, but then took hold of one hand with the other, thereby preventing further gesturing. Throughout most of the rest of the segment, Mrs. L sat leaning back, with one hand holding the other. Her hands seemed to be acting out a struggle to prevent expression through gesturing, mildly reminiscent of the efforts of Dr. Strangelove to prevent his arm from making a Hitler salute. The hand being held continued to begin movements which were prevented by the holding hand. In fact, the held hand initiated more movements here than at any other period in the segment, and when these were prevented increased movement of the fingers was apparent, as if efforts were being made to achieve expression with smaller movements. Finally, the delusional thoughts came out in words (the only time such expression occurred while the patient was leaning back) again attributed to another doctor, then once more an embarrassed laugh, followed this time not just by a turn of the head, but by a turn of the entire body. These indicators all suggest that the struggle between expression and defense became increasingly intense as the segment progressed. Significantly, right after the last sequence, the patient said, in no way relating it to the previous content, that "in spite of everything, I want you to know I still pray." With the indirect aid of the deity and a reminder that she was after all a good girl, the conflict could be momentarily reduced.

FURTHER COMMENTS ON THE APPROACH

One feature of the approach described here which is important to note is that the observations described above derived from frequent repetitive observations of the same tape. The patterns described above, which eventually appeared obvious, went almost completely unnoticed in early observations. It was only after more than 50 observations of the same interview segment that they emerged with the present clarity. This suggests that using this method it is possible to see things that a therapist typically would not notice.

The approach thus differs not only from work based on unrecorded psychoanalytic observation (e.g., Reich, 1945), but also from approaches emphasizing what may be perceived by untrained observers (e.g., Ekman, 1965). If such intense, repetitive viewing is needed to isolate patterns such as those described above, then an untrained observer could hardly be expected to notice them. In this respect, then, the present work has much in common with that of Scheflen (1964, 1965), Birdwhistell (1952, 1963), Loeb (1966), and others who examine and re-examine movements recorded on film or tape.

Since this study was part of a project focussing on processes of change in patients, the primary interest was in what nonverbal behavior can tell us about the state, dynamics, and experience of the patient, rather than in the role of nonverbal behavior in the structure of social communication, as studied by Birdwhistell and Scheflen. As Mahl (1966) has pointed out, nonverbal behavior clearly has both intrapsychic and communicative–interpersonal aspects of importance. In this study, movement and postures were viewed as reflecting expressions of drive and defensive processes, as well as conscious and unconscious attempts to communicate with the therapist.

IMPLICATIONS

Let us briefly consider where further pursuit of the present approach may lead us. One important consequence hopefully will be to make us better observers of bodily events. Dittman, Parloff, and Boomer (1965) have reported that dancers are better able to make use of cues from the body than psychotherapists. There is an obvious need for psychologically trained people to develop greater skill in observing the body. Improvement of such skill may be expected to lead to better understanding of individual patients and the trends in an interview.

Beyond the sensitizing of therapists to subtle actions and characteristics of individual patients, one may hope for some insight into more general features of personality functioning as well. Freud was able to perceive universal characteristics of personality functioning by coming to grips with the idiosyncratic features of each patient. Bodily expression of personality dynamics, if studied closely, should be particulary revealing, since so much behavior occurs on this level without the conscious control efforts characteristic of speech.

Finally, some possibilities for practical improvement in psychotherapy technique seem to emerge from these observations. For example, Mrs. L gave hints of her increasing resistance by leaning back and by clasping her hands. Perhaps this is a relatively common expression of resistance, which may precede verbal indicators. It would be useful to have nonverbal clues to the beginning of resistance, for it could lead to more accurate determination of just what thoughts set it off. The verbal clues may come later, or may be more disguised, resulting in recognition of the changed quality of the interview only after the threatening material has been bypassed. It would seem useful to investigate further whether this is a fairly general phenomenon, with which patients, and under what circumstances it occurs.

COGNITION AND CHARACTER STYLE

Introduction to Part Four

The cognitive thrust in psychology was not quite as powerful when some of the chapters in this section were written as it is today. The moment of stimulus–response (S-R) behaviorism had already begun to decline, but the dominance of cognitivism had not been as fully established. Moreover, the impact of cognitive perspectives on *clinical* psychology, and especially on the practice of psychotherapy, was rather minimal. The vast proliferation of cognitive therapies has basically been a product of the past decade or so.

Today, for many therapists, the reliance on a cognitive point of view is frequently associated with a rejection of the psychodynamic approach. As behavior therapists began to grow dissatisfied with the strict S-R formulations that had been dominant early in the development of their movement, many sensed a need for a more complex mediational theory. The clinical phenomena they were encountering called for a perspective that could account for people's selective perception and recall, for the vagaries of attention, and for the evident importance of people's assumptions and fantasies, even—or perhaps especially— when they remain unacknowledged. The perspectives emerging from cognitive psychology seemed to fit the bill: With their origins in the experimental laboratory, they were eminently "respectable." Moreover, they provided an opportunity to consider internal states without turning to psychoanalysis, the point of view that to some degree behavior therapy was originally designed to replace.

Although there is clearly something very useful in the developing area of cognitive and cognitive–behavioral therapies, I have been troubled by the (sometimes explicit, sometimes implicit) opposition to the psychodynamic point of view that tends to be a part of the contemporary cognitive approach to therapy. There is in fact a good deal of potential overlap and a possibility for each to learn important things from the other.[1]

Most of the chapters in this section stem from a time when it was *psychoanalytic* investigators who were most interested in a cognitive point of view and most active in bringing such a perspective into clinical theory. This seemed perfectly natural at the time, since a central aim of the psychoanalytic approach is to understand how people *interpret* events, to elucidate how experiences are processed and transformed. Filtering and selectivity of attention are essential components of this point of view, which from the outset has insisted that people's behavior and experience are not directly determined in a one-to-one fashion by stimuli, but reflect a complex set of mediating processes.

Chapters 17, 18, and 19 are a closely related series of explorations that are concerned particularly with the structural aspects of attention deployment. Their starting premise is that our experience is determined not only by *what* we attend to, but by *how* we attend to it.

For many years the strongest emphasis in the psychoanalytic tradition was on content; Freud's discoveries about the particular kinds of thoughts and experiences that people tend to ward off from consciousness led naturally to a concern with discovering precisely what it was that patients were avoiding. The line of experimental investigation most relevant to this set of concerns is the work on "perceptual defense" that was prominent some years ago.[2] But over the years a complementary emphasis became increasingly prominent in psychoanalytic thought as well. As attention turned to the analysis of defenses, analysts became interested in the stabilized modes of defense that crucially determined people's character types. It became clear that individuals had characteristic ways of organizing their experiences, and that these stylistic features were centrally implicated in the person's efforts to defend against unacceptable experiences.

1. In this regard, it has seemed to me a very salutary development that some of the leading figures in the evolution of the cognitive approach, such as Donald Meichenbaum (e.g., Meichenbaum & Gilmore, 1984) and Michael Mahoney (e.g., 1980), have in recent years indicated an interest in the unconscious. Marvin Goldfried, another of the leading contributors to the cognitive–behavioral point of view, has been particularly active in the development of a rapproachment between that approach and the more insight-oriented or interpretive therapies, including playing a key role in the founding of SEPI.

2. For a review of some of that work and a discussion of the methodological critiques that led to its decline—as well as a reinterpretation of those critiques, which suggests that this line of work was in fact dismissed prematurely—see Wolitzky & Wachtel (1973).

In the research on cognitive style that was launched in the 1950s and 1960s at the Menninger Foundation and then at the Research Center for Mental Health at NYU, an attempt was made to explore these consistencies in cognitive style and to examine their implications for personality functioning. At approximately the same time, Herman Witkin was investigating in exhaustive detail one of these stylistic variables, called by him "field dependence-field independence" or, in a later reformulation, "psychological differentiation."[3]

Most of the chapters in this section are rooted in this work and represent some of the concerns that grew as I became very familiar with it through close contact with Witkin at Downstate Medical Center and with George Klein at NYU. Chapter 17 addresses the issue of breadth or narrowness of attention and considers some of the potential confusions that can arise due to several different ways in which attention can be broad or narrow. It examines in detail how the deployment of attention can yield different experiences in what, defined externally or "objectively," is the same situation. Understanding such differential modes of deploying attention is a key to understanding how defenses function and are maintained. The chapter also looks closely at how attention deployment is influenced by anxiety and at how variations in the deployment of attention may contribute to some of the difficulties experienced by different subgroups of schizophrenics.

Chapter 18 addresses a problem that has been a debilitating one for much of the work in the cognitive-style area, and particularly for work on the most widely investigated style, that of field dependence-independence or psychological differentiation. Much of the excitement generated by the cognitive-style work derived from what seemed to be a means to tap experimentally very basic differences in psychological orientation. Close examination of the work, however, suggested to me that in fact much of it did not really deal with "separate but equal" styles, but rather with certain cognitive abilities and their implications. This in itself was hardly an uninteresting or unimportant line of inquiry. But considerable confusion was introduced by efforts to press this ability measure into the then "sexier" rubric of style. The close links between the measures of field dependence and scores on the Wechsler intelligence scales, cited by Witkin himself as a repeatedly replicated finding, were consonant with a number of other indications that there was a considerable amount of

---

3. The most sophisticated and articulate exposition of the *clinical* implications of styles of perception and cognition was provided by David Shapiro (1965, 1981; see also Wachtel, 1982a, for a review that highlights the implicit challenge Shapiro's approach presents to classical psychoanalytic formulations).

sheer ability variance in what was being presented as something less value-laden. Even today, one finds this confusion occurring not infrequently when cognitive-style research is reported, and I believe that this accounts at least in part for the fact that the seemingly enormous potential of the cognitive-style work still remains substantially unfulfilled.

Chapter 19 carries the implications of this analysis of the cognitive-style research further. Expanding its field of inquiry beyond the single dimension of field dependence–independence, it considers how *most* of the measures purporting to capture cognitive style in fact require the individual to make use of a particular mode of functioning. They assess not the person's *preference* for such a mode in a situation in which more than one approach is feasible, but rather his or her *ability* to utilize a particular mode in a situation where the task requirements rather obviously call for it. Thus, "many of the cognitive-style tests . . . tap styles or preferences only indirectly; what they most directly provide is a picture of the degree to which an individual possesses the basic tools and attributes upon which particular styles and strategies must rest" (pp. 380–381).

The chapter goes further in considering how the typical experimental situation constrains the individual in ways that obscure the very things most of interest to the student of personality. The analysis here of the limits of the experimental method as it is usually employed can be seen as a precursor to the more extended analysis of these problems that appears in this volume in Chapter 13. This effort to consider why the cognitive-style work had yielded disappointing fruits was, I now see, an important step along the path toward a more integrative approach. An essential message of the chapter is that one must understand internal states in relation to the person's context, but that in turn one must also understand how that context is defined and even to some degree created by the individual himself or herself.

Chapter 20 is in one sense not part of the same "series" of papers as the other three chapters in this section. It belongs together with them, however, by virtue of its effort to link clinical phenomena to cognitive processes. In this instance, however, the perspective of Piaget figures prominently. Chapter 20 is also the only selection included in the book that was written in collaboration with someone else. The coauthor, Robert Sollod, is a psychologist with a considerable breadth of interests, and his knowledge of Piaget is quite considerable. We each brought a differing perspective on Piaget's significance to the writing of the chapter. I learned a great deal from working on this paper with Bob. I hope he had a similar experience.

17

Conceptions of Broad and Narrow Attention

Concepts of narrowing and broadening of attention have begun to figure prominently in research on schizophrenia (McGhie & Chapman, 1961; Payne, Matussek, & George, 1959; Venables, 1963, 1964), in discussions of the effects of arousal and anxiety (Agnew & Agnew, 1963; Callaway, 1959; Callaway & Dembo, 1958; Callaway & Thompson, 1953; Easterbrook, 1959; Korchin, 1964), and in clinical and laboratory studies of cognitive style (e.g., Gardner, Holtzman, Klein, Linton, & Spence, 1959; Schlesinger, 1954; Shapiro, 1965). The breadth-of-attention concept has been extremely useful in integrating a wide range of findings, and this success may tend to obscure some confusion and unanswered questions which remain. The present chapter examines some representative uses of concepts of broad versus narrow attention in the recent literature, and it is suggested that greater clarity is needed in distinguishing between different meanings of "broad" and "narrow."

The study of attention is essentially the study of selectivity in perception and cognition and of variations in overall responsiveness to stimulation. Because of man's limited capacity for information processing (Broadbent, 1957; Miller, 1956), "a sharp distinction must be drawn between the physical stimuli impinging . . . and the effective stimuli which control . . . behavior" (Mackintosh, 1965). The "new look" perception studies have extensively explored perceptual selectivity in terms of *content*, examining the variables which make a stimulus with one particular meaning for an individual more or less likely to be perceived than another stimulus with a different mean-

Reprinted by permission from *Psychological Bulletin*, 1967, *68*(6), 417–429.

I wish to express my gratitude to J. G. Schimek, P. K. Oltman, and H. A. Witkin for their valuable comments on earlier drafts of this chapter.

ing. In contrast, the studies discussed below deal primarily with the *structure* of attention, emphasizing the manner in which an individual's style of approach to stimuli (reflecting enduring personality features and/or momentary organismic states) influences what is perceived independent of content.

SCANNING AND FOCUSING

Concepts of breadth of attention have been prominent in research on cognitive styles, much of which can be regarded as the study of attention deployment. One of the early important studies in this area was that of Schlesinger (1954), and its later reinterpretation by Gardner et al. (1959) may highlight some of the complexities in the use of a concept of narrowed attention.

Schlesinger (1954) attempted to demonstrate the operation of a cognitive-control principle which he called "focusing," a "preference for experiencing the world in a narrowed, discriminating way," related to the psychoanalytic concept of isolation (Freud, 1926/1959). Subjects showed consistent individual differences in their accuracy on a size-estimation test in the presence of "neutral" (color, weight, etc.) and "emotionally loaded" (pictures of a nude woman, an electrocution, etc.) irrelevancies, and this performance was unrelated to accuracy in judging the size of a disk which contained no irrelevancies. Further, accuracy in the presence of irrelevancies was associated with a greater number of ratings of "indifferent" in judging likes and dislikes for pictures and with less awareness of feelings as indicated on a personality inventory.

Schlesinger viewed accurate size estimation as reflecting reduced influence of irrelevancies with narrowly focused attention. Gardner et al. (1959), following Piaget (Piaget, Vinh-Bang, & Matalon, 1958), suggested a different interpretation. They suggested that accuracy depends upon overcoming the effects of excessive centration on the standard stimulus and hence upon the extensiveness of attention deployment. Other studies have led to a similar conclusion (e.g., Gardner, 1959, 1961; Gardner & Long, 1962b). Gardner et al. (1959) thus reformulated the focusing control principle discussed by Schlesinger:

> The earlier definition implied that in extreme focussing irrelevancies are "shut out" of experience. The reinterpretation of the principle suggests, *in contrast* [italics added], that subjects originally called "focussers" may actually deploy attention to relatively

many aspects of stimulus fields. The focusser is broadly aware of many aspects of the stimulus field because he is constantly scanning the field, whereas the nonfocusser is more narrow in his deployment of attention. For these reasons the dimension of individual consistencies originally observed by Schlesinger may be more aptly described in terms of a scanning principle. (Gardner et al., 1959, p. 47)

Gardner et al. concluded from their studies that "scanning" is a more appropriate characterization for the cognitive style characteristic of obsessive personalities than is "focusing." They cited Schafer's (1948) description of the isolator as having an increased repertoire of consciously accessible ideas, and suggested that such broadened awareness is similar to the broad attention exhibited by high scanners. They seemed to suggest that individuals who rely heavily on isolation have broad *rather than* narrow attention. As Gardner et al. themselves noted, however, Schafer's description also includes the isolator's tendency to keep ideas separate from each other without becoming aware of their relatedness, and they noted that Freud (1926/1959) conceived of this as being accomplished by a narrowing and focusing of the field of attention.

Other observers since Freud have also noted a narrowness in the attentional field of the obsessive individual (e.g., Shapiro, 1965). Do Gardner et al.'s observations regarding scanning mean that all these observers are wrong? They do not, for the broadness of attention implied by high scanning scores is not at all inconsistent with a narrow and focused style of attention. Elaborating this point is made easier by Hernández-Peón's (1964) analogy between attention and a beam of light.

Hernández-Peón (1964) suggested that

attention may be compared to a beam of light in which the central brilliant part represents the focus surrounded by a less intense fringe. Only the items located in the focus of attention are distinctly perceived whereas we are less aware of the objects located in the fringe of attention. (p. 167)

Using this metaphor, we may see that scanning, as described by Gardner and his colleagues, is a measure of how much the beam moves around the field, while the focusing inferred from Freud's writings by Schlesinger (1954) refers in some way to the width of the beam. These are two logically distinct dimensions, and they should not be equated.

It is thus confusing to describe the attentional field of obsessives, or of any individual for that matter, as either broad or narrow, for there is more than one kind of breadth or constriction. Clinical observations would suggest, for example, that some obsessive personalities show considerable breadth of attention along the scanning dimension but, metaphorically speaking, tend to view with a narrow and sharply focused beam. Thus, on the one hand, they are able to allow a great many different thoughts into consciousness; they are intellectually active and gather a great deal of information; and they are careful to gather a broad sampling of information before acting. On the other hand, they are likely to concern themselves with small details and to be inattentive to the relationship between the many thoughts and ideas they entertain. The latter trait may be conceived of as resulting from an attentional style characterized by a broadly ranging but narrowly focused beam. Many items are brought into the light, but few may be brought to light at once. A wealth of highly articulated, discrete, but unrelated ideas and percepts is the result. Two adjacent objects (ideas) are not seen together, but rather one at a time.

It is important to note that attention is here discussed as focusing not only upon external stimuli, but upon internal processes as well. Attention to internal processes has been a central focus of the psychoanalytic view of attention and has been emphasized as well by such physiologically oriented researchers as Hernández-Peón (1964). Withdrawal of attention from offending thoughts, memories, or other "drive derivatives" is a basic feature of the psychoanalytic concept of defense (Freud, 1915/1959; Rapaport, 1951). Several studies (e.g., Gardner et al., 1959; Holzman & Gardner, 1959) have suggested that individuals show a consistent attentional style to both internal and external excitation, and these studies have tended to view intrapsychic defensive processes as but one expression of a coherent organization of cognitive processes, with attention as a key organizing concept. They may prove to be a much more fruitful way of approaching defense phenomena than most of the large body of "perceptual-defense" studies. The latter, with their emphasis on such measures as tachistoscopic recognition thresholds for briefly presented stimuli, seem to be of limited scope, for they generally do not take into account the role of such defensive manifestations in the overall economy of the personality; the importance of defense is largely in its effect on other aspects of personality functioning. More studies are needed which view defense as a problem of distribution of attention, exploring the relative emphasis on a wide variety of stimuli (internal and external, threatening and nonthreatening), rather than dichotomously focusing upon the recognition or lack of recognition of a single brief external stimulus.

TWO KINDS OF BROAD AND NARROW ATTENTION

The metaphor of a wide or narrow beam is useful in representing a dimension of narrowed attention which is conceptually distinguishable from the dimension of scanning described by Gardner and Klein and their colleagues, and helps to highlight the distinction. Separate consideration of the width of the beam and the movements of the beam clarifies the *specific* sense in which limited scanning represents narrowed attention, and avoids the confusion which may otherwise result. The metaphor may itself be misleading, however, if taken too literally. There may indeed be differences in how much individuals may take in at one "glance" (Granger [1953], for example, reported findings of contraction of visual fields in anxiety), but such differences probably have limited implications for general psychological functioning. The major phenomena which the beam-width analogy is meant to distinguish from scanning phenomena are those of *integration* of the objects of attention, expressing the degree to which an individual can bring various factors to bear on each other and can use them simultaneously to weave together a more complete and balanced picture of his inner and outer world. Such a concept is clearly related to Nunberg's (1931) notion of the synthetic function of the ego.

Consideration of Feffer's (1967) discussion of the role of decentering in cognitive and interpersonal behavior may further clarify what is meant by the width of the attentional beam, for his conception seems closely related. Feffer discussed a classic study by Piaget (1950) in which after children had put an equal number of beads into two identical vases, one vase was emptied and the contents put into a taller, thinner vase. Some children then stated that one of the vases had more beads than the other, citing the greater height or smaller circumference of the new vase, depending on the direction of their judgment. Piaget claimed that the failure to show constancy of quantity was here due to the excessive influence of one aspect (height or circumference) upon judgments of the entire situation.

Interestingly, when the beads were transferred to progressively taller and thinner vases, the direction of the children's estimates would at times reverse. Children who claimed, for example, that the "taller" (and thinner) vase must have more beads, at a later point might decide that the "wider" (and shorter) vase had more. Such fluctuation in judgment was viewed as reflecting the child's sequential focusing upon one aspect of the situation at a time. In order to achieve constancy in the situation according to this view, it is necessary to consider height and circumference together in relation to each other, thus providing a "mutually corrective influence of different, simultaneously experienced centerings" (Feffer, 1967). Feffer has suggested that many psychopathological symptoms can be understood as instances of failure to achieve such integrative functioning.

In terms of our beam-width analogy, the greater the number of aspects of a situation which can be subject to simultaneous decentering, the wider the beam of attention. Procedures similar to Piaget's quantity-constancy experiment may be useful in studies attempting to clarify the implications of the beam-width notion. Also of relevance are studies such as Bemporad's (1967), in which subjects were presented with cards showing a number formed by the pattern of different-sized dots against a field of dots of contrasting colors. Whereas normals easily perceived the numbers, even when their outlines were somewhat hazy and unclear, schizophrenics tended to notice just the parts, calling the cards merely a collection of dots, bubbles, etc., sometimes described in great detail. Here what is at issue is not specifically reconciling contradictory cues in a mutually corrective overall view, but responding to a higher-order percept instead of separate parts.

In contrast to these procedures, scanning has been assessed by methods such as recording movements of the eyes while estimating size (Gardner & Long, 1962a, 1962b) or looking at pictures (Luborsky, Blinder, & Schimek, 1965). The scanning notion is also derived from Piaget's concept of decentration, but is concerned with the changes in focus and searching for additional data which are necessary but not sufficient for the achievement of what Feffer referred to as *simultaneous* decentering.

Actually, scanning itself is a complex dimension. Gardner and Long (1962b), in their study of individual strategies in size estimation, used several different estimates of degree of scanning, such as time to make size judgments, number of stops in the course of adjusting the comparison circle, number of separate centrations on the standard, total time of centrations on the standard, percentage of time on the standard, mean time per centration on the standard, and time spent checking the judgment after the final adjustment. Luborsky *et al.* (1965) also used several measures of how their subjects looked around at the pictures presented. These included time spent looking at background features, percentage of time spent looking at the central area of the picture, number of areas of the picture fixated at least once, distance from the point of one fixation to the next, and duration per fixation. In the Gardner and Long study, with an *n* of 60, most of the measures were significantly intercorrelated. The Luborsky *et al.* study, with a smaller *n* (16), showed fewer significant intercorrelations but did suggest some consistency in the tendency of individuals to "venture to look around." Those measures which were most highly intercorrelated also tended to have similar correlations with measures of defense as assessed by the Rorschach, but there were some exceptions. It appears that an overall dimension of scanning may be a useful conceptual tool, but that it may nonetheless prove fruitful to explore further whether in particular individuals or in particular circumstances certain components of scanning may be emphasized more than others. To illustrate somewhat schematically, one may rapidly shift from one of two foci to the other many times, or one may at a slower pace cover a greater variety of stimuli, lingering longer at each, but covering a greater area. The implications of such distinctions may prove as fruitful an area of research as the study of the implications of the overall scanning dimension.

ANXIETY AND ATTENTION

It was noted above—for example, in the case of some obsessive personalities—that description of an individual's style of attention as either broad or narrow, without distinguishing between different dimensions of breadth, may be incomplete and confusing. Similar difficulties may arise in efforts to describe the effects of anxiety on attention. Korchin (1964) discussed extensively the cognitive effects of anxiety and came to the conclusion that at moderate levels of anxiety there is a narrowing of the attentional field, but that at more extreme levels there is a general breakdown of organized behavior and attention becomes more diffuse: "The anxious patient is unable to concentrate, hyper-responsive, and hyper-distractable."

Korchin's clinical observations are acute, and his description of the anxious patient is consistent with those of other observers. Theoretically, however, the postulation of a narrowing and focusing of attention at moderate levels of anxiety and a diffusion at higher levels presents some difficulties, for it seems to imply a sudden discontinuity at some critical level of anxiety. To avoid postulating such a discontinuity, it might be argued that the change from focusing to diffusion could be expressed as a continuous inverted-U function in which attention becomes more and more focused until it reaches a peak, at which point it gradually diffuses. When the implications of such a formulation are examined, however, it leads to predictions which are inconsistent with observed facts.

Consider Easterbrook's (1959) explanation of the classic Yerkes-Dodson law (Yerkes & Dodson, 1908).

> For any task . . . , provided that initially a certain proportion of the
> cues in use are irrelevant cues . . . , the reduction [in the number
> of cues in use] will reduce the proportion of irrelevant cues em-
> ployed and so improve performance. When all irrelevant cues have
> been excluded, however, . . . further reduction in the number of
> cues employed can only affect relevant cues, and proficiency will
> fall. (Easterbrook, 1959, p. 193)

If we view moderate anxiety as leading to a narrowing of attention,
everything is fine. We would expect that as anxiety increases, performance first improves (as irrelevant cues are excluded) and then gets
worse (as relevant cues are also excluded). This is consistent with a
large body of experimental literature. But what happens when anxiety increases still further and (as Korchin suggested) attention begins to diffuse? As the attentional field widens again, the relevant
cues which had been excluded should come back into the range of
attention, and performance should begin to improve, worsening only
after many irrelevant cues begin to be employed again. This "two-
humped camel" curve relating anxiety to performance has never
been found empirically.

The dilemma may perhaps be resolved if instead of talking of
diffusion or narrowing of attention in general, we again consider
separately changes in the two dimensions of breadth discussed thus
far. If we postulate that a primary effect of anxiety is to narrow
specifically what has been referred to as the width of the attentional
beam, then we might expect that at extremely high levels of anxiety,
the attentional field may become so narrow that no stable orientation toward the environment can be maintained. A smiling mouth or
a frowning mouth can be experienced as two entirely separate entities when not anchored in the context of the single individual who
can smile one minute and frown the next. Without the capacity to
stabilize his world by making use of the larger integrated units which
remain relatively constant, the extremely anxious individual becomes a slave to minor variations in the perceptual field, which
demand most of his attention and leave him confused and disorga-
nized. He might then indeed be "unable to concentrate, hyper-
responsive, and hyper-distractable" (Korchin, 1964), but the diffusion
of his attention would be along a different dimension (roaming of the
beam) than the narrowing, and largely a consequence of it.

The description of the very anxious individual's attention as like
a narrow beam which roams all over the field bears similarities to the
description given earlier of the attention of some obsessive individuals. There is, however, one major difference. The scanning of the
field exhibited by the obsessive is highly planful and organized,

whereas that of the anxious individual appears scattered and poorly controlled. The patterning and degree of organization of an individual's scanning is a difficult but highly important problem to explore.

AROUSAL AND THE RANGE OF CUE UTILIZATION

Korchin's (1964) discussion of the effects of anxiety on attention may be largely viewed as a special case of Easterbrook's (1959) formulation that "emotional arousal acts consistently to reduce the range of cues that an organism uses and that the reduction in range of cue utilization influences action in ways that are either organizing or disorganizing, depending on the behavior observed." The range of cue utilization was defined as "the total number of environmental cues in any situation that an organism observes, maintains an orientation towards, responds to, or associates with a response."

According to Easterbrook, emotional arousal is neither consistently facilitating nor consistently disrupting. Whether one effect or the other is observed depends upon the level of arousal and the characteristics of the task.[1] The only consistent effect of arousal is reduction in the range of cue utilization. For some tasks this reduction improves performance.

> Irrelevant cues are excluded and drive is then said to be organizing or motivating. In other tasks, proficiency demands the use of a wide range of cues and drive is disorganizing or emotional. There seems to be an optimal range of cue utilization and hence an optimal level of arousal for each task. (Easterbrook, 1959, pp. 197–198)

Thus, by means of this attentional concept, Easterbrook was able to make meaningful and coherent a large body of diverse and often seemingly contradictory observations.

One may question, however, whether the process of attentional narrowing is as passive as Easterbrook seemed to imply. As Easterbrook described it, narrowing appears to be an invariant effect of arousal and has little to do with the individual's active efforts to cope with his environment. It has been demonstrated (e.g., Klein, 1954, 1958) that efforts to describe the effects of drive without taking into account individual differences in control processes may lead to error. Studies are now being planned by me to investigate possible individual differences, rooted in differences in cognitive style, in the effect

---

1. Kausler and Trapp (1960) have suggested further variables that may be involved.

of anxiety on the breadth of attention. In an earlier study, not focusing on individual differences (Wachtel, 1968a), a form of narrowing of attention was evident when anxiety was induced in a fashion that left the subject no way of coping, but not when subjects had a way to cope with the threat. These results suggest that narrowing may not be automatic at all times, but rather that the range of attention deployment may be somewhat under the control of the individual when the arousal is associated with an explicit task. In fact, the capacity to maintain an attention span appropriate to the demands of a task performed under stress may be an important adaptive asset,[2] and automatic and invariant narrowing of attention as arousal increases may signify serious ego weakness.

It is also important to consider just what kind of narrowing arousal may produce. In Easterbrook's formulation, attentional changes were again described along a single dimension of breadth or narrowness. But if, as suggested here, there is more than one kind of broad or narrow attention, then the considerable usefulness of the arousal-narrowed attention formulation should be increased by attempts to explore the effects of arousal on each of these dimensions separately.

Consideration of the specific type of attention-narrowing effect which may accompany arousal in particular instances has important practical implications. As Easterbrook (1959) pointed out, in many cases impairment in functioning may be viewed as reflecting the individual's use of only a limited portion of the cues necessary to guide behavior effectively. If this limitation is due to reduced scanning,[3] it should be possible to point out other aspects of the situation to the individual and improve his efficiency by providing him with perspective. One, so to speak, turns the person's attentional beam for him, enabling him to notice that which he has missed. Once he has viewed the needed material, he should be able to make use of it to perform like the more efficient and successful person. If the impairment is due to a "narrowed beam," however, such efforts may prove less fruitful. In order to take into account any cue pointed out to him, such an individual may then have to almost totally ignore those cues

---

2. I do not mean to suggest that *no* attentional changes accompany arousal in these cases. Along with an attention span maintained at an adequate level for the required task, increased thresholds might appear for nonrelevant stimuli; these increased thresholds would reduce the chance of distraction from an important activity.

3. Phenomenological theorists (e.g., Combs, 1949; Combs & Taylor, 1952) have described the effects of threat as limiting the perceptive field of the threatened individual to the area of threat, leaving him unable to explore a wide range of potential percepts. Such a description seems essentially to be one of restricted scanning of the field.

he had previously been using, for his capacity to use many cues together is impaired. He may then evidence behavior guided just as one-sidedly, in effect going overboard in the other direction. Obsessive indecision may be an instance of such a phenomenon. In a sense, it would be as if a dialectic process were continually beginning but never reaching the synthesis stage. Such an effect has been noted by Mayman and Gardner (1960) for individuals with brain damage. Easterbrook (1959) also described several studies in which brain-damaged subjects showed impaired "integration of simultaneous stimuli."

By restricting his generalization to situations in which "the direction of behavior is constant," Easterbrook (1959) seemed to be confining his discussion to a narrowed beam, for the direction of behavior seems here to be roughly equivalent to movements of the beam. He seemed to be saying that given no movements of the beam, its width decreases with arousal. The overall spirit of his paper seems consistent with this interpretation as well. There is, however, one important difference between the direction of behavior and the direction of attention as here conceived. At the level of observation implied by Easterbrook, the direction of behavior is constant if the subject continues to perform the assigned task throughout the test period. A more microscopic analysis of his attention, however, might suggest that while performing this overall task, continuous subtle fluctuations are occurring, with now this aspect of the situation more salient, now that. Thus, it is not necessary to demonstrate differences in, say, gross eye movements or to observe major shifts in the subject's attention from the assigned task to something else in order to postulate that a scanning explanation may be possible. The "direction of behavior" may remain constant, but shifts of attention, movements of the attentional beam along conceptual as well as physical dimensions, may occur throughout.

In most of the studies cited by Easterbrook, it is difficult to determine whether the narrowing consists of some limitation of scanning processes (thus keeping the subject focused on certain features of the field most of the time, instead of sampling many aspects focally) or of some reduction in how much information can be handled in an integrated fashion. Consider, for example, Bahrick, Fitts, and Rankin's (1952) study of the effect of incentive motivation on a perceptual–motor task. High-incentive subjects did better on a continuous tracking task, but more poorly in reporting the occurrence of occasional stimuli in the periphery. The overall direction of behavior remained constant—subjects performed the assigned task, with its central and peripheral aspects. The focus of attention, however, might have shifted often during the task. While tracking, subjects might occasionally have reminded themselves that they had better be ready for the peripheral stimuli, thus shifting the center of their attention to these stimuli although still tracking. In the present scheme, such phenomena are viewed as attentional scanning as much as phenomena of eye movement or other sense organ adjustments. Reduced responsiveness to the peripheral stimuli under high incentive may have been a product of a reduction in this kind of scanning, or it may have reflected reduced capacity to handle the tracking and peripheral stimuli at once. Experimental procedures of this sort (e.g., Bursill, 1958; Wachtel, 1968a) do not lend themselves to determination of such an issue.

An effort to experimentally differentiate the effects of motivation on different aspects of attention was made by McNamara and Fisch (1964). These investigators distinguished between (1) the "span of attention," related to extensity and breadth of attentional activity and concerned with "the total number of stimulation elements and/ or the gross amount of stimulus information perceived in that span of time and/or space between proximal stimulation and the relevant response," and (2) a scanning process or mechanism, related to "discrimination of small nuances in and between cue elements . . . and acquisition and acceptance or rejection of specific cue elements relevant to a task." The former aspect, identified by McNamara and Fisch with Easterbrook's conception of range of cue utilization, was assessed by means of a pathways test, a test for memory of serial order of a list of nonsense syllables, and an incidental-learning task involving learning the serial order of words encircled in the middle of cards and later testing for learning of other "irrelevant" words written in other areas of the card. The "scanning" process, viewed by McNamara and Fisch as closely related to Solley and Murphy's (1960) notion of attentional act, was assessed by means of a modification of the Wechsler–Bellevue Digit Symbol subtest in which each symbol had a minute imperfection that had to be reproduced, and by a memory-for-designs test involving discrimination of seen designs from very similar new ones. Monetary incentive and threat of shock both led to poorer performance on the "span-of-attention" tasks; there was little evidence for such impairment on the "scanning" task.

Careful examination of McNamara and Fisch's experimental procedures indicates that these, too, leave some ambiguity with regard to the process underlying good or poor performance. The incidental learning task, for example, viewed by them as reflecting processes similar to receptor–effector span (Woodworth, 1938), may also depend upon looking around the card and shifting one's focus of attention back and forth from the central word to the other words on the card. This is the type of process referred to here as scanning[4] or movements of the beam, and distinguished here from span-type measures. McNamara and Fisch's study may be viewed as one more demonstration that *some* kind of narrowing of attention may occur under high drive, but much more experimental work is needed to determine just what kind of narrowing occurs under what conditions in which individuals.

NARROWING AND SELECTIVE ATTENTION

The discussion thus far has emphasized the distinction between two kinds of phenomena (reduced scanning and narrowing of the beam of attention) which, with some confusing consequences, have both been referred to as "narrowed attention." There is still a third group of phenomena which have also been referred to as "narrowed attention," and it may be important to distinguish this dimension from the other two.

An important series of studies exploring the arousal–narrowed-attention relation was performed by Callaway (1959; Callaway & Band, 1958; Callaway & Dembo, 1958; Callaway & Stone, 1960; Callaway & Thompson, 1953). A wide variety of measures were used to indicate narrowing or broadening of attention, including the Stroop Color–Word Test (Stroop, 1935), and embedded-figures tests (Thurstone, 1944; Witkin, 1950). The inclusion of better performance on the Stroop and embedded-figures tests with the rest of the indicators of narrowed attention seemed justified by the pattern of results obtained in these studies, and there is sense to the rationale, for example, that good Stroop performance depends on narrowing attention so that the printed name of the colors is excluded from focal attention. Agnew and Agnew (1963), manipulating arousal by threat of shock and challenging instructions rather than by stimulant drugs as did Callaway, also found indications that drive or arousal leads to better Stroop performance and attributed the finding to narrowed attention. Oltman (1964, 1965) found that arousal due to white noise led to improved scores on the rod-and-frame test, and attributed the finding to narrowed attention, the effect of the (peripheral) frame on judgment of the rod being reduced.

---

4. McNamara and Fisch's use of the term "scanning" obviously differs from its use here. They were referring to some sort of discriminative process by scanning, and the process described by them, although an attentional process, does not seem directly related to concepts of *broad and narrow* attention.

The above studies introduce further complexity into ideas of broad and narrow attention. Good performance on the Stroop, embedded-figures, and rod-and-frame tests requires selective responding to one portion of the stimulus field and ignoring or inhibiting response to the rest. The controversy over whether such good performance reflects the capacity to extract items from an embedding context (Karp, 1963; Witkin, Dyk, Faterson, Goodenough, & Karp, 1962) or represents a more general capacity to selectively direct attention to relevant rather than compelling irrelevant stimuli (Gardner, Jackson, & Messick, 1960) need not concern us here. There is considerable agreement that good performance is associated with a more differentiated and highly articulated style of cognition and with reduced responsiveness to the misleading or disrupting irrelevant cues. Further, in such tasks it takes an active effort on the part of the individual to ignore the compelling pull of the frame, embedding figure, or printed name. Studies such as Gardner's (1961) factor analysis suggest that the mere wearing of psychological blinders is not sufficient for good performance on such tasks. Gardner found that field articulation, the cognitive control associated closely with performance on such tests as rod and frame or embedded figures, represents a different factor than does scanning. This has been suggested by other correlational studies as well, such as the finding that the number of centrations in a size-matching procedure showed low and nonsignificant correlations with mean solution time on the embedded-figures test (Gardner & Long, 1962a). Thus, it would seem of value to distinguish between narrow attention in the sense of limited scanning and narrow attention in the sense of reduced responsiveness to compelling irrelevant stimuli.

Regarding the Stroop test, Gardner and Long (1962a) actually found a tendency for extensiveness of scanning (*broad* attention) to be associated with the kind of Stroop performance Callaway referred to as indicating *narrowed* attention. Callaway and Band (1958) did get opposite findings (i.e., individual consistency in broad or narrow functioning on both size-matching and Stroop performance), but they used only 10 subjects, and their size-matching task and rationale for accurate matching were not quite the same as Gardner's. Callaway and Band had subjects match a nearby standard with an adjustable distant object and reasoned that overestimation of the standard results from reduced influence of distance cues on judgments. Callaway's conception of narrowed attention has much merit. His emphasis (Callaway & Dembo, 1958) on the *relative influence* of aspects of the field, rather than on merely whether or not a stimulus is sensed, and his recognition that reduced influence of peripheral factors may be evident in factors peripheral in time and meaning, as well as space, represent a useful conceptual approach. Discussion of narrowed attention as only a single dimension, however, is subject to the difficulties noted above.

To be sure, Callaway has found that in size matching, as well as embedded figures, EEG arousal is associated with enhanced influence of some cues and decreased influence of all others. Further, the Gardner studies examined the intercorrelations of test scores for normal subjects not experimentally aroused, and may not be relevant to characterizing changes in functioning under the conditions employed by Callaway. The common qualities of such phenomena, which enable them to be grouped under the rubric of broad or narrow attention, are important to note, particularly since these phenomena may share common antecedents (such as arousal). Nonetheless, there is evidence that decreased scanning and greater field articulation are forms of narrowed attention which have different consequences for psychological functioning, and grouping them together under a single label obscures these differences. Further exploration may even reveal that in different circumstances, or for different individuals, the effect of arousal may be specific to one of these types of narrowing.

Selective Attention and Beam Width

The dimension of broad and narrow attention represented by performance on tests such as the rod and frame or embedded figures can be distinguished not only from the scanning dimension, but also from what has been referred to as the width of the attentional beam. Global, unarticulated functioning, such as is seen in field-dependents (Witkin et al., 1962) or hysterics (Shapiro, 1965), should not be confused with broadly integrative functioning. This type of confusion has been discussed with reference to the meaning of Rorschach W responses by Blatt and Allison (1963; Allison & Blatt, 1964). Responses to the entire blot as a whole have been theorized to reflect "abstracting, surveying and integrating abilities" (Rapaport, Gill, & Schafer, 1946), but as Blatt and Allison noted, W responses may be global and diffuse or highly articulated and differentiated, and it is only the latter response which, for example, relate highly to intelligence measures. The capacity to integrate and deal with many facets of a situation simultaneously (broad beam) is clearly not the same as an inability to reduce the influence of irrelevant distracting or misleading stimuli, which is the sense in which the description "broad attention" is applicable to influence of a frame in setting a rod to the vertical, influence of written color names in calling out the actual color of a stimulus, or influence of an embedding figure upon finding a smaller figure embedded within it. In fact, field-independent subjects (low influence of frame or embedding figure) seem to show superior integrative capacity to some extent, as Witkin *et al.* (1962) have indicated and as a recent study by Schimek of overall integrative capacity in the Rorschach also indicated (Schimek, 1967).

Broad and Narrow Attention in Schizophrenia

Venables (1964) organized his important review of input dysfunction in schizophrenia around a model of broadening or narrowing of attention along a single dimension. He placed McGhie and Chapman's (1961) descriptions of acute patients' inability to select among incoming stimuli on the broad end of the continuun, with narrowing represented by such findings as decreased incidental learning (Greenberg, 1953; Topping & O'Connor, 1960; Winer, 1954), decreased size constancy for distant objects (e.g., Hamilton, 1963; Lovinger, 1956; Weckowicz, 1957, 1958), and disruption of distance estimation (Hamilton, 1963; Weckowicz, Sommer, & Hall, 1958). The latter two effects were interpreted by Venables as possibly reflecting decreased appreciation of peripheral cues.

But acute schizophrenics' inability to shut out noises from next door or inability to focus upon figure apart from ground (McGhie & Chapman, 1961) is not the same as using peripheral cues to gain fuller, more balanced awareness of a situation, though both are in some sense broad rather than narrow. Particularly in schizophrenia, where the organization of thought and the sorting of stimuli according to salience is such an issue, it is necessary to distinguish the degree to which irrelevant stimuli are screened out (seemingly related to field dependence or field articulation) from the other dimensions of attention discussed here.

Silverman (1964) and Broen (1966) have emphasized a similar distinction in their discussions of schizophrenia. Silverman based his discussion of attention in schizophrenia upon Gardner *et al.*'s (1959) concepts of scanning and field articulation. He noted that either of these cognitive controls may be exaggerated for purposes of defense and that schizophrenics tend to be extreme on measures of these controls in ways consistent with the kind of schizophrenia they exhibit. Thus, paranoid schizophrenics tend to show extensive scanning and high field articulation, whereas simple schizophrenics evidence extremely minimal scanning and an undifferentiated style of attention consistent with minimal field articulation. He suggested that a pattern of attention deployment that is not too extreme on either of these dimensions is a good prognostic sign and noted as well that style and extremity of attention deployment are complexly related to the process-reactive dimension and to degree of chronicity.

If we consider Silverman's description of the extensive-scanning, high-field-articulation paranoid schizophrenic, for example, it is clear that such an individual cannot be simply categorized as exhibiting either broad or narrow attention. His attention is both broad and narrow, and both aspects are consistent with the way in which he protects himself from anxiety and maintains his delusional system. By broadly scanning, he is able to gather "evidence" for his ideas (and also to be on the alert for the dangers he often anticipates); by narrowly selecting what he finds consistent with his delusional ideas, screening out and ignoring all other aspects of potential percepts, he uses his extreme field articulation to make sure that the evidence indeed fits. It is thus not surprising that a less extreme degree of field articulation is associated with better prognosis in such a patient, for not only does it signify that a less extreme mobilization is necessary to cope with his anxiety, it also implies that events are more likely to be experienced as having meanings beyond the hidden signs and clues which he seeks (Shapiro, 1965), for such meanings would be less thoroughly screened out.

Broen (1966) presented a conceptual scheme which, as he noted, bears many similarities to Silverman's. He demonstrated that some apparently contradictory findings regarding schizophrenia may be reconciled by assuming that all schizophrenics exhibit response disorganization, "a lack of clear hierarchical ordering of competing response tendencies," and that chronic schizophrenics attempt to deal with this deficit by observing fewer stimuli. As Broen pointed out, response disorganization and minimal field articulation are somewhat similar concepts, for the former implies an inability to selectively focus attention on relevant stimuli.

Broen did not emphasize preschizophrenic attentional styles and their exaggeration for defensive purposes in schizophrenia, and thus the explanatory implications of his description seem to differ to some extent from Silverman's. He noted, for example, that Gardner (1961) has shown consistent individual differences among normals in the scanning dimension, but emphasized general decrease in scanning with chronicity rather than amplification of individual tendencies among schizophrenics. Like Silverman, he noted that paranoids scan and select more than other schizophrenics, but viewed this as their suffering somewhat less response disorganization, rather than as reflecting the exaggeration of a different attentional style.

Degree of organization and breadth of observation were viewed by Broen as more directly related to each other than in Silverman's formulation. Silverman stressed that field articulation and scanning are aspects of attention which operate independently of each other, though the particular pattern of controls of an individual presumably attains some measure of functional coherence. Broen, on the other hand, viewed the minimal scanning he attributed to chronic schizophrenics as a more or less direct response to and effort to cope with the primary disorganization of response hierarchy. The differences between these two conceptions reflect, in part, Silverman's interest in individual attentional styles' showing some continuity between normals and schizophrenics and Broen's interest in general processes which account for schizophrenic pathology. Like Silverman's, however, Broen's discussion demonstrates the gain in conceptual and terminological clarity which accrues from a multidimensional scheme for describing attentional processes. He noted, for example, that chronic schizophrenics have been described both as attending to a narrower range of stimuli than normals (Venables, 1964) and as being more distractable than normals (Chapman, 1956). As Broen implied, however, these descriptions are not incompatible if it is recognized that failure to observe certain stimuli because of some limitation in scanning processes is not the same as selectively ignoring them because they are of little relevance to ongoing concerns. Failure to consider this distinction can obscure meaningful coherence in the findings of different investigators.

CONCLUDING COMMENTS

Several writers have noted that attention has generally been treated as a stepchild by modern psychologists (e.g., Berlyne, 1960; Mackintosh, 1965; Solley & Murphy, 1960). The studies reviewed suggest that a healthy revival of interest in attention has been occurring. While authors such as Easterbrook (1959) and Mackintosh (1965) have indicated that attentional concepts may be consistent with a sophisticated behaviorist point of view, the work of people like Shapiro (1965) demonstrates that attention is also a key element in attempting to understand the experience of other people. Indeed, William James (1890) commented: "My experience is what I agree to attend to."

Perhaps it is because attentional phenomena are so closely linked to the ever-shifting world of experience that they have been so difficult to pin down precisely. Terms like "breadth" or "narrowness" of attention are seductive because they reverberate with common experiences of us all. The above discussion, however, suggests strongly that a single dimension such as breadth of attention fails to do justice either to the complexities of experience or to the demands of a precise science. The separable dimensions of breadth of attention discussed here are tentative and probably incomplete. They will doubtless be refined as research becomes more precise and differentiated. In order to advance beyond the promising beginnings inherent in the work reviewed, such precision and differentiation are clearly necessary.

18

Field Dependence and Psychological Differentiation: A Re-Examination

The dimension of individual differences variously referred to as field dependence–independence, psychological differentiation, or field articulation has been one of the most extensively studied constructs in the area of personality and psychopathology. The concept of field dependence arose out of the correlations noted between performance in a variety of seemingly diverse tasks, such as the rod-and-frame test (RFT), the embedded-figures test (EFT), the body-adjustment test, and human figure drawings (Witkin, Dyk, Faterson, Goodenough, & Karp, 1962). Witkin *et al.* have postulated that the characteristic of psychological functioning underlying the relationship between performance on all these tasks is the degree to which the world is experienced in differentiated fashion, with aspects of the person's life space experienced as discrete from the context in which they appear. These authors have described a large body of research indicating that individual differences on these tests are related to behaviors in a wide variety of situations. The present chapter will examine the conceptual and methodological assumptions which have been the basis for most of the work in this area and will suggest some alternative interpretations and strategies. Prominent in our inquiry will be a consideration of the kinds of questions which have *not* been asked as a function of these assumptions.

Reprinted by permission from *Perceptual and Motor Skills*, 1972, 35, 179–189. Copyright © 1972 by *Perceptual and Motor Skills*.

Many of the ideas presented in the present chapter were enhanced and clarified in many discussions with valued colleagues. I wish especially to express my gratitude to Leo Goldberger, Nancy R. Israel, George S. Klein, Carole Shulman, Lloyd Silverman, and David L. Wolitzky. The able assistance of Cheryl Kurash greatly facilitated my work. Preparation of this chapter was facilitated by Grant No. 5-P01-MH17545 from the National Institute of Mental Health.

COGNITIVE STYLE AND COGNITIVE CONTROL

Before proceeding further into the theoretical edifice which has been constructed around the basic measures, it may be of value to stop at the entrance and note the name on the door. Throughout his writings, Witkin refers to the field dependence–field independence dimension as a "cognitive style," indicating that by that term he is referring to a mode of functioning evident across many situations (e.g., Witkin & Oltman, 1967). On the other hand, in the work of Gardner, Klein, and their associates (e.g., Gardner, Holtzman, Klein, Linton, & Spence, 1959), this same dimension, designated as field articulation, is referred to as a cognitive *control*, and the term "cognitive style" is reserved for a higher-order characterization of the individual. In that work, cognitive style refers to a particular meaningful ordering or patterning of cognitive controls, of which field articulation is just one. Such a patterning is a reflection of the individual's adaptive strategy, and goes a long way toward defining his unique approach to the world.[1]

The difference is more than merely one of terminology. It goes to the heart of one of the key conceptual difficulties inherent in much of the work on field dependence. The conception of style put forth by Gardner, Klein, and associates implies that a high field-independence score may have vastly different implications for personality when seen in the context of one configuration of cognitive controls than in another. From this point of view, the search for even relatively invariant personality correlates of a particular cognitive-control dimension is likely to be a rather risky business. Field independence may have quite different functions for a field-independent, extensive-scanning sharpener than for a field-independent, minimal-scanning leveler (Gardner, *et al.*, 1959).

Witkin's use of the term "style," on the other hand, is consistent with the view, expressed in some of his writings, that the measures he uses pick up an indication of divergent directions of psychological development and preferred modes of perceiving. He states that he is going beyond the problem of individual differences to the study of "psychological individuality" and asserts that "it is now possible to offer a fairly comprehensive characterization of people who show a typically field-dependent orientation on the rod-and-frame test" (Witkin *et al.*, 1962).

Thus, much of the work deriving from this view of cognitive style represents a rather ambitious attempt to capture the style of

---

1. This distinction in terminology has also been discussed in another context by Santostefano (1969).

life of a person by using a few highly reliable and objective laboratory instruments. Although it is made quite clear that field dependence is not *all* that is involved by any means, this orientation does imply that people who differ in their performance on these tests differ in the very direction of development of their personalities, in the way they prefer to deal with life situations, in their strategy for living.

However, it has been pointed out on a number of occasions (e.g., Gardner, Jackson, & Messick, 1960; Mayman & Voth, 1969; Mischel, 1968; Wachtel, 1968; Witkin, 1965) that the instruments generally used to assess field dependence do not really offer the subject a choice to see how he prefers to deal with a situation. Rather, they *require* the individual to perform in a particular way and assess how *able* he is to meet the task requirements. Both the EFT and RFT have clear demands for the subject to respond to some aspects of the stimulus field in isolation from the context in which they are embedded. The individual who does not disembed is demonstrating that he *cannot*, and *not* that he *chooses* not to, especially in light of other evidence that individuals who do poorly on EFT or RFT tend also to be people particularly eager to do what they are supposed to do.

Thus, in many respects, what is most directly assessed by the tests of field dependence is not so much a style of functioning as an ability to function well in certain types of tasks, something we might well think of as a component of intelligence. Indeed, the tests of field independence most commonly used correlate just as highly with the Block Designs, Object Assembly, and Picture Completion subtests of the Wechsler Adult Intelligence Scale (WAIS) as they do with each other.

This intelligence-like property of tests like the RFT and EFT seems inconsistent with the idea of a style reflecting differing directions of psychological development. It is consistent, however, with another of Witkin *et al.*'s (1962) concepts, that of psychological differentiation. Witkin *et al.* view the more differentiated individual as having progressed from a relatively primitive and unstructured state to one of greater articulation and complexity. "Other things being equal, the differentiated person has richer, more diversified resources for coping than the less differentiated person" (Witkin *et al.*, 1962, p. 21). Thus, the concept of differentiation implies not differences in direction or strategy of development but in *degree* of development. It is a more-or-less concept rather than one of equal alternative strategies.

There are, then, two separate strands of theory woven into the research in this area. One emphasizes style and direction of development and the organization of personality. The other centers around abilities and the across-the-board quality of certain developmental limitations. Although these two views of the data of field-dependence research are not irreconcilable (an attempt at reconciliation appears below), it seems that a good deal of confusion does exist among workers in this area. The lack of clarity is reflected in and further aggravated by some extremely persistent methodological limitations, which are discussed next.

METHODOLOGICAL LIMITATIONS IN FIELD-DEPENDENCE RESEARCH[2]

Need for Converging Measures: Test versus Construct

Many studies have not been clear about the distinction between one's position on the hypothetical dimension field dependence–independence and one's score on a particular *test* which is related to the dimension. Witkin and other workers with this concept have made it quite clear that the construct "field dependence" refers to the variance shared by several measures, not the variance in performance on any one of them. In fact, the obtained correlations among even the most trusted measures of field dependence tend to have an upper limit of about .60, indicating that approximately two-thirds of the variance in any of these measures is due to something other than field dependence.

Thus, when a correlation is found, for example, between EFT and some social or cognitive measure, there is no solid basis for assuming that field dependence is implicated in that correlation. The variance which the EFT shares with that other variable might not be the same variance it shares with the RFT or with figure drawings. The need for this caution is further highlighted by a number of recent studies indicating sources of variance not intrinsic to the field-dependence construct which may differentially affect performance on RFT or EFT (e.g., Jacobson, 1966, 1968; Kurie & Mordkoff, 1970; McAllister, 1970; Silverman, 1968). The disturbing number of studies which assess "field dependence" with only one test pay a high price in interpretability for eschewing the use of several converging measures of the construct.

Even where a variety of measures are used, failure to distinguish between test and construct can lead to confusion. For example, in

2. The methodological problems discussed in this section are evident in literally hundreds of studies in this area. Therefore, except when specific illustrations are necessary for clarification, references to particular studies showing these difficulties will not be included.

discussing a factor analysis of cognitive measures with children, Santostefano (1969) makes much of the "finding that a measure of Focal Attention played a subordinate role in defining the factor of Field Articulation, and that a measure of the latter in turn contributed to the construction of the Leveling–Sharpening factor." This "finding" is based, for example, on a loading of .40 of a block designs test on a factor interpreted as reflecting the cognitive control Leveling–Sharpening. Since "this test is interpreted as involving the selective directing of attention to relevant and irrelevant cues and defines the context of Field Articulation," it seems to be assumed that wherever the test appears in the definition of a factor it brings with it its property of being a measure of Field Articulation. It seems more reasonable to assume that the test is factorially complex and that the variance it shares with tests involving Leveling–Sharpening is different from that shared with other tests of Field Articulation. (Actually, this block designs test does not even load on one of the factors defined by Santostefano as a "Field Articulation" factor.) This particular error of interpretation has led to some questionable proposals about the developmental and adaptive properties of cognitive controls.

Insufficient Controls for Intelligence

As indicated above, the traditional measures of field dependence may be viewed as tests of ability and correlate as highly with some intelligence test subscales as they do with each other. Despite this, a large number of studies of field dependence fail to control sufficiently for the effects of intelligence in their findings.

In this regard, it has frequently been argued that, although RFT and EFT significantly correlate with full-scale IQ scores, this correlation is "carried" primarily by the 3 WAIS subtests noted earlier (Block Designs, Object Assembly, and Picture Completion), which in factor-analytic studies have defined an "analytic" or "perceptual-organization" factor. The correlations between the field-dependence measures and other WAIS subtests, though usually also positive, tend to be smaller and have attained standard significance levels in some studies and not in others. This has led to the argument that field-independent individuals are not *generally* more intelligent, but rather better endowed in a particular component of intelligence (e.g., Witkin *et al.*, 1962).

For many purposes, such a factor-structure approach to intelligence is extremely useful. But despite the many advantages of the more differentiated picture of intellectual ability provided by factor scores, consideration of full-scale IQ as a variable in its own right is not without its place. However one conceives of the components which enter into the total IQ score, that score is an estimate of the *sum* of the intellectual resources available to an individual and provides at least a rough estimate of his total adaptive assets or overall coping skills. Although it is correct to point that field independence is not a measure of overall IQ, sufficient care has not been taken in most studies to empirically distinguish the *correlates* of field independence and those of overall IQ, nor has sufficient attention been paid to examining whether superiority in *other* specific aspects of intelligence might also yield similar relationships.

Many studies fail to control for intelligence at all. Others typically attempt to assure that field dependence, and not verbal intelligence, is the variable responsible for differences noted between groups by equating verbal intelligence in the field-dependent and field-independent group or by covarying it out. But equating groups for scores on the verbal subtests while distinguishing them on scores on the analytic subtests is *guaranteed* to yield groups differing in overall IQ. Thus, in such a situation, one cannot be certain that personality differences between "field-dependent" and "field-independent" groups are due specifically to their differing in analytic ability rather than to their having a greater total stockpile of intellectual resources. Perhaps any group having an overall greater range of adaptive skills (as the "field-independent" subjects in the typical study are selected to have) would show the same personality attributes.

Future studies might do well to check inferences about the specific consequences of analytic ability by also examining (1) groups equated on analytic IQ, but differing in verbal IQ and/or (2) groups which differ in analytic IQ (as in the typical study) but which are equated in *overall* IQ. Such a comparison would not confound the influence of analytic ability and overall ability as does the verbal IQ control. The suggested procedures would enable investigators to discern much more clearly what are correlates of field independence per se and what are correlates of the posssession of outstanding ability in general.

STYLE, ABILITY, AND DEVELOPMENT

Limits of Generality of Differentiation Construct

The above-noted methodological limitations create difficulty in evaluating the theoretical notions which have developed from the field-dependence research. The most elaborate and influential theoretical position currently guiding research in this area centers on the view that the many variables which show a relationship to the original field-dependence measures are all reflections of a single underlying process of development toward greater psychological differentiation (e.g., Witkin, 1969; Witkin *et al.*, 1962). According to this "differentiation hypothesis," performance on such commonly used laboratory tests of perceptual–cognitive performance as RFT or EFT may be viewed as reflecting the person's position on the overall differentiation dimension. Seen as part of this dimension of psychological development are, for example, the articulation of the body concept, the sense of separateness of self, knowledge of one's own needs and feelings, reliance on one's own experiences for definition of one's attitudes and judgments, and reliance upon "specialized" defenses such as isolation rather than denial and repression (Witkin, 1965).

Such a formulation has considerable heuristic power, and serves to introduce impressive coherence in a maze of diversity. But the large number of studies evidencing the test–construct confusion noted earlier create difficulties in assessing how much of the data of field-dependence research is properly regarded as the unfolding of a single developmental process. When a correlation is found, for example, between the EFT and some other variable, it may be tempting to assume that a further extension and elaboration of the differentiation construct has been obtained. Such a finding may, however, represent instead a relation completely external to the field-dependence or differentiation construct, and reflect instead some specific characteristic of the embedded-figures *test*. Few of the studies in this area are factor-analytic studies, in which such a question could more readily be examined, and those that are tend to deal almost exclusively with the more purely cognitive variables rather than those involving more general aspects of personality.

One may attempt to overcome these limitations and include the large number of single-test field-dependence studies by examining the *pattern* of findings that have been obtained, which does seem plausibly organized and simplified by the concept of differentiation, at least as a rough first approximation. Such post hoc conceptual analysis is an essential part of the scientific process, but one whose dangers should be clear. The notion that development proceeds from the global and undifferentiated to the structured and articulated is itself a rather global conception which is thereby not readily discomfirmable. For example, Witkin *et al.* (1962) discuss an unpublished study by De Varis in which field-dependent boys were more accurate than field-independents in identifying cut-out photographs of their own eyes, noses, mouths, etc., among a group of similar photographs of parts of other people. As Witkin *et al.* point out, such a finding seems at first contradictory to the idea that field-independent people have a more articulated concept of their own selves and bodies.

Witkin *et al.* then go on to present a very interesting and ingenious account of how these same findings may be viewed as consistent with the differentiation hypothesis: If field-dependent people are more concerned about how they look to others and conceive of people in terms of external characteristics, they might pay more attention to the appearance of their own faces as well as to others.

There is nothing wrong with the logic of this interpretation of the data. In fact, I find it a rather compelling and impressive piece of theoretical assimilation. But it is assimilation, and exactly opposite findings could also be readily assimilated.

The point is not that the De Varis finding is crucial to the differentiation hypothesis. Witkin *et al.* describe the study largely as a problem for further investigation and base their theoretical position on a vastly broader base of data. But such an instance of assimilating "superficially" contradictory data to the plus side of a theory points to the problems in the structure of inference in this area. Inferential hazards such as that illustrated by the De Varis finding above are evident throughout the research on psychological differentiation, even where the use of only one measure of field dependence is not an issue. Does looking more for others' reactions or watching their faces reflect a less developed sense of one's own identity? It could. But it could also represent the recognition on the part of a person who knows himself well that he lacks certain skills and had best check whether he is performing adequately when these skills are required. Does a more articulated figure drawing reflect a more complete and intimate knowledge of one's own body? It could. But it could also represent the possession of a particular ability regarding representation of form in space (cf. Sherman, 1967).

Thus, while the studies cited in a number of presentations of differentiation theory (e.g., Witkin, 1965, 1969; Witkin *et al.*, 1962; Witkin & Oltman, 1967) can readily be seen as consistent with the view that the correlations which have been observed reflect "diverse expressions of an underlying process of development toward greater psychological complexity" (Witkin, 1965), they do not compellingly require such a single-process interpretation. At the very least, it may be said that the explanatory limits of this view are unclear; deciding just which observations of self-consistent behavior are profitably viewed as reflections of psychological differentiation is a far from simple task.

Differentiation and Adaptive Strategy

A related difficulty with the differentiation hypothesis is that in its focus upon progress along a single dimension, and particularly a dimension postulated to characterize the degree of development of the psychological system as a whole (Witkin, 1969), it is in certain respects poorly suited for exploration of the very problem it was originally designed to deal with—that of style. It is difficult to organize ideas about different directions of development upon a framework which includes only one dimension, and only the possibility of "more" or "less." The concept of mobility versus fixity of functioning (Haronian & Sugerman, 1967; Witkin, 1965), which points to the question of why some people consistently operate at a highly differentiated level and others are more variable, was an effort to deal with this difficulty. So too was my own (Wachtel, 1968) focus upon the distinction between those who *can* function in a field-independent fashion and those who *must* function that way.

But fuller understanding of the meaning of performance on tests like the RFT or EFT, and of the correlates of such performance, requires a broader perspective on the interactive role of developmental advances along a variety of dimensions. Such a perspective, in which consideration of style and adaptive strategy becomes possible, may be built upon more explicit recognition of the RFT and EFT as ability tests.

Field Articulation: An Ipsative Perspective on Style[3]

Viewed as ability tests, the EFT and RFT do not directly reveal stylistic preferences or adaptive strategies, though such preferences may correlate with the possession of the ability, especially as ways of *adapting to its presence or absence*. Viewed developmentally, however, the possession of the ability may itself be the product of a series of choices which reflect or define the individual's adaptive strategy. Here it is useful to recall the earlier point that three subtests of the WAIS (Block Designs, Picture Completion, Object Assembly) may be regarded as alternative measures of field independence. We may then bring to bear the logic of WAIS scatter analysis to clarify the present position. Rapaport, Gill, and Schafer (1945) have described the assumptions of scatter analysis as follows: In the course of development, as the individual begins to emphasize particular adaptive strategies and particular defense preferences, he begins to invest in particular skills and perhaps to actively underplay others, as in the hysteric, for whom memory is impaired as a function of defensive needs. The particular pattern of peaks and valleys in the individual's

---

3. Broverman's (1960, 1962) efforts along somewhat related lines may be of interest to the reader.

skills, then, points to or defines the particular personality style he has developed.

Considering the three analytic subtests (Block Designs, Picture Completion, Object Assembly), it makes considerable difference in assessing the meaning of a particular mean score on these three subtests whether they are among the highest, among the lowest, or around the mean for that individual. Thus, an individual whose scaled scores on those subtests averaged 13 (scores range from 0 to 19, with a mean of 10) would likely appear as field-independent on the RFT and EFT. If this were a person whose other subtest scores clustered around 9 or 10, it would make sense to characterize this person as someone whose personality style places great importance on analytic skills. This would be a person who has invested in this particular kind of skill, and it seems likely his personality would reflect this emphasis.

On the other hand, consider an individual with the same mean of 13 on the analytic subtests, but whose other scores were all 17, 18, or 19. Such an individual, though "field-independent" in the sense of having more analytic skill than average, may be viewed as well as someone who has de-emphasized this particular skill—someone who, relative to his general level, actually shows a *deficit* in this area of functioning. The implications of his score on the RFT or EFT would likely be very different.

The above line of thought points to the difficulty in examining the implications of an individual's position on the dimension field dependence–field independence without consideration of other aspects of his cognitive and personality makeup. We may now see more clearly why efforts to find those situations in which it is best to be field-dependent have had limited success. Such efforts stem from the idea that field dependence represents a different direction of psychological development than field independence, or that tests like the RFT or EFT directly assess separate but equal adaptive orientations. From such a viewpoint one would indeed expect that field-dependent individuals must, in the modern idiom, have "their thing" too. But if it is recognized that the RFT and EFT are largely ability tests and that they assess personality orientation only *indirectly*, then the fact that there are far fewer studies indicating the superiority of field-dependents is understandable.

For only *some* subjects does poor performance on the EFT or RFT reflect a directional style. All that is directly shown by such measures alone is a deficiency in a particular aspect of cognitive functioning. Field dependence is designated by the *lack* of something, and assessed (almost by definition) in situations well suited to the adaptive capacities of *all but* field-dependent persons. If all we know about a person is what he *can't* do well, there is generally little basis for predicting what he can do, given the variety of possible alternative outlets for his talents. Certainly field-dependent people aren't simply inferior individuals, but studies which overestimate the value of RFT and like instruments, and attempt to characterize people on the basis of such measures alone, provide few clues to the positive attributes of these people. Useful understanding of diverse strategies for living requires that we stop thinking of them as "field-dependents" and fully recognize that ability or inability to articulate and disembed from a complex gestalt is but one aspect of an overall approach to dealing with the world.

At this point in the development of a theory of individual differences in style of adaptation, it is necessary to go beyond the description of consistencies and consider more carefully the nature of the consistencies observed. In particular, it is important to distinguish those consistencies which express the *limitations* of the individual's adaptive capacity and those which reflect *choices and strategies*. As we have seen above, the distinction between a capacity and a stylistic preference is not an absolute one; the pattern of an individual's currently fairly stable strengths and weaknesses may itself be the residue of earlier strategic choices. Nonetheless, it is clarifying to make the distinction, and somewhat confusing to see the consistency described sometimes as a *style* of life, *preferred* mode, or *direction* of psychological development and sometimes as a difference in how *capable* an individual is of functioning at a high level, how much *progress* he has made in some general aspect of psychological development, etc. The self-consistency which is assessed when EFT and RFT performance is related to other realms of psychological activity is, as we have seen, of both varieties. Future research must focus more sharply on the differing implications of these two types of consistency, in order to understand more fully the dialectic process by which strategies of adaptation and adaptive strengths and assets determine each other.

19

Cognitive Style and Style of Adaptation

The concepts of cognitive style and cognitive control have played a leading role in efforts to link psychoanalytic ideas to laboratory research. In the monograph which was a seminal influence in this area, Gardner, Holzman, Klein, Linton, and Spence (1959) note that "the essential question we have posed concerns the individual's style of adaptation—his mode of coming to terms with the world . . ." This concern with the adaptive significance of cognitive controls has been an implicit concern of most of the research which has been done, but explicit discussion of the role of cognitive controls in the person's adaptation to his life situation has been relatively uncommon. The present chapter addresses itself to this issue.

In any attempt to understand adaptation, the first stumbling block which is likely to be encountered is the question: adaptation to what? To any psychologist unsatisfied with the simplification of this question by stimulus–response theory, this is an exceedingly difficult question to answer. For if one takes seriously the idea that each individual, through his perceptual–cognitive activity, constructs and creates his phenomenal world, then the world to which he is adapting and his mode of adapting to that world are not two separate realms but part and parcel of the same set of processes. In response to the adaptive demands a person perceives, he develops a perceptual–cognitive strategy; and this strategy in turn leads to his encountering a new set of demands, created in part by the new view of the

Reprinted by permission from *Perceptual and Motor Skills*, 1972, 35, 779–785. Copyright © 1972 by *Perceptual and Motor Skills*.

I wish to express my gratitude to my colleagues at the Research Center for Mental Health, who helped to clarify these ideas in many discussions. This work was supported by a United States Public Health Service Grant (No. 5-P01-MH17545) from the National Institute of Mental Health.

world which his strategy has afforded him. The continual integration of these two realms of events is that flux which we designate as personality.

Fortunately for the investigator of personality (but sometimes much to the consternation of the therapist), by the time most of us have achieved adult status, the flux to which I have referred bears much closer resemblance to some kind of super molasses than to a rushing river. Thus we are able, despite the fact of continuing change, to speak of "personality structure." Here Rapaport's (1967) view of personality structures as "processes at a slow rate of change" is very useful.

From the above point of view, one may consider the current stable features of personality as a residue of a long process of interaction between individual and environment. For better or worse, most individuals eventually manage, by a combination of altering themselves, altering the world, and choosing their situations, to achieve a relatively stable equilibrium in their commerce with the world. Once this is achieved, barring new disturbances (such as a sudden influx of drive, the decline of a heavily relied-upon skill through ill health or aging, or some change in the world he encounters) it is possible to describe the individual in terms of consistent styles of thinking, seeing, behaving, etc. To be sure, the consistencies may be rather more situation-specific than is often assumed (e.g., Klein, Barr, & Wolitzky, 1967; Mischel, 1968), but consistency is nonetheless evident, and as I shall indicate later, the typical research strategy may be leading us to underestimate the extent of consistency which exists.

The vast research literature on cognitive style represents an effort to map out one aspect of this consistency—that in the realm of formal properties of thinking and perceiving. Two large questions may be seen as guiding the work in this area. First is the question of whether it is in fact *possible* to characterize individuals by such features as whether they scan the environment broadly or confine themselves to rather limited segments of stimulus information; whether they respond to a stimulus array globally or articulate discrete elements independently of the context in which they are embedded; whether they are alert to subtle changes in successive stimulus configurations or readily assimilate new information to old schemas; etc. Included in this line of questions is the effort to specify precisely the dimensions of cognitive functioning which most efficiently can describe the ways in which people differ. Studies along this line have relied heavily on correlational methods, especially factor analysis.

The second kind of question to which workers in cognitive style have addressed themselves involves consideration of the adaptive significance of an individual's mode of cognitive functioning. As indicated earlier, this question has, in principle, been an integral part of the intent of most studies in this area, including those seeking to clarify the dimensionality of individual differences in cognitive functioning. I will attempt to demonstrate, however, that much of the work on the structure of cognitive controls has been unclear, and at times even misleading, with regard to the adaptive implications of the individual differences assessed. To be sure, it is necessary to demonstrate that consistencies *exist* in order to be justified in studying their consequences. But it is necessary to study their existence in ways amenable to the next step.

The theory underlying the investigations of cognitive style has pointed to consideration of how individuals experience the world in terms of differing modes and strategies for organizing the vast influx of (internal and external) stimuli. This work is a child of the "new look" perceptual research, with its emphasis on the influence of personal needs upon perception. Like the original "new look" work, the cognitive-style approach views perception as an active process whose final product is determined by the (momentary and enduring) characteristics of the perceiver as well as by external stimulus conditions. But the cognitive-style approach goes beyond the early work in correcting for the early overemphasis on the *distorting* effects of need. The influence of drives is not solely autistic. Were it, the individual would be least in touch with reality just when he needed to be most. Rather, the effect of variations in drive state is mediated by cognitive structures which guarantee and effect contact with environmental cues, but contact of a sort most useful to the organism at the moment. For the theory underlying the cognitive-style approach (e.g., Gardner *et al.*, 1959; Klein, 1958) implies that individuality in perception is not necessarily "unrealistic." The implicit epistemology of this work assumes that all men are in touch with only a limited glimpse of reality, and that a variety of possible ways of seeing things are included within the "normal."

Thus, although this approach does set the task of considering adaptive failures as well as successes (and in fact largely derives from psychoanalytic theory, with its grounding in the study of neurosis), its forte lies in the effort to characterize equally viable alternative modes of adaptation. Its superiority to approaches considering only distortion or defense lies in the recognition that there is no one way to truth, no single best or healthy kind of personality from which all lower types deviate. Within any strategy of adaptation, success or failure is possible, and while defenses are grounded in and consistent with varying cognitive styles, the degree of defensiveness or of pathology is relatively independent of the particular direction of development one takes.

The promising theoretical approach outlined above, however, has not been reflected in much of the empirical work, due to an emphasis on measures which have clear better-or-worse implications and are more accurately characterized as tests of ability than of style. Consideration of the adaptive task set for the subject taking the rod-and-frame test (RFT), the embedded-figures test (EFT), the color-word test, the schematizing test, and several other measures prominent in research in this area indicates that in each case a particular mode of functioning is required of the subject, and what is assessed is how *able* he is to perform as requested. I have discussed in detail elsewhere (Wachtel, 1968, 1972) some of the implications of viewing the measures of the field-dependence dimension as primarily tests of ability. When viewed in this fashion, many of the cognitive-style tests may be seen to tap styles or preferences only indirectly; what they most directly provide is a picture of the degree to which an individual possesses the basic tools and attributes upon which particular styles and strategies must rest.

Thus, it would be difficult to anchor one's approach around a highly intellectualized, analytic, dissecting view of the world if one did not possess the basic ability to experience items discretely from the context in which they are embedded and to keep distinct and separate the succession of changing configurations of stimuli which impinge. Or, as Gardner and Holzman (1959) point out, the defense of repression, which is associated with the assimilation of new stimuli readily into the schema of forbidden drives, is more likely to occur and be relied upon in the context of leveling (i.e., a *general* tendency to assimilate new information to old schemas, even in "neutral" situations).

But knowing that a person is a leveler or a sharpener, field-dependent or field-independent, more or less interference-prone, etc., only tells us those strategies for which a person is best equipped. It does not tell us which strategy he will necessarily adopt, nor how he will balance his reliance upon the variety of skills he possesses. The confusion between possession of a particular cognitive ability and the proclivity to utilize it arises from the homogenization of adaptive intentions (Klein, 1958) which ability tests produce. When you are asked to perform in a particular way, as you are on RFT, EFT, color-word tasks, etc., the range of possible adaptive intentions is vastly reduced in comparison to the intentions in a complex interpersonal context.

Somewhat similar difficulties are evident even in research on those cognitive-control dimensions which do not have such clear better-or-worse implications. For example, in examining individual differences in extensiveness of scanning or in preference for broad versus narrow categorization, most studies have ascribed particular characteristics to an individual, and then attempt to investigate the "generality" of the particular characteristic across situations. But such a search for generality again ignores the subject's adaptive intention, though such intentions were a prime interest leading to the cognitive-control conception. The vitality of work in this area is seriously diminished by a research strategy of seeking the person's average approach in an average expectable environment (Hartmann, 1939/1958). To know the adaptive implications of a particular dimension of cognitive control, it is necessary to know when the person functions in a way *not* typical for him, how readily he can make such shifts when the situation calls for it, and precisely what the consequences of either persisting in or changing his typical mode of functioning might be in any situation he might face. Very few studies have considered such issues. Among the noteworthy exceptions are those of Berger and Israel (1970), Santostefano (1969), Silverman (1964), and Wild (1965).

I believe the above considerations highlight an important limitation upon determining something about a person's life-style via the traditional kinds of cognitive-control measures. By imposing specific adaptive requirements, and arousing a limited set of adaptive intentions, many of these measures effectively short-circuit a vitally important element of individuality. I am referring to the considerable degree to which people *choose* the adaptive requirements they will try to meet, exhibiting adaptive intentions congruent with the situations *they* have created and selected.

To be sure, in almost any imposed situation, including cognitive-control tests, there is room for some individuality in defining and meeting its requirements, and in some of these tests, like object sorting, there may even be a great deal of latitude for individual variation in ways of meeting the experimenter's requirement. But this is still a far cry from the range of choices and consequences we face when we encounter another human being (or choose *not* to encounter him). In everyday social intercourse, the number of different ways we may structure the situation is enormous, especially since our own perceptions and responses exert a continuing influence upon what the situation is that we are engaged in.

What distinguishes the world of everyday interpersonal events and the world of the psychology experiment is the far greater fluidity of the former. In the laboratory, events are to a great degree preprogrammed. Things *happen to* the subject, and what happens during his stay in the laboratory tends to be rather minimally in his control. Experiments do, of course, often provide a *contingent* environment, as for example in the case of operant conditioning. But such a situation, in which independent and dependent variables can so clearly be labeled, presents the subject with a range of options so reduced compared to those of normal social intercourse as to be qualitatively different.

Unfortunately, the conditions of the psychological experiment do approximate in many ways conditions which are all too common a feature of the modern world. From the concentration camp to the assembly line to, ironically, some classrooms and psychoanalytic couches, human beings do often face largely implacable situations in which the options are exceedingly narrow, sometimes only between grin-and-bear-it or die trying. For explicating the behavior of men in these to my mind extreme, yet frequent, situations, the traditional laboratory experiment may be of considerable utility. Many aspects of modern life do indeed make of us simply creatures of habit, reflexly responding to the stimuli or demands presented to us.

But things are not all that gray. In much of our interpersonal lives, the people we meet are not preprogrammed in quite the same way. They don't just happen to us; they respond to us, to who we are, and to how we behave. As is implicit in the criticisms of traditional characterology by behaviorists such as Mischel (1968), this response may be quite specific to variations in the social stimulus we present. And, of course, our behavior is conversely quite specific to the social stimuli we receive from others.

But it would be a serious mistake to conclude, on the basis of evidence that people's responses differ greatly in different stimulus situations, that notions of character or style are illusory. On the contrary, recognition of the importance of situational specificity may lead to more sophisticated descriptions of consistency. The consistency evident in the lives of most human beings is due not to an overriding static structure which operates as in a vacuum, without regard to changes in the situation; it is due rather to our considerable ability to recreate the *same situation* over and over again. Psychoanalytic concepts such as transference and repetition compulsion have developed out of recognition of this quality in our interpersonal lives. Further understanding of this phenomenon is provided by Horney, Sullivan, and others, who have emphasized that not only do we recreate old situations perceptually, by seeing things in terms of past experiences and expectations, but also by the provocative quality of the behavior which flows from these perceptions. For example, if we expect rebuff, we may act in a hostile or disdainful manner, and thereby elicit rejection from others. Our expectations are thereby "confirmed" and our likelihood of seeing others as rejecting increased still further, for due to our actions we have once again "really" met with rejection. Thus, although we are very largely responding to the current stimulus situation, and perhaps even could act differently if the situation were different, we do not allow it to be different. In the laboratory, where our personal force field does not as readily change and mold the stimulus situation we face, it is not surprising that consistency is less evident.

The outcome of the cognitive-style research which has been performed thus far has been viewed as consistent with an interpretation of personality functioning which de-emphasizes organizing structures and stresses stimulus determinants to an extreme (Mischel, 1968). This has in large part been due to an empirical strategy in cognitive-style research in which cognitive functioning is studied in situations where cognition is an end in itself, rather than part of a continuing sequence of adjusting to old situations by creating new ones. Only by examining such sequences and giving full consideration to the interpersonal aspect of consistency will the important theoretical efforts (e.g., Klein, 1958) underlying the cognitive-control work be fully realized. This theoretical perspective, with its stress on viewing motivation, cognition, and behavior as part of an integrated pattern, provides a framework for understanding personality structure and stimulus conditions as complementary and interactive, rather than competing, keys to human behavior.

20

A Structural and Transactional Approach to Cognition in Clinical Problems (with Robert N. Sollod)

The study of cognition by psychologists has been largely isolated from the study of either action or desire. In most of the dominant models and approaches in the area of cognition, man is viewed as a kind of information-processing machine that transforms and organizes perceptual input. In pursuing such models, contemporary cognitive psychologists have achieved a good deal of sophistication, and the efforts by an increasing number of psychotherapists to incorporate these new developments into their clinical approach are likely to prove quite productive. But in applying these models to clinical problems, it will be necessary to pay a good deal of attention to the continuous interplay between cognitive processes and other activities of the organism.

For a period in the late 1940s and 1950s, such a research program was widely pursued. The studies, which were frequently described under the rubric of the "new look" in perception and cognition, attempted to examine how cognitive functioning interacted with the individual's motivational states and enduring motivational dispositions. For more than a decade this kind of work was pursued by a great many researchers, including some of the most prominent names in psychology. Then, within a few years, this research largely dropped out of sight, and references to it today are rare.

The reasons for the decline and abandonment of the "new look" work are complex and fascinating. Some of the early work on "per-

Reprinted by permission from M. Mahoney (Ed.), *Psychotherapy Process: Current Issues and Future Directions*. New York: Plenum, 1980.

ceptual defense" (e.g., comparisons of perceptual thresholds for supposedly neutral and taboo words) was methodologically rather naive,
and criticisms tended to be both abundant and cogent. In response to
this early criticism, however, the work became increasingly sophisticated. In a certain sense, so too did the criticisms. But—unnoticed
apparently by either the critics or the defenders of this work—the
criticisms became increasingly irrelevant to the clinical concerns that
stimulated this line of inquiry in the first place. More and more
debate began to be concerned with fine points of definition in distinguishing between "perceptual" and "response" effects, while leaving
untarnished the clear demonstrations—still not successfully refuted—that motivational factors could influence people's *experiences*
(Wolitzky & Wachtel, 1973). Whether one called the processes "response processes" or "perceptual processes," it was clear that in
ambiguous situations—as so many of the important interpersonal
and affective matters of concern to the clinician are—people's motives and expectations influenced how they categorized and labeled
what they encountered, and hence how they proceeded to deal with
life events. As in clinical practice, so too in experimental research
there exists a sound foundation for inquiring further into the link
between motives and cognitive processes, but of late there has been
relatively little fruitful work along these lines.

   One of the prime reasons for the derailment of this line of
inquiry was the reliance on methods like the tachistoscope, which are
generally more suited to examining the fine points of perceptual
theory in the motive–perception relationship than to exploring the
issues of concern to the clinician.[1] In most tachistoscopic studies, acts
of perception, or the cognitive processes involved in evaluating a
stimulus, are treated as end points, rather than as part of a *sequence* of
events in which cognitive processes lead to actions by the person
(based on his appraisal of the situation), which in turn influence and
change the situation that is to be appraised (and further acted upon).
Such a continuous series of feedback-governed processes is characteristic of most of the problems dealt with by the clinician. Some
problems, such as certain simple phobias, do seem to involve appraisals of events that are essentially nonreactive to the patient's behavior
(e.g., the danger inherent in a small room or on a high floor of a
building). Such problems may perhaps be fairly well understood in
terms of a model which looks at the mediating processes per se. But
in most clinical problems, the faulty mediating processes are influ-

1. A notable exception is the work of Silverman (e.g., 1976), who has used tachistoscopic methods to explore matters of great clinical relevance and has reported some
rather extraordinary findings.

enced not only by motivational factors (as noted above), but also by feedback from the consequences of actions taken on the basis of the appraisal. For such problems the isolated study of cognitive processes can be not only incomplete, but at times misleading. One of us has discussed how lack of attention to such issues has limited the clinical relevance of research on cognitive style (Wachtel, 1972a, 1972b) and has led to misleading conclusions about a whole range of experimental studies on personality processes and psychopathology (Wachtel, 1973a, 1973b).

To a substantial degree, the overreliance on such methods as the tachistoscope by the "new look" researchers reflected their incorporation of the dominant trends in psychodynamic thought, which were largely intrapsychic in their emphasis. Like academic researchers on cognition, intrapsychically oriented psychodynamic thinkers tend to focus upon the internal mediating processes per se or on how they are activated by particular kinds of environmental input. They do not stress cyclical processes (Wachtel, 1977a), or what Bandura has called "reciprocal determinism" (Bandura, 1978).

As noted above, the broad psychodynamic assumptions of the "new look" work (e.g., regarding defensive processes that alter awareness) were validated to a much greater degree than is generally recognized. But the intrapsychic emphasis placed limits on the kinds of questions that were asked. Following the lead of clinical theorists such as Sullivan, Horney, and Erikson, it is possible to incorporate the clinical observations from which predominantly intrapsychic theories derive into a framework that is more interpersonal or transactional. Attending to the full implications of such a conceptual strategy suggests new models for research (Wachtel, 1977a) and for therapeutic intervention (Wachtel, 1977b). Of particular importance are the possibilities such a conceptual strategy offers for integrating psychodynamic and behavioral approaches to clinical problems.

Such an integration is further facilitated by the greatly increased interest in cognitive processes by behavior therapists in recent years. Though labeled as "cognitive," this trend seems to us to reflect more generally an interest in internal mediating processes, and thus potentially to open the way for behavior therapists to consider the full range of processes that have been of concern to psychodynamic theorists for many years. The initial impressively trim, spare lines of models derived from laboratory experimentation have had to be modified to accommodate the complexities encountered by behavior therapists in their increasingly diverse clinical practices. We do not expect cognitive-behavior therapists to "rediscover" psychoanalysis. Coming from a different tradition—both substantively and epistemologically—we expect that they will bring the particular strengths and perspectives of their origins to bear on their approach to clinical issues. They will see and add things that analysts—viewing things from a different vantage point—have long missed. But they are also likely, it seems to us, to find that their concerns about covert self-statements, constructs, and images dovetail to a substantial degree with the concerns of psychodynamic thinkers.

A number of prominent behaviorally oriented clinicians and researchers have already made important contributions to the analysis of complex mediating processes in personality and behavior change (e.g., Bandura, 1969; Goldfried & Davison, 1976; Lazarus, 1971; Mahoney, 1974; Meichenbaum, 1977; Mischel, 1973). . . . This chapter will have relatively little to say about this work directly. But the emphasis we will place on the importance of viewing cognition transactionally—on recognizing that cognitive structures are formed, maintained, and changed in relation to the individual's actions on the environment—does constitute in places an implicit critique of (or at least a friendly reminder regarding) aspects of the emerging tradition of cognitive-behavior therapy.

In general, we regard this work as highly promising, but we see a danger that in its "rediscovery" of cognition, some of the virtues of the *behavioral* perspective from which it began will be lost. Of particular concern is the necessity to retain the emphasis on *action* that has characterized the behavioral approach to clinical problems. We suspect, for example, that future research will reveal that far more of the success of Ellis's (1962) rational-emotive therapy—which has been so attractive to cognitively oriented behavior therapists—is due to its emphasis on structured real-life tasks and to the therapist's vigorous urging that the patient do things differently than to the rationalistic analysis of the patient's "irrational" ideas. We are heartened by the increasing interest of behavior therapists in their patients' internal processes, and agree strongly that the underlying assumptions and attributional tendencies that people bring to situations are crucial. But we regard a lot of the current work as holding a far too rationalistic model of how people make sense of their world and reach conclusions about what is going on and what they should do.

We suspect that cognitive-behavior therapy will go through an evolution similar to that which occurred in psychoanalysis: Freud, too, started with efforts to *persuade* his patients and to rely on insights of a rather cognitive sort. Increasingly, however, psychoanalytic work revealed the limitations of such an approach (while highlighting its value as a *part* of how change occurs). Saying the right words was not enough. Intellectual insight alone produced little change.

From the beginning, of course, Freud recognized to some extent that insight must be accompanied by affect, that it could not be effective if it was coldly rational. But it took many years of clinical work to develop fully the implications of this recognition and to find ways to prevent lifeless intellectualization from draining the process of its efficacy.[2] In a parallel way, contemporary practitioners of cognitive-behavior therapy and rational–emotive approaches are aware of the need for insights to be put into action in the person's daily life, but still seem to us to be at a point where they overvalue cognitive clarity per se, as Freud did. The truth shall make us free— but only if we not only *know* it, but also *feel* it and *act* upon it.

A TRANSACTIONAL PERSPECTIVE ON COGNITION AND PERSONALITY STRUCTURES

We have stressed thus far that cognitions must be understood in relation to other aspects of psychological functioning. Cognitive processes can appropriately be viewed as either cause or effect. Cognitions influence our emotional reactions, as Ellis (1962), Beck (1976), and others have pointed out, and cognitions are *influenced by* emotional processes, as indicated by psychoanalytic observations, "new look" perceptual research, research on hormonal influences on thought, etc. Cognitions play a major role in determining how we will behave, and our actions and their consequences feed back to influence our cognitions. Cognitions are influenced by environmental input, and they actively shape the environment we encounter, both by interpreting and giving meaning to it, and by leading to actions that select among alternative environments and alter environmental conditions that are encountered. Cognitive processes are neither epiphenomena (or mere "way stations") nor the absolute center of the causal nexus of behavior. They are an essential and integral part of a quite complex set of chains of causal events in which feedback loops and repeated cycles of events figure prominently (Wachtel, 1977a).

A generally similar perspective has recently been offered by Bandura (1978), though it is hardly the exclusive province of social learning theory. Among theorists beginning from a broadly psychoanalytic perspective, Shapiro (1965)[3] and Klein (1970) have been

2. And of course the task is still far from complete, and the critical distinction between "intellectual" and "emotional" insight still far from fully understood.

3. Shapiro (1970, 1975) has subsequently clarified ways in which his "holistic" approach *differs* from a psychodynamic approach, but his original starting point was clearly that of psychoanalytic ego psychology.

particularly concerned with cognitive processes, and with how the individual's way of organizing perceptual input and construing the events of his life both determine and are determined by his behavior and his experiences. Shapiro, for example, notes that the neurotic person

> seems to think in such a way and his attitudes and interests are such as to continue to sustain the neurotic process and to make the characteristic neurotic experiences inevitable. . . . [His] attitudes and interests will be of a sort that guarantees that the next neurotic act—which from an objective standpoint may sustain and continue the neurotic process—will appear as the only plausible next thing to do. (pp. 18-19)

> The neurotic person is no longer merely a victim of historical events . . . his way of thinking and his attitudes—his style, in other words—have also been formed by that history, are now integral parts of that neurotic functioning and move him to think, feel, and act in ways that are indispensable to it. (p. 21)

For Klein,

> the behavioral unit appropriate to the study of cognitive attitudes is the patterned sequence of behavioral events that eventuate in an experienced attainment. The child's creeping after a toy exemplifies such a complex yet integrated unit of responses; back actions from objects en route provoke new stimulations, inhibit some, facilitate others, and finally produce a terminal experienced attainment. (p. 213)

He notes that motor response

> does not necessarily *follow* perception. Neither is it necessarily the executor of perception, although it is an indispensable component of a more comprehensive adaptive effort. . . . In the Object Assembly test of the Wechsler-Bellevue test, trial-and-error movements may provide opportunities for *perceptual* restructuring; the subject may move a block and *then* see the crucial relation. . . . The role of perception and motor activity in reflecting the adjustive requirements of intention is lost when we rigidly adhere to the older model of stimulus, followed by perception, followed by motor response. (p. 212)

A potentially even more thoroughly cyclical or reciprocal view of the role of cognition in clinical problems can be derived from the interpersonal theory of Sullivan (1954), from Horney's (e.g., 1939, 1945) descriptions of vicious circles in neurosis, from White's (1959) concept of efficacy, and from a variety of related views. Wachtel (1977a, 1977b) has discussed how the cognitive and motivational structures that have been of interest to psychodynamic theorists and clinicians can be understood in a thoroughly transactional way as both the cause and the product of the person's way of living. On the basis of particular assumptions about the likely consequences of various ways of interacting with others, the individual engages in interpersonal transactions which are very likely to yield feedback that confirms the original assumptions and makes the whole process likely to occur again. Thus, the shy young man who tells himself that women are not likely to be interested in him, that he is not handsome enough, or dynamic enough, is likely to approach women in an awkward, hesitant manner that evokes responses that seem to confirm his view that he is not sufficiently appealing. Or the hostile, hard-driving man-on-the-make, who tells himself that everyone is out for himself and no one can be trusted with confidences, is likely to find that experience confirms this—without clearly realizing that it is his own behavior toward others that evokes such an antagonistic and competitive attitude on their part (or that the same people who, in his experience, do try always to top him and to take advantage of every weakness or even of simple openness on his part, are capable of acting quite differently with others who have established a different relationship with them and evoke a different set of responses).

Recognition of the role of such cyclical transactions has important clinical implications. It allows the clinician to recognize that the patient's erroneous assumptions about the world are not so erroneous for his particular idiosyncratic slice of life. In the patient's world, the things he (seemingly wrongly) anticipates often *do* in fact happen, at least to some degree. Efforts to help the patient examine and correct his assumptive world must take into account how its behavioral implications make it more accurate than it would otherwise seem. Such an analysis is still relevant and important but must be presented to the patient in a broader, transactional context. If you explain your therapeutic strategy in a way that makes clear to the patient that you do understand what kind of experiences he has been having, you are likely to elicit greater cooperation with the therapeutic work.

The above should not be taken to imply, however, that the patient's assumptions are necessarily "correct." *Some* distortion or error most often does play a role in maladaptive behavior patterns. Some clarification is introduced, we think, by applying the Piagetian notion of schema to interpersonal transactions. As Wachtel (1977b) has noted in applying this concept to phenomena labeled as transference by analysts, the notion of schema

> implies that not only do we assimilate new experiences to older, more familiar ways of viewing things (as is implicit in the concept

of transference), we also do eventually accommodate to what is actually going on.

Thus, as in transference phenomena, new people and new relationships tend to be approached in terms of their similarity to earlier ones; and frequently, particularly in the special conditions of the psychoanalytic situation, one sees what appear to be quite arbitrary assumptions and perceptions occurring. But in principle, I would suggest, accommodation is always proceeding apace and would, with non-reactive sources of stimulation, eventually lead to a fairly accurate picture of what one is encountering. The problem is that other people are *not* non-reactive. How they behave toward us is very much influenced by how we behave toward them, and hence by how we initially perceive them. Thus, our initial (in a sense distorted) picture of another person can end up being a fairly accurate predictor of how he or she will act toward us; because, based on our expectation that the person will be hostile, or accepting, or sexual, we are likely to act in such a way as to eventually draw such behavior from the person and thus have our (initially inaccurate) perception "confirmed." Our tendency to enter the next relationship with the same assumption and perceptual bias is then strengthened, and the whole process likely to be repeated again. (pp. 53–54)

THE CLINICAL RELEVANCE OF PIAGET'S MODEL OF COGNITION

The utility of a concept borrowed from Piaget for explicating and developing the point of view we have been stressing is far from a casual accident. Piaget's developmental and cognitive perspective has a good deal in common with the point of view we have been advocating. Piaget's approach is very centrally concerned with how the developing person's cognitive structures at once shape and are shaped by his actions on and in the world. The dual functions of assimilation and accommodation reflect this continuing interaction. Neither can occur alone. One always finds some molding of the person to the shape of the world he encounters, and some changing, selecting, and redefining of what is encountered to make it fit the available structures that the person brings to bear. Piaget's integrative theoretical orientation always views cognitive functioning within the context of the individual's biological development and maturation, the activity of the individual, his or her interaction with other people, and the qualities of the physical environment.

Only recently has the potential clinical relevance of Piaget's work begun to be tapped. No doubt the stylistic difficulty of Piaget for American readers, as well as the divergence between the underlying philosophical and methodological assumptions of structuralism and those of American psychology, have contributed to the limited use of Piaget's ideas by clinicians on this side of the Atlantic. Even in the areas of education and developmental psychology—where Piaget's work seems more directly applicable—American psychologists began to show a substantial interest only decades after the publication of Piaget's early works. In clinical areas, receptivity has been even slower in developing.

Piaget himself was strongly inclined, except very early in his career, *not* to study abnormal or pathological phenomena. In an autobiographical statement Piaget (1952) indicated that as a consequence of his mother's poor mental health he always detested any "departure from reality." At first, he says, "it was this disturbing factor which . . . made me intensely interested in questions of psychoanalysis and pathological psychology. Though this interest helped me to achieve independence . . . I have never since felt any desire to involve myself deeper in that particular direction, always much preferring the study of normalcy." Largely as a result of this attitude on Piaget's part, rather than on the basis of any theoretical necessity, the Geneva School has, with few exceptions, avoided clinical areas.

In attempting to spell out the implications of Piaget's work for understanding clinical problems, it should be noted that Piaget has had rather little to say concerning the relationship of cognition to emotion. In fact, Piaget recently wrote, "nor have I been interested in affective life (except to live it!)" (1975). Nonetheless, Piaget's framework has much of value to the clinician. It is important to recognize that, although Piaget is widely viewed in America as primarily a child psychologist, his interests have ranged far more broadly. Though he did devote much effort to mapping out and describing the stages of normal cognitive development, his was not just a descriptive theory. He was especially interested in the *process* of cognitive development, and thus in evolution and change. His work is firmly rooted in an understanding of biological adaptation, and thus is, in principle, quite applicable to maladaptation as well, and to its correction.

Piaget's approach shares with behavioral approaches an emphasis on understanding the individual's actual behavior in response to environmental stimulation. But he stresses far more the particular adaptive demand that is experienced in relation to the stimulation encountered, and the way in which the individual's present mode of understanding both defines and informs the response required to meet the challenge of external change. Piaget's approach presumes the presence of underlying cognitive structures, and he sees behavior and interaction with the environment as a function of these structures and also as leading to change and development in them. Like the behaviorists, Piaget sees learning as integrally related to the individual's actions in the world, rather than rising out of an internal mental process. But behavior and interaction with the environment lead to significant learning, in Piaget's view, only when there is already present a readiness of the individual, reflected in the existence of sufficiently developed cognitive structures and the ability to perform certain cognitive operations. The ability to master the concept of conservation, for example, occurs in children who—in other ways—show the potential for operational thought. The clearly preoperational child, when exposed to a conservation problem, is unable to answer it correctly. Even if taught the correct answer (as a discrete response) in training sessions, the child proves unable to generalize to different problems involving the same concept. Mastery of conservation involves the ability to consider more than one aspect of a situation. Development of conservation requires not only suitable experience and behavior, but also a certain pre-existing level of cognitive functioning.

Similar behaviors, in Piaget's view, have different significances for individuals with different cognitive levels. Piaget is thus very careful in his studies of cognitive development in children not only to observe whether an individual solves a given problem (the actual behavior), but also to inquire as to the underlying rationale for the solution. In the conservation example, the ability is considered fully attained when the child gives the correct answer and also indicates a suitably logical basis for the answer.

The more recent cognitive–behavioral approaches have much in common with the Piagetian approach in their emphasis on the importance of cognitions and the relation of such cognitions to behavior and adjustment. Compared to most current cognitive-behavioral theorists, however, Piaget places more stress on the overall cognitive level and organization or the total set of cognitive operations of which an individual is capable. Cognitive–behavioral theorists tend to emphasize *specific* cognitions or thoughts and the consequences of such cognitions for either the individual's behavior or emotional experience. They either do not emphasize or do not fully elaborate the concept of cognitive framework or structure in which the specific cognition is embedded. The therapeutic focus of Beck (1976) and Ellis (1962), for example, is on changing specific irrational thoughts; Meichenbaum (1977) has focused on specific statements of internal dialogue. Therapeutically, they aim at changing the specific irrational thoughts or on modifying statements of internal dialogue. Piaget's complementary emphasis is on the more general cognitive framework—the cognitive structure of an individual and the kinds of cognitive operations in which an individual can engage. The irrational thought "I must be perfect" or "Everything must happen exactly as I wish" may be changed without necessarily implying any enhancement of the more general ability to look at oneself from a variety of perspectives that would be emphasized in a clinical approach incorporating Piaget's concepts.

APPLICATIONS TO CLINICAL WORK WITH CHILDREN

Perhaps the most direct and obvious area of application of Piaget's work is in clinical work with children. In order to work effectively with children, it is necessary not only to empathize with their feelings but also to have some appreciation of the model of reality which they have constructed, and also some understanding of the kinds of cognitive operations they can perform. Children are not merely smaller versions of adults. The Piagetian tests of cognitive functioning are explicitly developed to indicate how the child actually goes about apprehending reality, rather than the particular facts or specific skills he has attained or the speed and persistence with which he functions. For example, the conservation tests assess whether or not a child comprehends the fact, say, that the weight or mass of a piece of clay remains the same regardless of how its shape may be modified, or that a quantity of water remains constant when poured from a cup to a flat dish.

A child who attains conservation has not merely learned a new piece of information, but is able to use his mind in a qualitatively different way from the preconservation child. In order to attain conservation, a person must be able to reflect on or have the ability to disengage from the immediate perceptual given. Without this ability, a person is absorbed in the immediate perception. The preconservation child, when asked to compare two equal quantities of water—one spread out in a flat dish and the other in a cup—after having watched the water in the flat dish being poured from an identical cup, may be so impressed by the vastness of the water in the flat dish that he will say that there is more water in the dish, or may be so struck that the water in the cup is "higher" that he thinks that the cup contains more water. The child who has attained conservation will be able to step back from the immediate perception of a single aspect of the situation (say, the perceived vastness of the water in the dish). He will be able to realize that the water there could be poured back into the cup from which it came, or that no water had been added or subtracted in the manipulation there. Such a child has a different way of making sense of reality and dealing with it than the preconservation child.

There is some evidence that the ability to conserve in children does have more general implications for overall functioning. Goldschmid (1968) has shown that children who achieved conservation earlier were more mature emotionally and more popular than others. In addition, he demonstrated that children rated as neurotic achieved conservation later than normal children. It has also been found (Dudek, 1972; Dudek & Dyer, 1972) that children who showed regression on Piaget's conservation tests—after having first attained conservation—were more concrete, cautious, careful, and unimaginative than other children, as evidenced by their Rorschach responses.

Piaget's fundamental understanding that children have a variety of levels of ordering their experience and ways of using their minds is a rich source of insight for the clinician. This perspective is often complementary to (or an elaboration of) perspectives already important in traditional clinical approaches, though at times it can point to rather novel considerations. Consider, for example, how Piaget's view can add to our understanding of the special difficulty children can have in dealing with parental conflict, separation, or divorce. Guilt and self-recrimination are common outcomes for such children. Their sense of responsibility for what has happened is often quite disproportionate to their actual role in the events. Traditionally, clinicians have frequently attempted to understand this phenomenon by focusing upon the child's *wishes* and his limited ability to distinguish between the consequences of wishes and those of actions. When there is a (largely coincidental) congruence between what the child wished and what actually occurred, the child feels responsible. Such a view includes both motivational and cognitive-developmental considerations. It is not only the particular content of the child's wish that is relevant, but his tendency to erroneously estimate the impact of his wishes on events. Piaget's concept of egocentrism, with its focus on the child's tendency to see *all* events as centrally concerned with him, and on his difficulty in understanding the point of view of others and their broader range of concerns, nicely complements the more traditional focus.

The Piagetian concept of egocentrism is applicable in understanding a fairly broad range of characteristics of child behavior and cognition. "Egocentrism," as Piaget uses the term, does not mean narcissism or selfishness and has no moralistic connotations, but is rather as Looft (1972) has stressed, "an embeddedness in one's own point of view." There are different levels of egocentrism. In the earliest stages of infancy, there is presumed to be a total lack of subject–object differentiation, which gradually yields to the formation of the object concept as something apart from the child's own ego. At a more advanced level of growth out of egocentrism, the child learns to distinguish between his own viewpoint and that of others. Laurendeau and Pinard (1970) have studied the development of growth out of egocentrism in the area of spatial perspectives. In the earliest stage, the child is unable to imagine a three-dimensional scene from any but his own point of view. Next, the child is able to indicate awareness that other points of view exist, but is not able to imagine accurately how the three-dimensional scene might appear to them. The higher stages of this ability involve greater degrees of accuracy in imagining exactly how the scene might appear from other viewpoints.

The ability to imagine with some accuracy what the viewpoint of another might be is based on the cognitive capacity to decenter—that is, to be able to step back from one aspect of what is perceptually given and to consider other aspects. As we have indicated, the same ability to step back from what is immediately given is required to pass a test of conservation.

Chandler (1976) has developed a test of egocentricity in which a child is shown a series of picture sequences and asked to make up stories to accompany them. The egocentric child is unable to imagine the existence of more than one viewpoint (of a child protagonist in the sequences) and cannot understand that the behavior of the child might seem inexplicable to another (who has a different perspective because he is not privy to all the child's experiences). For example, in one of Chandler's picture sequences, a child is shown as being sad after her snowman melts. She runs to a nearby street where she is drawn to the smells coming from a bakery. The friendly baker offers her gingerbread-men cookies which remind her of the melted snowman. She becomes sad again and suddenly runs out of the bakery; the baker is puzzled by her behavior.[4] The egocentric child assumes that the baker is aware that the child ran out of the bakery because of her experience with the snowman melting. Thus, such a child cannot account for the baker's puzzled expression. The child who has grown out of this degree of egocentrism is aware that the baker and the child have two separate viewpoints, and he thus is able to understand why the baker is puzzled that the child suddenly left the bakery.

The concept of egocentrism can be useful in understanding why a child is so often vulnerable to the role of "identified patient." The child's being chosen as identified patient serves a purpose in the

---

4. The sequence of events is represented only by pictures, and the child must explain what has happened.

family, as therapists operating from a family systems perspective have frequently pointed out; but in addition to the *family* dynamics, the child's accepting and playing into the role is made more likely by the general tendency toward egocentricity in his cognitive functioning. In such an egocentric stance, the child is unable objectively and accurately to assess the nature of family interactions and to sort out the relative role and weight of each family member in such interactions. As a result, he is likely to assign excessive responsibility to his own role in family conflict, to feel guilty and responsible for the family's behavior, and thus to accept readily the family's belief of his responsibility for their behavior.

For therapy with young children, egocentrism is a normal aspect of the child's functioning in the session. For example, preschool children often do not explain their thoughts and feelings because they assume that the therapist views the world the way they do. It is necessary for the therapist to probe quite thoroughly in order to elicit their thoughts and feelings. In addition, they are often very concerned that anything they tell the therapist will automatically be known by the parents. In one case, an egocentric but nonpsychotic 5-year-old boy expressed some negative thoughts about his parents and then immediately left the therapy room to see if his parents in the waiting room were angry over what he had said. It is thus difficult for young children, who are normally egocentric, to form open, trusting relationships with therapists; in addition, their explanations of both internal and external phenomena are almost exclusively self-referential.

The areas of play and social interaction with others are both clarified and emphasized by Piagetian concepts. In any therapeutic work with children, it is necessary for clinicians to have a clear sense of what is age-appropriate behavior. Parents often have unrealistic expectations for the functioning of children at different ages. The Piagetian cognitive-developmental approach provides a clear conceptual framework which can guide clinicians in their appreciation of the quality of play and interaction with others appropriate for children at different ages. There is, furthermore, an emphasis on the encouragement of social interaction to facilitate cognitive development. In Piaget's (1950) view, it is social interaction with others—especially in the early concrete operational period—that leads to a diminution of egocentrism. Flavell (1963) has indicated that the child, through interaction with others (particularly through conflicts and arguments), is forced to examine his own percepts and concepts from other viewpoints and thus gradually divests himself of cognitive egocentrism. This approach would support the clinician's working not only in a direct symptom-focused way with children who fail to show certain age-appropriate reciprocity or who show deficits in other aspects of social interaction, but also by a more indirect encouragement of social interaction generally. Selman, Newberger, and Jaquette (1977) have described a quasi-educational therapeutic program which specifically focused on the encouragement of structured social interaction as a means of changing the qualitative nature of cognitive functioning.

APPLICATIONS TO ADULT PSYCHOTHERAPY

The applications of Piagetian concepts to psychotherapy of adults rest on a number of considerations. If adults' cognitive functioning were both monolithic and uniformly complete, there might be little application of Piaget to adults. But in fact the complete attainment of formal operational thinking in adults has been found not to occur universally. Adults show a wide range of levels of cognitive functioning. A recent study by Kuhn, Langer, and Kohlberg (1977) indicated that 15% of normal adults gave no evidence of formal operations and 55% showed only partial or incomplete acquisition of formal operational thinking. Formal operational thought had been completely attained by only 30%. Thus, with regard to the development of those abilities specifically pinpointed by Piaget, there is a wide range of individual variation among adults, with many displaying significant deficits in functioning.

In addition, there is much evidence for wide variation of cognitive functioning within an individual. Even though Piaget used emotionally neutral tasks in his studies, he was aware that a person might perform differently on tasks of a similar type but involving different content. For example, a child may be able to attain conservation of weight but not conservation of number. Such intraindividual differences appear to be a function not only of the intrinsic difficulty of a task, but also of the person's history of experience with a given area, as well as the emotional significance of the task. As we have learned in recent years (e.g., Mischel, 1968), conceptions of personality that assume a monolithic consistency do not stand up very well in clinical or real-life situations removed from the experimental laboratory.

Even though a person may, in general, perform at a formal operational level, such a level of functioning cannot be assumed to be invariant across all situations. Weiner (1975) has reported several cases in which anxiety and conflict in particular areas led to regressions in cognitive functioning.

Childhood modes of construing, experiencing, and behaving are thus not entirely eradicated in adults. Adult thought and behavior arise from long experience in more childlike modes. Piaget has shown that such development is dependent not merely on biological maturation alone, but also on the nature of interaction with the environment. Lack of sufficient experience or experience of a limiting kind in a certain area may impede full cognitive development in that area. The concept of "horizontal decalage" refers to the fact that the level of cognitive functioning may be higher in one area of application than another. For example, a girl who has been taught that playing with mechanical devices is unfeminine may carry into adulthood rather oddly magical or global notions of the working of an automobile or of household devices; in this area she may have an incapacity to see the relationship of the workings of one part of a device to another, even though in other respects she is quite capable of such analytic thinking. Piaget's approach emphasizes that such a deficit is not simply one involving lack of knowledge about the working of machines, but involves the way the person construes reality and thus influences her perception of mechanical devices and the nature of her interaction with them, as well as her thinking about them. Similarly, a withdrawn or shy person, or one who has grown up in an environment with insufficient opportunity for interpersonal interaction, can be viewed not merely as having an impoverished repertoire of social behavior and little information about social reality, but also as having an inadequately developed construction of social reality, with many egocentric and childlike features present.

In addition to gaps from lack of experience in certain areas of cognitive-developmental growth, certain types of upbringing may actively prevent cognitive growth more generally. Lidz (1973) has pointed out, for example, that many types of disturbed families actively encourage egocentric thinking in the adolescent. In fact, egocentric thinking is a plausible way for the adolescent to explain the constant overreaction of the family to his most trivial behaviors. Such a person is likely to carry the same type of egocentric thinking to other situations. Lidz has pointed to this process particularly in the families of young schizophrenics and, like Feffer (1967), has considered many forms of schizophrenic symptomatology, including ideas of reference and certain delusional patterns, in terms of an underlying cognitive egocentricity.

In addition to the appreciation that all adults do not always function uniformly at the highest level of formal operational thinking, Piagetian concepts have further relevance to understanding what occurs in psychotherapeutic work with adults. Inasmuch as psychotherapy may be seen as a process of cognitive development, general Piagetian concepts such as egocentrism, schema, cognitive structure and the processes of assimilation and accommodation, as well as Piaget's ideas about the growth and transformation of structure through new interaction and experience, are applicable to understanding the psychotherapeutic process.

An interesting perspective is provided, for example, by viewing psychotherapy as a social interaction encouraging growth out of egocentrism. In a wide variety of therapies, the patient becomes aware of and gradually learns to imagine the viewpoint of the therapist regarding his behavior and experience. Regardless of the particular theoretical stance of the therapist, the very process of learning to consider one's behavior and experience from different viewpoints represents growth out of cognitive egocentrism, with implications, as Looft (1972) has pointed out, for more effective and wider-ranging social interaction. Watzlawick (1976) has developed the technique of reframing, which he defines as changing "the conceptual and/or emotional setting or viewpoint in relation to which a situation is experienced and to place it into another frame that fits the facts of the same concrete situation equally well or even better, and thereby changes its entire meaning." Even short of such explicitly emphasized techniques, the very process of a patient speaking to a therapist about his thoughts and feelings and listening to the therapist's theories, views, and interpretations concerning such thoughts and feelings encourages decentering. This is particularly true when those thoughts and feelings revealed during the therapeutic process have been kept out of discussions with others.

As noted earlier, the view of transference as the employment of schemas in which assimilation predominates is another example of the application of Piagetian concepts to psychotherapy. These concepts lead to an appreciation of why, from a purely cognitive point of view, change in psychotherapy may be difficult and slow. Kuhn (1962), informed by a Piagetian approach, has discussed scientific paradigms and indicated that they change only with great difficulty and only after much contrary evidence has accumulated. A given paradigm assimilates many facts or findings, and thus its proponents are reluctant to abandon it, even though it may not explain *all* the relevant data. It is precisely those facts which cannot be explained by a given scientific theory—but which can be incorporated into a new theoretical framework—which are most crucial for change in scientific paradigms. The shift from Newtonian to Einsteinian physics, for example, was marked by an emphasis on those few areas of physical phenomena—such as the motion of the planet Mercury—which were not adequately accounted for in the Newtonian framework. An analogy can be drawn between the historical development of scientific theory and individual progress in psychotherapy. The individual has certain schemas which assimilate many facts. One therapeutic task is to draw the patient's attention to facts which cannot so easily be assimilated into these extant schemas and, by so doing, encourage accommodation of extant cognitive structures to these facts. In this view, certain aspects of resistance to psychotherapeutic change can be seen as due to insufficient accommodation or too ready assimilation.

To return to a prior theme, it may also be noted that as the patient learns to attend to discrepancies between his view of the world and what actually goes on in his life, he may not only correct specific errors in his prior view but also develop a fuller awareness and appreciation of the nature of his actual organizing cognitions about others. This process may be considered as one of helping the patient to move away from cognitive egocentrism. Rather than being embedded in his view of others (regardless of its accuracy or adequacy), the patient can develop a growing awareness of the relativistic nature of that point of view.

PIAGETIAN PERSPECTIVES ON SCHIZOPHRENIA

One emerging area of application of Piaget's ideas is a reconceptualization of schizophrenic functioning (Blatt & Wild, 1976; Sollod, 1979). Strauss and Carpenter (1978) have recently concluded that the functioning of schizophrenics may be thought of not only in terms of pathological symptomatology, but also in terms of the quality of the patient's thinking as well as his or her social adjustment. This emphasis on the level of thought organization as well as symptomatology has origins in the work of Hughlings Jackson (1887), who referred to both the "negative mental element" and the "positive mental element" in insanity. He concluded, "we have to consider not only the absurdity but also the elaborateness of the mentation remaining possible" in the insane. Since that time, a number of investigators, including Vigotsky (1934) and Werner (1957), emphasized the salience of looking at cognitive and/or perceptual organization in schizophrenia in addition to symptoms of psychopathology. Piagetian approaches follow in this tradition of the application of cognitive-developmental considerations in understanding schizophrenia. They add to these more traditional approaches a more refined articulation of stages of development directly, and a comprehensive theory indicating the relation of functioning at various levels of cognitive functioning to areas of adaptation.

Piaget's elaborate and highly articulated model of cognitive development has recently begun to be operationalized with standardized empirical tests (Goldschmid & Bentler, 1968; Laurendeau & Pinard, 1963, 1970). These tests very generally indicate qualitative stages of cognitive functioning. Schizophrenic thinking has been explored using a variety of Piagetian tests—including a study by Piaget (1923) himself—and it has been established that there are differences between schizophrenics and normal adults, with the performance of schizophrenics being structurally similar to those of normal children (Trunnel, 1964, 1965). In addition to nosological differences, Kilburg and Siegel (1973) found that reactive schizophrenics performed better than process schizophrenics on tests of formal operational thinking.

Sollod (1976) reported that 21% of the chronic paranoid inpatients ($n = 28$) and 39% of other chronic schizophrenic inpatients tested ($n = 23$) did more poorly on tests on conservation than the average 7-year-old child as reported by Goldschmid and Bentler (1968). The poor functioning of schizophrenics on Piagetian tests did not appear in these studies to be primarily a function of low IQ. Trunnel (1964), for example, reported similar IQs in the normal and schizophrenic groups. Sollod (1976) found that Wechsler Adult Intelligence Scale (WAIS) vocabulary scores were much more highly correlated with years of formal education than were scores on concrete operational thinking.

In addition to the exploration of differences between diagnostic groups (Sollod and Lapidus, 1977), the determination of a level of cognitive functioning in schizophrenics appears to have some utility in predicting adaptive capacity of subjects both within and between diagnostic groupings. Sollod (1976) found that of a group of chronic hospitalized schizophrenics, patients who, regardless of assigned diagnosis, had achieved at least day-pass status were all successful on a series of tests of concrete operational thinking. Patients not on day pass were mixed with regard to concrete operations. Thus, success on these tests was found to be a necessary but not sufficient condition for day-pass status. Such a finding was consistent with Piaget's theoretical emphasis that the ability to solve conservation problems was not an isolated aspect of mental functioning, but reflected a qualitative level of mental organization with consequences for the nature of the person's functioning in daily life.

Functioning on Piagetian tasks was also found to predict particular aspects of symptomatology. For example, patients at the preoperational level were found to be largely free of significant delusional ideation, fear–worry, or anger–hostility as measured by the Structured Clinical Interview (Burdock & Hardesty, 1969). Suchotliff (1970) has reported that schizophrenic subjects with difficulty in decentering shared communication deficiencies both in comparison to normals and to schizophrenics without comparable deficiencies.

Such findings strongly suggest the salience of cognitive functioning in schizophrenics as measured by Piagetian tests, both as an outcome variable and as a criterion variable in a variety of studies. The use of level of cognitive functioning to categorize schizophrenics would reduce the high variance typical of this area of research. Investigations of cognitive functioning in schizophrenics make it clear that the conventional diagnostic groups, though different in their mean cognitive scores, each contain subjects at many different levels of cognitive functioning. In spite of similarities based on pattern of pathology or course of illness, such subjects—one, for example, functioning at a preoperational level and another at a formal operational level (equivalent in some respects to the difference between a normal 5-year-old and a normal 16-year-old)—would be expected to respond very differently to a variety of both clinical situations and experimental stimuli.

In exploring, for example, the question of the efficacy of psychotherapy for schizophrenics, the patient at the formal operational level might be expected to respond differently to a variety of therapeutic modalities than a patient functioning at the concrete operational level. Putting both of these patients in the same group in a study should lead to a great deal of response variability to a specified therapeutic modality. The patient able to function at the formal operational level is able to reflect on his or her own thinking, and thus should be more amenable to an insight-oriented approach than an patient unable to engage in such thought.

Such cognitive differences should be salient not only in response to psychotherapy, but in treatment and discharge planning within the hospital. Consider, for example, two patients who are being prepared for a community-care home. Although both have about the same degree and type of manifest psychopathology, it is found that one is markedly egocentric, unable to understand or imagine the possible impact of his behavior on others or to be responsive to more subtle interpersonal cues; the other is sociocentric, able rather accurately to imagine a variety of viewpoints other than his own and to be aware of the impact of his behavior on others. The former patient, even though trained or programmed for a community home, is lacking in the ability to adjust sensitively to the requirements of others. It is possible that an impasse in regard to his adjustment to others might arise; for example, he might engage in a routine unpleasant to the other occupants of the home and appear rather intransigent to their expressed displeasure. A worthwhile predischarge endeavor in such a case would be not only to see to what extent the patient could be "programmed" to engage in appropriate daily behavior, but to encourage him to engage in sociocentric thinking. Should such efforts be without success, a greater emphasis on rule following would appear in order, as well as working with the staff of the home to be extremely direct and emphatic in necessary communications with the patient. Such an approach would not be required in the case of the more sociocentric patient, who could function quite well on the level of normal social interaction.

APPLICATIONS TO THE AGED

Considerations of the level of effective cognitive functioning appear to be relevant as well to psychogerontology. Deficits in both formal and concrete operational thinking in the aged have been found in many studies (Papalia, 1972; Papalia & Bielby, 1974). Ajurieguerra and Richard (1966) found that the loss of cognitive abilities occurs in reverse of the order of acquisition in normal development. The differing levels of effective functioning in the aging seem to be salient (in much the same way as previously discussed for schizophrenics) as a predictor variable both for daily adjustment—in particular, the quality of social interaction—and for experimental studies of cognition. D. Jackson (1974), for example, studied cognitive functioning in elderly subjects from private nursing home facilities on a battery of Piagetian tasks. He found that the subjects who were successful at conservation had more social interaction and were institutionalized for shorter periods than the nonconservers.

One area of possible application for the elderly is in the area of person–environment fit and the choice of appropriate residences or nursing homes. A person with a high degree of sociocentric thinking, or, more generally, with the ability to engage in decentered thought, is able to engage in diverse and complex social interactions such as games, conversations, and the like, the significance of which will be lost on the more regressed elderly patient.

Although there certainly are important motivational and interpersonal factors that contribute to the difficulties the elderly have in functioning, a sensitive understanding of their predicament requires as well an accurate assessment of their cognitive abilities and limitations. Piagetian tests and concepts are likely to enhance our understanding of the cognitive capacity of elderly patients.

Saccuzzo (1977) has discussed similarities between the functioning of the aged and schizophrenics, and has suggested that the common feature of cognitive regression could well explain these findings. It has not yet been determined how much of this regression in the elderly is due to a biologically programmed deterioration and how much to the nature of the physical and social environment in which they are found. It seems likely that both of these interact in a vicious circle. The initial reduction in activity and lapses of cognitive functioning due to aging lead slowly and inexorably to an environment increasingly lacking in the kind of stimulation that is required for the maintenance of effective cognitive functioning and the motivational support to implement it. Particularly in hospitals and nursing homes—but frequently even when living alone or with their families—the elderly are often given few responsibilities and little opportunity for challenge, stimulating social interaction, or the exercise of their mental capacities. The monotonous conditions under which many elderly people live can at times approximate the conditions of a sensory-deprivation experiment, in which the efficacy of cognitive functioning is sharply reduced.

Thus there is present in the elderly a combination of biological deficit or deterioration, withdrawal from social interaction, and reduced interaction with the physical environment. These factors are the reverse of the biological maturation, social interaction, and active exploration of the world that Piaget has described in normal cognitive development. A view of cognitive regression in the elderly most consistent with Piaget's approach would emphasize the interaction of these factors rather than assigning a unique causal importance to any one alone.

DISPROPORTIONATE DISABILITY

Another area in which cognitive functioning has recently been connected with a clinically significant phenomenon is "disproportionate disability," a syndrome in which there is catastrophic disability as a result of minimal residual physical impairment from a work-related injury. This phenomenon has long been observed by clinical workers. Ellenberger (1970) reports that Freud studied a number of cases of railroad workers who suffered a catastrophic reaction to injury termed "railway spine." Freud did not address the quality of cognitive functioning in considering these cases.

The adaptive significance of the quality of cognitive functioning was highlighted in a recent study of disproportionate disability by Shands and Meltzer (1975). A group of subjects were chosen who, in spite of the most minimal physiological impairment, evidenced severe psychological reaction characterized in many cases by extreme disorganization, withdrawal, and isolation. In one typical case, a saleswoman who fractured her leg in a fall and developed some residual swelling and stiffness in her leg became depressed and suicidal, gained 15 pounds, and was subject to weeping spells and anxiety attacks. She was preoccupied with her condition, repetitively expressed the wish that the accident had never occurred, and checked and rechecked her leg to see if it had completely returned to normal. She felt that she had become a "different person" since the accident.

When compared with a matched group of psychiatric patients, the disproportionate-disability patients showed marked difficulty on the Verbal Similarities subtest of the WAIS. Although their overall measured IQ was similar to the psychiatric controls, they demonstrated an inability to engage in abstract thinking. The explanation provided by Shands and Meltzer is that those patients' self-concept reflects their inability to disengage from the most concrete aspects of reality. Swelling of a leg, loss of a digit, or the development of a noticeable scar would represent irremediable damage to their self-concept. The concept "I am a person with a damaged leg or finger" becomes for them the equivalent of "I am a damaged person." Whereas from a psychoanalytic perspective their reaction might be viewed as displacement of castration anxiety, for Shands and Meltzer the patients' concrete and global thinking is seen as most salient.

Although the findings of this study are far from conclusive, they suggest that level of cognitive ability may be an important indicator of adaptive capacity for a wide range of stresses involving threats to bodily integrity. Such threats might include injury, reconstructive or cosmetic surgery, rapid weight change, or serious illness. In addition, the quality of cognitive functioning may prove to be a predictor of ability to adjust effectively to a variety of stresses other than physical impairment.

IMPLICATIONS FOR PSYCHOLOGICAL ASSESSMENT

Assessment of intellectual functioning is another area in which Piagetian concepts and approaches have clinical relevance (Phillips, 1975). In place of a quantitative score, Piaget's tests indicate a qualitative level of functioning (Pinard & Laurendeau, 1964). Items in standard intelligence tests are chosen to differentiate between children at specified ages, with the score expected of a given age determined empirically. In Piagetian testing, the items are chosen to reflect certain types of cognitive processes, with the age of attainment determined after the construction of the test. The conventional test is designed to score whether an answer is right or wrong, whereas the Piagetian tests explore the reasoning behind both right and wrong answers. Among the merits of a Piagetian approach to intelligence testing is a somewhat greater generality of application, as the stages are not as closely linked to the content of traditional schooling as are the Wechsler and Stanford–Binet. In spite of reported intercultural similarities at the concrete operational level (Voyat & Silk, 1970), there do appear to be substantial differences between cultures with regard to these tests, particularly at the formal operational level (Dasen, 1973).

Using Piagetian approaches to assessment, it might be determined that a culturally deprived, lower-class child, with an IQ score in the retarded range, was merely demonstrating a measured lack of certain specific skills and abilities associated with a middle-class environment or classroom learning. Such a child might, however, evidence operational thought, even though he scored lower on the Wechsler Intelligence Scale for Children (WISC) than a highly motivated and well-socialized middle-class child who was preoperational. The Piagetian tests, more clearly than the WISC, would point to environmental and motivational explanations for the poor performance of the ghetto child in more conventional tests and might rule out a diagnosis of retardation suggested by the results of the WISC.

Christ (1977, 1978) has described his work with both psychotic and brain-damaged children and adolescents and indicated that assessment of the level of effective cognitive functioning—rather than IQ alone—is necessary to determine the most effective therapeutic intervention. Emotionally disturbed adolescents with near-normal IQ scores may have a preoperational level of cognitive functioning. In the brain-damaged population, Christ has noted that two 15-year-olds with about the same IQ may function at different cognitive levels. According to Christ, insight-oriented psychotherapy can be used with brain-damaged youngsters who have attained concrete and formal operational thinking, but children who function at the sensory–motor and preoperational level require supportive and instructional approaches.

Sollod (1977) has explored the integration of Piagetian tests with a standard psychological battery in adult schizophrenic patients. He suggested that Piagetian tests usefully complement the more structured intelligence tests, as well as the projectives. In the case of the WAIS, the Piagetian concept of level of cognitive organization provides a framework within which the intelligence test results can be understood. The comparison of results on projectives with those of Piagetian tests indicates the relation of emotions, feelings, and fantasy in a variety of thematic areas to the more abiding cognitive-structural aspects of personality. An adult patient at a low cognitive-developmental level, on the basis of structural considerations alone, should be expected to demonstrate many areas of regressed and primitive thought in projective tests; in a patient with a higher cognitive-developmental level, equivalently regressed projective responses would have a primarily dynamic rather than a structural significance.

CONCLUDING COMMENTS

We have emphasized the importance of understanding cognitive functioning in context—as part of a continuing interplay between cognition, overt behavior, and environmental input and feedback. In exploring the implications of such a perspective for clinical research and practice, we have noted some important convergences (though also differences) between the work of cognitive-behavior therapists, particular versions of psychodynamic theory, and the psychological theories of Piaget. Piaget's work has not been heavily relied upon by clinicians thus far, but we have tried to indicate some important potential areas of applicability. Even as the importance of internal mediating processes has been increasingly stressed by clinicians who previously played down such processes, the importance of the individual's actions in the world has continued to be stressed by a wide range of clinicians and theorists. Piaget's theories provide a particularly well-developed perspective on how to integrate internal cognitive structure, overt action, and interaction. Indeed, in Piaget's terms, it is impossible to even speak of one without the other. We have emphasized some of the transactional implications of Piaget's work, in which cognitive structures are viewed as the result of a continuing series of transactions between extant structures and the events that are encountered by them (and, to a substantial degree, brought about by them). In our view, further progress in developing a cognitive perspective for clinical psychology depends greatly on the degree to which it is understood that cognitive structures are developed and modified by real-world actions that are in turn constrained and guided by extant structures; on the integration of affective and motivational considerations into such a perspective; on an understanding of the wide range of levels of cognitive organization that underlies people's attitudes and belief systems; and on the development and selection of intervention methods that are suited to the particular way in which the individual goes about making sense of the world.

Finally, a note of caution: We have emphasized Piaget's approach in this chapter more than some other perspectives because we feel that it has been particularly underutilized and that little effort has been made to integrate it with other perspectives on clinical phenomena. But it is essential that the reader not take this as a starting point for treating Piaget's approach as a new "answer" or "system." Even in this chapter we stress other perspectives as well, and in our work generally the potential contribution of Piaget's concepts is just beginning to be explored. We do think that concepts such as cognitive structure, egocentrism, equilibrium, accommodation, and assimilation have significant potential for clinical thinking; but that potential will be quickly eroded if one's gaze is fixed too exclusively on Piaget, without the "decentering" that will permit a more useful and balanced understanding of his contribution.

THE SOCIAL CONTEXT

Introduction to Part Five

Our understanding of the psychological experiences of individuals cannot be divorced from an understanding of the larger social order that constitutes the setting for those experiences. Matters of class, race, and ethnicity, as well as the overall status of the economy and the prevailing tenor of social relations, play a major role in shaping our psychological lives. Widely shared assumptions and values contribute far more significantly to the psychological functioning of individuals than one would gather from most of the major theories that have guided our understanding of personality, mental illness, and psychotherapy.

The chapters in this section explore how the values and assumptions of society at large influence the tenets of our psychological theories; they also consider how in turn those theories can help shed light on some of the dilemmas we face as a society. These chapters complement the more extended application of psychology to social problems in my 1983 book, *The Poverty of Affluence: A Psychological Portrait of the American Way of Life*. Over the years I have written a number of other pieces that have looked at how a psychological perspective can shed light on social questions, or at how our psychological theories reflect or are shaped by widely shared values in our society. Some of these pieces, however, were concerned with social conditions that have continued to evolve since they were written and therefore require new ways of addressing them; others reflect a perspective that now feels tied to a particular period in our recent cultural development and therefore seem at least somewhat dated. Those that I have selected for this volume seem to me still to be relevant to the issues we presently face as a society and as individuals living in a cultural milieu one of whose most significant characteristics is that it discourages the very act of noticing that milieu.

Solution of our social problems is impeded by two key characteristics of the implicit psychology that guides social thought and decision making in our society: an overemphasis on individualism, and an
underestimation of the role of conflict. To the second of these errors,
psychoanalysis is a needed corrective; to the first it is a prime contributor. Psychoanalysis illuminates for us how pervasive is conflict
in our psychological life and how invisibly, yet powerfully, it works
its way through our thoughts and feelings. But, in many of its forms,
it also points us to think about people in highly individualistic ways
that do not accord a sufficient role to the significance of context or to
the ways in which we mutually determine each other's experience.
Its overemphasis on autonomy as both a desirable and an achievable
goal parallels features of the society at large.

The chapters in this section address issues of individualism and
of conflict in a number of ways. Chapter 21 first appeared in *The New
Republic* as a "reconsideration" of Karen Horney's work on the 40th
anniversary of the publication of *New Ways in Psychoanalysis*. Much of
it is devoted to addressing the sentimentality that weakens Horney's
work and that, though not really intrinsic to her theoretical position,
has made it easy for opponents to dismiss her work and ignore the
radical implications for psychoanalysis that it conveys. The chapter
shows that the *substance* of Horney's theory, as opposed to her rhetoric, is far from the sugary pablum some have suggested; in fact, her
account addresses the human potential for cruelty and self-deception
in a tough-minded fashion. Horney, however, looks for an explanation in the ironic circles in which we become trapped—and then
continue to trap ourselves—rather than in our genes or the events of
earliest childhood.

The chapter traces the competing implications of Freud's and
Horney's approaches through a variety of instantiations, from the
meek but secretly rageful neurotic of the consulting room, to the
fictional but psychologically resonant complaints of Alexander Portnoy, to the problematic formulations of the psychohistorians. In
arguing for the continuing importance of the neo-Freudian movement in psychoanalysis, the chapter asks why the work of Horney
and related theorists has not attracted the quality of followers that
continue to rally to the Freudian banner. The answer, I suggest, has
much to do with individualism:

> The most interesting and distinctive of [the neo-Freudians'] ideas
> were ultimately dissolved . . . in a watered-down Freudianism, in
> which conceptions of an autonomous self, developing according to
> its own inner laws, replaced the more contextual descriptions of
> the earlier years. More accurately, they succumbed not so much to

Freudianism per se as to the pervasive individualism of modern
Western culture, which both they *and* Freud shared. (pp. 426–427)

The chapter was written during the Carter years, when the
memory of Richard Nixon's assaults on decency remained quite
vivid, and his name seemed a particularly potent symbol of the
socially corrosive effects of an individualism that serves to rational-
ize a lack of compassion for those in need. Unfortunately, we have
now achieved a new stage in America—selfishness with a smiling
face. Now, in response to Ronald Reagan's stage-managed geniality
and carefully rehearsed whisper of sincerity, I find myself almost
longing for Nixon's jowls and prodigiously obvious hollowness and
cynicism. It is a measure of how far backward our society has proceeded in a few short years that the mention of Nixon's name in this
chapter could evoke in me something approaching nostalgia.

Chapter 22 develops further the social implications of the individualism that lies at the heart of most theories of personality and of
psychotherapy. The chapter was originally an invited presentation at
an International Conference on the Psychotherapies in Bogota, Colombia, and it provided an opportunity to consider some of the issues
in an international context and to get feedback on the ideas from
thinkers who represented a range of cultural experiences.

The chapter addresses a number of ways in which our psychological theories unwittingly adopt modes of thought deriving from
the ideological imperatives of an industrial and market-oriented society. The centrality of the imagery of "growth" in discussions of
personality and psychotherapy reflects this influence, as does the
emphasis on autonomy, on motivation arising from deep within the
psychological interior, and on the need to separate from one's family
in order to achieve psychological maturity.

In its original form, the chapter was presented orally from notes
and simultaneously translated into Spanish for the primarily Span-
ish-speaking audience in Bogota. I would like to thank Lynn Simek-
Downing for her effort to render the transcript of my oral presentation into a form suitable for publication. Ultimately, I relied heavily
on the version published in Spanish by the press of the Universidad
de los Andes and prepared from the Spanish transcript by Augusto
Perez Gomez. Laura Benkov ably translated that version back into
English, and it became the working draft from which the present
version was derived.

Chapter 23 appeared originally in *The Nation* under the title "The
Politics of Narcissism." Its central concern was to provide a corrective to the misleading arguments of Christopher Lasch, which have
had such currency in recent thinking on social problems from a

psychological perspective. Lasch, it seemed to me, had wrapped a moralistic argument in deceptive psychoanalytic clothing and had attacked as "narcissistic" trends that I regarded as potentially progressive. It has become fashionable in recent years to argue that America has become excessively preoccupied with psychology, that we have produced a "psychological society," a "culture of narcissism," a "me generation." There is a certain measure of truth to these criticisms. An excessively narrow definition of psychological well-being and an interpretation of psychological imperatives that overemphasizes autonomy and the seeking of individual gratification are tendencies to which we have at times been prone.

But behind and beneath this surface psychologizing lies a great lack. Our culture is in fact *deficient* in concern for the psychological dimension of life and overly concerned with the economic. This has led us in directions that yield continuing dissatisfaction and a way of life whose consequences for the environment are potentially disastrous. As discussed in more detail in *The Poverty of Affluence*, we have misunderstood the nature of our needs and have attempted to use economic growth to solve problems that are better approached psychologically. The problems we face are not the result of an overemphasis on psychology or on the development of the self; they derive rather from a reliance on a particular *kind* of psychology—one that echoes the very values and assumptions that it should be psychology's role to help us look at critically. Our society's "narcissism"—to the extent that this confusing and much-abused term has any clear reference at all—stems not from an overemphasis on self, but from a failure to understand how much the needs of the self are intertwined with the person's immediate and larger social milieu. As the alert reader will readily note, this constant interplay between self and context is the red thread that runs through this entire volume.

21

Karen Horney's Ironic Vision

Forty years ago, Karen Horney published a probing re-examination of some of the basic precepts of Freudian psychoanalysis. The issues she addressed, both in *New Ways in Psychoanalysis* and in her other major works, were not matters for the psychoanalyst alone. Her questioning of some of the key Freudian assumptions had relevance as well to a rather broad range of issues in American cultural life—both because an unexamined Freudianism is implicit in much of our general intellectual discourse, and because Freud himself reflected some of the dominant assumptions in the Western tradition, assumptions which in her own way Horney challenged.

Now this may seem like a heavy burden to place on the work of a thinker and therapist who has tended to be seen as an interesting, but nonetheless minor, figure. And, to be sure, there is a good deal in Horney's writings that does seem rather naive and simpleminded. The most unfortunate consequence of this feature of her work is not so much the limitations her simplifications introduce—though they are significant—but the way in which they enabled her to be categorized and dismissed, so that her more important ideas were not taken quite as seriously as they should have been.

Perhaps the most glaring of the difficulties with her approach was her tendency to lace her work with a syrup of gratuitous optimism—gratuitous both in the sense that it had no firm basis in observation or argument and in the sense that it was not called for by the logic of the rest of her work.

Horney's use of such terms as "self-realization" or the "inherent urge to grow" was consonant with the trends among the other "neo-Freudian" writers of the time, and seems best understood as a reac-

Reprinted by permission from *The New Republic*, January 6, 1979, pp. 25–28.

tion to the equally groundless pessimism in much of Freud's writings. The problem with such terms is not that they are wrong—on what grounds could one ever decide that?—but that they are vacuous. Precisely *because* they cannot really be assessed, they amount to little more than sentimental slogans, useful perhaps for motivating patients, but debilitating to serious intellectual inquiry.

But Horney's vision, if examined in its entirety, is not really so sunny. Horney does not deny that men have been venal, destructive, or callous. She differs from Freud not in her view of what men are capable of doing, but in her view of what the ultimate source of their behavior is. She rejects the simple conclusion that men have acted destructively because such behavior is the expression of something intrinsic and necessary, which must have its due one way or another. She chooses instead to search for an understanding of the conditions under which such impulses will arise. Although at times she makes rather simple environmentalist claims, her analysis suggests that those conditions are not wholly external but are in substantial part the result of our own actions, or, put differently, a consequence of our *character*.

Thus in Horney's view we are not doomed by fate. Neither neurosis nor destructiveness is our inevitable destiny. But, as I shall try to explicate below, the choices we make are likely to be the wrong ones, and in pursuing their unfortunate consequences we are likely to affirm these bad choices even more strenuously as necessary and correct.

To understand why this should be the case, it is useful to begin with Horney's view of what are the strongest driving forces in human life. The actions and tendencies that Freud saw as peremptory by virtue of a biological imperative, Horney saw as an imperative of *anxiety*. "The observation underlying the conviction that certain drives are instinctual or elemental," says Horney, "is their seemingly irresistible strength, their enforcing themselves on the individual and driving him willy-nilly toward certain goals" (1939). But, she contends, it is not the search for satisfaction that makes these urges so compulsive, but the search for safety, for relief from the feeling of being alone and helpless in an arbitrary, hostile world.

If one pursues the question of just what the nature of the danger actually is, one discovers how much irony pervades Horney's view. For the anticipated dangers which we strive so hard to avoid are largely of our own making, and largely a result of precisely those defensive efforts which we think are necessary for our security. Were we not so rigidly engaged in striving for safety, our sense of safety would be much greater, and the need for the defensive efforts much less. We are stretched upon a wheel of our own making, a psychic perpetual-motion machine which revolves cycle after cycle. We groan but faithfully keep it going.

Take, for example, the kind of person who in the Freudian view might be said to exhibit strong reaction formations against rage and destructive urges. Such a person's overt behavior appears excessively nice, or meek, or cooperative, or self-debasing; yet his dreams, slips of the tongue, and inadvertent actions all suggest that behind his adherence (or overadherence) to social forms lie impulses that are decidely *anti*social. Traditionally, the rage is seen as deeper and earlier, deriving from instinctual sources and from the distant past. Horney would have us look elsewhere for its source; the way this person lives his life, she points out, is almost guaranteed to *continuously* generate rage, even as it continues to require that he find the rage unacceptable. For over and over again this kind of person creates circumstances in which his own desires are overridden, his own interests sacrificed, his efforts at self-expansion and even clear self-definition checked and pinched—and this not out of a meaningful expression of loving feelings but out of blind fear of offending, provoking, threatening, or losing those on whom he depends. Thus, the impulses he defends against—whatever their original source— are at this point the ironic product of the very defenses against them. Impulse leads to defense; defense leads to further stirring of impulse; and the person's life is an endless closed circle. Horney points in similar fashion to a variety of other ways of seeking security that tend ultimately to leave the person feeling less secure. The examination of how these self-protective efforts undermine themselves is at the heart of Horney's approach.

Reinhold Niebuhr has suggested that an ironic situation "is distinguished from a pathetic one by the fact that a person involved in it bears some responsibility for it. It is distinguished from a tragic one by the fact that the responsibility is not due to a conscious choice but to an unconscious weakness." The irony in Horney's view of the human dilemma is further compounded by her insistence that the weakness too is not intrinsic but is itself a function of unconscious choices.

Horney, like Freud, traces the origin of neurotic conflict back to early childhood. But for her, the critical feature of the early years is the child's helplessness and dependency on others, as well as his inability to comprehend what makes his parents so loving and available some times and irritable or withdrawn at others—so that the world often seems, even for the child with the best upbringing, frightening and capricious. This insecurity promotes patterns of defensive behavior which will restrict the growth of the personality and interfere with the more realistic efforts to achieve security that are also developing.

Freud, of course, also regarded early helplessness, dependency, and cognitive immaturity as critical factors in determining our fate, though he stressed more frequently the strength of instinctual urges which he felt must inevitably clash with the socializing, civilizing influence of parents. But his view of the way the experiences of early childhood color our adult lives differed from Horney's in a way that has important implications for understanding our responsibility for our lives and for any consideration of improving our condition, either as individuals or as a society.

For Freud, certain aspects of early development are crucial and determinative because, as a result of their being repressed, they are rendered impervious to modification by later experience. Only the ego is responsive to external reality; that which is id is unchanging, making the same blind demands upon us in spite of whatever real constraints we might perceive or consider. Repression, in Freud's view, creates a fateful psychic disunity, a splitting between ego and id that prevents any psychic process in the latter category from partaking of the organizing, synthesizing, reality-testing activities of the former. Thus, that which is repressed early in life is preserved in its original form, like a woolly mammoth frozen in the Arctic ice, the only difference being that the primeval denizens of the psyche continue to trumpet loudly and trample upon the prerogatives of the rational ego.

Horney's perspective, on the other hand, suggests that if we look closely we can see that in fact we remain childlike not *in spite of* what is going on today but precisely *because of* how we are presently leading our lives. The past is not something preserved and anachronistically imposing its influence upon the present; it is the starting point for a process that continues to generate consequences today.

The implications of this alternative view of how unconscious conflicts persist are illustrated in interesting fashion by considering Philip Roth's Alexander Portnoy. Portnoy is the quintessential post-Freudian man. Like so many contemporary intellectuals, he is trapped in a Freudian world view. His conviction that the familial past is determinative has reduced him to a highly articulate form of impotent whining. However much we may empathize with his plight, we cannot, so long as we accept his grounding assumptions, help him find a solution. What he fails to see, immersed as he is in a particular outlook, is how the early experiences he points to have led him to establish a way of life that—at this point—accounts for his dilemma far more substantively than does anything that happened in the past. It is in taking steps to change his current way of living that a resolution of his dilemma lies.

Freud cannot, of course, be held responsible for all the ways in which his ideas have been used (nor, certainly, did Roth intend to imply that Portnoy's complaint would leave Freud with no response). But the particular abuse of the Freudian perspective that Portnoy offers us to justify—and immobilize—himself is both widespread in our culture and not without some foundation in Freud's actual (admittedly far more complex) views. It illustrates well why a close second look at what Horney has had to say could be useful.

So too does the state of affairs in the field that has come to be known as psychohistory. Despite the valuable model provided by Erik Erikson (whose approach is, I would contend, closer to Horney's than to Freud's in many respects), the trend in psychohistorical writing has been reductionist and often verging on self-caricature. The fault, I think, lies not in the concept of psychohistory per se, (as some critics have argued,) but in the theoretical perspective that has informed most of this work.

The model that has been adapted by the psychohistorians has tended to be the "woolly mammoth" model, in which early experiences are viewed as lodged unchanging in the psyche, and causation is almost exclusively from inside out, with external reality serving only to trigger the reactions which are lying in wait. One gets little sense in most psychohistorical writing of the continuing and reciprocal influences described by Horney and by other neo-Freudian writers such as Harry Stack Sullivan.

Much psychohistory is all psyche. The history is merely the playing out of a drama whose climax was already written when the future historical figure was only 4 years old. Indeed, one sometimes gets the impression that Hitler's, or Nixon's, or Carter's, or whoever's *mothers* were the real historical figures, with the famous offspring merely an incidental link in the causal chain. Now this of course is *poor* Freudianism—but it is also common and rooted in certain features which really are part of the Freudian approach. The perspective of Horney and the other neo-Freudians lends itself far more readily to an assessment of the responsibility the historical figure under study has for the maintenance of the patterns which characterize his or her life. Moreover, it points us to the particular actions chosen by the historical figure: the particular associates selected as advisers and confidantes, the particular kinds of relationships established with those advisers and the particular side of the advisers that the historical figure brings out—how these choices and actions are essential if the pattern established in childhood is to be maintained. And it therefore also enables us to examine both how the earlier pattern *has* been changed by new circumstances, and how it genuinely might have been, had different historical circumstances been encountered (on both a personal and a national or international level). Rather than describing historic personalities as in lockstep with an old marching song, this approach points us to where personality and history really meet, and gives each its due.

Karen Horney was not blessed with the brilliant followers who helped keep the Freudian tradition vital even after Freud's death. Though I think that her revisions represented the most useful direction for psychoanalytic theorizing to take and that contemporary Freudianism continues to reflect some of the same difficulties Horney highlighted 40 years ago, the orthodox Freudian tradition continues to attract the best minds in psychoanalysis. Apart from her contributions to feminist theory—the one area where Horney's work has received the attention it deserves—her ideas are not now at the center of intellectual discourse.

To some extent the lack of first-rate followers may have been due to the interpersonal difficulties that also caused her to sever her relations with other like-minded theorists shortly after her split with the Freudian establishment. In addition, she undermined the impact of her own ideas by retreating in her later years from her emphasis on social and interpersonal factors to a renewed emphasis on intrapsychic considerations. This turn in her theorizing was partly spurred by her increasing interest in the role played in neurosis and human suffering by false idealized images of the self, and she made some important contributions in this regard. But the overall effect of this change in emphasis was a debilitating one. As applied to theory, it led to the substanceless emphasis on "self-realization" discussed earlier. At the level of therapeutic practice, her reliance on spontaneous growth once the blinders of self-deception were removed prevented her from developing the more active and directive approach which her keenest insights seemed to suggest. There became little to distinguish her approach from the Freudian one here. Elsewhere I have spelled out in some detail why I think that the most important insights of Horney and the other neo-Freudians suggested that every neurosis required "accomplices"—in the sense that feedback from others is crucial to the maintenance of any recurrent pattern of behavior—and why this suggested a far more active and varied role for the therapist than the purely analytic one for which Horney opted. In a sense it can be said that the brilliant followers of Horney and other neo-Freudians do exist—in the ranks of the family therapy movement, where far more intellectual vitality and creativity can be found than among the official followers of Horney or the other neo-Freudians.

The decline of the neo-Freudians as an explicit intellectual force was further related to a larger, extremely significant issue. The most interesting and distinctive of their ideas were ultimately dissolved—either in their own work or that of their followers—in a watered-down Freudianism, in which conceptions of an autonomous self, developing according to its own inner laws, replaced the more contextual descriptions of the earlier years. More accurately, they succumbed not so much to Freudianism per se as to the pervasive individualism of modern Western culture, which both they *and* Freud shared. In psychotherapy, as in the society at large, this individualism has both positive and negative features. It is valuable in that it leads to a respect for the patient's values and a hesitancy for the therapist to impose his own (and, on a social level, to such concerns as the protection of civil liberties). But it can also lead to an excessive emphasis on each person's responsibility for his own fate, which makes the therapist hesitant to extend explicit help and which, on a social level, leads to the help-is-crippling rationalizations of the Nixon welfare ethic and the destructive view that we should all go it alone, without feeling responsible for each other.

The reconciliation of these two features of individualism—the question of how to guarantee freedom while fostering cooperation and mutual assistance, of how to avoid the twin dangers of Sovietism and Nixonism—is perhaps the most crucial task facing us today. In confronting this dilemma, an examination of the work of Karen Horney—both of her still untapped insights and of her failures—has much to offer us.

22

Psychotherapy and the Social System

The potential range of questions that could be addressed by a contribution on the social impact of psychotherapy is enormous, and I can address only a portion here. My focus in this discussion is not on the practice of psychotherapy per se, nor on the question of the social impact of that practice in itself. At a conference held in a developing country, where a large segment of the population does not share the attitudes or the social and economic position of the patients for whom the major therapeutic systems were first devised, there are numerous questions that need to be addressed concerning the appropriate psychotherapy for the poor and uneducated. There are many in my own country also who do not have the privileges one might expect in an "advanced" country, and I intend to follow closely the presentations of those who have worked in the so-called "Third World."

In this presentation, however, I am mainly concerned not with practice per se, but with the values and assumptions that seem to be implicit in the majority of psychotherapeutic systems. I want to have us look at the assumptions, habits of thought, and conceptions of human nature that lie behind the dominant approaches to psychotherapy.

As many commentators have noted, the evolution of the Western world during the last few centuries has been marked by a decline in the dominion of religion. The influence of such secular institutions as science and medicine has correspondingly expanded to fill the vacuum. In more recent years, psychotherapy and the theories that underlie it have played an increasing role in people's efforts to

A version of this chapter was presented, under the title of "The Social Significance of the Psychotherapies," at the First International Conference on the Psychotherapies, Bogota, Colombia, February 1983.

find meaning in their lives and to reconcile their conflicting desires with their ideas of what is right and proper. In the United States, and increasingly in other parts of the world as well, psychotherapists function almost as a species of secular priesthood. The ideas that we therapists offer about the human condition have an impact that goes well beyond the effect on our individual patients. They contribute to molding how people in our society view themselves and how they conceive of human possibilities, desirable aims, and the appropriateness of various kinds of conduct. It is for this reason that I believe it so important to understand better what are the values and assumptions embodied in the dominant psychotherapeutic systems.

Discussions of matters related to psychotherapy tend to be couched in language that has a scientific and objective tone. Whether the dominant terms be the forces and energies of the Freudians or the stimuli and responses of the behaviorists, the typical language of psychotherapeutic discourse tends to obscure the role of values and of fundamental philosophical predilections. If we are to understand more fully the impact of our theories and practices on society, we must pierce this language of objectivity and seek the unspoken assumptions that lie behind it.

I wish here to focus particularly on a cluster of ideas and assumptions that underlies much of our thinking about psychotherapy and mental health. To begin with, I want to call attention to our use of the word "growth" in psychological discourse—our tendency to speak of the growth of the personality or of people growing through psychotherapy.

If we look closely, the word "growth" used to describe the psychological development of a human being appears to be a peculiar phrase, although we are all in the habit of using it. Consider the physical growth of a human being, or of any creature for that matter. Certainly growth is very important during a period of our lives. We all begin life very small and for a substantial portion of our lives we keep getting bigger and bigger; that is, we grow. But for an even longer period we do not grow; we maintain the same size and the same form. The adult's body maintains a dynamic equilibrium in which new cells are continually being produced, but in which they do not add to the size of the body but simply replace other cells that have died. Indeed, despite its providing us with the root metaphor for equating growth with development, the body also provides us with a cautionary image regarding an overemphasis on growth as a goal: When it is exclusively growth that continues to characterize some aspect of our bodily functioning, rather than dynamic equilibrium, what we have is cancer—our most feared disease.

Could it be that our use of the growth metaphor in psychological discourse derives at least in part from the strong emphasis on the idea of growth in our economic system? In what follows, I want to consider how the nature of the society in which modern psychotherapy developed may have influenced the nature of our therapeutic systems. Such a consideration of the shaping influence of the economic basis of society was, of course, central to the thinking of Marx. But one can see a similar strand of analysis in the writings of Erik Erikson, especially in his analyses of how various aspects of the child-rearing practices, values, and dominant modes of personality of different American Indian tribes could be understood as closely related to the way they earned their daily bread (or salmon, or bison).

In pursuing the task of relating aspects of our thinking about psychotherapy to our economic system and its ideological underpinnings, I wish to focus initially on the psychoanalytic tradition. In part I begin here simply because I find it easiest to; this is the tradition in which I was first trained and whose habits of thought probably still form the deepest layer of my professional psyche. But I also direct my attention to this tradition first because it has almost certainly been the most influential viewpoint guiding social criticism (as well as the therapeutic point of view that is most frequently the *object* of such criticism). Moreover, notions deriving from psychoanalysis can be seen to underlie even many of the trends in psychotherapy that arose *in opposition to* psychoanalysis. For example, most of the various "humanistic" therapies, from the pioneering work of Carl Rogers to the vast proliferation of humanist approaches in the 1960s and 1970s, are characterized by some of the same underlying assumptions and habits of thought that are addressed in my consideration of psychoanalysis. Even where my argument focuses most explicitly on psychoanalysis, it can be seen as quite relevant to these other therapies as well.

Although Freud's work has justly been described as presenting considerable challenges to the status quo of his society, there are also important (and not always noticed) ways in which his thinking served to maintain the status quo more effectively. Many commentators have noted that Freud's thinking was strongly influenced by the dominant scientific models of his day—by the science of forces and energies built very largely around the structure of classical mechanics. Less frequently explored has been the influence of the social and economic ideas that were current then. Perhaps this is because it is easier to gain some distance from the world view of 19th-century physics. Physics has changed enormously in this century. Contemporary physics, while not flatly contradicting the physics of Freud's student years, certainly provides us with a rather different set of dominant metaphors.

To be sure, economic and social thought have advanced over the years as well, but, as with all the social sciences, their progress has been slower. Some of the social ideas that dominated in the years when Freud's theories were taking shape are still in large measure influential today. Indeed, they permeate our own milieu to a sufficient degree that it may be difficult even to recognize them as specific assumptions, rather than just "what is." This makes it very hard to recognize their specific shaping influence on our psychological theories, because they have had a shaping influence on all of us as well.

I would like to focus particularly on the individualistic nature of Freud's conceptualizations about human behavior and on their relation to the fundamental premises of our social and economic system. If one looks closely at our newspapers or, say, at a presidential news conference, one appreciates the centrality in our society of an image of people as discrete entities who search for their own profit and gratification. Society, from this viewpoint, is a pale shadow located behind these individuals; it provides the *arena* for their individual efforts, but has little role in determining what those efforts will be.

The fundamental assumptions underlying a market economy such as ours correspond to a significant premise of many of today's dominant therapeutic systems. The latter, in conformity with the former, assume that the sources of human motivation and human choices are best understood as deriving from deep within ourselves rather than as significantly shaped by social forces. Within the economic sphere, these assumptions have derived from an essential premise (a false one, in my opinion) that the constantly multiplying wants that characterize people's lives in advanced industrial societies are not artifacts of the values and economic arrangements of our particular system—of advertising, the need to "create" jobs in order to prevent unemployment, etc.—but a simple expression of human nature.

This set of assumptions has yielded us a constellation of grave problems, both social and ecological. Over the decades, our material standard of living has increased rather continuously, but our personal satisfaction with what we have has not shown a corresponding rise. Indeed, through the 1970s, when per capita income in the United States was rising rather steadily (*after* correcting for taxes and inflation), there was a widespread perception of economic decline; people were feeling they could barely make ends meet who in fact had considerably more than their parents had at the same age or than was typical when John Kenneth Galbraith could describe us, to general assent, as "the affluent society" (Galbraith, 1958; Wachtel, 1983a).

The assumptions by which we are living have led to increasing discontent even as the economy grows, and to a correponding increase in selfishness and social regression. They have led us as well to stress continuing expansion of our industrial output in a futile effort to keep up with the desires our way of life generates. The toll on our life-sustaining environment of such ceaseless striving after more has been enormous. Three Mile Island, Love Canal, PCBs, acid rain, and dioxin have all become unwanted additions to our vocabulary. Yet, trapped in our present way of seeing things, we experience no alternative to relentless striving after economic growth except severe deprivation.

One might hope that psychotherapists, whose work involves studying the illusions that contribute to needless misery and investigating the genuine sources of satisfaction in people's lives, would, at least in a small way, be contributing to combating those aspects of our modern world view that lead us away from real satisfaction and into a labyrinth of self-deceptions and false solutions that only make things worse. Yet, in significant ways, the theories that guide most therapeutic systems actually tend to reinforce the modes of thought that are at the heart of our social and ecological dilemmas.

To be sure, we should not overestimate our capacity to affect large social events in our role as psychotherapists. Those who hold economic and political power clearly shape our society far more than we do. But we are not completely without influence. As noted above, our theories have partially filled the vacuum left by the decline of traditional religious beliefs. Our ideas do have an impact; for better or worse, they seep into the sea of general social assumptions and give it a particular coloration.

But, far more than we usually realize, the nature of the influence we wield serves to maintain rather than to combat the social patterns in which we are trapped. The proliferation of desires that characterizes our way of life gains legitimacy to the degree that we view our desires as spontaneous upwellings of human nature and minimize their also being products of our social system. Theories that stress internal determinants of behavior lead us to play down the role of social influences—whether they be the attitudes, expectations, or manifest behavior and way of life of friends or neighbors, or the impact of advertising, the job market, or the nature of housing and transportation. These influences play an enormous role in what we think we want for ourselves, but they find little place in most of the theories that guide the work of psychotherapists.

The individualistic biases inherent in most approaches to psychotherapy are evident in many ways. In stressing autonomy, for example, as a possible and desirable goal for human beings, our theories contribute to the illusion that our desires and attitudes can be *sui generis*. Ours is a society that overemphasizes independence as a characteristic of the successful and well-functioning individual. This not only leads us to be unsympathetic to those in need, but also contributes to our dominant tendency to prefer individual ownership to sharing. The stress on the unattached single-family house as the ideal, with the concomitant necessity (and desire) for each of us to have our own washer, dryer, etc., is part of a larger set of attitudes that contributes to our ecological crisis, requiring more and more to be produced. Our stress on independence also provides very unfertile ground for an understanding of the *inter*dependence that lies at the heart of an ecological point of view.

Psychotherapists are, of course, not responsible for the entire configuration of attitudes in our society; moreover, an interpretation of independence and autonomy that is fundamentally opposed to interdependence is at least in part a distortion of what is intended by most of the psychological theories that rely on those concepts. Nonetheless, it can at a minimum be noted that the stress on autonomy and on looking inward for the sources of our behavior does little to counter the prevailing trend and is likely to contribute in some ways to strengthening it, even if there are complex technical interpretations of the concept that do not strictly conform.

The same may be said regarding the emphasis on differentiation and separation–individuation that is also at the heart of much current therapeutic thinking. Ours is a society in which, to a degree that once would have been virtually unimaginable, people are expected to move away from their families of origin and usually even from the communities in which they were raised. There is a strong confluence between these tendencies and the tendency to outgrow our possessions and require new ones constantly (see Wachtel, 1983a, for a fuller discussion of these connections). And clearly there is a strong link between the latter tendency and the present strain on our environment. There has been increasing recognition among critically oriented therapists of the predisposition toward blaming of parents inherent in the major therapeutic approaches and of the bias toward separation from family as a sign of mental health. Once again, there are more complex and sophisticated versions of the point of view under discussion here—versions that attempt to incorporate both the need for separation and the need for connection and reconciliation. But if one looks not at the fine print but at the overall vector, one can see again how the views we promulgate are quite consonant with the major trends of the society at large.

It could, of course, be argued that the connotations and potential implications of our theories must take a back seat to their validity: If our theories are correct, then it is shortsighted to censor them because some of what they suggest is socially inconvenient; we will ultimately achieve a sounder basis for social justice and harmony with nature if our efforts are based on a correct assessment of human nature than if we try to pretend we are something other than what we are.

In response, several lines of argument are relevant. To begin with, we may note the rather tentative state of our knowledge at this point. Although psychological theories are often presented by their proponents with considerable force and conviction, almost all of our theories remain highly speculative. Much more evidence is required before we can even begin to argue that any particular theoretical position must be regarded as "the harsh truth," like it or not.

Indeed, an increasingly influential group of critical observers (see, e.g., Habermas, 1971) has argued that it is in principle impossible to attain a view of human nature that is independent of the blinders and particular interests that place limits on any theorist simply by virtue of his being a member of a particular society and class and of his living in a particular historical era. According to this view, any psychological theory will reflect not just some objective reality, but also very considerably the particular vantage point of the observer. An appreciation of how the theorist's psychological conceptions serve to bolster or challenge the dominant social order is thus seen not as some external judgment brought to bear on a theory arrived at simply with the truth in mind, but rather something intrinsic to understanding what the theory—any theory—is really about.

We may also note, in a different vein, that in fact an alternative to the highly individualistic theories of Freud and the various "humanistic" approaches exists, and that this alternative is capable of accounting for the same set of observations within a framework whose social implications are considerably different. I am referring to the theories generally described as "neo-Freudian," which were quite influential some decades ago but have declined in influence in recent years.[1] The theories of Horney, Sullivan, and Fromm, supplemented by those of Erikson (who is not usually grouped with the other three, but shares a number of important characteristics), provide the basis for a view of human behavior and experience that is considerably better able to provide a challenge to prevailing attitudes

1. As discussed elsewhere (Wachtel, 1979b, 1982c), the reasons for this decline lie less in failings of the theoretical approach per se than in a failure by its proponents to take it seriously enough and carry through on its most significant features.

and habits than is orthodox Freudianism or the currently influential object-relations theories.[2]

There are features of some of these "neo-Freudian" theories that I find problematic; however, in building upon them, one can construct a theory that takes full account of the value and uniqueness of the individual and the individual's subjective experience, but that does so in a way that fully integrates the individual's responsiveness to the world around him. Such an orientation does not conceive of an internal world split off from the events of the person's daily life, but rather presents the world of subjective experience and the world of environmental events as in continuous reciprocal interaction: Our subjective experience and behavioral inclinations are shaped by what happens in our daily lives, but the environmental events to which we respond are themselves in large measure determined by our own behavior and the behavior it elicits in others.

This type of theory presents an opportunity to employ psychodynamic insights in the service of a critique of the individualistic thinking that characterizes both classical psychoanalysis and the neoclassical economics that presently delimits our society's view of what is possible or desirable. The blather about "freedom to choose" (Friedman & Friedman, 1980) that currently passes for respectable social thought is leading us rapidly toward ecological disaster. As the late British economist Fred Hirsch (1976) noted in his perceptive analysis of the fallacies regarding economic growth, our efforts to solve our social problems individualistically are comparable to the efforts of a person who is standing in a crowd to see better by standing on his toes: Since he is thinking just of what he can do alone, such a course of action seems to make perfect sense. He will indeed see better on his toes than not. But of course he is not likely to be the only one to think of standing on his toes. Others too will attempt this individualistic solution, either in an effort to gain some improvement in their situation or, after not too long, defensively in response to the people in front of them having done so. The net result of all this will be that no one has a better view than before, but everyone is more tired from the effort of standing on his toes (and unable to stop doing so because of the positive *dis*advantage it would now entail in the face of everyone else's doing so).

2. There have been vigorous challenges to the point of view I am putting forth here, and several claims that in fact the neo-Freudians are shallow conformists and it is *Freud's* theory that is truly radical and challenging of the status quo (see, e.g., Jacoby, 1975; Lasch, 1977; Marcuse, 1955). In part, my response to these claims can be found in a number of my publications [including several chapters of the present book], but a full-scale analysis of the differing social implications of the Freudian and neo-Freudian positions is a project I hope to be able to launch before too long.

Much of what we face today fits well with Hirsch's paradigm. In an atmosphere in which we are encouraged to "look out for Number One," we all end up exhausted but ungratified. The varied and generally unrecognized ramifications of this social pattern are beautifully elaborated in Hirsch's book (see Wachtel, 1983a, for still other illustrations of our self-deceptions in this regard, and for a psychological perspective on this state of affairs that complements Hirsch's economic perspective). Particularly in an era in which the ecological consequences of our multiple individual choices are so enormous, it is urgent for us to find a way to achieve collective solutions to our problems that are not subject to the ironies of the individualistic course. Yet it is equally essential to avoid the converse danger of the loss of freedom that has characterized those countries whose regimes have elevated collectivism to a monolithic principle and in which individual experiences and desires are given short shrift. Here is precisely where a psychological perspective that is attentive to the subjective needs of the individual, yet alert to the nature of our profound interdependency, can prove useful. Such a psychology would not be an alternative to political and social action, but a guide and spur to such action and a guarantor of its humane direction. The further development of such a psychology, and exploration of its social and political implications, are tasks it behooves us to pursue.

23

The Concept of Narcissism in Discourse on Social Trends

One effect of the modern communications industry has been to reduce greatly the lag time between insight and cliché. No sooner does an interesting and original idea appear than its clones inundate our airwaves and periodicals. That has been the fate of discussions of narcissism in our culture and of our preoccupation with self-development and self-improvement. What was at first a useful insight into an emerging trend in our culture threatens to become a repetitive chorus of "Isn't it awful!" that provides little illumination and even less sense of what a constructive response to this state of affairs might be.

The critiques of social narcissism—what Tom Wolfe called the "me generation"—have encompassed an enormous range of phenomena, from jogging to encounter groups; from Proposition 13 to the worship of celebrities; from the increasing interest in psychotherapy to the shift among college students from social activism to preoccupation with grades. In a very broad, vaguely articulated way, these phenomena do seem to constitute a trend, and some aspects of this trend do seem antisocial and unhealthy. At a time when events point to the necessity of thinking ecologically and of recognizing our interdependence, much of what is surfacing in American life seems to reflect a misguided effort to revivify a form of extreme individualism that in myth or reality was a part of American life in earlier and simpler times. This is evident not only in attitudes toward taxes and welfare programs, but is implicit as well in many of the calls for self-improvement—in their emphasis on individual control over one's

Reprinted by permission from *The Nation*, January 3–10, 1981, pp. 13–15, where it originally appeared under the title "The Politics of Narcissism."

destiny and their depreciation of political concerns or commitment to a cause.

But personal experience can never really be apolitical. As many saw clearly in the 1960s, private experience and public politics are not thorougly separate realms; the two interpenetrate continuously and fatefully. The most important contribution of that tumultuous decade was the elaboration, in a sense considerably broader than R. D. Laing's, of a "politics of experience." This particular legacy of the 1960s is the impetus for the trends now being called "narcissistic"; they are both a reaction to and a continuation of that legacy.

I would thus take sharp issue with Christopher Lasch's claim that "the radicalism of the Sixties failed to address itself to the quality of personal life or to cultural questions" (1976, p. 8). Certainly there were some 1960s radicals whose vision was dark and monolithic, who saw concern with emotional life and personal relations as a corrupt bourgeois distraction from the cause of the revolution. But there was nothing new about these New Left figures. They were essentially old vodka in new bottles. What *was* new in the 1960s—or at least a rediscovery of what had been lost for many years—was precisely the coming together of strands of political radicalism and personal, experiential liberation. Eli Zaretsky, in his fine little book *Capitalism, the Family and Personal Life* (1976), is much closer to the truth than Lasch when he discusses how "currents of personal emancipation and cultural radicalism" became isolated from leftist politics after the Russian Revolution, only to be reunited in the radical ferment of the 1960s. Marshall Berman raised similar ideas in his *The Politics of Authenticity* (1970).

For a time, there was a broad segment of our youth whose desire for political change was expressed in large measure by their rejection of the style and role expected of them. Although more overt and traditional political activity was common as well, it was a time when every facet of personal life was fraught with political significance. Clothes, hairstyle, music, slang phrases and, most significantly, the kind of job one envisioned for oneself (and the anticipated role of work and career in one's life altogether)—all these were political statements. All indicated "which side you were on."

Sadly, it did turn out that much of the political commitment and disaffection from materialist, competitive values was not as deep as it had seemed. Many of today's rising young professionals and executives are people who 10 years ago looked so "different" from either their parents or the "teenagers" of the 1950s that it was hard to imagine what they would grow up to be. Not all approved of what they were up to, but only the most cynical pictured them simply

fitting in, becoming basically indistinguishable from previous co-
horts of "kids" who "grew up."

The cynics' prediction seems, on the face of it, to have been so
correct that it is already difficult to remember just how different the
youth of the 1960s seemed to be. But I think they really were
different, if not as different as they seemed, and they were different
because they were responding to a different set of conditions. The
Vietnam War was the catalyst, but more basic was a failure of
identification, a recognition on the part of many young people that
their parents' affluence did not bring the satisfaction and contentment they were led to expect it would. The vanguard of the movement in the 1960s was from the middle class rather than the working
class, because it was there that so many had reached the point of
diminishing returns, the point where further affluence did not bring
further satisfaction, and thus where some of the ruling assumptions
of American life began to lose their legitimacy and power to compel.
Preoccupation with personal growth and development was a natural
consequence of disillusionment with received values and an inability
to identify with and commit oneself to them.

The congeries of trends now being depicted as the "new narcissism" reflect in many ways a corrupted version of the idealistic (and
valuable) questioning of the 1960s. The radicalism of the 1960s
foundered because the political and the personal again began to
separate. As a result, the end of the decade saw more purely political
groups, sometimes given to terrorism and the rhetoric of class and
race war, along with an increased privatism as many retreated into
drugs, mysticism, and other purely solipsistic rebellions. The reasons
for this (I think temporary) failure of the binding synthesis merit a
great deal of discussion. But whatever the causes, and whatever the
problems that have followed from it, it is well to note that the
purported narcissism of the current decade is a continuation of
trends that, back in the 1960s, implied a serious search for alternative values.

The trends now being called narcissistic are essentially the same
ones that Philip Rieff (1966) earlier designated as "therapeutic"
because they reflected a shift from concern with things greater than
the individual to a primary concern with the self, a shift from "religious man" to "psychological man." Rieff also includes an intermediate stage in his account—that of "economic man"—but neither he,
nor those like Christopher Lasch who have built upon his ideas, have
made much of this latter idea. This is, I think, unfortunate, for an
understanding of the role of economic values tempers the view of

the present trends as decadent. The therapeutic may be more aptly named than even Rieff intended, in that it may reflect not the loss of transcendent values but a genuinely restorative effort to deal with that very loss—a loss largely the result of the rapacious individualism and crass materialism of economic man.

Seen in this light, many of the defects of the therapeutic or self-actualizing orientation are in fact vestiges of the earlier economic value system, which is still quite influential; thus, our problems result not from too much concern with self-actualization, but from too little. What passes for self-actualization is all too often a model of self-aggrandizement based not on experiential but on economic metaphors. Our new psychological hucksters are hucksters first and psychologists decidedly second, whether they be formally trained in psychology or more nakedly revealed as public relations types. The est-chatology of the profiteering gurus reflects a vision part P.T. Barnum and part robber baron, not a culmination of our understanding of the experiece of satisfaction, vitality, and relatedness.

I would thus take issue with Peter Marin's (1975) claim that est is "the logical extension of the whole human potential movement of the past decade." Est and its all too plentiful ilk are not a logical extension but a regressive drag on this movement. For the moment, they have prevented the progressive forces of the movement from generating much momentum. In his widely cited essay in *Harper's* on "the new narcissism," Marin expresses concern about "the ways in which selfishness and moral blindness now assert themselves in the larger culture as enlightenment and psychic health" and contends that what is missing from such approaches is "the ground of community, the felt sense of collective responsibility for the fate of each separate other" (1975). Marin's is in general an interesting and useful examination of the excesses and mistakes of this movement, and his discussion of the emphasis on the prerogatives of the self as a defense against the demands of conscience in an unfair world is an important idea deserving further exploration.

What he largely ignores, however, is that these movements did begin with a moral impulse, however much they may have subsequently strayed. In the 1960s, concern with self-awareness and personal growth reflected a rejection of the materialism that was seen as the basis for a social system that oppressed its minorities and wrought havoc around the globe. Today, this psychological and therapeutic emphasis continues to represent (at least potentially) an alternative to dominant values that point toward productivity instead of experience; that tell us that we can't "afford" social programs, though we somehow still can afford new cars, gadgets, and weapons; and that painfully push us to scrape raw our body politic against the rough edges of limited energy, toxic pollution, and misordered priorities which require us to make things we don't need in order to provide jobs.

Marin's use of the term "narcissism" reflects a moral judgment; he essentially equates it with "selfishness." In the few years since his essay, this moral concern has increasingly been conflated with the clinical psychological meaning of the term, creating two problems. First, the psychoanalytic perspective, which was intended to be value-neutral or to provide a sympathetic understanding, has been used instead in the service of pseudoscientific condemnation and dismissal of what the critic doesn't like. Lasch's writings on narcissism in particular show this trend. Second, the psychoanalytic accounts of narcissism that have primarily been relied on by social critics—the theories of such analysts as Heinz Kohut and Otto Kernberg—fix the origins of narcissistic personality traits almost exclusively in experiences with the mother during the first year or two of life.

Other analysts, however, see personality as much more responsive to the person's adult social context, a view that has quite different social implications. From their perspective, it may *appear* that personality traits are set very early, but this is because the social context we encounter is so often a self-created one. The individual who needs to bolster a shaky self-esteem by self-inflation and by desperately seeking admiration creates a particular kind of world for himself. Either he evokes similar puffery from others (thereby confirming his view that he must win a Nobel Prize just to tread water), or, even when he succeeds in winning a role as a "star," he is likely to make the basis of his acceptance in a social group be one in which his role is the "special" one; and there is even some truth in his implicit sense that what will win acceptance for "ordinary" people will not be regarded as acceptable in his case. The *origin* of such a "narcissist's" need to engage in such a pattern may well lie early in life, but the maintenance of the process requires a continuing cycle of events.

The full implications of such an alternative perspective cannot be spelled out here. At the very least it provides a much clearer sense of how present social realities—particularly our almost compulsive social and geographic mobility and our lack of clear guidelines as to what is expected of us, in work, in marriage, in parenthood—disrupt the continuing processes by which the self is defined and rooted in a community. And it points to how selfishness can arise from insufficient care for the real needs of the self even when what is observed manifestly is an excessive self-preoccupation. Let us by all means expose what is shallow, meretricious, and self-serving in the human potential movement. Particularly let us take heed that the self cannot thrive in a vacuum, that only in concert with others can we achieve the conditions for harmony within. But let us also recognize that the narcissist keeps looking into the mirror not out of delighted contentment but out of anxious concern, and that the suffering he causes himself and others cannot be reduced by denying the claims of the self but only by more accurately and sympathetically understanding them.

REFERENCES

Agnew, N., & Agnew, M. Drive level effects on tasks of narrow and broad attention. *Quarterly Journal of Experimental Psychology*, 1963, *15*, 58–62.

Ajurieguerra, J., & Richard, J. Quelques aspects de la désintégration des praxies idéomatrices dans les démences du grand age. *Cortex cérébral*, 1966, *27*, 438–462.

Alexander, F. *Psychoanalysis and psychotherapy*. New York: Norton, 1956.

Alexander, F. The dynamics of psychotherapy in the light of learning theory. *American Journal of Psychiatry*, 1963, *120*, 441–449.

Alexander, F., French, T., et al. *Psychoanalytic therapy*. New York: Ronald Press, 1946.

Alker, H. A. Is personality situationally specific or intrapsychically consistent? *Journal of Personality*, 1972, *40*, 1–16.

Allen, E. K., Hart, B. M., Buell, J. S., Harris, F. R., & Wolf, M. M. Effects of social reinforcement on isolate behavior of a nursery school child. *Child Development*, 1964, *34*, 511–518.

Allison, J., & Blatt, S. J. The relationship of Rorschach Whole responses to intelligence. *Journal of Projective Techniques and Personality Assessment*, 1964, *28*, 255–260.

Amacher, M. P. Freud's neurological education and its influence on psychoanalytic theory. *Psychological Issues*, 1965, 4(Whole No. 16).

Argyle, M., Trower, P., & Bryant, B. Explorations in the treatment of personality disorders and neuroses by social skills training. *British Journal of Medical Psychology*, 1974, *47*, 63–72.

Arkin, A. To thine own self be true: A review of *Advances in self psychology*. *Contemporary Psychology*, 1981, *26*, 785–787.

Arkowitz, H., & Messer, S. (Eds.). *Psychoanalytic therapy and behavior therapy: Is integration possible?* New York: Plenum, 1984.

Ayllon, T., & Azrin, N. *The token economy*. New York: Appleton-Century-Crofts, 1968.

Bahrick, H. P., Fitts, P. M., & Rankin, R. E. Effects of incentives upon reactions to peripheral stimuli. *Journal of Experimental Psychology*, 1952, *44*, 400–406.

Bandura, A. *Principles of behavior modification.* New York: Holt, Rinehart & Winston, 1969.

Bandura, A. Behavior theory and the models of man. *American Psychologist,* 1974, *29,* 859–869.

Bandura, A. On paradigms and recycled ideologies: Analogue research revisited. *Cognitive Therapy and Research,* 1978, *2,* 79–104. (a)

Bandura, A. The self system in reciprocal determinism. *American Psychologist,* 1978, *33,* 344–358. (b)

Bandura, A., & Walters, R. *Social learning and personality development.* New York: Holt, Rinehart & Winston, 1963.

Beck, A. *Cognitive therapy and the emotional disorders.* New York: International Universities Press, 1976.

Bem, D. Constructing cross-situational consistencies in behavior: Some thoughts on Alker's critique of Mischel. *Journal of Personality,* 1972, *40,* 17–26.

Bemporad, J. R. Perceptual disorders in schizophrenia. *American Journal of Psychiatry,* 1967, *123,* 971–976.

Berger, J., & Israel, N. *Leveling–sharpening and discrepancy in self-report and physiological indices of stress.* Paper presented at Eastern Psychological Association meeting, Atlantic City, N. J., April 4, 1970.

Berlyne, D. E. *Conflict, arousal, and curiosity.* New York: McGraw-Hill, 1960.

Berman, M. *The politics of authenticity.* New York: Atheneum, 1970.

Bibring, C. Psychoanalysis and the dynamic psychotherapies. *Journal of the American Psychoanalytic Association,* 1954, *2,* 745–770.

Birdwhistell, R. L. *Introduction to kinesics.* Louisville: University of Louisville Press, 1952.

Birdwhistell, R. L. The kinesic level in the investigation of the emotions. In P. Knapp (Ed.), *Expression of the emotions in man.* New York: International Universities Press, 1963.

Birk, L. Behavior therapy: Integration with dynamic psychiatry. *Behavior Therapy,* 1970, *1,* 522–526.

Birk, L. Intensive group therapy: An effective behavioral–psychoanalytic method. *American Journal of Psychiatry,* 1974, *131,* 11–16.

Birk, L., & Brinkley-Birk, A. Psychoanalysis and behavior therapy. *American Journal of Psychiatry,* 1974, *131,* 499–510.

Blanchard, E. B., & Hersen, M. Behavioral treatment of hysterical neurosis: Symptom substitution and symptom return reconsidered. *Psychiatry,* 1976, *39,* 118–129.

Blatt, S. J., & Allison, J. Methodological considerations in Rorschach research: The W response as an expression of abstractive and integrative strivings. *Journal of Projective Techniques,* 1963, *27,* 269–279.

Blatt, S., & Wild, C. *Schizophrenia: A developmental analysis.* New York: Academic Press, 1976.

Bowers, K. S. Situationism in psychology: An analysis and a critique. *Psychological Review,* 1973, *80,* 307–336.

Brady, J. P. Psychotherapy, learning theory and insight. *Archives of General Psychiatry,* 1967, *16,* 304–311.

Breger, L., & McGaugh, L. A critique and reformulation of "learning theory" approaches to psychotherapy and neurosis. *Psychological Bulletin*, 1965, *63*, 338–358.

Brenner, C. Some comments on technical precepts in psychoanalysis. *Journal of the American Psychoanalytic Association*, 1969, *17*, 333–352.

Breuer, J., & Freud, S. Studies on hysteria. In *Standard edition* (Vol. 2). London: Hogarth Press, 1955. (Originally published, 1895.)

Broadbent, D. E. A mechanical model for human attention and immediate memory. *Psychological Review*, 1957, *64*, 205–215.

Brody, N. *Personality*. New York: Academic Press, 1972.

Broen, W. E., Jr. Response disorganization and breadth of observation in schizophrenia. *Psychological Review*, 1966, *73*, 579–585.

Broverman, D. M. Cognitive style and intra-individual variation in abilities. *Journal of Personality*, 1960, *28*, 240–256.

Broverman, D. M. Normative and ipsative measurement in psychology. *Psychological Review*, 1962, *69*, 295–305.

Brown, N. O. *Life against death*. Middletown, Conn.: Wesleyan University Press, 1959.

Burdock, E., & Hardesty, A. *Structured Clinical Interview manual*. New York: Springer, 1969.

Bursill, A. E. The restriction of peripheral vision during exposure to hot and humid conditions. *Quarterly Journal of Experimental Psychology*, 1958, *10*, 113–129.

Callaway, E. The influence of amobarbital (amylobarbitone) and methamphetamine on the focus of attention. *Journal of Mental Science*, 1959, *105*, 382–392.

Callaway, E., & Band, R. Some psychopharmacological effects of atropine. *Archives of Neurology and Psychiatry*, 1958, *79*, 91–102.

Callaway, E., & Dembo, D. Narrowed attention: A psychological phenomenon that accompanies a certain physiological change. *Archives of Neurology and Psychiatry*, 1958, *79*, 74–90.

Callaway, E., & Stone, G. Re-evaluating the focus of attention. In L. Uhr & S. G. Miller (Eds.), *Drugs and behavior*. New York: Wiley, 1960.

Callaway, E., & Thompson, S. V. Sympathetic activity and perception. *Psychosomatic Medicine*, 1953, *15*, 443–455.

Carson, R. C. *Interaction concepts of personality*. Chicago: Aldine, 1969.

Chandler, M. *Egocentrism and childhood psychopathology: The development and application of measurement techniques*. Paper presented at the biennial meeting of the Society for Research in Child Development, Minneapolis, 1976.

Chapman, L. S. The role of type of distractor in the "concrete" conceptual performance of schizophrenics. *Journal of Personality*, 1956, *25*, 130–141.

Chapman, L. J., & Chapman, J. Genesis of popular but erroneous psychodiagnostic observations. *Journal of Abnormal Psychology*, 1967, *72*, 193–204.

Christ, A. Cognitive assessment of the psychotic child: A Piagetian framework. *Journal of the American Academy of Child Psychiatry*, 1977, *16*, 227–238.

Christ, A. Psychotherapy of the child with true brain damage. *American Journal of Orthopsychiatry*, 1978, *48*, 505–515.

Cohen, J. *Statistical power analysis for the behavioral sciences*. New York: Academic Press, 1969.

Combs, A. W. A phenomenological approach to adjustment theory. *Journal of Abnormal and Social Psychology,* 1949, 44, 29–35.

Combs, A. W., & Taylor, C. The effect of the perception of mild degrees of threat on performance. *Journal of Abnormal and Social Psychology,* 1952, 47, 420–424.

Dahl, H. A quantitative study of a psychoanalysis. In R. R. Holt & E. Peterfreund (Eds.), *Psychoanalysis and Contemporary Science.* Vol. 1. New York: Macmillan, 1972.

Dasen, P. Biology or culture? Interethnic psychology from a Piagetian point of view. *Canadian Psychologist,* 1973, 14, 149–166.

Davis, M. That's interesting! Towards a phenomenology of sociology and a sociology of phenomenology. *Philosophy of the Social Sciences,* 1971, 1, 309–344.

Davison, G. C. Appraisal of behavior modification techniques with adults in institutional settings. In C. Franks (Ed.), *Behavior therapy: Appraisal and status.* New York: McGraw-Hill, 1969.

Davison, G. C., & Wilson, G. T. Processes of fear reduction in systematic desensitization: Cognitive and social reinforcement factors in humans. *Behavior Therapy,* 1973, 4, 1–21.

de Charms, R. *Personal causation.* New York: Academic Press, 1968.

Dewald, P. *The psychoanalytic process.* New York: Basic Books, 1972.

Dittman, A., Parloff, M., & Boomer, D. Facial and bodily expression: A study of receptivity of emotional cues. *Psychiatry,* 1965, 28, 234–244.

Dollard, J., & Miller, N. E. *Personality and psychotherapy.* New York: McGraw-Hill, 1950.

Dudek, S. A longitudinal study of Piaget's developmental stages and the concept of regression: II. *Journal of Personality Assessment,* 1972, 36, 468–478.

Dudek, S., & Dyer, G. A longitudinal study of Piaget's developmental stages and the concept of regression: I. *Journal of Personality Assessment,* 1972, 36, 380–389.

D'Zurilla, T. J., Wilson, G. T., & Nelson, R. A. Preliminary study of the effectiveness of graduated prolonged exposure in the treatment of irrational fear. *Behavior Therapy,* 1973, 4, 672–685.

Easterbrook, J. A. The effect of emotion on cue utilization and the organization of behavior. *Psychological Review,* 1959, 66, 183–201.

Eissler, K. R. The Chicago Institute of Psychoanalysis and the sixth period of the development of psychoanalytic technique. *Journal of General Psychology,* 1950, 42, 103–157.

Eissler, K. R. Remarks on some variations in psycho-analytical technique. *International Journal of Psycho-Analysis,* 1958, 39, 222–229.

Ekehammar, B. Interactionism in personality from a historical perspective. *Psychological Bulletin,* 1974, 81, 1026–1048.

Ekman, P. Differential communication of affect by head and body cues. *Journal of Personality and Social Psychology,* 1965, 2, 726–735.

Ellenberger, H. *The discovery of the unconscious.* New York: Basic Books, 1970.

Ellis, A. *Reason and emotion in psychotherapy.* New York: Lyle Stuart, 1962.

Endler, N., & Magnusson, D. *Interactional psychology and personality.* New York: Halsted, 1976.

Eriksen, C. W. Individual differences in defensive forgetting. *Journal of Experimental Psychology*, 1952, *44*, 442–446.

Erikson, E. H. *Childhood and society*. New York: Norton, 1950.

Eysenck, H. J. Learning theory and behavior therapy. *Journal of Mental Science*, 1959, *105*, 61–75.

Eysenck, H. J., & Beech, R. Counterconditioning and related methods. In A. E. Bergin & S. L. Garfield (Eds.), *Handbook of psychotherapy and behavior change*. New York: Wiley, 1971.

Feather, B. W., & Rhoads, J. M. Psychodynamic behavior therapy: I. Theory and rationale. *Archives of General Psychiatry*, 1972, *26*, 496–502. (a)

Feather, B. W., & Rhoads, J. M. Psychodynamic behavior therapy: II. Clinical aspects. *Archives of General Psychiatry*, 1972, *26*, 503–511. (b)

Feffer, M. Symptoms expression as a form of primitive decentering. *Psychological Review*, 1967, *74*, 16–28.

Fenichel, O. *The psychoanalytic theory of neurosis*. New York: Norton, 1945.

Ferster, C. B. Clinical reinforcement. *Seminars in Psychiatry*, 1972, *9*, 101–111.

Ferster, C. B. A functional analysis of depression. *American Psychologist*, 1973, *28*, 857–870.

Flavell, J. *The developmental psychology of Jean Piaget*. Princeton, NJ: Van Nostrand, 1963.

Frank, J. D. *Persuasion and healing: A comparative study of psychotherapy* (Rev. ed.). Baltimore: Johns Hopkins University Press, 1973.

Franks, C. M. *On the importance of conceptual integrity and its mutual advantages to two fundamentally incompatible systems*. Paper read at the annual meeting of the Association for Advancement of Behavior Therapy, Chicago, November 17, 1978.

Franks, C. M., & Wilson, G. T. Behavior therapy: An overview. In C. M. Franks & G. T. Wilson (Eds.), *Annual review of behavior therapy*. New York: Brunner/Mazel, 1979.

Freedman, J., & Fraser, S. Compliance without pressure: The foot-in-the-door technique. *Journal of Personality and Social Psychology*, 1966, *4*, 195–202.

Freedman, N., & Hoffman, S. *Kinetic behavior in altered clinical states: An approach to the objective analysis of motor behavior during clinical interviews*. Unpublished manuscript, Psychiatric Treatment Research Center, Downstate Medical Center, 1966.

Freud, S. An outline of psycho-analysis. In *Standard Edition* (Vol. 23). London: Hogarth Press, 1964. (Originally published, 1940.)

Freud, S. Fragments of an analysis of a case of hysteria. In *Standard Edition* (Vol. 7). London: Hogarth Press, 1953. (Originally published, 1905.) (a)

Freud, S. Three essays on the theory of sexuality. In *Standard Edition* (Vol. 7). London: Hogarth Press, 1953. (Originally published, 1905.) (b)

Freud, S. *The origins of psychoanalysis: Letters to Wilhelm Fliess, drafts and notes, 1887–1902*. New York: Basic Books, 1954.

Freud, S. Beyond the pleasure principle. In *Standard Edition* (Vol. 18). London: Hogarth Press, 1955. (Originally published, 1920.)

Freud, S. The dynamics of transference. In *Standard Edition* (Vol. 12). London: Hogarth Press, 1958. (Originally published, 1912.) (a)

Freud, S. Observations on transference-love: Further recommendations on the technique of psycho-analysis. In *Standard Edition* (Vol. 12). London: Hogarth Press, 1958. (Originally published, 1915.) (b)

Freud, S. Two encyclopaedia articles. In *Standard Edition* (Vol. 18). London: Hogarth Press, 1959. (Originally published, 1923.) (a)

Freud, S. Inhibitions, symptoms and anxiety. In *Standard Edition* (Vol. 20). London: Hogarth Press, 1959. (Originally published, 1926.) (b)

Freud, S. On the history of the psycho-analytic movement. In *Standard Edition* (Vol. 14). London: Hogarth Press, 1957. (Originally published, 1914.) (c)

Freud, S. The question of lay analysis. In *Standard Edition* (Vol. 20). London: Hogarth Press, 1959. (Originally published, 1926a.) (d)

Freud, S. The unconscious. In *Standard Edition* (Vol. 14). London: Hogarth Press, 1957. (Originally published, 1915.) (e)

Freud, S. The ego and the id. In *Standard Edition* (Vol. 19). London: Hogarth Press, 1961. (Originally published, 1923.)

Freud, S. Further remarks on the neuro-psychoses of defence. In *Standard Edition* (Vol. 3). London: Hogarth Press, 1962. (Originally published, 1896.)

Freud, S. Introductory lectures on psycho-analysis. In *Standard Edition* (Vol. 16). London: Hogarth Press, 1963. (Originally published, 1916.)

Friedland, B. Toward a psychology of the self. *Contemporary Psychoanalysis*, 1978, *14*, 553–571.

Friedman, M., & Friedman, R. *Free to choose.* New York: Harcourt Brace Jovanovich, 1980.

Frye, N. *Anatomy of criticism.* New York: Athaneum, 1957.

Galbraith, J. K. *The affluent society.* Boston: Houghton-Mifflin, 1958.

Gardner, R. W. Cognitive control principles and perceptual behavior. *Bulletin of the Menninger Clinic*, 1959, *23*, 241–248.

Gardner, R. W. Cognitive controls of attention deployment as determinants of visual illusions. *Journal of Abnormal and Social Psychology*, 1961, *62*, 120–127.

Gardner, R. W., Holtzman, P. S., Klein, G. S., Linton, H., & Spence, D. P. Cognitive control: A study of individual consistencies in cognitive behavior. *Psychological Issues*, 1959, *1*(Whole No. 4).

Gardner, R. W., Jackson, D., & Messick, S. Personality organization in cognitive controls and intellectual abilities. *Psychological Issues*, 1960, *4*(Whole No. 8).

Gardner, R. W., & Long, R. Cognitive controls of attention and inhibition: A study of individual consistencies. *British Journal of Psychology*, 1962, *53*, 381–388. (a)

Gardner, R. W., & Long, R. Control, defence, and centration effect: A study of scanning behavior. *British Journal of Psychology*, 1962, *53*, 129–140. (b)

Gergen, K. J. Toward generative theory. *Journal of Personality and Social Psychology*, 1978, *36*, 1344–1360.

Gill, M. M. Psychoanalysis and exploratory psychotherapy. *Journal of the American Psychoanalytic Association*, 1954, *2*, 771–797.

Gill, M. M. Psychology versus metapsychology. *Psychological Issues*, 1976 (Whole No. 36).

Gill, M. M. *Analysis of transference.* New York: International Universities Press, 1982.

Goldberger, L. Experimental isolation: An overview. *American Journal of Psychiatry,* 1966, *122,* 774–782.

Goldfried, M. R. Resistance and clinical behavior therapy. In P. Wachtel (Ed.), *Resistance: Psychodynamic and behavioral approaches.* New York: Plenum, 1982.

Goldfried, M. R., & Davison, G. C. *Clinical behavior therapy.* New York: Holt, Rinehart & Winston, 1976.

Goldfried, M. R., & Kent, R. N. Traditional versus behavioral personality assessment: A comparison of methodological and theoretical assumptions. *Psychological Bulletin,* 1972, *77,* 409–420.

Goldfried, M. R., & Merbaum, M. (Eds.). *Behavior change through self-control.* New York: Holt, Rinehart & Winston, 1973.

Goldfried, M. R., & Padawer, W. Current status and future directions in psychotherapy. In M. R. Goldfried (Ed.), *Converging themes in psychotherapy.* New York: Springer, 1982.

Goldschmid, M. The relation of conservation to emotional and environmental aspects of development. *Child Development,* 1968, 579–589.

Goldschmid, M., & Bentler, P. *Concept assessment kit—conservation: Manual and keys.* San Diego, Calif.: Educational and Industrial Testing Service, 1968.

Granger, G. W. Personality and visual perception: A revision. *Journal of Mental Science,* 1953, *99,* 8–43.

Greenberg, A. *Directed and undirected learning in chronic schizophrenia.* Unpublished doctoral dissertation, Columbia University, 1953.

Greenson, R. The working alliance and the transference neurosis. *Psychoanalytic Quarterly,* 1965, *34,* 155–181.

Greenson, R. *The technique and practice of psychoanalysis.* New York: International Universities Press, 1967.

Greenson, R. The "real" relationship between the patient and the psychoanalyst. In M. Kanzer (Ed.), *The unconscious today.* New York: International Universities Press, 1971.

Greenson, R., & Wexler, M. The non-transference relationship in the psychoanalytic situation. *International Journal of Psycho-Analysis,* 1969, *50,* 27–40.

Greenspan, S. I. The clinical use of operant learning approaches: Some complex issues. *American Journal of Psychiatry,* 1974, *131,* 852–857.

Greenspan, S. I. A consideration of some learning variables in the context of psychoanalytic theory: Toward a psychoanalytic learning perspective. *Psychological Issues,* 1975, *9*(Whole No. 33).

Habermas, J. *Knowledge and human interests.* Boston: Beacon Press, 1971.

Hall, E. T. *The silent language.* New York: Doubleday, 1959.

Hamilton, J. Size constancy and cue responsiveness in psychosis. *British Journal of Psychology,* 1963, *54,* 25–39.

Haronian, F., & Sugerman, A. Fixed and mobile field-independence: Review of studies relevant to Werner's dimension. *Psychological Reports,* 1967, *21,* 41–57.

Hartmann, H. *Ego psychology and the problem of adaptation.* New York: International Universities Press, 1958. (Originally published, 1939.)

Hartmann, H., Kris, E., & Loewenstein, R. M. Notes on the theory of aggression. *Psychoanalytic Study of the Child,* 1949, *3/4,* 9–36.

Hernández-Peon, R. Psychiatric implications of neurophysiological research. *Bulletin of the Menninger Clinic,* 1964, *28,* 165–185.

Hilgard, E. R. Psychoanalysis: Experimental studies. In D. L. Sills (Ed.), *International encyclopedia of the social sciences* (Vol. 13). New York: Macmillan, 1968.

Hirsch, F. *Social limits to growth.* Cambridge, MA: Harvard University Press, 1976.

Hoffman, I. Z. The patient as interpreter of the analyst's experience. *Contemporary Psychoanalysis,* 1983, *19,* 389–422.

Holt, R. R. A review of some of Freud's biological assumptions and their influence on his theories. In N. S. Greenfield & W. C. Lewis (Eds.), *Psychoanalysis and current biological thought.* Madison: University of Wisconsin Press, 1965. (a)

Holt, R. R. Ego autonomy re-evaluated. *International Journal of Psycho-Analysis,* 1965, *46,* 151–167. (b)

Holt, R. R. Beyond vitalism and mechanism: Freud's concept of psychic energy. In J. Masserman (Ed.), *Science and psychoanalysis.* (Vol. 11). New York: Grune & Stratton, 1967.

Holt, R. R. Yet another look at clinical and statistical prediction: Or, is clinical psychology worthwhile? *American Psychologist,* 1970, *25,* 337–349.

Holt, R. R. Drive or wish? A reconsideration of the psychoanalytic theory of motivation. *Psychological Issues,* 1976 (Whole No. 36).

Holzman, P. S., & Gardner, R. W. Levelling and repression. *Journal of Abnormal and Social Psychology,* 1959, *59,* 151–155.

Horney, K. *New ways in psychoanalysis.* New York: Norton, 1939.

Horney, K. *Our inner conflicts.* New York: Norton, 1945.

Horwitz, L. Theory construction and validation in psychoanalysis. In M. H. Marx (Ed.), *Theories in contemporary psychology.* New York: Macmillan, 1963.

Jackson, D. Relationship of residence, education, and socialization to cognitive tasks in normal adults of advanced old age. *Psychological Reports,* 1974, *35,* 423–426.

Jackson, H. Remarks on the evolution and dissolution of the nervous system. *Journal of Mental Science,* 1887, *33,* 25–48.

Jacobson, G. R. Effect of brief sensory deprivation on field-dependence. *Journal of Abnormal Psychology,* 1966, *31,* 386–394.

Jacobson, G. R. Reduction of field-dependence in chronic alcoholics. *Journal of Abnormal Psychology,* 1968, *73,* 547–549.

Jacoby, R. *Social amnesia: A critique of conformist psychology from Adler to Laino.* Boston: Beacon Press, 1975.

James, W. *Principles of psychology.* New York: Holt, 1890.

Karp, S. Field dependence and overcoming embeddedness, *Journal of Consulting Psychology,* 1963, *27,* 294–302.

Kausler, D. H., & Trapp, E. P. Motivation and cue utilization in intentional and incidental learning. *Psychological Review,* 1960, *67,* 373–379.

Kellner, H., Butters, N., & Wiener, M. Mechanisms of defense: An alternative response. *Journal of Personality,* 1964, *32,* 601–621.

Kiesler, D. J. Some myths of psychotherapy research and the search for a paradigm. *Psychological Bulletin*, 1966, *65*, 110–136.

Kendall, P. C. Cognitive processes and procedures in behavior therapy. In C. M. Franks, G. T. Wilson, P. C. Kendall, & K. Brownell, *Annual review of behavior therapy* (Vol. 8). New York: Guilford Press, 1982.

Kilburg, R., & Siegel, A. Formal operations in reactive and process schizophrenics. *Journal of Consulting and Clinical Psychology*, 1973, *40*, 371–376.

Klein, G. S. Need and regulation. In M. R. Jones (Ed.), *Nebraska symposium on motivation*. Lincoln: University of Nebraska Press, 1954.

Klein, G. S. Cognitive control and motivation. In G. Lindzey (Ed.), *Assessment of human motives*. New York: Rinehart, 1958.

Klein, G. S. *Two theories or one? Perspectives to change in psychoanalytic theory.* Paper presented at the Conference of Psychoanalysts of the Southwest, Galveston, Texas, March 1966.

Klein, G. S. Peremptory ideation. *Psychological Issues*, 1967, *5*, (Whole No. 18/19).

Klein, G. S. Freud's two theories of sexuality. In L. Breger (Ed.), *Clinical–cognitive psychology*. Englewood Cliffs, NJ: Prentice-Hall, 1969.

Klein, G. S. *Perception, motives, and personality*. New York: Knopf, 1970.

Klein, G. S. *Psychoanalytic theory: An exploration of essentials*. New York: International Universities Press, 1976.

Klein, G. S., Barr, H. L., & Wolitzky, D. L. Personality. *Annual Review of Psychology*, 1967, *18*, 467–560.

Klein, M. H., Dittman, A. T., Parloff, M. B., & Gill, M. M. Behavior therapy: Observations and reflections. *Journal of Consulting and Clinical Psychology*, 1969, *33*, 259–269.

Klenbort, I. Another look at Sullivan's concept of individuality. *Contemporary Psychoanalysis*, 1978, *14*, 125–135.

Kohut, H. *The analysis of the self*. New York: International Universities Press, 1971.

Kohut, H. *The restoration of the self*. New York: International Universities Press, 1977.

Kohut, H. *How does analysis cure?* Chicago: University of Chicago Press, 1984.

Knight, R. Determinism, "freedom," and psychotherapy. *Psychiatry*, 1946, *9*, 251–262.

Korchin, S. J. Anxiety and cognition. In C. Scheerer (Ed.), *Cognition: Theory, research, promise*. New York: Harper & Row, 1964.

Kuhn, D., Langer, L., & Kohlberg, L. Attainment of formal operations. *Genetic Psychology Monographs*, 1977, *1*, 97–188.

Kuhn, T. *The structure of scientific revolutions*. Chicago: University of Chicago Press, 1962.

Kubie, L. S. The fallacious use of quantitative concepts in dynamic psychology. *Psychoanalytic Quarterly*, 1947, *16*, 507–518.

Kurie, G. D., & Mordkoff, A. M. The effects of brief sensory deprivation and body concentration upon two measures of field dependence. *Perceptual and Motor Skills*, 1970, *31*, 683–687.

Laing, R. D., Phillipson, H., & Lee, A. R. *Interpersonal perception*. New York: Springer, 1966.

Lang, P. J. The mechanics of desensitization and the laboratory study of human fear. In C. Franks (Ed.), *Behavior therapy: Appraisal and status.* New York: McGraw-Hill, 1969.

Lang, P. J. The application of psychophysiological methods to the study of psychotherapy and behavior modification. In A. E. Bergin & S. L. Garfield (Eds.), *Handbook of psychotherapy and behavior change.* New York: Wiley, 1971.

Langs, R. The patient's view of the therapist: Reality or fantasy? *International Journal of Psychoanalytic Psychotherapy*, 1973, *2*, 411–431. (a)

Langs, R. *The technique of psychoanalytic psychotherapy.* New York: Jason Aronson, 1973. (b)

Lasch, C. The narcissistic society. *New York Review of Books*, September 30, 1976.

Lasch, C. *Haven in a heartless world.* New York: Basic Books, 1977.

Lasch, C. *The culture of narcissism.* New York: Norton, 1979.

Laurendeau, M., & Pinard, A. *Causal thinking in the child.* New York: International Universities Press, 1963.

Laurendeau, M., & Pinard, A. *The development of the concept of space in the child.* New York: International Universities Press, 1970.

Lazarus, A. A. Behaviour therapy and graded structure. In R. Porter (Ed.), *The role of learning in psychotherapy.* London: Churchill, 1968.

Lazarus, A. A. *Behavior therapy and beyond.* New York: McGraw-Hill, 1971.

Lazarus, A. A. Avoid the paradigm clash. *International Journal of Psychiatry*, 1973, *11*, 157–159.

Lazarus, A. A. *Multimodal behavior therapy.* New York: Springer, 1976.

Lazarus, A. A., & Fay, A. Resistance or rationalization? A cognitive–behavioral perspective. In P. Wachtel (Ed.), *Resistance: Psychodynamic and behavioral approaches.* New York: Plenum, 1982.

Lazarus, A. A., & Serber, M. Is systematic desensitization being misapplied? *Psychological Reports*, 1968, *23*, 215–218.

Leitenberg, H., Agras, S., Barlow, D., & Oliveau, D. Contribution of selective positive reinforcement and therapeutic instructions to systematic desensitization. *Journal of Abnormal Psychology*, 1969, *74*, 113–118.

Leitenberg, H., Agras, W. S., Butz, K., & Wincze, J. Relation between heart-rate and behavior change during the treatment of phobias. *Journal of Abnormal Psychology*, 1971, *78*, 59–68.

Lewis, H. B. *Shame and guilt in neurosis.* New York: International Universities Press, 1965.

Lidz, T. *The origin and treatment of schizophrenic disorders.* New York: Basic Books, 1973.

Locke, E. A. Is "behavior therapy" behavioristic? (An analysis of Wolpe's psychotherapeutic methods). *Psychological Bulletin*, 1971, *76*, 318–327.

Loeb, F. *Grasping: The investigation of a recurrent behavior pattern.* Paper prepared for American Psychological Association convention, 1966.

Loevinger, J. Three principles for a psychoanalytic psychology. *Journal of Abnormal Psychology*, 1966, *71*, 432–443.

Looft, W. Egocentrism and social interaction across the life span. *Psychological Bulletin*, 1972, *78*, 73–92.

Lovinger, E. Perceptual contact with reality in schizophrenia. *Journal of Abnormal and Social Psychology*, 1956, *52*, 87–91.

Luborsky, L., & Auerbach, A. The symptom-context method: Quantitative studies of symptom formation in psychotherapy. *Journal of the American Psychoanalytic Association*, 1969, *17*, 68–99.

Luborsky, L., Blinder, B., & Schimek, J. G. Looking, recalling, and GSR as a function of defense. *Journal of Abnormal Psychology*, 1965, *70*, 270–280.

Luborsky, L., & Schimek, J. G. Psychoanalytic theories of therapeutic and developmental change. In P. Worchel & D. Byrne (Eds.), *Personality change*. New York: Wiley, 1964.

Luborsky, L., & Spence, D. P. Quantitative research on psychoanalytic therapy. In A. Bergin & S. Garfield (Eds.), *Handbook of psychotherapy and behavior change*. New York: Wiley, 1971.

Lustman, S. Psychic energy and mechanisms of defense. *Psychoanalytic Study of the Child*, 1957, *12*, 151–165.

Lynd, H. M. *On shame and the search for identity*. New York: Harcourt, Brace & World, 1958.

Lynn, S., & Garske, J. (Eds.). *Contemporary psychotherapies: Models and methods*. Columbus, OH: Charles E. Merrill, 1985.

Macalpine, I. The development of the transference. *Psychoanalytic Quarterly*, 1950, *19*, 501–539.

Mackintosh, N. J. Selective attention in animal discrimination learning. *Psychological Bulletin*, 1965, *64*, 124–150.

Magnusson, D., & Endler, N. (Eds.). *Personality at the crossroads: Current issues in interactional psychology*. Hillsdale, NJ: Erlbaum, 1977.

Mahl, G. Gestures and body movements in interviews. In *Research in psychotherapy* (Vol. 3). Washington, D.C.: American Psychological Association, 1968.

Mahoney, M. *Cognition and behavior modification*. Cambridge, MA: Ballinger, 1974.

Mahoney, M. Psychotherapy and the structure of personal revolutions. In M. Mahoney (Ed.), *Psychotherapy process: Current issues and future directions*. New York: Plenum, 1980.

Malan, D. *The frontier of brief psychotherapy*. New York: Plenum, 1976.

Marcuse, H. *Eros and civilization*. Boston: Beacon Press, 1955.

Marin, P. The new narcissism. *Harper's* October 1975.

Marks, I. M., & Gelder, M. G. Common ground between behavior therapy and psychodynamic methods. *British Journal of Medical Psychology*, 1966, *39*, 11–23.

Marmor, J. Psychoanalytic therapy as an educational process. In J. Masserman & L. Salzman (Eds.), *Modern concepts of psychoanalysis*. New York: Philosophical Library, 1962.

Marmor, J. Psychoanalytic therapy and theories of learning. In J. Masserman (Ed.), *Science and psychoanalysis* (Vol. 7). New York: Grune & Stratton, 1964.

Marmor, J. Dynamic psychotherapy and behavior therapy: Are they irreconcilable? *Archives of General Psychiatry*, 1971, *24*, 22–28.

Mayman, M., & Gardner, R. W. The characteristic psychological disturbance in some cases of brain damage with mild deficit. *Bulletin of the Menninger Clinic,* 1960, *24,* 26–36.

Mayman, M., & Voth, H. Reality closeness, phantasy, and autokinesis: A dimension of cognitive style. *Journal of Abnormal Psychology,* 1969, *74,* 635–641.

Mazer, M. The therapeutic function of the belief in will. *Psychiatry,* 1960, *23,* 45–52.

McAllister, L. W. Modification of performance on the rod and frame test through token reinforcement procedures. *Journal of Abnormal Psychology,* 1970, *75,* 124–130.

McGhie, A., & Chapman, J. Disorders of attention and perception in early schizophrenia. *British Journal of Medical Psychology,* 1961, *34,* 103–116.

McGuire, W. J. The yin and yang of progress in social psychology: Seven koan. *Journal of Personality and Social Psychology,* 1973, *26,* 446–451.

McNamara, H., & Fisch, R. Effect of high and low motivation on two aspects of attention. *Perceptual and Motor Skills,* 1964, *19,* 571–578.

Meehl, P. E. *Clinical versus statistical prediction: A theoretical analysis and a review of the evidence.* Minneapolis: University of Minnesota Press, 1954.

Meichenbaum, D. *Cognitive behavior modification.* New York: Plenum, 1977.

Meichenbaum, D., & Gilmore, J. B. Resistance: From a cognitive–behavioral perspective. In P. Wachtel (Ed.), *Resistance.* New York: Plenum, 1982.

Meichenbaum, D., & Gilmore, J. B. The nature of unconscious processes: A cognitive–behavioral perspective. In K. Bowers & D. Meichenbaum (Eds.), *The unconscious reconsidered.* New York: Wiley, 1984.

Menninger, K. *Theory of psychoanalytic technique.* New York: Basic Books, 1958.

Messer, S., & Winokur, M. Some limits to the integration of psychoanalytic and behavior therapy. *American Psychologist,* 1980, *35,* 818–827.

Miller, G. A. The magical number seven, plus or minus two: Some limits on our capacity for processing information. *Psychological Review,* 1956, *63,* 81–97.

Miller, N. E. Studies of fear as an acquirable drive: I. Fear as motivation and fear as reinforcement in the learning of new responses. *Journal of Experimental Psychology,* 1948, *38,* 89–101.

Miller, N. E. Liberalization of basic S-R concepts: Extensions to conflict behavior, motivation, and social learning. In S. Koch (Ed.), *Psychology: A study of science* (Vol. 2). New York: McGraw-Hill, 1959.

Millon, T. *Psychopathology.* Philadelphia: W. B. Saunders, 1969.

Mischel, W. *Personality and assessment.* New York: Wiley, 1968.

Mischel, W. *Introduction to Personality.* New York: Holt, Rinehart & Winston, 1971. (2nd Edition, 1976.) (a)

Mischel, W. *Specificity theory and the construction of personality.* Paper presented at the annual meeting of the American Psychological Association, Washington, DC, September 3, 1971. (b)

Mischel, W. Toward a cognitive social learning reconceptualization of personality. *Psychological Review,* 1973, *80,* 252–283. (a)

Mischel, W. On the empirical dilemmas of psychodynamic approaches: Issues and alternatives. *Journal of Abnormal Psychology,* 1973, *82,* 335–344. (b)

Mitchell, S. A. Twilight of the idols. *Contemporary Psychoanalysis*, 1979, *15*, 170–189.

Mitroff, I. I., & Kilmann, R. H. *Methodological approaches to social science.* San Francisco: Jossey-Bass, 1978.

Moscovici, S. Society and theory in social psychology. In J. Israel & H. Tajfel (Eds.), *The context of social psychology: A critical assessment.* New York: Academic Press, 1972.

Murray, E. J., & Berkun, M. M. Displacement as a function of conflict. *Journal of Abnormal and Social Psychology*, 1955, *51*, 47–56.

Muslin, H., & Gill, M. Transference in the Dora case. *Journal of the American Psychoanalytic Association*, 1978, *26*, 311–328.

Nessen, R. Rich guy's loophole. *The New Republic*, December 3, 1977, pp. 9–12.

Nunberg, H. The synthetic function of the ego. *International Journal of Psycho-Analysis*, 1931, *12*, 123–140.

Oltman, P. K. Field dependence and arousal. *Perceptual and Motor Skills*, 1964, *19*, 441.

Oltman, P. K. *Activation and cue utilization.* Unpublished doctoral dissertation, Yale University, 1965.

Orne, M. On the social psychology of the psychological experiment: With particular reference to demand characteristics and their implications. *American Psychologist*, 1962, *17*, 776–783.

Orne, M. Demand characteristics and the concept of quasi-controls. In R. Rosenthal & R. Rosnow (Eds.), *Artifact in behavioral research.* New York: Academic Press, 1969.

Piaget, J. *The psychology of intelligence.* New York: Harcourt, Brace & World, 1950.

Papalia, D. Status of several conservation abilities across the life span. *Human Development*, 1972, *15*, 229–243.

Papalia, D., & Bielby, D. Cognitive functioning in middle and old age: Review of research based on Piaget. *Human Development*, 1974, *17*, 295–301.

Paul, I. H. *Letters to Simon: On the conduct of psychotherapy.* New York: International Universities Press, 1947.

Payne, R. W., Matussek, P., & George, E. An experimental study of schizophrenic thought disorder. *Journal of Mental Science*, 1959, *105*, 627–652.

Pepitone, A. Aggression—A matter of stimulus and reinforcement control. *Contemporary Psychology*, 1974, *11*, 769–771.

Philips, J. *The origins of intellect: Piaget's theory.* San Francisco: W. H. Freeman, 1975.

Piaget, J. La pensée symbolique et la pensée de l'enfant. *Archives de Psychologie*, 1923, *18*, 273–304.

Piaget, J. *The psychology of intelligence.* New York: Harcourt, Brace & World, 1950.

Piaget, J. Jean Piaget (autobiographical sketch). In E. Boring (Ed.), *A history of psychology in autobiography* (Vol. 4). Worcester, MA: Clark University Press, 1952. (a)

Piaget, J. *The origins of intelligence in children.* New York: International Universities Press, 1952. (b)

Piaget, J. *The construction of reality in the child.* New York: Basic Books, 1954.

Piaget, J. Foreword to Weiner, M., *The cognitive unconscious: A Piagetian approach to psychotherapy.* Davis, CA: International Psychological Press, 1975.

Piaget, J., Vinh-Bang, & Matalon, B. Note on the law of the temporal maximum of some opticogeometric illusions. *American Journal of Psychology,* 1958, *71,* 277–282.

Piers, G., & Singer, M. B. *Shame and guilt.* Springfield, IL: Charles C. Thomas, 1952.

Pinard, A., & Laurendeau, M. A scale of mental development based on the theory of Piaget. *Journal of Research in Science Teaching,* 1964, 253–260.

Pine, F. The bearing of psychoanalytic theory on selected issues in research on marginal stimuli. *Journal of Nervous and Mental Disease,* 1964, *13,* 205–222.

Polanyi, M. *Personal knowledge: Towards a post-critical philosophy.* Chicago: University of Chicago Press, 1958.

Polanyi, M. *The tacit dimension.* Garden City, New York: Doubleday, 1966.

Rachman, S., & Hodgson, R. I. Desynchrony in measures of fear. *Behaviour Research and Therapy,* 1974, *12,* 319–326. (a)

Rachman, S., & Hodgson, R. I. Synchrony and desynchrony in fear and avoidance. *Behaviour Research and Therapy,* 1974, *12,* 311–318. (b)

Rapaport, D. *Organization and pathology of thought.* New York: Columbia University Press, 1951.

Rapaport, D. Review of J. Dollard and N. E. Miller's *Personality and psychotherapy. American Journal of Orthopsychiatry,* 1953, *23,* 204–208.

Rapaport, D. The theory of attention cathexis. In M. M. Gill (Ed.), *The collected papers of David Rapaport.* New York: Basic Books, 1967.

Rapaport, D. A historical survey of psychoanalytic ego psychology. *Psychological Issues,* 1959, *1*(Whole No. 1). (a)

Rapaport, D. The structure of psychoanalytic theory: A systematizing attempt. In S. Koch (Ed.), *Psychology: A study of a science* (Vol. 3). New York: McGraw-Hill, 1959. (b)

Rapaport, D., & Gill, M. M. The points of view and assumptions of metapsychology. *International Journal of Psycho-Analysis,* 1959, *40,* 153–162.

Rapaport, D., Gill, M. M., & Schafer, R. *Diagnostic psychological testing* (Vol. 2). Chicago: Year Book Medical Publishing, 1946.

Reich, W. *Character analysis.* New York: Orgone Institute Press, 1945.

Rhoads, J. M., & Feather, B. W. Transference and resistance observed in behavior therapy. *British Journal of Medical Psychology,* 1972, *45,* 99–103.

Rhoads, J. M., & Feather, B. W. The application of psychodynamics to behavior therapy. *American Journal of Psychiatry,* 1974, *131,* 17–20.

Rieff, P. *The triumph of the therapeutic.* New York: Harper & Row, 1966.

Rosenthal, R. *Experimenter bias in behavioral research.* New York: Appleton-Century-Crofts, 1966. (a)

Rosenthal, R. *Experimenter effects in behavioral research.* New York: Appleton-Century-Crofts, 1966. (b)

Rosenthal, R., & Rosnow, R. (Eds.). *Artifact in behavioral research.* New York: Academic Press, 1969.

Saccuzzo, D. Bridges between schizophrenia and gerontology: Generalized or specific deficits? *Psychological Bulletin*, 1977, *84*, 595–600.

Sarnoff, I., & Zimbardo, P. Anxiety, fear and social affiliation. *Journal of Abnormal and Social Psychology*, 1961, *62*, 356–363.

Santostefano, S. Cognitive controls versus cognitive styles: An approach to diagnosing and treating cognitive disabilities in children. *Seminars in Psychiatry*, 1969, *1*, 291–317.

Sawyer, J. Measurement *and* prediction, clinical *and* statistical. *Psychological Bulletin*, 1966, *66*, 178–200.

Schafer, R. *The clinical application of psychological tests*. New York: International Universities Press, 1948.

Schafer, R. *Aspects of internalization*. New York: International Universities Press, 1968.

Schafer, R. An overview of Heinz Hartmann's contributions to psychoanalysis. *International Journal of Psycho-Analysis*, 1970, *51*, 425–446.

Schafer, R. Internalization: Process or fantasy? *Psychoanalytic Study of the Child*, 1972, *27*, 411–436.

Schafer, R. Action: Its place in psychoanalytic interpretation and theory. *The Annual of Psychoanalysis* (Vol. 1). New York: Quadrangle, 1973.

Schafer, R. *A new language for psychoanalysis*. New Haven, CT: Yale University Press, 1976.

Schafer, R. The interpretation of transference and the conditions for loving. *Journal of the American Psychoanalytic Association*, 1977, *25*, 335–362.

Schafer, R. *The analytic attitude*. New York: Basic Books, 1983.

Scheflen, A. Communication and regulation in psychotherapy. *Psychiatry*, 1964, *27*, 126–136.

Scheflen, A. Quasi-courtship behavior in psychotherapy. *Psychiatry*, 1965, *28*, 245–257.

Schimek, J. *Cognitive and defensive aspects of psychological differentiation*. Brooklyn: Downstate Medical Center, Psychological Laboratory, 1967. (Mimeo)

Schimek, J. A critical re-examination of Freud's concept of unconscious mental representation. *International Review of Psycho-Analysis*, 1975, *2*, 171–187.

Schimek, J. G., & Wachtel, P. L. Exploration of effects of distraction, competing tasks and cognitive style on attention deployment. *Perceptual and Motor Skills*, 1969, *28*, 567–574.

Schlesinger, H. S. Cognitive attitudes in relation to susceptibility to interference. *Journal of Personality*, 1954, *22*, 354–374.

Schwartz, F., & Schiller, P. A psychoanalytic model of attention and learning. *Psychological Issues*, 1970, *6*(Whole No. 23).

Seligman, M. E. P., & Johnston, J. C. A cognitive theory of avoidance. In F. J. McGuigan & D. B. Lumsden (Eds.), *Contemporary approaches to conditioning and learning*. New York: Holt, Rinehart & Winston, 1973.

Selman, R., Newberger, C. M., & Jaquette, M. *Observing interpersonal reasoning in a clinic/educational setting: Toward the integration of developmental and clinical-child psychology II*. Paper presented at the biennial meeting of the Society for Research in Child Development, New Orleans, 1977.

Shands, H., & Meltzer, J. Disproportionate diability: The Freud–Charcot syndrome rediscovered. *Journal of Psychiatry and Law*, 1975, *3*, 25–37.

Shapiro, D. *Neurotic styles*. New York: Basic Books, 1965.

Shapiro, D. Motivation and action in psychoanalytic psychiatry. *Psychiatry*, 1970, *33*, 329–343.

Shapiro, D. Dynamic and holistic ideas of neurosis and psychotherapy. *Psychiatry*, 1975, *38*, 218–226.

Shapiro, D. *Autonomy and rigid character*. New York: Basic Books, 1981.

Sherman, J. Problem of sex differences in space perception and aspects of intellectual functioning. *Psychological Review*, 1967, *74*, 290–299.

Shevrin, H., & Dickman, S. The psychological unconscious: A necessary assumption for all psychological theory? *American Psychologist*, 1980, *35*, 421–435.

Silverman, J. The problem of attention in research and theory in schizophrenia. *Psychological Review*, 1964, *71*, 352–379.

Silverman, J. Toward a more complex formulation of rod-and-frame performance in the schizophrenias. *Perceptual and Motor Skills*, 1968, *27*, 1111–1114.

Silverman, L. H. An experimental technique for the study of unconscious conflict. *British Journal of Medical Psychology*, 1971, *44*, 17–25.

Silverman, L. H. Drive stimulation and psychopathology: On the conditions under which drive related external events trigger pathological reactions. In R. R. Holt & E. Peterfreund (Eds.), *Psychoanalysis and Contemporary Science*. Vol. 2. New York: Macmillan, 1972.

Silverman, L. H. Psychoanalytic theory: "The reports of my death are greatly exaggerated." *American Psychologist*, 1976, *31*, 621–637.

Skinner, B. F. *Science and human behavior*. New York: Macmillan, 1953.

Sloane, R. B. The converging paths of behavior therapy and psychotherapy. *American Journal of Psychiatry*, 1969, *125*, 49–57.

Sloane, R. B., Staples, F. R., Cristol, A. H., Yorkston, N. J., & Whipple, K. *Psychotherapy versus behavior therapy*. Cambridge, MA: Harvard University Press, 1975.

Solley, C. M., & Murphy, G. *Development of the perceptual world*. New York: Basic Books, 1960.

Sollod, R. Behavioral and psychodynamic dimensions of the new sex therapy. *Journal of Sex and Marital Therapy*, 1974, *1*, 335–340.

Sollod, R. A Piagetian approach to psychopathology: Concrete operational thinking and adjustment in hospitalized schizophrenics (Doctoral dissertation, Columbia University, 1974). *Dissertation Abstracts International*, 1976, 37B. (University Microfilms No. 76-29309.)

Sollod, R. *Piagetian tests in psychological assessment*. Paper presented at the 7th Annual Symposium of the Jean Piaget Society, Philadelphia, 1977.

Sollod, R. *A Piagetian perspective on schizophrenia*. Paper presented at the 9th Annual International Interdisciplinary UAP–USC Conference on Piagetian Theory and the Helping Professions, Los Angeles, 1979.

Sollod, R., & Kaplan, H. S. The new sex therapy: An integration of behavioral, psychodynamic, and interpersonal approaches. In J. L. Claghorn (Ed.), *Successful psychotherapy*. New York: Brunner/Mazel, 1976.

Sollod, R., & Lapidus, L. Concrete operational thinking, diagnosis, and psychopathology in hospitalized schizophrenics. *Journal of Abnormal Psychology*, 1977, *86*, 199–202.

Solomon, R. L., & Wynne, L. C. Traumatic avoidance learning: The principles of anxiety conservation and partial irreversibility. *Psychological Review*, 1954, *61*, 353–385.

Spence, D. P., & Greif, B. *Randomness of serial letters as a monitor of attention to distracting prose.* Unpublished manuscript, Research Center for Mental Health, New York University, 1968.

Staats, A. W. *Science standards or separatism? Questions on the conduct of psychology.* Unpublished manuscript, University of Hawaii, 1983.

Stone, L. *The psychoanalytic situation.* New York: International Universities Press, 1961.

Strauss, J., & Carpenter, W. The prognosis of schizophrenia: Rationale for a multidimensional concept. *Schizophrenia Bulletin*, 1978, *4*, 56–67.

Stroop, J. R. Studies in interference in serial verbal reactions. *Journal of Experimental Psychology*, 1935, *18*, 643–661.

Strupp, H., & Binder, J. *Psychotherapy in a new key.* New York: Basic Books, 1984.

Suchotliff, L. Relation of formal thought disorder to the communication deficit in schizophrenics. *Journal of Abnormal Psychology*, 1970, *76*, 250–257.

Sullivan, H. S. *The interpersonal theory of psychiatry.* New York: Norton, 1953.

Sullivan, H. *The psychiatric interview.* New York: Norton, 1954.

Toman, W. Mental or psychic energy and its relation to learning and retention: An experimental contribution. *Acta Psychologica*, 1954, *10*, 317–350.

Topping, G., & O'Connor, N. The response of chronic schizophrenics to incentives. *British Journal of Medical Psychology*, 1960, *33*, 211–214.

Thurstone, L. L. *A factorial study of perception.* Chicago: University of Chicago Press, 1944.

Truax, C. B. Reinforcement and nonreinforcement in Rogerian psychotherapy. *Journal of Abnormal Psychology*, 1966, *71*, 1–9.

Trunnel, T. Thought disturbance in schizophrenia. *Archives of General Psychiatry*, 1964, *11*, 126–136.

Trunnel, T. Thought disturbance in schizophrenia: Replication study utilizing Piaget's theories. *Archives of General Psychiatry*, 1965, *13*, 9–18.

Turkat, I. D., & Meyer, V. The behavior-analytic approach. In P. Wachtel (Ed.), *Resistance: Psychodynamic and behavioral approaches.* New York: Plenum, 1982.

Ullmann, L. P., & Krasner, L. *Case studies in behavior modification.* New York: Holt, Rinehart & Winston, 1966.

Ullmann, L., & Krasner, L. *A psychological approach to abnormal behavior.* Englewood Cliffs, NJ: Prentice-Hall, 1969.

Venables, P. H. Selectivity of attention, withdrawal, and cortical activation. *Archives of General Psychiatry*, 1963, *9*, 74–78.

Venables, P. H. Input dysfunction in schizophrenia. In B. Maher (Ed.), *Progress in experimental personality research* (Vol. 1). New York: Academic Press, 1964.

Vigotsky, L. Thought in schizophrenia (J. Kasanin, Trans.). *Archives of Neurology and Psychiatry*, 1934, *31*, 1062–1077.

Voyat, G., & Silk, S. Cross-cultural study of cognitive development on the Pine Ridge Indian Reservation. *Pine Ridge Research Bulletin*, 1970, *11*, 52–73.

Wachtel, E. F., & Wachtel, P. L. *Family dynamics in individual psychotherapy: A guide to clinical strategies.* New York: Guilford Press, 1986.

Wachtel, P. L. Conceptions of broad and narrow attention. *Psychological Bulletin*, 1967, *68*, 417–429.

Wachtel, P. L. Anxiety, attention, and coping with threat. *Journal of Abnormal Psychology*, 1968, *73*, 137–143. (a)

Wachtel, P. L. Style and capacity in analytic functioning. *Journal of Personality*, 1968, *36*, 202–212. (b)

Wachtel, P. L. Psychology, metapsychology, and psychoanalysis. *Journal of Abnormal Psychology*, 1969, *74*, 651–660.

Wachtel, P. L. Cognitive style and style of adaptation. *Perceptual and Motor Skills*, 1972, *35*, 779–785. (a)

Wachtel, P. L. Field dependence and psychological differentiation: A reexamination. *Perceptual and Motor Skills*, 1972, *35*, 179–189. (b)

Wachtel, P. L. On fact, hunch, and stereotype: A reply to Mischel. *Journal of Abnormal Psychology*, 1973, *82*, 537–540. (a)

Wachtel, P. L. Psychodynamics, behavior therapy, and the implacable experimenter: An inquiry into the consistency of personality. *Journal of Abnormal Psychology*, 1973, *82*, 324–334. (b)

Wachtel, P. L. Behavior therapy and the facilitation of psychoanalytic exploration. *Psychotherapy: Theory, Research and Practice*, 1975, *12*, 68–72.

Wachtel, P. L. Interaction cycles, unconscious processes, and the person-situation issue. In D. Magnusson & N. Endler (Eds.), *Personality at the crossroads: Current issues in interactional psychology.* Hillsdale, NJ: Erlbaum, 1977. (a)

Wachtel, P. L. *Psychoanalysis and behavior therapy: Toward an integration.* New York: Basic Books, 1977. (b)

Wachtel, P. L. Internal and external determinants of behavior in psychodynamic theories. In L. A. Pervin & M. Lewis (Eds.), *Perspectives in interactional psychology.* New York: Plenum Press, 1978. (a)

Wachtel, P. L. On some complexities in the application of conflict theory to psychotherapy. *Journal of Nervous and Mental Disease*, 1978, *166*, 457–471. (b)

Wachtel, P. L. Contingent and non-contingent therapist response. *Psychotherapy: Theory, Research and Practice*, 1979, *16*, 30–35. (a)

Wachtel, P. L. Karen Horney's ironic vision. *The New Republic*, Jan. 6, 1979, pp. 25–28. (b)

Wachtel, P. L. What should we say to our patients? On the wording of therapists' comments. *Psychotherapy: Theory, Research and Practice*, 1980, *17*, 183–188.

Wachtel, P. L. The politics of narcissism. *The Nation*, January 3–10, 1981, pp. 13–15. (a)

Wachtel, P. L. Transference, schema, and assimilation: The relevance of Piaget to the psychoanalytic theory of transference. *The Annual of Psychoanalysis*, 1981, *8*, 59–76. (b)

Wachtel, P. L. Phenomenological virtuoso: A review of *Autonomy and rigid character* by David Shapiro. *Contemporary Psychology*, 1982, *27*, 681–682. (a)

Wachtel, P. L. Resistance and the process of therapeutic change. In P. L. Wachtel (Ed.), *Resistance: Psychodynamic and behavioral approaches*. New York: Plenum Press, 1982. (b)

Wachtel, P. L. Vicious circles: The self and the rhetoric of emerging and unfolding. *Contemporary Psychoanalysis*, 1982, *18*(2), 259–273. (c)

Wachtel, P. L. What can dynamic therapies contribute to behavior therapy? *Behavior Therapy*, 1982, *13*, 594–609. (d)

Wachtel, P. L. *The poverty of affluence: A psychological portrait of the American way of life*. New York: Free Press, 1983. (a)

Wachtel, P. L. *The social significance of the psychotherapies*. Paper presented at the First International Conference on the Psychotherapies, Bogota, Colombia, February 1983. (b)

Wachtel, P. L. Integrative psychodynamic therapy. In S. Lynn & J. Garske (Eds.), *Contemporary psychotherapies: Models and methods*. Columbus, OH: Charles E. Merrill, 1985.

Wachtel, P. L., & Blatt, S. J. Energy deployment and achievement. *Journal of Consulting Psychology*, 1965, *29*, 302–308.

Watzlawick, P. The psychotherapeutic technique of "reframing." In J. Claghorn (Ed.), *Successful psychotherapy*. New York: Brunner/Mazel, 1976.

Weckowicz, T. E. Size constancy in schizophrenic patients. *Journal of Mental Science*, 1957, *103*, 475–486.

Weckowicz, T. E. Autonomic activity as measured by the mecholyl test and size constancy in schizophrenic patients. *Psychosomatic Medicine*, 1958, *20*, 66–71.

Weckowicz, T. E., Sommer, R., & Hall, R. Distance constancy in schizophrenic patients. *Journal of Mental Science*, 1958, *104*, 1174–1182.

Weiner, M. *The cognitive unconscious: A Piagetian approach to psychotherapy*. Davis, CA: International Psychological Press, 1975.

Weitzman, B. Behavior therapy and psychotherapy. *Psychological Review*, 1967, *74*, 300–317.

Werner, H. *Comparative psychology of mental development*. New York: International Universities Press, 1957.

Wheelis, A. Will and psychoanalysis. *Journal of the American Psychoanalytic Association*, 1956, *4*, 285–303.

Wheelis, A. *How people change*. New York: Harper & Row, 1973.

White, R. Motivation reconsidered: The concept of competence. *Psychological Review*, 1959, *66*, 297–333.

White, R. W. Ego and reality in psychoanalytic theory. *Psychological Issues*, 1963, *3*(Whole No. 11).

Wild, C. Creativity and adaptive regression. *Journal of Personality and Social Psychology*, 1965, *2*, 161–169.

Wile, D. *Couples Therapy: A nontraditional approach*. New York: Wiley, 1982.

Wile, D. Kernberg, Kohut, and Accusatory interpretations. *Psychotherapy: Theory, Research and Practice*, 1984, *21*, 315–329.

Wilkins, W. Desensitization: Social and cognitive factors underlying the effectiveness of Wolpe's procedure. *Psychological Bulletin*, 1971, *76*, 311–317.

Wilson, G. T., & Davison, G. C. Processes of fear reduction in systematic desensitization: Animal studies. *Psychological Bulletin*, 1971, *76*, 1–14.

Winer, H. R. *Incidental learning in schizophrenics*. Unpublished doctoral dissertation, Purdue University, 1954.

Witkin, H. A. Individual differences in ease of perception of embedded figures. *Journal of Personality*, 1950, *19*, 1–15.

Witkin, H. A. Psychological differentiation and forms of pathology. *Journal of Abnormal Psychology*, 1965, *70*, 317–336.

Witkin, H. A. Social influences in the development of cognitive style. In David A. Goslin (Ed.), *Handbook of socialization theory*. Chicago: Rand McNally, 1969.

Witkin, H. A., Dyk, R. B., Faterson, H. F., Goodenough, D. R., & Karp, S. A. *Psychological differentiation*. New York: Wiley, 1962.

Witkin, H. A., & Oltman, P. K. Cognitive style. *International Journal of Neurology*, 1967, *6*, 119–137.

Wolberg, L. Toward a comprehensive psychotherapy. *Journal of the American Academy of Psychoanalysis*, 1974, *2*, 349–360.

Wolf, E. Learning theory and psychoanalysis. *British Journal of Medical Psychology*, 1966, *39*, 1–10.

Wolitzky, D. L., & Wachtel, P. L. Perception and personality. In B. Wolman (Ed.), *Handbook of general psychology*. Englewood Cliffs, NJ: Prentice-Hall, 1973.

Wolpe, J. *Psychotherapy by reciprocal inhibition*. Stanford, CA: Stanford University Press, 1958.

Wolstein, B. Interpersonal relations without individuality. *Contemporary Psychoanalysis*, 1971, *8*, 75–80.

Woodworth, R. S. *Experimental psychology*. New York: Holt, 1938.

Yerkes, R. M., & Dodson, J. D. The relation of strength of stimulus to rapidity of habit formation. *Journal of Comparative Neurological Psychology*, 1908, *18*, 459–482.

Zaretsky, E. *Capitalism, the family and personal life*. New York: Harper & Row, 1976.

Zetzel, E. Current concepts of transference. *International Journal of Psycho-Analysis*, 1956, *37*, 369–376.

INDEX